Carceral Liberalism

DISSIDENT FEMINISMS

Elora Halim Chowdhury, Editor

*A list of books in the series appears
at the end of this book.*

Carceral Liberalism

Feminist Voices against State Violence

Edited by
SHREEREKHA PILLAI

Foreword by
DEMITA FRAZIER

© 2023 by the Board of Trustees
of the University of Illinois
All rights reserved
♾ This book is printed on acid-free paper.

Library of Congress Cataloging-in-Publication Data
Names: Pillai, Shreerekha, editor. | Frazier, Demita,
  writer of foreword.
Title: Carceral liberalism : feminist voices against state violence /
  edited by Shreerekha Pillai ; foreword by Demita Frazier.
Description: Urbana : University of Illinois Press, [2023] | Series:
  Dissident feminisms | Includes bibliographical references and
  index.
Identifiers: LCCN 2022057463 (print) | LCCN 2022057464
  (ebook) | ISBN 9780252045189 (hardback) | ISBN
  9780252087325 (paperback) | ISBN 9780252054556 (ebook)
Subjects: LCSH: United States—Social conditions—21st century.
  | Neoliberalism—United States—History—21st century. |
  Feminism—United States—History—21st century. | Social
  justice—United States—History—21st century. | Prison-
  industrial complex—United States—History—21st century.
  | Equality—United States—History—21st century. | Social
  stratification—United States—History—21st century. Power
  (Social sciences)—United States—History—21st century.
Classification: LCC HN90.S6 C358 2023 (print) | LCC HN90.S6
  (ebook) | DDC 305.50973—dc23/eng/20221208
LC record available at https://lccn.loc.gov/2022057463
LC ebook record available at https://lccn.loc.gov/2022057464

Dedicated to all those inhabiting and resisting the carceral, concrete and liminal

Contents

Foreword   ix
Demita Frazier

Acknowledgments   xiii

Introduction   1
Shreerekha Pillai

PART ONE: CARCERAL NARRATIVES AND FICTIONS

Poems: Honorée Fanonne Jeffers, "Pantoum for a
Black Man on a Greyhound Bus" and "Lost Letter #27:
John Peters, Boston-Gaol to Phillis Wheatley Peters,
Boston, December 3, 1784"   33

1. Carceral Trauma at the Intersections of Race, Class,
   Gender, Sexuality, and Maternity   35
   Cassandra D. Little

2. Layered Realities: Prison Writings and
   Anti-Terror Laws in India   52
   Shailza Sharma

3. Seeing Orange: Mediatizing the Prison Empire   70
   Shreerekha Pillai

4. Emptied Chairs and Faceless Inmates: A Critical
   Analysis of the Texas Prison Museum   93
   Beth Matusoff Merfish

Poems: Ravi Shankar, "Against Innocence"
and "Sunday School"   109

5. These Stories Will Not Be Confined   111
Joanna Eleftheriou

Poem: Solmaz Sharif, "Reaching Guantánamo"   125

PART TWO: CARCERAL BODIES AND SYSTEMS

Poem: Jeremy Eugene, "Space"   129

6. Cornered: Day Laborers, Criminalization,
and Legal Rituals of Democracy in Texas   131
Francisco Argüelles Paz y Puente, aka Pancho

7. Resisting Criminalization: Principles, Practicalities,
and Possibilities of Alternative Justices beyond the State   141
Autumn Elizabeth, D Coulombe, Zarinah Agnew

8. Going Carceral: Analyzing Written and Visual
Representations of Prison Yoga Programs   166
Tria Blu Wakpa and Jennifer Musial

9. Vacant Refuge, Unfinished Resettlement:
Ambivalence among Syrian and Iraqi Refugee
Women and Children in Houston, Texas   190
Maria F. Curtis

10. Social Control, Punishment, and Gender:
Silenced Memories of Peruvian Women in Wartime   211
Marta Romero-Delgado

11. Bad Girls of Pinjra Tod   230
Alka Kurian

Poem: Javier Zamora, "Citizenship"   249

Contributors   251

Index   257

Foreword

As one of the cofounders of the Combahee River Collective, a radical Black feminist collective based in the Boston area in the late 1970s and early 80s, I can report that some of our very best work was done in the women's prison in Massachusetts, MCI Framingham. An adult literacy program that was too short (institutionally unsupported) but nevertheless quite successful. A concert produced for the inmates that showcased the talents of Black women composers, musicians, and poets. Meeting the inmates' needs for creative expression and engaging in adult literacy educational activities fostered a sense of profound connection between the women of the Collective and the inmates, and the shared experience of the beat and the books enhanced positive community-building among the women inside. My interest in organization development sprang from what I learned was possible when you use creativity to illuminate the possibilities of connectivity. Connectivity mitigates isolation. Connectivity builds relational pathways of communication. Connectivity engenders compassion.

In 2017 the National Women's Studies Association recognized the fortieth anniversary of the publication of the Combahee River Collective Statement. The intergenerational panel of Black feminists, which convened to discuss the tensions between the activist and academic spaces, afforded me the serendipity of meeting Dr. Shreerekha Pillai, and over the subsequent days of the conference we discussed her work with prisoners, a key focus of her work at the University of Houston–Clear Lake. It was and has been a wonderful meeting of the minds! Meeting her has been a gift: an ardent South Asian–born feminist and passionate academic who is a committed community educator, who understands the ability of language to empower, and who shares the gifts of the academy with the incarcerated. When she asked me to write the foreword for this book, I didn't hesitate.

This book is timely. The burgeoning prison industrial complex, yielding more and more incarcerated and formerly incarcerated citizens, many coming from the margins and living lives compromised by the effects of poverty, socioeconomic disinvestment, and struggling public education systems, presents enormous challenges to us as a democratic society. The questions we must ask ourselves as a country in this regard, and in the coming decades, are raised by the authors, artists, activists, and academics in this wonderful book. Twentieth-century ideas of crime and punishment are fully intertwined with profit making; there's money to be made on the continuing influx of new prisoners, and failing to provide substantive community needs-driven support services assures that the subsequent recidivism provides a revolving door of bodies and significant profits for the privatized prison system. The resulting disinclination to stem that flow of bodies has a predictable cascading effect on the families and communities the imprisoned come from, across generations. The writers, cultural workers, and thinkers in this volume are interested in critically interrogating those structures, processes, and ideas, and dare to imagine new approaches dedicated to achieving true justice, beyond the established, deeply flawed justice system currently in place.

Current statistics show that one in four Americans are related to or know someone who is or has been incarcerated. The last thirty years of carceral commodification has prompted renewed interest in contemplating progressive approaches to dealing with the millions of community members who will one day be freed and reenter our communities. The restorative justice movements, with their roots in the community justice practices of Indigenous peoples, have subsequently informed and shaped the thinking of everyone involved in these movements, including Black and other women of color intersectional feminists, queer communities of color, and radical prison abolitionist groups here and across the world.

Modern-era Black feminists have continued a long tradition of being in the forefront of progressive and radical interrogation of the modern carceral industrial complex. Black feminist artists, filmmakers, poets, and thought leaders in the movements for social justice have, through their works, inspired the reimagination of many systems; radical Black women historians and critical race legal scholars have called forth fresh ideas and approaches to creating a society "coupled with justice from the beginning," free from racist, sexist, class-based oppressions and founded on creating systems addressing necessary and fundamental human rights: to health care, housing, education, food, and livable wages, along with meaningful democratic socio-civic engagement. In this book, the authors have come to this work with new ideas that rest on a foundation of radical inquiry, in an era of increased awareness of the impact of structural racism and the link to the overpolicing and the excessive incarceration of Black and brown people.

The central premise of this volume is that the powers of art, language, and critical inquiry can and should be made available to the imprisoned, to promote the development of life skills, creative self-expression, and adult literacy, in furtherance of the inmates' recovery of their sense of agency. The contributors believe in the power of art to open the portal of self-awareness, which in turn bolsters self-esteem and empowerment. The cognitive benefits that accrue from discussing and sharing perspectives, along with the strengthening of spirit, can help to mitigate the unrelenting negativity of the carceral environment.

I encourage you to read this book and be inspired by the energy and visions for a better future contained herein. I hope it creates a springboard for new thinking about the purposes and functions of the carceral state, and the possibilities for a different world.

Demita Frazier, JD

Acknowledgments

Much of this project germinated as I wandered far afield, in an academic sense, from my disciplinary boundaries. Early in my career as a faculty at University of Houston–Clear Lake, I began teaching in its long-standing program for incarcerated students at a men's state prison in Texas, a program recently renamed "Transforming Lives by Degrees" (TLD). At about the same time, I began attending the National Women's Studies Association's (NWSA) annual conference through the Women of Color Leadership Project (WocLP) just as the power balance shifted and Black feminists led the charge at NWSA. Angela Davis presided as keynote and honored Beverly Guy-Sheftall's feminist work that is coterminous with the organization's birth in 1977. Nearly a decade later, NWSA continued the celebration of iconic feminists of color marking the forty-year anniversary of Combahee River Collective (CRC), bringing some of the founding members in conversation with Movement for Black Lives (M4BL) in its annual conference held in Baltimore in 2017. I owe much to the impactful conversations on social justice and carcerality nurtured within and through NWSA. Thanks in part due to the safe and dynamic spaces of critical exchange fostered there, I created and led a panel on carcerality at the 2017 conference, which led to the inception of this volume. At the heels of this animated session at NWSA, I sent out my call for papers in early 2018, and the rest is history. I owe much of what I have learned through the years to my students in my prison-classrooms and to my sister-scholar-activists at NWSA.

Encouraged by the radical aspirations of WocLP, we launched the South Asian Feminist Caucus. The members of this caucus and the Transnational Feminists Caucus have been critical coconspirators along the way. University of Illinois Press editor Dawn Durante and series editor Elora Halim Chowdhury nudged me along. I owe special gratitude to Elora for her unfailing encouragement and fierce advocacy of our work. This volume would not have seen the light of day without the leadership and guidance of current editor Dominique Moore, who carried us to the finish line. We owe much to the endless hours of work performed by the double-blind peer reviewers whose critical insights through many cycles of reviews have strengthened this manuscript, and the skilled team at UIP whose meticulous work strengthens this volume, especially Jennifer Argo, Jen Rogers, Roberta Sparenberg, and Dustin Hubbart. Most importantly, I thank the contributors, whose patience and hard work through the years is finally seeing the light of day. To the contributors who started with me in 2017 and the ones who joined in later stages of our journey, I owe you all the biggest and loudest thanks. Thank you for believing in this project and sticking with me through it all! I believe this volume stands apart due to the poets whose work partners with the scholars' and activists' work in beautiful and profound ways; I owe a special debt to the poets and want to thank my dear sister-friend Honorée Fanonne Jeffers, whose ready gift of poems to this volume occurred before the volume even took shape and whose friendship has been formative in my life. Demita Frazier's steady presence, searing intellect, and radical vision has kept me buoyed through the lengthy gestational period of this volume.

I am grateful for the support provided through fellowships and awards at University of Houston–Clear Lake and the sincere support of colleagues from my home program of Humanities as well as Women's and Gender Studies and Cross-Cultural and Global Studies in the College of Human Sciences and Humanities. I thank my friends near and far for their solidarity: Rachel Afi Quinn, Eesha Pandit, Jane Chin Davidson, Anupama Tuli, Sehba Sarwar, Anita Wadhwa, and Neneh Kowai-Bell. I remember my late friends Cheria Vonique Dial and Sarah Ann Heilbron, women with whom I began my teaching career in Baltimore and whose laughter still keeps me inspired. No words can suffice for the endless hours spent on this manuscript's many incarnations by my dear colleague, mentor, and sister-sojourner, Christine Kovic. To my parents, Mr. and Mrs. Pillai; appa and amma, Mr. and Mrs. Shankar; my brother, Unni; my niece, Parvathi; cousins and family everywhere, debts of love are not to be repaid, only rejoiced in. To Santosh, through thick and thin, and my now-grown babies, Sarvesh and Sumana, you are my light and my way out.

Carceral Liberalism

Introduction

SHREEREKHA PILLAI

In 1977, the Combahee River Collective (CRC) published a manifesto for social change to communicate the power of radical Black feminist consciousness to activists, scholars, and social justice workers across the nation and well beyond its borders.[1] That call to action, much like Audre Lorde's poetry and memoir,[2] have been formative in my understanding of feminist collective work in the Civil Rights era and its wake. In that signal emergence we discern modes of collective politics informed by personal stories, especially of women of color, who undertook leadership roles in local communities to broaden and deepen coalitional networks of resistance to inequality and injustice. For many of the women's rights activists and grassroots workers, arguing for spaces greater than the domestic site assigned to women was, in fact, an argument against the carcerality of domesticity. In putting together this book for some years now, what has become clear to me is the ubiquity and banality of carcerality in our everyday lives.

The CRC's practice of coalition building charged the consciousness of struggles for peace and justice during the bleak Reagan years, the period that marks my entry into the United States as an immigrant in New York City. I was a freshman in high school when the unforgettable Howard Beach incident happened. Three Black men were chased by a group of white teenagers simply because they were "existing while Black." Part of my acclimation to Americana in those days involved being subjected, mainly by cousins, to screenings of horror films like *The Exorcist*. That ritual cultural experience was disturbing enough, but I was deeply aware of an inchoate, more real and material sense of horror in learning about the story of Michael Griffiths, who ran for his life while being chased by an angry mob of white boys.[3] As he fled for his life, he ran onto the Belt Parkway, the very highway that brought me to my new home after I landed at Kennedy Airport. This stuff of nightmares memorialized my early experience of distance and remove from the American dream. Those were years in which the Central Park jogger case came to public attention as a site for the untrammeled expression of ideological interpellation, where a so-called mob of Black youth were wrongly convicted by not just the system but a city and its citizens.[4] As a new immigrant,[5] observing the marginalization and rampant brutalization of the resident people of color only made me feel that much more precarious as a brown entrant from elsewhere. The coinage of "wilding" to describe the activities of the youth did not go easy either; as an immigrant, I was used to correcting questions on the "wild spaces" of my homeland. My new home was a small apartment on an island that was a bastion of white supremacist discourse, and one did not imagine that such discourse would find a cozy home in the White House as we progressed toward the future.[6] Part of the secret learning as an immigrant is that the bright lights of the American dream also include dreams deferred and American nightmares. The liberalism within American grammar also promised the carceralization of its people of color. The lessons learned from the work of radical Black feminism—specifically, an intersectional analysis of race, class, and gender—is what clarifies the violence of the American liberalist project at its roots. Liberalism is always-already carceral. What I bring to the term *carceral liberalism* and the maxim above builds on the work done by the CRC and radical Black feminist consciousness that points its finger at the violence against Black and brown bodies on which the nation is premised. Carceral liberalism is the hidden script of neoliberalism; it is an ideology that wreaks violence on the most vulnerable while promising freedom and a higher quality of life for all.

Classrooms offered refuge; teachers and mentors made me feel privileged instead of endangered. At twenty-one, I began my first full-time job as a teacher in a Baltimore high school designated as SURR.[7] Barricaded and structured like a penitentiary, this school was located in the homogenous concrete row houses of Westside Baltimore, a school that accounted for more teenage funerals than graduations, a school where students observed police searches of the premises on a routine basis, where over a dozen teachers were stomped during my first year, and also where I encountered some of the most dedicated teachers I have met, and some of the most unforgettable students—in sum, the classroom where I learned the craft of teaching. Not only did Black feminist consciousness inform my teaching—I brought the memoirs of Audre Lorde and Assata Shakur[8] to my high school classroom— but it also gave me ground to stand on and room in which to move and think. As an elsewhere-person, I relied on ideas of pan-Africanism, solidarity, and the productive work of communities of color to stage dialogues, frame arguments and counterarguments, to explore nodes of connection, and yes, to learn compassion. In those years, I did not use the term *carcerality*, but I pointed cheekily to the high school field trips to the downtown jail[9] and how the educational system was systematically preparing a particular stratum of students for the penitentiary rather than high office. Some of the more outspoken students often joked I was going to incite a riot; instead, I received from my young organic intellectuals the most subtle, charged, and passionate art and poetry about their daily lives. For the young Black men and women in my classrooms who became larger than life in the narratives they shared through their words, the carceral formed the unconscious of their lived experiences. It was as though for the self-conscious and aware youth reared in the dark side of the American dream, going to prison was a rite of passage to adulthood, and the concomitant scarring, losses, and hardening a given; structural racism and systemic oppression was the lived reality for these students who were key translators of American liberalism in my journey.

In many ways, acclimating to American culture meant absorbing the banality of the carceral. It is prolific and everywhere, part and parcel of the daily fabric of life in the United States. For the Black and brown people in communities of color most familiar to me, food, finances, national identity, and so many other intersections of the self translated into insecurities of daily living that spelled out the carceral in the everyday. In Baltimore, those of us who taught and those who were our students compared notes on all the sites and moments that reminded us of prisons—from the narrow slits of windows and fortified structure of the high school to the highly policed neighborhood corners to the Scared Straight field trips to the downtown jail to the various confinements from lack of basic necessities or possibility of any luxuries for most of our students at home.

At my current institution, University of Houston–Clear Lake, we have had a program to teach classes at the prison itself, "Transforming Lives by Degrees," aimed at having our incarcerated students earn bachelor's and master's degrees. In fifteen years of teaching at the university and its ancillary campus at the prison, I have often encountered the deepest thinkers at the prison, people who bring to life the purpose and value of a humanities education. In a Freirean sense, my students evince a pedagogy of the oppressed.[10] In year one of teaching in the prison classroom, the students blew me away with their intuitive and precise reading of Toni Morrison's acclaimed novel *Beloved*. Since then, the students, most of whom are autodidacts deeply desirous of critical thinking and learning, have outmatched students in the

Introduction 3

"free world" in their capacity to work, write, engage, and grow. Frustrated often at being given a chapter instead of the entire text, the students in the prison classroom exemplify a curiosity to learn paired with compassion and desire to progress as a collective. The prison classroom becomes a sacral site of learning, a classroom entombed within the prison but full of light, a place where the discursive order produced by the student points to the intimacy of liberalism with carceralism, a place where the close relationship between freedom and unfreedom becomes as clear as day. Over and over, many of the students evince a familiarity with the prison long before they arrived as "offenders" inside its structure and speak of its haunting in their lives lived at the interlocking nexus of poverty, inequality, individual and communal illness, and despair. For most, American liberalism came as a twin paired with American carceralism; what felt new was their relationship to learning as a way to resist the violence through an epistemology grounded in pedagogies of the oppressed, a pedagogy that makes clear the workings of carceral liberalism.

In 2017, I attended the annual conference of the National Women's Studies Association,[11] which interestingly enough for me happened in the city of my beginnings, Baltimore. I had organized a panel on carceral dissident feminisms,[12] and that is where my panelists generated such productive energy that we thought of moving our work forward into a book project. It is not merely serendipitous that our seminar came together at the conference titled "Forty Years after Combahee: Feminist Scholars and Activists Engage the Movement for Black Lives." The many thousands of attendees at the conference listened to conversations between some of the remaining living legends behind the CRC, crafted after nearly a decade's work of radical Black feminist activism in Boston—women like Barbara Smith, Margo Okazawa-Ray, and Demita Frazier—and the young leaders at the helm of social justice movements today, such as Charlene Carruthers, Mary Hooks, and Professor Kimberlé Crenshaw. Demita Frazier shone with her humor and acerbic take on academic discourse that tends to wall off public participation and cements carceral logic by keeping people out of conversations. Her contributions to the discussion were illumined by years of life in the liminal zones between the academy and the so-called real world. She is one of the voices in the Combahee River Collective that prefers to speak with its original pitch: "Combahee gave us an opportunity to be uncensored in our radical agenda." For Demita Frazier, Combahee—a name that remembers Harriet Tubman's insurrection in 1863 in South Carolina that helped free 750 enslaved people—was their way of crafting freedom. To her sister soldiers on stage and in the audience, she quipped, "You youth are the sweet water. We are the salty water." Frazier went on to distinguish the markers of mainstream feminism from radical Black feminist thought and called on the audience to seize the narrative. As the elders were asked to impart some wisdom before leaving the stage, Frazier shared a set of pithy maxims that encapsulated her criticism of those who prefer the golden handcuffs of elitism. The logic of capital was everywhere, along with the critique of patriarchy and systems of racialized inequality—Frazier remembered how as a Black feminist she wanted to be in spaces where the activists were as animated about racial issues as they were about gender. Frazier shared four maxims:

- Be insurrectionists
- Observe the powerful closely
- Be critical thinkers, interrogate received wisdom mercilessly
- Embrace humility, forego hubris.[13]

Frazier conjured the political and material reality that haunts generations of activists who wish to bring about systemic changes to destabilize historically rooted systems of inequality. This book, generated from the productive energy found at each year's annual gathering of NWSA, and more specifically, the panel on carcerality where I first met Jennifer Musial and Autumn Elizabeth, was so significant that by the time the manuscript arose in some shape out of the collective work on carcerality, it was fitting to have Demita Frazier as our first word. Frazier's dialogue on stage, much like the animated conversations had in Boston living rooms that led to the collective writing of the CRC, brought to light the brickwork that fortifies capitalism, patriarchy, and liberalism through connecting nodes of hegemonies at work; the CRC's radical Black feminism is the resistance to these existing powers. I argue that all these hegemonies work in tandem to produce the ideology of carceral liberalism; the CRC's Black radical feminist vision offers an antidote to the violence of carceral liberalism. Our book was born in these sweet and salty waters.

What Is Carceral Liberalism?

I guess that that's the privilege of policing for some profit
But thanks to Reaganomics, prisons turned to profits.
—Killer Mike, "Reagan"

My central premise is that the marriage between new forms of imperialism, vis-à-vis gendered and racial otherings and neoliberalism, is a very specific type of American export that we can name "carceral liberalism." In many ways, the resistance encoded in rap attests to an insurrectionary knowledge that counters normative discourses and offers critical readings of history and

Introduction   5

the present, as made apparent in Killer Mike's lyrics. His song sums up the Reagan era, which marks the boom in the prison industry consequent to the Republican-engineered war on drugs, which can also be renamed, more appropriately, a war on the poor. Rather than freedom, it is carceral liberalism that is at work, moving forward the projects of imperialism, anti-blackness, neoliberalism, and patriarchy within the capillaries of power at home and abroad. Carceral liberalism, unlike the more prevalent and commonly invoked idioms of western life, freedom, liberty, and justice, undergirds the union in the United States. Carceral liberalism makes clear the violence at the founding of the nation and after as a continuing force. I am arguing that carceral liberalism is a powerful but unnamable ideological export, a hyperobject[14] that is not explicit but always already at work in local and global sites, producing its own forms of dissident resistance against the organized violence of the state made apparent within and beyond the walls of prisons.[15] Neoliberalism spins a mythology of freedom for all things, people, capital, resources, and progress. However, in the contemporary iteration of neoliberalism that has allowed for the free movement of goods and commodities, the most vulnerable people on the transnational stage have experienced carceral conditions when it comes to breathing, border-crossing, and surviving.[16]

At the intersections of the carceral and patriarchal systems, the syllogism points to the high rate of women's incarceration, twice that of men and located more in local jails than state prisons, as seen in recent decades.[17] At the crossroads of neoliberal and patriarchal orders, women's role in the workplace, home, the street, and the land remain tenuous, tense, and a continual site of struggle. What I am positing is that carceral liberalism emerges from the distillation of the three systems: neoliberalism, carcerality, and patriarchy built along nodes of anti-blackness, anti-woman, and anti-worker, which is to say, carceral liberalism is the Reuleaux Triangle, the heart of the Venn where all three systems of power intersect to generate a new subscript for "freedom." Carceral liberalism is the perfect ruse at the ideological heart of this structure, the discursive order that waves the feminist flag while keeping most women still at the margins, that speaks of a post-race society while one in three Black men remains warehoused in state apparatuses,[18] that speaks of capital while its dispossessed remain mired in debt. Carceral Liberalism, in so many ways, usurps, hollows, and repackages the "free" of freedom so that it comes to stand as code for the dominant impulse of the neoimperialist law-and-order state, a state of lockdown, immobility, and dispossession for many. In the old order of colonialism, the colonized resisted and finally fought through anti-colonial movements that lasted in some areas for centuries before entering a phase of self-rule under the umbrella of putative liberation.

Under the new logic of imperialism, the impacted subjects cannot even be named "imperialized," let alone resist coherently these multiple systems of lockdown. Hardt and Negri speak of a new form of imperial sovereignty that erases old racial inequalities but, in its place, gives us the "smooth space of Empire, [where] there is no place of power—it is both everywhere and nowhere. Empire is an *ou-topia*, or really a non-place."[19] For example, this ou-topia can deny old racisms forged out of the fires of specious nineteenth-century science experiments on racial hierarchies while keeping in place social, cultural, and societal determinants on racial otherizations.

Carceral liberalism is a logic of empire-building, fluent in the language of neoliberalism, patriarchy, and a new Jim Crow.[20] It is such a logic that can have a nation and a world audience riveted and traumatized by the repetitive play of George Floyd's murder at the hands of police officer Derek Chauvin as he kept his knee on Floyd's neck for nine minutes and twenty-nine seconds. While Black lives have been vulnerable throughout American history, and more recently brought to light through the simulacral witness of video recordings and social media, since the murder of Trayvon Martin there has been a more earnest reckoning of the long record of Black men, women, and children who have lost their lives at the hands of the police or white supremacist vigilantes. George Floyd's cold-blooded and calculated killing recorded on numerous cameras for all the world to see somehow awakened a global conscience that rallied around BLM and led to a resurgent Civil Rights Movement inspired by a violent act that became the springboard for trans-national resistance starting on May 25, 2020. It is such an event, broadcast repeatedly for an entire year, that led to a televised trial where witnesses and prosecutors had to articulate the humanity of George Floyd in a structure that systematically dehumanizes and punishes Black lives. The nine minutes and twenty-nine seconds it took to murder Floyd, while the longest nine minutes for a man, a community, and nations, also laid bare the vulnerability and marginalization of Black lives—the struggle to consume goods when poor, the challenges of conducting one's most banal daily transactions, the high cost of one possibly counterfeit $20 bill, the capital punishment doled out to those without capital. While the catalog of Black lives taken by police, civilian, or vigilante violence continues to grow, perhaps attended to with a transnational awakening after the tragedy of George Floyd, what has become clear in the resurgence of the contemporary Civil Rights Movement around BLM is that Black lives remain vulnerable. What I am arguing is that carceral liberalism is the secret formula of neoliberalism that says one thing but does another. It promises a post-race society that still kills based on racialization of brown and Black bodies. The most vulnerable people are interpellated by

Introduction   7

carceral logic that comes in the ruse of free thinking and freedom but offers more walls. Resistance, within and beyond walls, requires an imagination that dares to leap beyond the hyperobject of carceral liberalism.

In the years it took to labor and bring this book to life, the term *carceral liberalism* has come into circulation and been used by scholars in articles and online discussions. Sarika Talve-Goodman contextualizes the canonic work of South African writer Alan Paton in articulating how his groundbreaking texts that bespoke twentieth-century liberalism rested on the material reality of prison expansion and carceral state building.[21] Talve-Goodman stitches together Foucault's philosophy on prisons with those of Angela Davis, Joy James, Achille Mbembe, and Naomi Murakawa to connect the tropes of Black criminality and racial pity that reveal how contemporary liberalism rests upon the construction of color-blind systems of governance. Most recently, Korey Tillman conceptualizes carceral liberalism in his article by that title from his three years of participant-observer ethnography collected on the streets of Clark County in Southern Nevada while working on providing resources through a nonprofit organization, Give, to individuals experiencing homelessness.[22] Tillman theorizes carceral liberalism as the amalgam of contemporary U.S. policing based on coercive techniques rooted in anti-Black colonial ideologies alongside a transnational historical past that relied on racialized economic subjugation. He highlights the intimacy between coercive benevolence offered to its most vulnerable individuals and the carceral state whilst unpacking the anti-Black roots of liberalism citing scholars such as Sylvia Wytner, Savannah Shange, and Cedric Robinson. My position resonates with Tillman's; what I seek is to intentionally unsettle white supremacy offered in the academy under the alibi of continental philosophy. In citing radical Black feminism as the force that pushes against the violence of neoliberalism, patriarchy, and carcerality, my conceptualization of carceral liberalism cites, acknowledges, and moves the labor forward in solidarity with radical Black feminism. In citing Combahee as the epistemic force against power, my argument unmasks state violence through carceral liberalism and simultaneously centers radical Black feminism.

In addition, I wish to acknowledge the work of several scholars whose work brings to light the veiled violence at the heart of liberalism. Elizabeth Bernstein provides critical insights into the violence that is reproduced in antitrafficking campaigns wherein the policies designed to protect women reinscribe violence through militarized humanitarian campaigns.[23] Bernstein makes explicit the logical nodes that connect carceral politics and neoliberalism with her ethnographic work on antitrafficking or what she terms "carceral feminism." Jason Vick's work is instrumental in making visible the cruelty inherent in a system of exile that renders the wounds, often psychological in nature, invisible to the general public. Vick reminds us that though the birth of the modern prison as conceived by Jeremy Bentham and Cesare Beccaria in the nineteenth century rested on the impulse to dissolve earlier systems of corporeal depredations, the modern prison empire rests on rendering this cruelty behind walls and doors invisible.[24] From the state of Texas where I reside, the struggles to unmask the inherent cruelty and violence of the carceral state are ongoing in numerous examples of incarcerated individuals fighting for their right to exist with dignity, such as Dennis Hope, who has been residing in the tiniest of spaces for nearly three decades of solitary confinement,[25] a punishment considered to be a human rights violation by the UN in rules named after the suffering most famously emblematized by Nelson Mandela.[26] Sara Benson furthers these points in her book that speaks of the literal entombment promised by incarceration through a close critical reading of the Victorian Gothic aesthetic of many historic federal prisons in the United States.[27] With an entrance through doors into dark and subterranean worlds, the stuff of literary and media-fueled dramas, the prison promises a form of "civil death" and becomes code for what Sara Benson terms "carceral democracy."

This book is the collective effort of a group of people who are thinking from the margins about carcerality, sharing their stories from different perches in the academy, local communities, and activist spaces. This book includes the voice of one subject to the power of carcerality as well as the analyses of these subjections from interviews, lived experiences, imaginaries, and poetic visions. We continue the dialogue inaugurated by Julia Sudbury in her watershed anthology *Global Lockdown: Race, Gender, and the Prison-Industrial Complex.*[28] In that anthology, Sudbury's introduction offers the reader a theoretical toolkit for thinking about systems of anti-globalization and anti-carcerality as working in concert. Her volume brings together an illuminating array of voices: those incarcerated with scholars and public intellectuals locally and globally whose work makes clear the simultaneous oppression of carceral and capitalist regimes of power.[29] *Carceral Liberalism* adds to the dialogues begun by Sudbury's collective while updating and including momentous scholarship produced in the interim informed by Michelle Alexander's work that inaugurated conversations within and beyond the academy to the more recent works of Talitha LeFlouria, Erica Meiners, Emily Thuma, Elizabeth Hinton, Brittney Cooper, and Jackie Wang.[30] The thematics of racialism, class, age, national markers, and location all work as a form of hierarchy to cement carcerality as the subtext of liberalism. *Carceral Liberalism* asks us to read carcerality as the language that arises in the heady mix of neoimperialist political structures alongside nationalist policies generating a liberalism that is always already marked and limited by punitive state structures that hinge on violence, penality, and retribution.[31] I invoke Trinh T. Minh-ha's argument that alerts us to the theoretical functions performed in poetry and the poetic labor present in theory, reducing the distance between the academic and poetic sites.[32]

The five poets in this volume do heavy lifting in bringing forth their visions urging us to look back into history, as in Honorée Fanonne Jeffers's reconstructions of Phillis Wheatley's life and our present times, that is, the work of the rest of the poets, who help us look at the carceral in the daily racialized lives of the undocumented, the vulnerable, the refugee, the exiles, the detained, and other disposable bodies.[33] On the significance of poets and their ability to acknowledge pain, Martin Espada shares in his interview in *Policing the Planet: Why the Policing Crisis Led to Black Lives Matter*, "I believe that poets can inform social movements by doing what poets do: invoking the power of language, the musicality of language, the vividness of language, to move people, to win the proverbial hearts and minds, because that, indeed, is what social movements must do in order to effect social change."[34] Jeremy Eugene's poem, poignant for its power of invoking the racialized and gendered violence that ended Sandra Bland's life in a Texas jail, attests to the truth Espada reminds us, "If people want to know what really happened, they can always consult the poets. We spoke against it. I'm speaking against it."[35] The poets, in bringing to light the lives of the racialized other, trace the arc of disposability and oppression to the larger epoch of slavery. Jeffers's razor-sharp poetic focus on Phillis Wheatley's life and times is a poetics of enslavement and survival, bodies on whose labor, brutalization, and pain the nation was built.[36] In so many ways that are apparent or implicit, carceral liberalism points to the continuities between the old regimes of industrialization, capitalism, enlightenment, and slavery and the contemporary regimes of neoimperial racialization, gentrification, neoliberal development projects, and heteropatriarchal hegemonies. The lives that are subject to the power of the system, bodies marked as the other under what Michelle Alexander terms the New Jim Crow[37] directed at all who are racialized, vulnerable, and poor,[38] point to an alliance between the ideals of neoliberalism and the aims of the carceral apparatus.

Carceral Liberalism asks us to recognize the intimate relationship between the tenets of neoliberalism, patriarchy, and the shackles of carcerality; in doing so, this book brings together imaginative reflections narrativized in films, novels, and televised serials, all compelled to explore the idea of time as the only available cipher of retributive justice and condign punishment.

Angela Davis connects the turn in nineteenth-century punitive methods from corporeal, gruesome, and sadistic to private, psychic, and reformist to systemic structural changes shadowing the progress of capitalism: "The conditions of possibility for this new form of punishment were strongly anchored in a historical era during which the working class needed to be constituted as an army of self-disciplined individuals capable of performing the requisite industrial labor for a developing capitalist system."[39] Davis connects anti–capital punishment positions with her opposition to imprisonment itself, a complex of putative punishment that all in all needs to be rehauled, reexamined, and reimagined. In my chapter on the television series *Orange Is the New Black*, the condition of carcerality is obliquely the refrain in Regina Spektor's theme song that reflects on women's incarceration in America's carceral chambers[40] as she repeats these lines, "The sun is out, the day is new, and everyone is waiting, waiting on you. And you've got time."[41] The prison industrial complex (PIC) has been critiqued across disciplines and through interdisciplinary endeavors that coalesce as carceral epistemology. We trace our theoretical commitment of this volume to the ethical resistance manifest in the insurgent vision of radical Black feminism expressed in the CRC.

Dissident Feminist Projects of Liberation

The chapters in this volume evidence a diverse array of feminist resurgences and resistance framed within, at the threshold of, or outside state violence. Carceral liberalism, a primary ideological export of U.S. vintage and construction, gaining traction through the levers of neoliberalism and classical forms of patriarchy and systemic inequalities, is the wall that feminisms push up against, often coming up for air and light. Dissident feminisms are our counterinsurgency against the impositions and subjections of carceral liberalism, a praxis and theory of the radical imagination at work on the part of the poets, scholars, and activists in this book.

Demita Frazier, a scholar-activist whose political work began in her youth as a volunteer with the free breakfast program created by the Black Panther Party in Chicago in the 1960s and continued in reproductive justice, antiviolence, children's rights, and numerous other social justice projects over the decades since, and who was one of the primary authors behind the CRC, presents the foreword for this volume. One of the great privileges of editing this volume has been the honor not only of being in concert with the work inaugurated by the CRC, but of knowing one of its authors to be a continuing and infinite source of light and all-around humanity, a mentor, teacher, and most importantly, a dear friend. Under the sign of transnational feminist solidarity, our conversations attest to the borderlessness of activist communing. Our dissident friendship inspires all that we write, individually and in concert with each other.

The authors in this volume travel a range of intellectual sites: from academics to activists and one piece by a formerly incarcerated woman, now a life coach and social worker. The volume includes five poets: Honorée Fanonne Jeffers, Ravi Shankar, Solmaz Sharif, Jeremy Eugene, and Javier Zamora. These poets reflect on a range of carceral themes that tackle the vulnerability of Black, brown, and poor bodies in carceral contexts, subject to the violence of the state. On a macro level, the poems address the violence at the genesis and nature of the state itself, a state that is conceived willfully through genocide, enslavement, and appropriation of land that literally turns carcerality from a state of mind to a state of being. Jeffers's pantoum considers the intimacy of violence between kin and community from the vantage point of a Black American woman who is attempting to reconcile the losses, absence, and trauma of bearing witness. Ravi Shankar, who narrated his carceral experience in a memoir aptly named *Correctional* (2022), ponders the rage and silencing experienced by communities of color in "Against Innocence," and gives a primer on carcerality in "Sunday School." Solmaz Sharif's poem "Reaching Guantánamo" reflects the violence experienced by bodies, texts, and lives of those detained, especially in exceptional states of carcerality as in Guantánamo Bay Detention Camp. Sharif's epistolary poem from the beloved to the detained mirrors the "lost letter" Jeffers creates from John Peters to his famous poet wife begging for her words. These poets embody the violence of the carceral in these fictive letters. Jeremy Eugene's "Space," like Shankar's primer on rage, is incantatory as it addresses the violence of white supremacy that displaces and erases Black humanity. Javier Zamora's poem comes from his book *Unaccompanied* (2017), in which he recalls the long walk north from El Salvador that he made at the age of nine to join his family in the United States. To that child at the border, the militarized site of the repressive state is a paradox: the "fence" is a place of two-way crossings with dreamers on both sides of the border. What is common to all these poems is the beating heart of rage and beauty that leaves a lump in the throat, and that inchoate longing for a better world where such emanations can be reconciled as a thing of the past.

The eleven chapters in this volume are divided into two parts. The first part, "Carceral Narratives and Fictions" focuses on narratives of the self, emerging from the world of fiction, poetry, memoir, media, and museums, all serving as sites of seeing and curating the self and the other. The first part opens with Honorée Fanonne Jeffers's poems and closes with a poem by Solmaz Sharif. Between Merfish's chapter analyzing prison objects and Eleftheriou's meditating on the subjects in prison, I include Ravi Shankar's poetics on carcerality. The second part, "Carceral Bodies and Systems," attends to alternatives, programs, and systems at work within and ancillary to the state in pieces that are located in the local and the global. This part opens with a poem written by Jeremy Eugene in the wake of Sandra Bland's killing in a Houston jail. It closes with a poem from Javier Zamora on the artificiality of boundaries of a state that doles out hunger and violence to its own and the other. Part one includes memoir, analysis of memoir, the museum, and mediatized texts engendering a discursive order around the workings of carceral liberalism within narratives and fictions. Bracketed by the poetry of Jeffers, Shankar, and Sharif, part one focuses on the individuals interpellated by states of violence. Part two is site-specific, bracketed between poems of death and exile, depicting violence torpedoed between a Houston jail (Eugene), migrant day laborers seeking work on street corners (Argüelles), Indian women's hostels (Kurian), and home itself as a state of carceralized exile (Curtis). Bridging from a study of prison yoga programs to one about Peruvian post-war survivors to one on the nature and substance of intentional communities, part two interrogates the relationship between bodies and systems of power within carceral regimes.

Part One: Carceral Narratives and Fictions

The chapters in this volume argue toward an evocation of carceral liberalism that makes clear the visible, invisible, and otherwise implicit carceral structures that operate within and beyond prison walls. The opening and closing chapters of this section are first-hand accounts of carcerality, the first one authored by a woman who survived to speak about her sentence, and the last one by an educator who writes of her experience teaching in a state prison. Cassandra Little's memoir bears witness to a singular life, that of a Black, queer, educated mother who reaches and realizes her dream of self-care and care for others in running an organization to foster the children abused by the foster-care system, only to have it all unravel under charges of financial malfeasance. She serves a nearly two-year sentence in a federal penitentiary in California. Little's narrative is bracketed within larger historical moves by the powerful to shore up power. Little's life speaks to a comprehension of the vagaries and inflexibility of the carceral system, and her narrative hopes to move forward the march toward abolition democracy.

Shailza Sharma draws attention to a body of prison writings emerging in India. She connects the effects of a host of anti-terror laws to state-sanctioned

Introduction   13

violence specifically against Muslim citizens or activists allied with anti-state resistance movements. Through a closer look at the memoirs written by Seema Azad and her husband, Arun Ferreira, Anjum Habib, and Mohammad Aamir Khan, she examines the degradations of carceral subjections but also the way punishments are differentiated based on caste, class, and other such privileges as read by the surveillance apparatus that continues with colonial logic. In the context of the rising tide of militant Hindu supremacist notions that are being validated by the ruling party in the current climate where Muslims and minorities are directly subject to state violence, regulated and vigilante, Sharma attests to the forms of resistance that emerge from incarcerated voices, marking the prison itself as a site of political confrontation.

My chapter examines the Netflix-produced show focused on a women's prison, *Orange Is the New Black*, an adaptation of Piper Kerman's memoir by the same name. Kerman interrogates the injustices of the PIC; Kohan's show, while working diligently to construct an entire microcosm of women's lives subject to carceral hegemony and its vagaries, centers the white woman's gaze as its native informant. My analysis reveals the tacit connections of carceral liberalism within the more radical plenitude of abolition democracy that brings to light the racialized punishment that is at the heart of the American carceral system. I address the distance between the memoir written by a prison activist and a show meant to tug at heartstrings and draw the largest number of binge watchers; inadvertently, the emphasis shifts from the memoir's community-focused approach at narration to the show's singular propulsion of innocent "white" protagonist corrupted by the hard "dark" lives within the bars.

Beth Merfish attends to the project of disappearing bodies, stories, and identities through the systematic appearances of museums and sites of public culture in her study of the Texas Prison Museum. Merfish unpacks the tourist purview of the prison museum located in the city that is also the nucleus of the Texas carceral structure, Huntsville. In her analysis, we come to understand how carceral liberalism conducts its ideological work through the objects emplaced in the museum site away from their points of origin—the prison without the prisoner, the invisible carceral complex without the visibility of familial presence. The gaze of the spectator/voyeur/tourist works to reify the righteous ideology governing the Texas carceral logic. Thus Merfish's chapter tunnels into the further perpetuation of imperial logic at work.

In closing part one, Joanna Eleftheriou's narrative speaks to her experiences teaching creative writing to incarcerated graduate students. As a free woman with the privilege that comes from professional independence and class status, she speaks of captivity as forced seclusion resulting from having made mistakes. She wrestles with the contradictions present at every facet of the carceral experience, laying bare the ideologies of state violence writ large on bodies and walls. While Eleftheriou's piece leaves out reflections on race, class, and the intersection of multiple identities that lead so many lives locked in the prison nation, her narrative sheds light on the prison classroom as a site contesting carceral liberalism and questions the morality of prison as punishment. Eleftheriou urges the reader to reckon with their conscience and invites a fellowship in meditation on the criminality of a system that capitalizes on suffering and profits from punishment.

Part Two: Carceral Bodies and Systems

The individual stories and fictions of the first part of the book attest to the systems at work, systems structured by carceral liberalist ideologies. Neoliberalism, patriarchy, and carceral logics work in tandem in systems produced and functioning for profit as a legacy of imperialism. Emerging from the sweet and salty waters of Combahee, a collection of individuals who pointed their fingers at the systems of injustice, the latter half of this book focuses on systemic inequities while keeping the Black radical feminist vision of the CRC as a compass for envisioning a path forward. These chapters in part two focus on carceral bodies and systems. Jeremy Eugene's poem on the complex negotiation between being and erasure faced by Black bodies is an encomium to Sandra Bland, the Black activist who died in a Texas jail after being pulled over for not signaling while changing lanes. The first chapter is a short and powerful piece by a human rights worker in Houston who has dedicated the better part of his life to uplifting the voices and material conditions of migrants, especially those who are poor, undocumented, disabled, and disenfranchised. This chapter by Francisco Argüelles (Pancho) is the singular piece that brings together the poetic and theoretical, the scholarly and activist streams of this volume in his reflections on the struggle to ensure the legal right of Indigenous Mayan day laborers (jornaleros) to stand at the corner seeking work. In Pancho's retelling of this journey alongside the Jornaleros de las Palmas through attempts at restoring their revolutionary dignity, he reveals the workings of U.S. democracy as a ritual that nods toward white supremacy and capitalism rather than systematize freedom.

What follows this is a chapter on alternative justice systems in a San Francisco intentional community, collectively written by Autumn Elizabeth, D Coulombe, and Zarinah Agnew. Troubled by the historical systems of racial injustice informing state-formed systems of criminal justice and the PIC, these members express their experiences of setting up an alternative

Introduction   15

justice model, arising out of anarchist criminology, in opposition to state-appropriated models of alternatives such as restorative and transformative justice. Alt-J critiques victim-offender dyadic forms of criminalization that erase community-based implications and larger contexts of the genesis of violence and harm. The chapter conducts a thorough case study of two homes in the Embassy Network of intentional communities. Alt-J communities counter carceral liberalism through attempts to dismantle reigning discursive structures that pit victim against criminal and further disenfranchise the racialized, poor, and dispossessed, finding instead alternatives toward forging community and collective healing.

Tria Blu Wakpa and Jennifer Musial's chapter focuses on the appropriations evident in prison yoga programs. In "Going Carceral," Blu Wakpa and Musial speak of the problematic framing of incarcerated people as fallen, flawed, and unable to rescue themselves as well as New Age appropriations of eastern philosophies and Yogic practices as an antidote to the impoverishment of ailing prison cultures. The authors point to how the yoga industrial complex erases colonial histories of religious oppression, severs yoga from its religious contexts, and appropriates and erases South Asian bodies while rendering white hegemony natural by presenting whites as teachers who can better the lives of imprisoned Black and brown bodies. The authors speak to how rehabilitative strategies offered by privileged actors in the free world are deeply complicit with apparatuses of state violence, contrasting with productive alternatives such as the ones offered by activists emerging from abolition democracy.

The final three chapters reference local and global sites as they bring in new subjects and modalities for thinking about the carceral. Maria Curtis brings attention to the perspectives and conditions of refugee resettlement of Syrian and Iraqi women and children in Houston. Marta Romero-Delgado highlights the specific methods of punishment and its aftermath for women, especially those involved in activism against state violence in wartime Peru, and Alka Kurian draws our attention to a new wave of youth resistance against state and patriarchal forms of control in India that lock women down in dormitories and residences, barring access to mobility, opportunities, and the rights ascribed to the people of the postcolonial democratic nation.

Curtis reveals the liminal carceral zones occupied by Syrian refugees in Houston. She speaks of the exiled carcerality faced by women and children reeling from PTSD as they resettle in a city and a nation that they can never fully claim as their own. Caught in a web of macro-policy aggressions that profile Arab migrants and microaggressions that involve the educational, city, housing, and employment sectors that continually vilify and keep the women marooned, the refugees battle a sense of terrible displacement in their "vacant refuge." This chapter addresses these states of exception in a city considered to be a putative sanctuary. Curtis speaks of how ideologies of carceral liberalism keep these refugees torqued between memories of violent state repression and a subtle form of rejection that leaves them in a state of perpetual exile.

Marta Romero-Delgado interviews women serving sentences and those who have completed their sentences as members of two left-wing anti-government groups, the Communist Party-Shining Path and the Tupac Amaru Revolutionary Movement, during the Civil War that besieged Peru from 1980–2000. Through her research, Romero-Delgado came to see the differential gendered and racialized treatment accorded female revolutionaries and the suffering they endured once free because they were marked with aberrant femininity. With the harrowing treatment received by these female participants in revolutionary groups once in the prison, the women bore witness to state strategies to annihilate all dissent. The communal forms of confinement often led to a form of continued resistance whereby the women could support, nurture, and protect one another.

Alka Kurian reckons with a dissident feminist youth group rising up in India called "Pinjra Tod," or "Break the Cage" movement. Kurian defines this as a fourth-wave feminist resurgence against patriarchal and state-sanctioned prescriptions that keep young women and girls in carceral conditions under the sign of paternalism. The women rise up against cages of patriarchal and statist confinement, linking themselves to global movements for liberation against what I term as the great American ideological export, carceral liberalism. Kurian's fourth wave demands freedom without apology, state control, or surveillance, and reclaiming of public spaces for pleasure. Pinjra Tod resonates with the vision and call of the CRC as a bold futuristic aspiration advanced by a collective of women who think beyond carceral regimes of surveillance of women's bodies to imagine radical new futures for all women.

Carceral liberalism is the lattice fortifying structures of oppression within and beyond prison walls, as made clear through each chapter in this volume. In so many ways, this volume continues the discussions begun by Julia Sudbury and her colleagues in *Global Lockdown*. Our volume continues to engage in a dialogue that is about enlivening and charging the conversations stemming from radical imaginations at work. Not all the scholar-activists in here are perfectly aligned with one another, are in the same discipline, or explicate the same vision for liberation and/or solidarity. Here, I invoke Max Haiven and Alex Khasnabish's *The Radical Imagination* where they speak of the nexus between ontology, epistemology, and methodology so that radical

Introduction   17

imagination is not something that is possessed, but something that is done. They advise, "We can think about the research imagination not so much as being defined by clear, comprehensive and cohesive alignments between ontology, epistemology, and methodology, but by conflict, contention, difference and debate,"[42] and in that spirit, I believe that the epistemological framework of *Carceral Liberalism* along with the diverse array of research, theories, and poetics brought forth in here evoke dialogue through contestations, affirmations, difference, and tensions. *Carceral Liberalism* is a way of radically rereading the sign of American freedom and democracy and charging that along with the touted exports of ideas, culture, and other signifiers of freedom, the idiom of carcerality is packaged alongside liberation. For those who are at the receiving end of the power of the state, the sign reminds the dispossessed at home and abroad of a carceralized logic that speaks of the very lack of the notions purported as the hallmarks of its identity and its nationhood.

Theories of Resistance

Indeed, in the very line of dialogue launched by Julia Sudbury, and related research published in more recently,[43] the prison industrial complex has continued to grow despite federal and national consensus on prison reform from both sides of the aisle. Despite some momentous shifts in policies around clemency, sentence reduction, and nonviolent offenses, the carceral apparatus is booming.[44] The rehabilitative part of the criminal justice enterprise remains miniscule compared to the larger machinery of justice that grinds lives through abjection, dehumanization, and absolute despair. In a range of chapters that reflect on the carceral in the everyday, this book engages these problematics through interrogation of various sites of power, from a downtown Houston jail, as in Jeremy Eugene's poem dedicated to Sandra Bland,[45] to the bodies subject to power of self-improvement through prison yoga programs, as given in Blu Wakpa and Musial's chapter, to the memories of formerly incarcerated women in Peru, as in Marta Romero-Delgado's chapter. This book offers a range of theories of resistance, interdisciplinary and poetic and theoretical, wide-ranging, capacious, and focused through the pointed analysis offered in research and creative momentum unleashed in poetry.

In the 1970s, thinkers, activists, scholars, and many other Black women came together in various Boston homes and in safe spaces they created to write collectively what is now canonically taught in women and gender studies classes across the United States and beyond. The statement of the Combahee River Collective, crafted in solidarity with Black, working class, and third world women, provides a blueprint for revolutionary thinking. The CRC speaks of an integrated analysis and practice and opens with the acknowledgment and understanding of interlocking systems of oppression that inaugurate political movements of various shades, a method to combat multiple oppressions as envisioned in 1970s. In bringing together the work of radical Black liberation, Civil Rights, and feminism through empathy to all suffering people of the world, the CRC evinces a position of universality that merits distinction because it counters the European hegemonic singularity that till then stood as alibi for imperial colonialist expansions. The CRC speaks of an empathy that stands to uplift all because by the logic of CRC, if Black women are lifted, all will be lifted:[46] "We realize that the liberation of all oppressed peoples necessitates the destruction of the political-economic systems of capitalism and imperialism as well as patriarchy."[47] The CRC envisions the parts needed to assemble the tools to dismantle, brick by brick, the ideology cemented and now named as "carceral liberalism."

Cassandra Little's opening chapter on her subjections, privations, and survivals from the carceral regime attests to the ongoing work necessitated within the CRC's vision. While Curtis accounts for the pain and losses suffered by Syrian and Iraqi immigrants in Houston who come into what she calls a "vacant refuge," Elizabeth, Coulombe, and Agnew speak of an intentional community in San Francisco formed on principles of alternative justice as another form of refuge. *Carceral Liberalism* extends and broadens the conversations inaugurated by Sudbury and continued through the years by Ruth Wilson Gilmore, Sarah Haley, MaDonna Maidment, and others. Sarah Haley connects the dots in an intersectional analysis of Black women's subjection in her book *No Mercy Here: Gender, Punishment, and the Making of Jim Crow Modernity*, through a close reading of the history of Black women's violations in the late nineteenth century during Jim Crow. "By examining the gendered complexities of the carceral state, new continuities with slavery emerge. Although Black women's reproduction was not directly responsible for the reproduction of prisoners, the rape of Black women was crucial to the establishment of white superiority and Black women's representation as subjects who reproduced Black criminality was critical to Black criminalization."[48]

In so many ways, liberal notions of carcerality flow from the colonial logic of imperial machinery institutionalized under the cloak of civilizing missions that include uplift, education, conversion, and other "liberal" tasks that act as alibi for the violence of the colonial apparatus. Our contributors make plain the imperial logic that is always already at work in the heart of the carceral state, which masks its violence under the more palatable flag of liberalism and

Introduction 19

its cousins, development, free market, and progress. Ruth Wilson Gilmore and Craig Gilmore remind us of historical context: "Indeed, from the origin of professionalized policing in the early twentieth century, when Progressivism and Jim Crow arose as an interlocking system of benefit and exclusion, through the gendered racial and regional hierarchies of the New Deal, and on to the courtroom and legislative triumphs of the Civil Rights Movement, the location of the 'thin blue line' has moved but never disappeared as a prime organizing—or disorganizing—principle of everyday life."[49]

Merfish's chapter gives us analytics on reading the prison museum as a site where the violence of the state is rendered invisible and instantiated, normalizing prison in the everyday as a given and necessary agent of "law and order." Recent decades have seen an "increased criminalization to mark the poor as ineligible and undeserving of social programs."[50] The "thin blue line" manages to sever the most dispossessed of their fundamental rights to exist where they choose or render them from their so-called inalienable rights of choice and freedom. The prison is a site of excisions, removals, and exclusions, and in many ways the prison museum is a site where the symbolic order of these exclusions remains embalmed, on exhibit. Through the critical lens brought to bear on the Texas Prison Museum in the prison city, Huntsville, Beth Merfish catalogues artifacts that include creative tools made by the incarcerated and speaks of objects shorn from their original contexts, embodying the inclusions and exclusions practiced on the subjects of the penal system. Merfish's chapter helps conclude part I and moves us into part II of the volume, in gesturing at the discursive order that disappears bodies and reappears them in systems of carceral entombment through the prison museum. Eleftheriou's chapter on the prison classroom raises questions of parallel nodes of reflections arising from the incarcerated/student vis-à-vis free/teacher in a site of another set of inclusions and removals.

In my chapter on the televised serial based on a prison memoir, *Orange Is the New Black*, the imaginary emerges from the radical potentialities of prison abolition. In the figure of Sophia Burset, specifically the trans-figure portrayed by trans-rights activist Laverne Cox in the TV serial, the narrative grapples with the limitations of rights that stop at the prison doors for all who are incarcerated, with the cost most heavily paid by the trans-figure, who remains liminal—their identity questioned by the state as well as their peers who participate in gender policing within the carceral complex. Stanley and Smith's volume *Captive Genders* argues that the critical focus of both trans liberation and work on the carceral complex has to be prison abolition, and in the many testimonies offered in powerful relief throughout, they argue for a remapping of heteronormative neoliberal ideologies that incarcerate alongside the PIC, embodied in the epistolary dialectic by Dillon, who sums up the volume's argument:

> The reasons that he is there in a 9-by-12-foot cage for twenty-three hours a day and that I am here in the "free world" writing to him are not the result of random coincidence, personal choice, or isolated luck. Rather, I am here and he is there because of the (institutionalized) disparate distribution of wealth and poverty; health and illness; freedom and subjection; mobility and captivity; and life and death that is intimately informed by our skin, gender, class, queerness, and so much more. White supremacy, heteropatriarchy, and neoliberal capitalism have made the coerced disintegration of his mind and body acceptable, mundane, unseen, and unknown.[51]

In effect, Dillon sums up the crux of the carceral liberalist ideology at work that marks certain bodies as punishable and others as free.

Shailza Sharma argues in her chapter on the PIC in India that in the legal and carceral chokehold faced by the marginalized bodies exiled from public discourse, the prison memoir becomes the site of a counterdiscourse and a contestation. In the multiple stories of women's lives that are interpellated through state violence and state sanction in the television serial, I point to an early training into carceral logic: for those who are poor and vulnerable, they are always already used to the policing of their bodies long before formal entry into a brick and mortar prison.[52] In naming the ideology of the free state as that of *Carceral Liberalism*, the book strategically points to the parallels with the colonial state that historically carried out its violent machinations under the sign of benevolence and civilization, whilst marauding and violating native bodies, knowledge, and industries. What the state names benevolent often has deleterious effects on the bodies of the poor and the vulnerable, and that's where Black feminist praxis and a transnational feminist consciousness are the stratagem for naming the violence and moving toward possibilities of collective liberation. The CRC's insurgent vision, a Black radical feminist vision in concert with transnational critiques and resistance in locations within and beyond prison walls, forms the nucleus of *Carceral Liberalism*.

Notes

1. Keeanga-Yamahtta Taylor (2017) reinaugurates the intense activist labors of 1970s feminist collectives in her recent book that interviews the living members of Combahee alongside the young activists allied in the Movement for Black Lives, making clear the continuous line of power and resistance in radical black consciousness.

2. *Zami: A New Spelling of My Name* and *Sister Outsider: Essays and Speeches.*

Introduction   21

3. Roberts (2017) reports the obituary of one of the killers, Jon Lester, who moved to England and died under suspicious circumstances at the age of 48 after his release in 2001.

4. Tillet (2019) reflects on how the panic around the case led to the unjust indictment of the black teenagers quickly deemed as the culprits in a case that moved forward with Kafkaesque speed, a case that emblematizes the readiness of a system to punish its Black and brown children.

5. Fisk (1991) reports that the change in New York City due to immigration was remarkable in a decade that marks a rise in immigrant populations from elsewhere—notably Asia, Africa, and Latin America—balancing and remapping a city grappling with white flight and a marked change in demographics.

6. Here I invoke the incisive and prescient analysis of Christopher Lebron (2014), who unpacks the famous Baldwin-Buckley debate of 1965 through the discursive order of racial inequality and shifts the weight from those who are always under examination, the marginalized, "to the ones who benefit from others' marginalization" (156) to account for the violence of living as "raced" subjects through American history and the contemporary period. For Lebron, the cozy nexus of state power and white supremacy that comes to dominate the American political scene is perhaps far from unexpected. The benefits for those who profit from others' marginalization have been writ large in this period from the Oval Office.

7. Schools Under Registration Review (SURR) is an appellate devised by the school board for particular schools in the city of Baltimore troubled by student performance and other sociocultural issues that marked urban public schools in the desegregation era since the 1960s. For more, read Kozol (1992).

8. Shakur (1987).

9. Part of the "Scared Straight" initiatives that remained popular in states like Maryland and California until they were outlawed about a decade later due to their deleterious effects on the teens who were supposed to be discouraged from a life of criminality. African American boys from our high school in Baltimore also were selectively chosen to take field trips to the downtown jail.

10. Freire (2000).

11. https://convention2.allacademic.com/one/nwsa/nwsa17/.

12. "States and Prisons/States as Prisons: Critiques of Carcerality." https://convention2.allacademic.com/one/nwsa/nwsa17/.

13. Demita Frazier, "Combahee Revisited, Movement for Black Lives and Current State of Black Feminist Organizing and Leadership: Intergenerational Conversation," plenary at conference Forty Years after Combahee: Feminist Scholars and Activists Engage the Movement for Black Lives, Baltimore, MD, Nov. 17, 2017.

14. Morton (2013).

15. In *Misdemeanorland* (2018), Issa Kohler-Hausmann argues that there is a larger and more invisible penal structure in which the lives of the poor and the criminalized populations are automatically interpellated through a managerial model of surveilling lives and funneling them into the concrete prison, especially by letting a

person go after citing them for "disorderly conduct." This becomes a type of "get out of jail" card, but the next time the person has police contact, they are more likely to be charged with something more serious, as explained by a public defender in NYC in the 1990s during the "Broken Windows" policing period: "Next time you don't have a bullshit arrest, and you have less truth—less real exclusionary power or whatever. And you can't litigate it, because you're going to lose. You're not going to get the dis con because you took it on your bullshit arrest, which you should have litigated, especially for, like I said, people who are getting stopped and searched all the time" (97). Brett Story (2019) argues that what needs interrogation is not only the structure of the prison, but the societal structures that make these prisons a necessity, and how failed tropes such as "community policing" do the very opposite of what they promise. The term *community* attached to *policing*, like a more insidious version of the bird in the *Portlandia* skit, "denotes nothing in particular, but it hints at positive values such as community control and police de-escalation." As he argues, however, not only does community policing do very little to curb violence or decrease tension, but "as an ideological framework it is essential to support [of] broken windows policing, mass incarceration, and America's system of anti-Black state violence."

16. Here I am indebted to the lifelong work of migration studies scholar Christine Kovic and human rights activist and contributor to this volume Francisco Argüelles, based in Houston, Texas. Their photo essay (2010), written by Kovic and photographed by Argüelles, bears witness to the north-south route stretching from the United States south of the Texas borderlands through Mexico and Central America undertaken by vulnerable migrants who risk life and limb for the treacherous journey north to earn a living. In charting the simultaneous invisibility and hypervisibility of the vulnerable migrants, Kovic speaks of the criminalization of the migrants while noting that they are targeted by thieves who are often "police and other government officials" (89). Regarding the effects of NAFTA-impacted neoliberal policies, Kovic writes, "While goods and capital move freely between the United States and Mexico, the free movement of poor workers from the global south is prohibited" (94).

17. "Incarcerated Women and Girls" (Sentencing Project 2020) details the alarming statistics of the last three decades that show a higher rate of incarceration for women and surveillance through the probationary and jail systems rather than state prisons.

18. Sentencing Project (2022).

19. Hardt and Negri (2000), 190.

20. Alexander (2012).

21. Talve-Goodman (2019).

22. Tillman (2022).

23. Bernstein (2010, 2012).

24. Vick (2015).

25. Batt (2022).

26. Gilmour (2015).

27. Benson (2019).

Introduction   23

28. Sudbury (2004).

29. Genevieve LeBaron and Adrienne Roberts (2010) write in order ". . . to carve out a heuristic space in FPE (Feminist Political Economy) to come to a deeper understanding of carcerality in capitalism . . ." (21).

30. As Wang notes in her text *Carceral Capitalism* (2018), "Black racialization, then, is the mark that renders subjects as suitable for—on the one hand—hyper-exploitation and expropriation, and on the other hand, annihilation" (122). Recommended texts include, but are not limited to, the following: Erica Meiners (2016); Emily L. Thuma (2019); Elizabeth Hinton (2016); Brittney Cooper (2019).

31. Scholars in the 1970s who had begun to envision a society with a reduced reliance on prisons, and alternatives to the punitive state apparatuses, were noting the pernicious effects of imprisonment on human life. Paul Keve (1974) observes, "There is a slang phrase which probably originated far from any prison but which applies better to prison life than do any other two words in the English language—'put-down.' It eloquently describes the emotional effect of being squelched, and as a noun it tells sadly, bitterly just what prison is" (15).

32. Minh-ha (1989).

33. As Danielle Sered (2021) explains, with pathos and political insight, solving societal ills through violent containment of supposedly violent crimes misses the larger picture of pain and trauma of U.S. history. She writes, "America has a long history of disregarding the pain that people experience. I am talking about the America Langston Hughes evokes, the America James Baldwin evokes, the America, frankly, that Donald Trump evokes" (192).

34. In Camp and Heatherton (2016), 279.

35. In Camp and Heatherton (2016), 280.

36. Simpkins's (2016) acute interventions center on the experiences of Black women and how carcerality emerges at the very intersections of race, gender, citizenship, and geography, identifications and subjections begun in the work of Combahee and continuing in current research invigorate the centrality of Black female experiences to the discussion.

37. Alexander (2012).

38. Mark Jay and Philip Conklin (2017) provide an urgently needed historical reflection on the origins of "Broken Windows" policing through the genesis of such systematic racialized policing as it emerges in the mid-twentieth century in Detroit, which, read alongside other forms of structural disenfranchisement, works to further disempower marginalized residents of Detroit while also squelching working-class radicalism and dissent. They write, "The state's primary tactic for dealing with this burgeoning racialized surplus was aggressive criminalization" (32).

39. Davis (2003), 46.

40. Carolyn Sufrin, as a doctor who serves incarcerated women and has studied the conditions under which maternity is surveilled and governed within the jails and prisons, argues (2018) that "mass incarceration disrupts reproduction and motherhood, while simultaneously promoting an idealized, normative motherhood—one

that is largely unattainable for the people being shuffled in and out of prisons and jails" (57).

41. Spektor (2013). You've Got Time lyrics © Sony/ATV Music Publishing LLC, Warner/Chappell Music, Inc., 2013.

42. Haiven and Khasnabish (2014), 218.

43. Gilmore (2007); Gottschalk (2016); Carlton and Russel (2018); Taylor (2018); Moran (2018).

44. Despite talk about reducing the carceral state, Daniel Kato (2017) speaks of a mere realignment in play, rather than any substantive changes that will significantly reduce the carceral state.

45. As Michael Onah (2018) charts in his rigorous look at nineteenth- to twentieth-century policy shifts, especially after the implementation of the IMD Exclusion Act of 1965, state-provided care of the mentally ill is drastically reduced in order to value "dollars over lives." He states, "While the IMD Exclusion is poorly conceived and effectively facilitated the dramatic rise in the incarceration of the mentally ill, the provision was originally the lynchpin of an earnest movement to reform a deteriorating public mental healthcare system."

46. Marquita Smith's (2018) gifted analysis of Ava DuVernay's film *Middle of Nowhere* (2012) speaks to the film's ability to help audiences contend with the tentacular hold of carcerality to make subjects beyond the prison walls, which often includes women and children for the 93% population of incarcerated men, as embodied in the protagonist Ruby, who gives up her career aspirations of medical school in order to keep visiting and supporting her husband, Derek. Smith writes, "Under the carceral state, collectives matter as sources of resistance and support" (9) and further, notes how the carceral extensions reify the supporting family also into a state of social death. "The social death that Ruby undergoes highlights how carceral care unfixes notions of care from attentions to the body" (Smith 11).

47. Combahee River Collective.

48. Haley (2016), 251.

49. Gilmore and Gilmore (2016), 174–75.

50. Gilmore and Gilmore (2016), 175.

51. Dillon (2015), 197.

52. In a text emerging from the Canadian context, *Doing Time on the Outside* (2006), Maidment points to communities as an always-already site of punishment that continually criminalize the poor, "The community can be as repressive a site for punishment and control as the prison. Underlying penal rationales that fail to depart from the traditional goal of punishment, neoliberal governance strategies that wage war on the poor, women, and racialized groups, neoconservative policies that call for even tougher crime control tactics, and economic motives that view communities as a means of meting out cheap so-called justice usurp even the most benevolent of intentions" (32).

Bibliography

Alexander, Michelle. *The New Jim Crow: Mass Incarceration in the Age of Colorblindness*. New York: New Press, 2012.

Anzaldua, Gloria, and Cherrie Moraga, eds. *This Bridge Called My Back: Writings by Radical Women of Color*. New York: Kitchen Table/Women of Color Press, 1983.

Batt, Madeline. "The Truth behind Dennis Hope's Decades of Torture in Solitary Confinement." *Solitary Watch*, February 17, 2022. https://solitarywatch.org/.

Benson, Sarah. "The Architecture of Liberalism and the Origins of Carceral Democracy." In *The Prison of Democracy: Race, Leavenworth, and the Culture of Law*, 15–33. Oakland: University of California Press, 2019.

Bernstein, Elizabeth. "Militarized Humanitarianism Meets Carceral Feminism: The Politics of Sex, Rights, and Freedom in Antitrafficking Campaigns." *Signs* 36. no. 1 (Autumn 2010): 45–71.

———. "Carceral Politics as Gender Justice? The 'Traffic in Women' and Neoliberal Circuits of Crime, Sex, and Rights." *Theory and Society* 41, no. 3 (May 2012): 233–59.

Blackmon, Douglas. *Slavery by Another Name: The Re-Enslavement of Black Americans from the Civil War to World War II*. New York: Anchor Books, 2009.

Camp, Jordan T., and Christina Heatherton, eds. *Policing the Planet: Why the Policing Crisis Led to Black Lives Matter*. New York: Verso, 2016.

Carlton, Bree, and Emma Russel. *Resisting Carceral Violence: Women's Imprisonment and the Politics of Abolition*. Cham, Switzerland: Palgrave MacMillan, 2018.

Childs, Dennis. *Slaves of the State: Black Incarceration from the Chain Gang to the Penitentiary*. Minneapolis: University of Minnesota Press, 2015.

Combahee River Collective. "The Combahee River Collective Statement." In *Home Girls: A Black Feminist Anthology*, edited by Barbara Smith, 264–65. New Brunswick, NJ: Rutgers University Press, 2000.

Cooper, Brittney. *Eloquent Rage: A Black Feminist Discovers Her Superpower*. New York: Picador, 2019.

Crenshaw, Kimberlé. "Demarginalizing the Intersection of Race and Sex: A Black Feminist Critique of Antidiscrimination Doctrine, Feminist Theory and Antiracist Politics." *University of Chicago Legal Forum* 1989, no. 1, article 8. http://chicago unbound.uchicago.edu/uclf/vol1989/iss1/8.

Davis, Angela. *Are Prisons Obsolete?* New York: Seven Stories Press, 2003.

———. *Abolition Democracy: Beyond Empire, Prisons, and Torture*. New York: Seven Stories Press, 2005.

Davis, Angela, and Gina Dent. "Prison as a Border: A Conversation on Gender, Globalization and Punishment." *Signs* 26, no. 4, Globalization and Gender (Summer 2001): 1235–41.

Dillon, Stephen. "The Only Freedom I Can See: Imprisoned Queer Writing and the Politics of the Unimaginable." In *Captive Genders: Trans Embodiment and the Prison Industrial Complex*, edited by Eric A. Stanley and Nat Smith, 195–210. Oakland, CA: AK Press, 2015.

Fisk, Edward B. "New York Growth Is Linked to Immigration." *New York Times,* February 22, 1991. https://www.nytimes.com/.

Freire, Paulo. *Pedagogy of the Oppressed,* trans. Myra Bergman Ramos. New York: Bloomsbury, 2000.

Gilmore, Ruth Wilson. *The Golden Gulag: Prisons, Surplus, Crisis, and Opposition in Globalizing California.* Berkeley: University of California Press, 2007.

Gilmore, Ruth Wilson, and Craig Gilmore. "Beyond Bratton." In *Policing the Planet: Why the Policing Crisis Led to Black Lives Matter,* edited by Jordan T. Camp and Christina Heatherton, 173–99. New York: Verso, 2016.

Gilmour, Andrew. "The Nelson Mandela Rules: Protecting the Rights of Persons Deprived of Liberty." *UN Chronicle,* December 2015. https://www.un.org/en/un-chronicle/.

Gottschalk, Marie. *Caught: The Prison State and the Lockdown of American Politics.* Princeton: Princeton University Press, 2016.

Haiven, Max, and Alex Khasnabish. *The Radical Imagination: Social Movement in the Age of Austerity.* London: Zed Books, 2014.

Haley, Sarah. *No Mercy Here: Gender, Punishment, and the Making of Jim Crow Modernity.* Chapel Hill: The University of North Carolina Press, 2016.

Hardt, Guy, and Antonio Negri. *Empire.* Cambridge, MA: Harvard University Press, 2000.

Hartman, Saidiya. *Scenes of Subjection: Terror, Slavery, and Self-Making in Nineteenth-Century America.* New York: Oxford University Press, 1997.

———. *Lose Your Mother: A Journey along the Atlantic Slave Route.* New York: Farrar, Straus and Giroux, 2007.

Hill, Marc Lamont. *Nobody: Casualties of America's War on the Vulnerable, from Ferguson to Flint and Beyond.* New York: Atria Books, 2016.

Hinton, Elizabeth. *From the War on Poverty to the War on Crime: The Making of Mass Incarceration in America.* Cambridge, MA: Harvard University Press, 2016.

JanMohamed, Abdul. "The Economy of Manichean Allegory." In *The Post-Colonial Studies Reader,* ed. Bill Ashcroft, Gareth Griffiths, and Helen Tiffin, 19–23. New York: Routledge, 1995.

Jay, Mark, and Philip Conklin. "Detroit and the Political Origins of 'Broken Windows' Policing." *Race and Class* 59, no. 2 (2017): 26–48. SAGE Publications.

Kato, Daniel. "Carceral State 2.0?: From Enclosure to Control and Punishment to Surveillance." *New Political Science* 39, no. 2 (2017): 198–217. EBSCOhost.

Keve, Paul W. *Prison Life and Human Worth.* Minneapolis: University of Minnesota Press, 1974.

Killer Mike. "Reagan." By EI-P, Killer Mike, and Jason Demarco. Recorded 2011–2012. Track 6 on *R.A.P. Music.* William Street Records. https://www.youtube.com/.

Kohler-Hausmann, Issa. *Misdemeanorland: Criminal Courts and Social Control in an Age of Broken Windows Policing.* Princeton, NJ: Princeton University Press, 2018.

Kovic, Christine, and Francisco Argüelles. "The Violence of Security: Central American Migrants Crossing Mexico's Southern Border." *Anthropology Now* 2, no. 1 (2010): 87–97. Accessed June 12, 2021. JSTOR.

Kozol, Jonathan. *Savage Inequalities: Children in America's Schools*. New York: Harper Perennial, 1992.

LeBaron, Genevieve, and Adrienne Roberts. "Toward a Feminist Political Economy of Capitalism and Carcerality." *Signs* 36, no. 1 (2010): 19–44.

Lebron, Christopher. "Equality from a Human Point of View." *Critical Philosophy of Race* 2, no. 2 (2014): 125–59. JSTOR.

LeFlouria, Talitha L. *Chained in Silence: Black Women and Convict Labor in the New South*. Chapel Hill: University of North Carolina Press, 2016.

Lorde, Audre. *Zami: A New Spelling of My Name*. New York: Crossing Press, 1982.

Lorde, Audre, and Cheryl Clarke. *Sister Outsider: Essays and Speeches*. New York: Crossing Press, 2007.

Maidment, MaDonna R. *Doing Time on the Outside: Deconstructing the Benevolent Community*. Toronto: University of Toronto Press, 2006.

Mbembe, Achille. "The Intimacy of Tyranny." In *The Post-Colonial Studies Reader*, ed. Bill Ashcroft, Gareth Griffiths, and Helen Tiffin, 66–69. New York: Routledge, 1995.

Meiners, Erica. *For the Children? Protecting Innocence in a Carceral State*. Minneapolis: University of Minnesota Press, 2016.

Minh-ha, Trinh T. *Woman, Native, Other: Writing Postcoloniality and Feminism*. Bloomington: Indiana University Press, 1989.

Moran, Dominique. *Carceral Geography: Spaces and Practices of Incarceration*. New York: Routledge, 2018.

Morgan, Robin, ed. *Sisterhood Is Powerful: An Anthology of Writings from the Women's Liberation Movement*. New York: Random House, 1970.

Morton, Timothy. *Hyperobjects: Philosophy and Ecology after the End of the World*. Minneapolis: University of Minnesota Press, 2013.

Onah, Michael. "The Patient-to-Prisoner Pipeline: The IMD Exclusion's Adverse Impact on Mass Incarceration in United States." *American Journal of Law and Medicine* 44, no. 1 (2018): 119–44. Gale.

Parenti, Christopher. *Lockdown America: Police and Prisons in the Age of Crisis*. New York: Verso, 2008.

Perkinson, Robert. *Texas Tough: The Rise of America's Prison Empire*. New York: Metropolitan Books, 2010.

Petrella, C. "Courting Carcerality: The Rise of Paraprisons in the Era of Neoliberal Racial Statecraft." PhD diss., University of California Berkeley, Spring 2016. http://www.escholarship.org/.

Roberts, Sam. "Jon Lester, Convicted in Howard Beach Race Attack, Dies at 48." *New York Times*, October 23, 2017. https://www.nytimes.com/.

The Sentencing Project. "Incarcerated Women and Girls." November 24, 2020. https://www.sentencingproject.org/publications/incarcerated-women-and-girls/.

———. "Criminal Justice Facts." 2022. https://www.sentencingproject.org/criminal-justice-facts/.

Sered, Danielle. *Until We Reckon: Violence, Mass Incarceration, and a Road to Repair.* New York: New Press, 2021.

Shakur, Assata. *Assata: An Autobiography.* Chicago: Zed Books, 1987.

Shankar, Ravi. *Correctional.* Madison: University of Wisconsin Press, 2022.

Simpkins, Antwann M. *Under Siege: Black Women, the Choreography of Law, and the Public Carceral Sphere.* Los Angeles: University of California Press, 2016.

Smith, Marquita R. "'Don't Be a Martyr.'" *The Black Scholar* 48, no. 1 (2018): 6–19. EBSCOhost.

Spektor, Regina. "You've Got Time." Sire Records, 2013. Single.

Stanley, Eric A., and Nat Smith. *Captive Genders: Trans Embodiment and the Prison Industrial Complex.* Oakland, CA: AK Press, 2015.

Story, Brett. *Prison Land: Mapping Carceral Power across Neoliberal America.* Minneapolis: University of Minnesota Press, 2019.

Sudbury, Julia, ed. *Global Lockdown: Race, Gender, and the Prison-Industrial Complex.* New York: Routledge, 2004.

Sufrin, Carolyn. "Making Mothers in Jail: Carceral Reproduction of Normative Motherhood." *Reproductive Biomedicine and Society Online* 7 (Nov. 2018): 55–65. https://www.sciencedirect.com/.

Talve-Goodman, Sarika. "Cold War Carceral Liberalism and Other Counternarratives: The Case of Alan Paton's *Cry, the Beloved Country.*" *Safundi* 20, no. 2 (2019): 153–73. https://doi.org/10.1080/17533171.2019.1557449.

Taylor, Chlöe. *Foucault, Feminism, and Sex Crimes: An Anti-Carceral Analysis.* New York: Routledge, 2018.

Taylor, Keeanga-Yamahtta. *How We Get Free: Black Feminism and the Combahee River Collective.* Chicago: Haymarket Books, 2017.

Thuma, Emily L. *All Our Trials: Prisons, Policing, and the Feminist Fight to End Violence.* Urbana: University of Illinois Press, 2019.

Tillet, Salamishah. "'When They See Us' Transforms Its Victims into Heroes." *New York Times,* May 30, 2019. https://www.nytimes.com/.

Tillman, Korey. "Carceral Liberalism: The Coloniality and Antiblackness of Coercive Benevolence." *Social Problems* (February 2022). https://doi.org/10.1093/socpro/spac003.

Vick, Jason. "Putting Cruelty First": Liberal Penal Reform and the Rise of the Carceral State." *Social Justice* 42, no. 1 (2015): 35–52. JSTOR.

Wacquant, Loïc. *Punishing the Poor: The Neoliberal Government of Social Insecurity.* Durham, NC: Duke University Press, 2009.

Wang, Jackie. *Carceral Capitalism.* Semiotext(e) Intervention Series 21. South Pasadena, CA: Semiotext(e), 2018.

Zamora, Javier. *Unaccompanied.* Port Townsend, WA: Copper Canyon Press, 2017.

PART ONE

Carceral Narratives and Fictions

PANTOUM FOR A BLACK MAN ON A GREYHOUND BUS
Honorée Fanonne Jeffers

I just met him and he looks out the window, cries,
tells me he spent fifteen years behind prison walls.
What I can say to him is a weak *welcome home.*
I can't find vocabulary to resolve absence.

He left fifteen years behind prison walls.
Anne Sexton used to call her asylum a jail.
I wish there were vocabulary to resolve absence,
to name the fight past newborn insanity.

Anne Sexton used to call her asylum a jail.
I don't want to know how this brother earn his cell.
He's fighting his way past newborn insanity,
weeping for his mother and her useless songs.

I don't want to know what earned him a cell.
My real brother's mother died on her kitchen floor.
What of that night? What of her useless songs?
Did my brother hear the prayers breaking in her hands?

I think of my stepmother murdered on her floor:
at twenty-nine, my brother became his father's son.
What of those prayers breaking in Camille's hands?
For whose sake should my brother be forgiven?

At twenty-nine, my brother became his father's son,
the trail of blood beginning at the sire's gate.
For whose sake should my brother be forgiven?
Am I a woman or am I my brother's keeper?

My brothers spill blood at their sisters' gates
while we watch our doors with uneasy eyes.
Are we supposed to be our brothers' keepers
when those children return as sullen men?

And here I watch my door with uneasy eyes,
hoping I can welcome my brother home:
a child who returns as a grown man,
who looks out the window and cries to himself.

LOST LETTER #27: JOHN PETERS, BOSTON-GAOL
TO PHILLIS WHEATLEY PETERS, BOSTON, DECEMBER 3, 1784
Honorée Fanonne Jeffers

Wife,

Please write and let me touch your care.
There is no need for fear, for no one dares
to read your letters. We are Negroes and poor.
No one awaits to take our love and spin its ink
on a broadside. Please do not be filled with temper.
I should have written sooner, but paper and ink
are scarce and I shall not think of what I must do to secure
the means *[i have never been on a ship but these jailors*
bear the look of sailors they are greedy to touch They offer
terrible means and i want to come home to you clean
be patient with me woman please let me be clean] Wife
please write me. I know what your silences mean,
your disappointment and sacrifices but I wait
each day for your letters and poems. I told the men
in this heaving cell that my wife is the famed Negro
Poetess. They laughed until your first favor arrived
and then I read your lines to them. Wife, please write
me. *[i am still your man i have tried woman don't you*
understand i love you i have tried surely you know I have
tried there was no money after the war everyone was starving
but i gave my meals to you I have tried i love you do]
Christmas is coming soon, and snow will drift
through these bars. Please send a poem my way.
Your words are my only want.

Your John

PS Woman, please write.

During and after the American Revolutionary War, the former British colonies were
plunged into an economic crisis leading to poverty among Americans of all cultural
backgrounds. John Peters was in and out of debtors' prison during much of his
six-year marriage to the famous poet Phillis Wheatley (Peters). He probably was in
Boston's jail—then, "gaol"—when his wife passed away on December 5, 1784.

1

Carceral Trauma at the Intersections of Race, Class, Gender, Sexuality, and Maternity

CASSANDRA D. LITTLE

As a Black, Queer, educated mother who was given the opportunity to experience the carceral state very early in childhood—so early that my subconscious mind stored evidence of what was paved before me—I must admit that it took some of the most epic soul-searching and heartfelt conversations for me to find the root of my personal experience with also being labeled as a felon. My introduction into the prison industrial complex began when I was nine years old in the fall of 1973, right around the time my parents' divorce was still fresh in my mind, and the United States was in political turmoil. I was constantly trying to drown out everything that was deemed important, including the headline news, concerning the president's transgressions—which seemed to follow me everywhere. They played the news about the Watergate scandal at the corner store, at our neighborhood candy store, in my grandparents' car, and at my friends' houses. Back in those days, it seemed as if I had to bury my head completely in the sand to not hear about an impending impeachment.

At home, which I shared with my maternal grandparents, mother, and two younger sisters, my grandfather's FM radio often played in the kitchen. He'd sit at the table, which his legs, alternating right and left, would shake. At the same time, he'd have a cup of coffee with the newspaper in front of him, while the television blared from his and my grandmother's bedroom. This happened constantly. I recall hearing President Nixon declare from multiple media devices, "I am not a crook!"[1]

My grandmother adopted the word "crook" alongside a trail of other ungodly nouns and finally "God bless you!" repeatedly echoed from my brown-skinned, big-boned grandma's mouth thereafter. If ever anyone crossed her, they got a tongue lashing. I instinctively knew to trust her wisdom because of her martyrdom, her bleeding heart. She catered to her skirt-chasing husband in between managing six misguided adult children, and to her, they all deserved her adoration. I paid attention to my role models with a fiery defiance that flipped how I felt about responsibilities and relationships. My elders were living in survival mode, and as a young girl, I knew it—it was innate. During this impressionable period of my life, I began visiting any given uncle in San Quentin prison. I was young but fully aware of the consequences of breaking rules and laws. As the oldest child, I was an outgoing, very independent, strong-willed little girl, and I knew that my grandmother's New Orleans tendencies volleyed between martyrdom and courage. Looking back, I see how my grandparents essentially became full-time babysitters. My father became an alcoholic and remarried, and my mother began a life of abusing drugs, which included serving time in jail and prison—for multiple, nonviolent, drug-related offenses. In 1975 my sisters and I were being raised by both maternal and paternal grandparents because the writing was on the wall. My family dynamic was dysfunctional at a level that was too far gone for me not to embrace. By 1977 my mother had two additional little girls—the youngest was born addicted to heroin and picked up from the hospital by my aunt, while my mom went to serve time in prison.

There were occasions when I witnessed my mother's criminal activities firsthand. One of those times happened toward the end of summer in 1980. My mother took my sisters and me shopping for school clothes and ended up getting arrested for using someone else's checks and identification for the purchases. Instead of allowing my grandparents to pick us up, as I had begged the officers to do, they made me drive my mother's car to the police station as she sat in the back of the police car. There was one police car driving in front of me with my mother yelling and screaming in the back seat—and another police car trailed behind me. Once we arrived at the police station, all I could think about was the marijuana joint my mother had given me to hide in my pocket. I feared being caught and thrown in jail, too—so I pushed the joint all the way into the corner of my pocket. As we sat at the police station all I could think about was the consequences associated with having that joint in my pocket. I was pissed off at my mother, I couldn't comprehend why she did this to me. That was the pivotal moment when I decided that I would never trust her again.

Once I turned 18, my grandmother told me that she wasn't about to visit my mom in jail anymore, and that I was old enough to take my two younger sisters to the California Institute for Women without supervision. My grandmother had grown tired of my mom's drug habits, which included illegal activities ranging from drug dealing to identity theft. She passed the torch to me, and at the time I didn't want it either. I was stuck in between doing what was right for my family and doing what was right for me. I recalled feeling resentful of my parents' inability to provide me with two functional, loving parents. My dad remarried a single mother with two daughters and a son—right around the same ages as my two younger sisters and me. He found another family, while my sisters and I remained at the mercy of a reckless, drug-addicted mother who become too entrenched in her addictions to adequately raise kids.

I grew up in East Palo Alto (EPA), California—a safe hood, located approximately 32 miles from Oakland. During my childhood, I witnessed a slow yet impactful evolution of the effects of living in a carceral existence. Up until 1985, my hometown had an ambiance of a broken village, but thereafter, EPA became a war zone. In 1992, East Palo Alto made headline news for birthing the highest homicide rate in the country.[2] Crack cocaine, incarceration, ongoing killings, and broken families were scattered throughout my community. The aftermath of growing up in such trauma haunted me and my strides toward reaching the American Dream.

Douglass James Fort, a criminologist who also grew up in EPA and relates to my upbringing, writes, "The Crack Epidemic was capitalized upon the criminal justice system, triggering policy makers to make laws that put a lot of family and friends in prison for a long time, and in many ways are still sitting in these prisons today."[3] His personal insight speaks to me. Growing up in an environment peppered with drug abuse, trauma, and routine prison visits may have assisted me in becoming familiar with an environment that never left my psyche nor my direction in life. I was bound to familiarize myself with the prison industrial complex, no matter how optimistic I was about paving the way for a life free of restrictions by conducting myself properly, which entailed being a law-abiding, ambitious person—against all odds.

I graduated high school in 1982, then went to college in Southern California on a basketball scholarship. I played basketball for four years and graduated with ideas of who I wanted to be, as well as how I was going to help my sisters and other children, especially little brown kids who grew up in circumstances similar to mine. There was nothing more encouraging for me than when my youngest sister would greet me with such love and joy when I walked through the door, wrapping herself around my legs to hinder me from leaving again for college. I promised myself that I was going to take care of them, all of my sisters, but first I had to find the means to take care of myself.

After I graduated from college in December 1987 with my bachelor's degree in sociology, I started working full-time at a child welfare agency called

1. Carceral Trauma   37

Childhelp USA.[4] Two months later I received a very distressing call from one of my sisters. During that call she informed me that my maternal grandmother had decided that she could no longer take care of all of my mother's children, four by then; one of my sisters had a toddler of her own and the other, like my mother, was using drugs. That next weekend I hopped into my car and loaded it up with three of my four sisters, my toddler nephew, and all of their belongings. We started our new lives in my two-bedroom apartment in Redlands, California. For the next two years, with the help of my sister, we raised our two baby sisters until my mother was once again free and could meet their needs adequately.

After my sisters returned to my mother's care, I decided to move to Reno, Nevada, with a woman I loved. For the first time in years, I felt free to create the life of my dreams. I secured a job in Reno working at a treatment center for youth. My life began to move forward positively in the next two years. During this period, I was also struggling with my identity as a Queer Black woman in Nevada. After two years my girlfriend, who was beginning to find herself, decided to leave Reno to pursue graduate school in another state. I decided to stay back. My Queerness for me has always been about how I loved and who I loved. Not until I entered graduate school to pursue my master's in social work did I embrace my identity as a Queer Black woman. I attribute a lot of my growth during that period to a professor who introduced me to Audre Lorde, June Jordan, James Baldwin, and more. I spent most of my time in the library reading and absorbing any and every bit of information I could on Queerness and how it intersects with being Black and a woman in America. This period was crucial to the formation of my Black feminist identity. It was not that I had not been exposed to people who were Gay in my youth. I had an aunt who was openly Gay and would often bring her girlfriends to visit my grandmother's home. It was more about trying to develop my identity outside of my family, especially my mother. My Queerness has always been my strength; I knew I did not fit in everywhere so I developed a way of being that would not require me to explain who I am to anyone. I overachieved and excelled at any and everything I put my mind into doing. My thought was that my excellence would make me unsurpassable.

Time flew by, and I found myself juggling the last year of my master's program and plans for my future. Once again, I received a distressing call from my baby sister, who was now a sophomore in high school, this time stating that she needed to leave my mother's home. It had become unbearable for her, and she shared she could not take living with my mother anymore. This time when I sought my mother's permission to take in my sister, I knew she would not be returning to that home. Two years later, under my care, my

38   LITTLE

baby sister successfully graduated from high school. From there, she joined the Navy. I have never regretted my choices to pause and help my sisters. They have been my main purpose in life and my lifeline.

Upon graduating with my master's in social work, I obtained my clinical license and worked as a licensed social worker in the field of child welfare for five years. During my college years, one of my sisters fell victim to crack-cocaine addiction. In the terrible years of 1987–1999, she gave birth to nine crack-exposed babies. After I was notified that she had given birth to her youngest child and that he was going into foster care and was very ill with a heart problem, my partner at the time and I decided that we would take custody of my nephew. I agreed to accept custody once my sister obtained long-term birth control. After six months of completing legal paperwork and preparing our home for the baby, we were allowed to take Aaron home from Fresno to Reno. My partner, a registered nurse by training, had two incredible sons of her own, aged nine and ten. Bringing Aaron home was the perfect addition to our little family. When I initially saw Aaron, it was love at first sight. I remember holding him for the very first time, and how his little hands seemed to be touching every area of my face as we smiled at each other. It was an immediate connection, one that reflects the beauty of a mother-son relationship. That maternal feeling has always kept me centered and whole.

In 2000 I decided I wanted to pursue my doctorate in counseling educational psychology. This was in line with my long-term goal to eventually become a professor at a university. By 2002 I had acquired enough expertise, professional relationships, and courage to start my own foster care agency. I felt a strong desire to offer a nurturing yet therapeutic environment that provided not only the basic requirements of shelter, food, clothing, access to a team of health care professionals, and education—but also life and relationship-building skills. Because of my childhood, I felt it was necessary to guide abused children to dream beyond their suffering and trauma.

On March 5, 2003, I opened Ujima Youth Services to provide services for abused kids in the foster-care system. Aside from bringing home my son, it was one of the proudest moments in my life, to align myself with the results of all the hard work it took to even consider opening a community-based business. I borrowed the name Ujima from a Kwanzaa principle that means "collective work and responsibility."[5] My goal was to provide a safe, loving, supportive, purposeful program for all youths who were considered by many in the community to be "unsalvageable." It reminded me of my childhood days of helping my grandmother and her friends at the co-op community store in our neighborhood. And I had wonderful memories such as communities working together to help each other and listening to Angela Davis's speech in East Palo Alto after she was released. I remember her standing on a podium in front of the co-op with her big, beautiful afro and her fist raised signifying Black power.

Many of the youth who were referred to Ujima were severely traumatized. Ujima had nearly ten youth in the program, and we were running short of beds. This population was rapidly increasing as cycles of drug abuse and incarceration continued to separate children from their parents. My "adopted" city had a growing need for providers such as myself, and I had all the available resources to manage a successful business that would benefit the youth, alongside the community in which we all resided. By 2009, Ujima had grown to sixty-five youths from ages five to twenty-two years old, and over fifty staff members. My goals and dreams were becoming a reality; I had my four sisters by my side, many of my family members, and close friends—who provided love and care to the youths in Northern Nevada. Seven years had passed with the promise of continued service. Then, one fateful day in October of that same year, an IRS agent and a Medicaid fraud investigator[6] entered my office asking about the whereabouts of my brother-in-law—who was also the chief financial officer of Ujima Youth Services. This inquiry wrecked years of my dedicated work and service. Overnight I shape-shifted from being a mother, community leader, caring foster mother, licensed clinical social worker, and professional to a suspect in a white-collar crime.

In April 2010, I received the dreaded letter stating that my agency would no longer receive funding and that the youths then in my program would have to be removed by May 20, 2010. My dreams turned into nightmares. For the next two years I spent most of my time in my blue lounge chair, contemplating suicide, mindlessly watching television, praying like I've never prayed before for answers as to why this was happening to me and what was going to happen next. I knew I was traumatized by the sudden investigation into my business affairs. I wasn't prepared for the most intense anxiety I would ever experience as an adult. The mystery of not knowing what was going on with my life catapulted me into a major depressed and paranoiac state. I began to feel like my house was being watched, and frequently peered through the blinds in my upstairs room. I was fully convinced that my home was under surveillance every time I saw a police car drive down the street. I didn't speak much on the phone because I began hearing strange noises during conversations, and I was sure someone was listening in on my calls. I'd often receive messages that investigators were speaking to friends, family, community members, and some of my former foster care youths to gather information about me and my organization. One day I received a frantic call from my nephew, who was in one of my offices that I had converted to a music studio for kids in the community: Federal Bureau of Investigation (FBI) agents were raiding my office. I got into my car and drove to see what was going on. By this time my agency had been closed over a year. When I reached the office and asked what was going on, the young Medicaid Fraud Control Unit (MFCU) investigator abruptly told me that I was not the one to ask questions, they were. He proceeded to ask me if I had a bomb or weapons on the premises. Nervously, I laughed and said, "NO! that's ridiculous." They handed me a warrant, told us to leave the premises, and stated that they had keys to lock the door. I was astounded. What was going on? You would have thought I had murdered someone.

The investigation lasted for another two years, during which time I had no frame of reference as to the toll of this ongoing surveillance. I tried to gain insight into what I had done that was legally or even morally wrong. I began to feel personally attacked. Did the government wage war against me because of the color of my skin? Was it due to my gender or sexual preference? In the past I had very little concern over how people judged me, but this was completely different. My freedom and livelihood were in their hands, rendering me powerless; I had no income, no business, and no job. I was so financially in the hole, I couldn't afford an attorney, leaving me at the mercy of the system. As in my childhood, the carceral state was in full control of the narrative, and all I could do was sit in my blue lounge chair and wait for the unknown. The only thing that kept me hopeful was the time spent with my son, my grandkids, and close family members.

In 2013, the same two investigators appeared at my doorstep. They asked if they could enter my home and handed me an indictment. *The United States v. Cassandra Little* was underway and all I could say to myself was, "Finally!" At least I was in the position to find out what the government wanted from me. As I read the indictment my hands began to shake. I could not get past the heading, "The United States v. Cassandra Little." It was the scariest document I have ever held in my hands. The next day I called the Federal Public Defender's Office and arranged to meet with someone who could assist me with understanding exactly what was happening with my case, and how I could possibly fight it.

My assigned public defender was very helpful. She was about to retire and did not waste any time telling me that everything would move quickly. Every time I presented her with my argument countering the government's assertion, she'd remind me that the carceral state was not about the truth. It was about what they could and would try to prove. In other words, I was at their mercy and therefore powerless.

1. Carceral Trauma   41

After many sleepless nights researching and trying to understand being processed by the prison industrial complex, I succumbed to the reality that the federal government has a 93% conviction rate.[7] It's damn-near impossible to win a criminal case against the system, so I had to accept the judgment handed to me with the same resolute confidence that was part of my persona. I decided that as a poor Black woman in Reno, Nevada, I would not stand a chance at a fair trial. I found out that it would be less punitive for me to plead guilty to my original indictment, which entailed twenty-eight counts of healthcare fraud and ten counts of money laundering, totaling $84,000, than to take a chance on defending myself in a biased jury trial. After enduring a 2.5-hour discovery hearing,[8] which I had requested to force the government to prove their assertion that my work for the past seven years was fraudulent and therefore required me to pay over one million dollars in restitution, I was sentenced by the judge to serve thirty-three months instead of the sixty months the Government suggested. In addition, I had to pay $84,000 in restitution according to the original indictment charge. I question the system's decision to incarcerate me as well as requiring me to repay the $84,000. When you look at it, taxpayers paid for the government's three-year investigation, the court hearings, my twenty-three months of incarceration, and my five months at a halfway house. Let's not forget about the sixty-four youth, many of whom had to be placed in higher-level, high-cost facilities, and the many staff members who were forced to get on welfare, food stamps, or unemployment. My case reveals the flaws of the state's logic, which demurred on leniency to a Queer Black woman but stood ready to bail out big banks.

That fateful day finally came, and I found myself incarcerated at a federal prison camp in Victorville, California. I decided to actively participate in a process that was constructed to destroy my consciousness and way of being. I deemed myself a conscientious prisoner by practicing radical acceptance, which is defined as accepting life without resistance. There's no need to do anything to change outcomes as it's fruitless. Radical acceptance is about saying yes to life, just as is. I survived the worst period of my life and somehow escaped suicide or insanity. After the closing of Ujima Youth Services, my dream and my life's work were over. I visualized myself peacefully lying in a shiny casket, wearing my Sunday best, as my loved ones cried and spoke about what a wonderful and loving person I was. As I walked away from a life I had planned my entire childhood, I was heading closer to what I had been avoiding as a person of color in the United States. As I looked back and waved goodbye to my close friend, my designated person, Rebecca, I took a deep breath and pulled open the heavy door. My heart raced as I slowly stepped into a world I had always feared. I recall thinking that it would be great to just drop dead from a heart attack, right there in the hallway. That way I would bypass my federal prison camp sentence of thirty-three months for healthcare fraud and money laundering.

After waiting anxiously for nearly two hours to be processed, I was escorted to the women's bathroom by one of the correctional officers, where she nervously instructed me to strip off my clothing. As a middle-aged woman, I had grown into being conservative about who I exposed my body to, but when she asked me to bend over, tears filled my eyes, and I decided to complete my intake with as little eye contact as possible. I stuck out my tongue without regard for my privacy and coughed directly in front of me while looking through the correctional officer. When asked to lift my breasts for contraband, I held them toward my face without pause. I was operating outside of my body, which was fine with me, now. The emotional impact of that three-minute ordeal remains with me to this day. After it was clear that I was free of any unauthorized materials, I was handed a black mesh laundry bag that had a green smock dress, three pairs of large men's tube socks, four panties, travel-size toiletries, a pair of oversized and used slip-on tennis shoes, and a pair of black used crocs. As I searched through the bag for something to wear, the officer said, "Welcome to the BOP."[9]

Orange Is the New Black (2013) came to Netflix at the same time I was being indicted. I spent many of my days attempting to research the federal criminal justice system and the federal prison system. Most of the information that was provided was specific to the experiences and the needs of men. The show was based on a book by Piper Kerman, who was imprisoned within the federal prison system. I was intrigued when I heard of the book; it was the first current point of reference that was available to me at the time. After reading Piper Kerman's memoir, I had a difficult time watching the Netflix series, as it played mostly toward entertaining the masses, but I was torn because at least there was something that spoke to the experiences of women. At that moment I decided that it was my duty to share my story and my truths, so that women like me could have a narrative that would speak to our experiences from a space of truth, not entertainment.

I was amazed as I walked pass the prison TV room where women were lined up in green plastic chairs, sitting with clear transistor radios from the overpriced commissary, radios that were programmed to pick up the audio signals from the televisions that were mounted on the white concrete barren walls. Often to my dismay the women would be watching shows such as *Lockup*. I would always feel deeply offended when I would walk by the small, crowded room and see the women intently watching these shows. Quite often I would ask many of them how they could watch a show that provides a chronicle to those on the outside that we belonged in prisons. As an educated woman I understood how media was providing a narrative that would desensitize the general population to the dehumanizing and traumatic aspects of incarcerating Black and brown bodies. This show continues to give Americans the okay to not complain about people being locked in cages and treated as animals.

I am not writing about my journey to entertain or persuade anyone in one way or the other. I understand that it is very difficult for individuals to overcome prejudices or preconceived ideas about mass incarceration. The one thing I have learned through my journey within the prison industrial complex is that my lived experience does matter. It may not make you laugh or cry nonstop. It will make you think: Could this happen to me? And if it does, here is what I can do to survive.

During my incarceration, I created a daily routine which I followed to the T. That routine began with walking the dirt track outside of the recreation room every morning. I would then return to the unit, shower, dress for my so-called work detail, a euphemism for legalized slavery. Then, I spent the rest of the afternoon reading Angela Davis, James Baldwin, Buddhist teachings, and whatever other material spoke to my heart. Drawing and writing were my daily rituals to keep my faith and my soul intact.

There was no routine or personal strength, however, that could protect any loving, caring woman from being impacted by the visceral behaviors, routines, or rules within the federal prison camp, from the daily human counts to being berated and treated in a dehumanizing manner by correctional officers to hiding food in your locker so you could have something to eat when the hunger pangs started to hit, and many other freedom-snatching atrocities that those on the outside could never ever fully understand. These types of traumatic occurrences would often remind me of my childhood and the experiences of many of those foster youth I cared for over the years, who were taken out of their homes and mistreated in foster care. I would often think: Who in the world will hold the American Criminal Justice System accountable for being abusive and neglectful to those they oversee within the prison walls? The state can punish us for our "individual" crimes, but who will punish the state for its crimes?

The Bureau of Prisons has a written policy that, if possible, incarcerated persons will not be sent more than 500 miles away from their hometown and support.[10] Yet I was sent to Victorville, which was 475 miles away from my son. I was hoping to be sent to the facility in San Francisco, which was 218 miles away and easier for my family members to bring my son to visit me. I did not see my son for nearly eight months after I surrendered myself to the prison camp. The day before he was coming to visit I could not sleep, and I was questioning my decision to have him come see me imprisoned. I didn't have the freedom to wear any other clothing except for prison attire and a Kool-Aid smile.

On our last day together before I had to leave to drive to California and self-surrender to the Bureau of Prisons, I loaded up the car with my son's things and my suitcase.[11] While driving my son to his new, temporary home, I looked at him and told him that he had everything he needed while I was away. He quietly put his head down, started crying, and said, "Yeah, I have everything except my mom!" I couldn't respond, since deep down inside I knew he was rightfully saddened by our separation.

I had never been away from my son for more than a weekend. The first month away from him caused me a tremendous amount of anxiety. I learned to savor every minute we spoke on the phone, while trying to maintain composure. At night I would stare at his picture that I taped on the brick wall. I would say a silent prayer for my son and myself, and our healing. I prayed for his safety and I prayed that he knew that even though I was absent from his life, I deeply loved him. I reminded myself that my son was just as resilient as myself, and we would get through this period of our lives.

As I made my way to my visit, I wondered how visiting me would impact him. Would it be traumatic? How would I feel once he left, and I had to go back to the unit? Fortunately, it all went well. When I walked into the visiting room and saw his chocolate face I could not help smiling. As I sat next to him, he leaned over and put his head on my shoulder. By this time, he had grown to be a very handsome, 6-foot-tall young man. We talked about school and football and his plans for the next weekend. It was wonderful to see him face to face, to kiss and hug him. Prior to my incarceration, we had our nightly routine where I would come in and tuck him in and discuss the plans for the next day. I missed those days and promised myself that once I returned home I would never take any of our moments together for granted. At the end of the visit on the second day I prepared myself to say goodbye and I hugged him as long as he allowed, then watched as he exited the visiting area. I distinctly remember hearing mothers crying after their visits with their children. I can still hear their voices trying to reassure their children that everything was going to be okay. I considered myself a professional mother. I took that role seriously and understood clearly what my absence for nearly two years would do to my son and to our relationship. I understood the sense of vulnerability and fears a mother can have when parting from her children, and all I could do was be present—in the moment, as a witness, and move with some sort of grace. I also felt a kinship with

1. Carceral Trauma   45

the expecting mothers. During my incarceration there were six pregnant, nonviolent, low-level offenders.

One of the pregnant women did not know she was pregnant until she received the news from the physician assistant at the federal prison camp. After her initial shock and frustration at being told that she was pregnant, she quickly started counting her good days to see if she would be released from custody prior to her baby being born. After she realized that for nine months she would have to rely on the marginal medical care at the prison camp, she started crying. She explained to me that she had been fighting her indictment for nearly three years and was just relieved to get it over with. As the days and weeks and months went by, I continued to check on her diligently and she would always smile and reassure me that they were both doing okay.

The maternity care in prison was nearly nonexistent. I would pray daily that the women would go into labor before 5 p.m. on the weekdays—after 5 p.m., and on the weekends, we were basically on the federal camp with one guard who would spend most of his time in the office or socializing with colleagues from other prisons. For my own sanity, I started asking questions about what needed to happen in case one of the women went into labor during off hours. I was told that the red phone on the wall was used for emergencies, but every one of the women on the camp knew that no one ever responds to the red phone calls.

I was released on September 5, 2015, and went to a halfway house in San Francisco, California. I was extremely cognizant that again I was being thrust into another aspect of my childhood. My temporary shelter was located near my mother's old stomping grounds, the Tenderloin, a drug-infested area that was also in the middle of gentrification. I've witnessed homelessness, blind eyes, and the juxtaposition of the two. I eventually went home with a felony, ankle monitor, and fifteen months of supervised probation.

Since my release from the federal prison camp, I have not been able to watch any shows, realistic or comedic, that focus on the lives of incarcerated people. I tried to watch the later seasons of *Orange Is the New Black* but fell short because I found myself becoming angry. I was frustrated with the tales about the relationships women have in prison and the lack of characters who had deep and profound reactions to being incarcerated. A woman's life within a prison is very hard to make entertaining. There is nothing funny about not being able to see your child or hearing that someone in your family has died or never being physically touched, held, or kissed while you are incarcerated.

I continue to boycott such shows and at the same time express that I appreciate the fact that there are more conversations about the incarceration

46   LITTLE

of women. I just hope that we can have a balance of stories and that mine and those of other women such as Susan Burton,[12] Donna Hylton,[13] and Christine Rathbone, who have written authentically about their experiences, are heard also.

On April 15, 2018, I was released from supervised release and from the legal shackles of the carceral state. The collateral consequences of being a Black Queer woman and felon at times have felt insurmountable. Since my release and return, I have lost my home, my business, my career, and my clinical license. I have been fired from a minimum wage job. I have been refused assistance by the Equal Employment Opportunity Commission. I have not been able to secure employment in my field of practice after submitting over a hundred applications. I wonder about the women who do not have the education, clinical experience, resources, and support that I have. I have a saying that reminds me that I was born and raised to move through anything, anywhere, at any given time. I have an innate ability to tap into my childhood resiliency and use my education to enhance and empower me. But I truly have a clear understanding of how and why recidivism occurs. I continue to share my story and my methods for not just surviving but thriving through one of the most horrendous periods in my life.

Dr. Angela Davis has made apparent in her work that the prison industrial complex is doing exactly what it is structured to do, and that is why it must be abolished.[14] The carceral state has affected generations of families, specifically Black Americans. My journey serves as an example of how our government policy concerning mass incarceration is a detriment to all Americans.

I'm free, but in a lot of ways I'm far from being free. The collateral consequences for formerly incarcerated persons are often more challenging than incarceration itself. Because of my childhood, I have always strategically placed myself in a position to be financially secure and gainfully employed. After returning home from prison, the first thing I was told by my probation officer was that to remain in compliance with my probation, I must obtain a job. In the past, prior to my being a felon, I never worried about employment or creating a job for myself. Now I was faced with seeking employment with a list of restrictions and a felony. My employment restrictions barred me from working in child welfare, being self-employed, working for a friend, working for family, or working in the healthcare field. The structural barriers within the criminal justice system and collateral consequences for being labelled a felon made it very difficult for me to obtain gainful employment upon my release. After applying for over fifty jobs, I finally got hired at Patagonia Clothing for $12.65 an hour. I had never been paid so little since college, but I was so happy to be employed and once again being a productive citizen in my community. After three months I was summoned into an office with the area manager, human resource manager, and my supervisor. The area manager informed me I was being fired because they were notified by someone on Facebook of my indictment. I will never ever forget his words to me when he stated, "We never would have hired you if we knew you had a record." I was appalled and heartbroken, not because I was losing the $12.65 an hour job but mainly because this young man felt authorized to speak to me in such a dehumanizing and disgusting manner. I quickly gathered myself emotionally and regally told him that he was missing out because I am an incredible, wonderful woman and it was his company's loss. As I was escorted out of the Patagonia Clothing building, I kept telling myself don't cry, don't curse them out, don't scream, "Fuck you!" just peacefully leave. As I walked to my car, I took three deep breaths and I thought about all that I had been through and survived. I got into my car, cried, and returned home to my son.

I have memories that are still marred with questions, and a host of emotions associated with my incarceration. I've healed the bridge that connected my childhood to my adult experiences. All is well on that end, but for the life of me, I can't understand the lack of humanity within our government agencies. I guess that will have to remain a question, one which has forever changed my life. Today I find myself gravitating toward assisting other women who share my story. I am telling my stories through poetry and participating in panel discussions, conferences, and workshops as much as possible. Writing this chapter is my first step toward my book. My hope is that my experiences can help someone find solace and strength through their journey until necessary changes are made within our government's penal system that would benefit all Americans. I urge those who're seeking help to reach out to whatever support is available. I pray that all the women and children traumatized by living in a carceral society[15] find peace, passion, and purpose on their journeys to repairing and healing their lives.

In July 2018, I was hired by an incredible agency, Root and Rebound, as an education and leadership specialist.[16] Many of the people I am tethered to question my choice to not pursue my own agency or a higher position as I have in the past. It is very difficult to explain to others the impact of carceral trauma and its impact on me. It is not normal for a loving human, woman, and mother to endure the insolence, pain, and dehumanizing system without having some residual pain. At this phase in my journey, I welcome the security of being a part of a team of social justice advocates. When I speak about my journey it is not just about my time spent in prison. I endured trauma both before and after incarceration, within my re-entry, as well as during that period. The realization that as a Black woman in America who did not have millions of dollars, I had no value. I will never forget that for a period in America, I was not Dr. Cassandra Little, a community worker, mother, foster mother, sister, aunt, friend, academic, or woman. I was just inmate 47078-048.[17]

My favorite writer, James Baldwin, was once asked during an interview if he felt that being Black, poor, and gay made him feel disadvantaged as a writer, and he replied, "No, I thought I hit the jackpot, it is so outrageous, I have to find a way to use it."[18] Like Mr. Baldwin, I too feel strongly that I have hit the jackpot and I must find a way to use my story to inform others about the atrocities of the criminal justice system and our need as a nation to oppose an unjust, carceral society. Like Mr. James Baldwin, I want to write about the necessity for all of us to hold America accountable for its behaviors and treatment of those of us who live in this country. My time spent in prison allowed me to assess and reevaluate how to utilize my innate strength, redirect my life's passions and goals, and stand up against the wrongful mass incarceration of women. We, as persons in the United States, can begin to induce necessary changes to bring about healing for self and for our future generations.

Notes

1. Carroll Kilpatrick, "Nixon Tells Editors, 'I'm Not a Crook,'" *Washington Post*, November 18, 1973, https://www.washingtonpost.com/.

2. Warren, "E. Palo Alto Murder Rate."

3. Fort, "East Palo Alto and the Crack Epidemic."

4. Childhelp is a nonprofit organization that "exists to meet the physical, emotional, educational and spiritual needs of abused, neglected and at-risk children. We focus our efforts on advocacy, intervention, treatment, prevention, family resilience and community outreach" (https://www.childhelp.org/our-mission/).

5. InterExchange, "History, Principles, and Symbols of Kwanzaa."

6. See Office of Inspector General, Health and Human Services, "Medicaid Fraud Control Units," https://oig.hhs.gov/fraud/medicaid-fraud-control-units-mfcu/.

7. "Of the 87,709 defendants terminated during Fiscal Year 2012, 80,963, or 93 percent, either pled guilty or were found guilty. . . . The rate of conviction remained over 90 percent, as it has since Fiscal Year 2001" (Offices of the U.S. Attorneys, "U.S. Attorneys' Annual Statistical Report 2012," 8).

8. In a discovery hearing, one side of a legal case is able to obtain certain evidence held by the other side, usually before a trial begins.

9. The Federal Bureau of Prisons.

10. Federal Bureau of Prisons, "Designations."

11. "When you are ordered by the Court to voluntarily surrender, you will be notified by the U.S. Marshals Service (USMS) of your surrender date and provided

with the name of the institution where you are to surrender, OR you will be directed to surrender to the USMS" (Federal Bureau of Prisons, "Voluntary Surrenders").

12. Following the accidental death of her young son, Burton, whose own childhood had been traumatic, turned to drugs and spent almost twenty years moving in and out of incarceration.

13. Hylton and accomplices kidnapped a man in 1985. They brutalized and ultimately killed him while holding him for ransom. She spent more than twenty-five years in prison for murder and kidnapping convictions.

14. Davis, *Are Prisons Obsolete?*

15. DeVeaux, "Trauma of the Incarcerated Experience."

16. "Root & Rebound's mission is to restore power and resources to the families and communities most harmed by mass incarceration through legal advocacy, public education, policy reform and litigation—a model rooted in the needs and expertise of people who are directly impacted" (https://www.rootandrebound.org/our-mission -values/, accessed 15 August, 2022).

17. Federal prisoners are given individual numbers by the United States Marshals Service and the Federal Bureau of Prisons. Someone wishing to contact or visit an inmate needs that inmate's number in order to do so.

18. Dedalus05, "James Baldwin."

Bibliography

Across Women's Lives Staff. "Why Are More Women Incarcerated Now Than Ever Before?" *USA Today*. April 7, 2018. Accessed July 21, 2018. https://www.usatoday .com/story/opinion/policing/2018/04/06/women-incarceration-drugs-policing -usa/494565002/.

Cherney, Max. "I Went on a Police Ride-Along in San Francisco's Worst Neighborhood." January 16, 2014. Accessed July 21, 2018. https://www.vice.com/.

Davis, Angela Y. *Are Prisons Obsolete?* New York: Seven Stories Press, 2008.

Davis, Angela Yvonne, and Robin D. G. Kelley. *The Meaning of Freedom*. San Francisco: City Lights Books, 2012.

Dedalus05. "James Baldwin: On Being Poor, Black, and Gay." YouTube. September 29, 2009. Accessed July 21, 2018. https://www.youtube.com/.

DeVeaux, Mika'll. "The Trauma of the Incarcerated Experience." *Harvard Civil Rights- Civil Liberties Law Review* 48, no. 1 (December 1, 2013): 257–77.

Federal Bureau of Prisons. "Designations." Accessed August 15, 2022. https://www .bop.gov/inmates/custody_and_care/designations.jsp.

———. "Education." Accessed July 21, 2018. https://www.bop.gov/.

———. "Voluntary Surrenders." Accessed August 15, 2022. https://www.bop.gov/ inmates/custody_and_care/voluntary_surrenders.jsp.

Florida International University. "Slavery and the Prison Industrial Complex- Angela Davis." YouTube. June 10, 2011. Accessed July 21, 2018. https://www.youtube.com/.

Fort, Doug. "East Palo Alto and the Crack Epidemic That Tried to Kill the Black

Family." Silicon Valley De-Bug. February 4, 2015. Accessed July 21, 2018. http://archives.siliconvalleydebug.org/.

Gramlich, John. "The Gap between the Number of Blacks and Whites in Prison Is Shrinking." January 12, 2018. Accessed July 21, 2018. https://www.pewresearch.org/fact-tank/2018/01/12/shrinking-gap-between-number-of-Blacks-and-whites-in-prison/.

InterExchange. "The History, Principles, and Symbols of Kwanzaa." December 18, 2014, updated July 20, 2020. https://www.interexchange.org/articles/career-training-usa/history-principles-and-symbols-of-kwanzaa/.

Law, Victoria. "Pregnant and behind Bars: How the US Prison System Abuses Mothers-to-Be." *The Guardian*. October 20, 2015. Accessed July 21, 2018. https://www.theguardian.com/us-news/2015/oct/20/pregnant-women-prison-system-abuse-medical-neglect.

Morse, Leila, and Richard Rothstein. "Mass Incarceration and Children's Outcomes: Criminal Justice Policy Is Education Policy." Economic Policy Institute. December 15, 2016. Accessed July 21, 2018. https://www.epi.org/publication/mass-incarceration-and-childrens-outcomes/.

Office of Inspector General. "Medicaid Fraud Control Units." U.S. Department of Health and Human Services. Accessed July 21, 2018. https://oig.hhs.gov/fraud/medicaid-fraud-control-units-mfcu/.

Offices of the United States Attorneys. "*United States Attorneys' Annual Statistical Report Fiscal Year 2012.*" *U.S. Department of Justice. Accessed 15 August 2022. https://www.justice.gov/sites/default/files/usao/legacy/2013/10/28/12statrpt.pdf.*

Wagner, Peter, and Wendy Sawyer. "Mass Incarceration: The Whole Pie 2018." Prison Policy Initiative. March 14, 2018. Accessed July 21, 2018. https://www.prisonpolicy.org/reports/pie2018.html.

Warren, Jennifer. "E. Palo Alto Murder Rate Worst in U.S.; Drug Wars Blamed." *Los Angeles Times*. January 5, 1993. Accessed July 21, 2018. http://articles.latimes.com/1993–01–05/local/me-833_1_east-palo-alto.

Williams, Timothy. "Number of Women in Jail Has Grown Far Faster Than That of Men, Study Says." *New York Times*. December 21, 2017. Accessed July 21, 2018. https://www.nytimes.com/.

Zarya, Valentina. "This Is Why Women Are the Fastest-Growing Prison Population." *Fortune*. December 10, 2015. Accessed July 21, 2018. http://fortune.com/2015/12/10/prison-reform-women.

2

Layered Realities

Prison Writings and Anti-Terror Laws in India

SHAILZA SHARMA

> How does one reveal to the world outside, the creative power
> of these prisoners? What do these walls convey to those
> outside? Do they tell of the [wo]men behind them? Do they
> communicate that prisoners are not merely the accused and
> punished, but are also those who dream and have vision?
> —Varavara Rao 2010, 99

Introduction

Prisons are complicated spaces. Prisoners' lives are even more so.

Prisoners' writings question our hegemonic understanding of prisons as spaces of totalizing control, violence, and darkness, the exact opposite of how everyday life is characterized—hopeful, free, and full of possibilities. Prison writings also problematize our unidimensional understanding that reproduces binaries of guilt and innocence, oppression and resistance, violence and justice.

This chapter offers a reading and analysis of a select set of prison writings from India to highlight the role that prisoners' writings can play in knowledge production about the layered realities of prison life. Such accounts are central to understanding political subjectivities of prisoners, forms of state control within prisons, and the gendered dimensions of imprisonment, among other things.[1] While literally, a prisoner is subjected to imprisonment and isolation within the boundaries of a prison, the analysis in this chapter points to the insufficiency of conducting scholarly research from within the walls of a discipline, particularly since the subjectivity of a prisoner is under constant transformation and is constituted via a nexus of the social, economic, cultural, and political environment she or he is in. As a law practitioner eventually foraying into political theory, I was often bothered by neat disciplinary boundaries. I found that analyzing prison writings was a useful tool to dissolve those boundaries and identify the legal and political layers of interpretation within such analysis.

The prison writings analyzed here can be located within a specific political context, which is the operation of anti-terror laws in India and their nexus with state violence. The legacy of anti-terror legislations in colonial and postcolonial India exposes state practices which create exceptions within legal procedures. This is achieved through ambiguous language and perpetuity of anti-terror laws. Agamben's characterization of the "state of exception" instructs that we consider anti-terror legislations as a "space devoid of law" where "all legal determinations are deactivated" (2003, 50). However, contrary to being "spaces devoid of law," a review of various anti-terror legislations reveals the "elaborate regulatory efforts" (Johns 2005, 614) made by legal authorities and state agencies to regulate ideologies by utilizing legal (and extralegal) contraptions of state surveillance and incarcerating dissenting individuals and groups. While recognizing this legal context within which these writings are situated or the legal procedures that prisoners are required to navigate, this chapter is not specifically concerned with legal technicalities or precedents laid down by courts in India. Instead, what this chapter will investigate is the sphere of legal contraptions that subsume the lives of prisoners, be it repeated court visits or rules under various colonial prison manuals. The political context that the memoirs are set in also alludes to ways in which the carceral state operates to create conditions that seek to criminalize individuals and communities.

This chapter also pays attention to the practices adopted by prisoners that resist and challenge the pervasiveness of the legal regime on their bodies and minds. Writing as a form of expression provides a window into the political subjectivities of the prisoners. Foucault's assertion that we should analyze "power relations through antagonism of strategies" is instructive in order to focus on the "*forms* of resistance and attempts made to disassociate these [power] relations" (Foucault 1982, 780, emphasis mine). Considering traditions of writing as a palpable form of resistance adopted by prisoners in India against state power, this chapter will analyze prison writings to specifically construct prisoners' accounts of the (political) self, the gendered nature of prisons, and the violence/control associated with prison life. In my inquiry, not only do I consider prisons as a terrain of violence and control but, taking a cue from Bargu's (2014) political ethnography of methods of protest utilized by political prisoners in Turkey, I identify prisons as sites of "political confrontations." To understand resistance, I draw on subaltern historiography, which "treats everyday forms of resistances as significant markers of protest. Protest is located not just in the grand acts of defiance but is also implicit in the minute texture of everyday life" (Bandyopadhyay 2010, 139–40).

The first part of this chapter will give a brief overview of the set of prison writings that have been selected for analysis. The second part will contextualize these writings within the political-legal framework mentioned above. The third part will conceptualize the prison writings to interrogate the following collective assumptions: While prisons are "institutions of discipline," can the "docile bodies of the prisoners" (Foucault 1977, 286), which are objects and targets of power, also be categorized as thoughtless beings? What happens when "an individual's sense of justice, as a prisoner, is antagonistic to the idea of justice that the state upholds in the interest of the collective good?" (Bandyopadhyay 2010, 23). By studying a culture of writing memoirs, autobiographies, diaries, and letters, one can assemble and compare across time and space the narratives of prisoners and understand the prison as a terrain of violence and control. Therefore, in that part of the chapter, through analysis of the narratives I look at how, when prisoners are made into instruments of social control, it is necessary to look at their writings to tease out instances of their response, resistance, and condemnation to the control of their private lives and ideology.

Prison Writings: 2011–2017

Seema Azad, a journalist and the organizing secretary of People's Union for Civil Liberties in Uttar Pradesh,[2] was arrested along with her husband, Vishwavijai, in Allahabad on February 6, 2010. The accusation levelled against them was that they were members of the banned Communist Party of India (Maoist), and they were charged under various sections of the Indian Penal Code, 1860, and Unlawful Activities (Prevention) Act, 1967 (UAPA). In August 2012 they were let off on bail by the Allahabad High Court. In June 2017 Azad and her husband published their jail diaries, both of which are called *Zindanama* (which roughly translates to "Document of Life" or "Life Stories").[3] Azad's narrative of prison life is not only full of practices of everyday resistance but also contains descriptions of the reproduction of caste and religion-based hierarchies inside prison, along with a sociological analysis of class position of women constables, among other things.

Arun Ferreira,[4] a cartoonist, political activist, and lawyer based in Mumbai, was arrested in May 2007 under UAPA for charges of being a Naxalite.[5]

As the foreword to his book tells us, his political views during his teenage years were shaped by debates around liberation theology. Over the course of almost five years he spent in prison, ten cases were slapped against him. In September 2010, he was acquitted in all cases but after being released was rearrested by the police for a criminal case, the facts of which indicated that he was still in prison when the alleged crime happened. In January 2012 he was finally let off on bail by the Bombay High Court. He has written about his ordeal in the book *Colours of the Cage: A Prison Memoir* (2014): "Vividly illustrated with the author's drawings, the book documents his experiences of custodial torture, fighting the battle against false charges, the grim conditions of Indian prisons where corruption is endemic, and the everyday life that prisoners create in these dismal conditions" (Shah and Jain 2017, 1212).

Anjum Zamarud Habib is a political activist from Kashmir who was arrested in 2003 in Delhi. She was sentenced under the Prevention of Terrorism Act, 2002 (POTA) by Justice Ravinder Kaur to a five-year jail term. After a challenge to the judgment in the Delhi High Court, she was released in December 2007. Habib writes an account of being imprisoned in Tihar Central Jail in her book titled *Prisoner No. 100: An Account of My Nights and Days in an Indian Prison* (2011). In the author's own words, the book is neither a diary nor a journal nor a memoir.[6] It is rather a compilation of experiences within prison, written from the vantage point of a Kashmiri-Muslim woman jailed in an Indian prison.

Mohammad Aamir Khan was picked up by Delhi police in February 1998 and was charged in nineteen cases of terrorism. He spent fourteen years in prison being wrongfully accused. He wrote his account of prison life in his coauthored book titled *Framed as a Terrorist: My 14-Year Struggle to Prove My Innocence* (2016). Khan's telling of his experiences demonstrates the glaring bias of the state machinery against Muslim youth in the country. The book is not described as either a diary or a memoir. In fact, the context set by the coauthor Haksar details the political and legal conditions that led to Khan's arrest, while proposing that the larger picture, which demonstrates the Indian state's increased violence against Muslim youth (in the backdrop of global war on terror), requires "national outrage" (Khan and Haksar 2016, 33), thus transforming the book into a testimonial of injustice suffered by Khan and many others like him.

In his prison writings, Ngugi Wa Thiong'o, a Kenyan writer, recognizes that "a narration of prison life is, in fact, nothing more than an account of oppressive measures in varying degrees of intensity and one's individual or collective responses to them" (1981, 100). However, his own account and the ones analyzed here tell us more than the conditions of oppression and the

2. Layered Realities   55

prisoner's struggles against them. I see these writings as a testimonial of the resilience of the body and mind to extreme pain and suffering. Specifically, the prison writings discussed here are evidence against the legal and political infrastructure that the prisoners are embroiled in. As discussed later in the chapter, these writings are a tool to expose the extralegal efforts made by the state and its machinery to present a discourse of national safety and security while oppressing religious, caste, or political minorities in the country. Carceral liberalism as conceptualized in this edited volume is the instinct of the state that dictates ideas of citizenship, rights, criminality, care, protection, and social good resulting in privileging the upper caste and class of society. Such carceral instincts can simultaneously dehumanize certain acts and individuals while allowing the state to implement its liberal visions.

There is also a need to comment on the form or the genre of the books when contemplating the orientation or perspective of the reader. For the purposes of writing this chapter I have referred to these authors' books in the manner that they have themselves chosen to refer to them. However, certain points of inquiry are not easily resolved: "Should a reader approach these accounts with sympathy?" or "Should factual details be corroborated or taken as given?" These challenging points of inquiry dissipated with the realization that these narratives cannot be limited to an analysis of the form of the text. Instead, a recurring pattern of state violence, surveillance, and control was visible, which among other things dissolved the need for confirmation of factual details in prisoners' accounts. This aspect of bringing together (while not necessarily comparing) varying narratives across space and time exposes their unique and shared way of confirming marginal discourses about issues of power, subjectivity, and resistance, making the analysis in this chapter necessary.

Perpetual Permanence and the Annihilation of Exception

Such laws are held out to be a reflection of a strong state with strong laws; however, "it is perhaps in the paradoxical nature of such laws that they are justified as being indispensable for democracy" (Singh 2007, 16). Singh here is referring to "extraordinary laws" in India, such as the Prevention of Terrorism Act, 2002 (POTA), the Terrorist and Disruptive Activities (Prevention) Act, 1985 (TADA), or the Unlawful Activities (Prevention) Act, 1967 (UAPA).[7] To analyze the functioning of such extraordinary laws in India, it is crucial to acknowledge the debates and analysis regarding the colonial legacies of the Indian state and its functioning. The justification of these laws by a democratic nation is marked by the legacy and logic of colonial rule.

The postcolonial Indian nation-state is a "successor to both the British colonial state and the movement of Indian nationalism" (Kaviraj 2010, 222). Kaviraj claims that the British left behind "three apparatuses of persuasion and control, entirely unreformed i.e., the education, the police, and the bureaucracy" (222). The introduction of rule of law in the colonies was itself an exercise in control and subjugation of dissent; "it was central to the 'civilising mission' of imperialism, particularly British imperialism, of the nineteenth and early twentieth centuries" (Darby 1987 in Merry 1991, 890). Hussain also explains how the introduction of English law in the colonies was a story of "haphazard introduction of a rule of law, its colonial mutations, and its enduring consequences," whereas "to the late 18th century English political imagination, the virtue of a rule of law was as settled a fact as its Englishness" (2003, 2); and "when the British turned India into a crown colony, the colonial state explicitly assumed the rights of sovereignty as understood in European discourses of the nineteenth century" (Kaviraj 2010, 217).

Given the colonial legacy and an "ineluctable continuance" of the British Indian legal system, the phenomena of "juristic *dependencia*" (dependence) manifested itself "in planning or initiating through legislative or judicial processes, evident in copycat drafting of laws" (Baxi 1982, 42–43). Post-independence the Indian nation-state also retained "in a virtually unaltered form the basic structure of the civil service, the police administration, the judicial system, including the code of civil and criminal law, and the armed forces as they existed in the colonial period" (P. Chatterjee 1993, 204). So, in what ways was the postcolonial nation-state different from its predecessor? It claimed its legitimacy through planning, viewing it as "a single will and consciousness—the will of the nation—pursuing a task that was both universal and rational: the well being of the people as a whole" (205). This meant that the postcolonial nation-state could "confront exceptions to this project" of development "ranging from strikes and insurgencies to separatist movements, with its inherited arsenal of emergency powers and with an application that was at least as vigorous as that of its predecessors" (Hussain 2003, 137). In fact, while the constitution-building exercise of the "world's largest democracy" was underway, the expectant democratic nation was already sending its armed forces in the area known as Telangana (the biggest princely state at the time) to crush a peasant struggle which began in 1946 against "forced labour, illegal extractions, eviction by feudal landlords and oppression by village patels [headsman], among other things and later developed into an agrarian liberation struggle to get rid of feudal landlordism" (Banerjee 1984, 19). Thus, since the heyday of colonial rule, "India has lived under a series of draconian preventive detention laws" (Seminarist 2002) and

2. Layered Realities   57

consequently independent India has mirrored the British in its application of emergency and security laws: "While India's post-independence constitution includes an extensive array of fundamental rights protections, its emergency and security provisions incorporate a number of the same basic principles found in the Government of India Act of 1935: extraordinary powers that may be exercised during declared periods of emergency, but supplemented by several layers of preventive detention and other security laws that readily afford the government multiple options to exercise similar powers even outside of formally declared periods of emergency" (Kalhan et al., 2006, 132).

Although the Indian National Congress–led governments "initially made efforts to repeal the emergency powers enacted before 1935, by 1937 they increasingly began to rely upon the same kinds of measures used by the British to maintain order and exercise social control" (132). Given the fact that legal practices and codes were carried forward wholesale in independent India, the security state apparatus remained a continuation of its British colonial legacy.

This colonial legacy is evident in the application of extraordinary laws, such that "court processes are inevitably subverted, and the much-trumpeted 'rule of law' is transformed into 'rule by discretion,' which is a euphemism for 'rule by caprice'" (Kannabiran 2003, 83). One such law, the Terrorism and Disruptive Activities (Prevention) Act (1987) (TADA), was promulgated to "combat terrorism in the Punjab region," but it is telling that 19,263 individuals detained under the act were in Gujarat, "in a state without any significant terrorism problem" (Kalhan et al., 2006, 147). Additionally, the selective application of TADA was apparent from the fact that "TADA was not brought into force when large-scale violence against Muslims took place in Bombay riots" in 1993 (Singh 2007, 53). When the law was reviewed on the basis of its application in different regions, it was found that in many states the conviction rate was less than even one percent (Kalhan et al., 2006). Therefore, the law became an instrument of abuse of power, torture, and application of preventive detention laws indiscriminately. TADA was finally allowed to lapse in May 1995.

The next instalment of anti-terror legislations came (conveniently) in the backdrop of the September 11 attacks in the United States—although previous governments had unsuccessfully tried to "replicate TADA through the Criminal Law Amendment Bill, however no action was ultimately taken" (Kalhan et al., 2006, 151). The 9/11 attacks, UN Security Council resolution number 1373, and the attack on the Indian Parliament building on December 13, 2001, gave an impetus to the promulgation of the Prevention of Terrorism Ordinance (POTA 2001–2004). Even under vehement opposition, ignoring the human rights abuses under TADA, "the perception of a national security threat created by the 9/11 attacks, the Parliament attack, and the deteriorating conditions with Pakistan all served to blunt the opposition to the ordinance," and it finally became law on March 26, 2002 (Verma 2004, 437); thus POTA came into existence.

This law based on a perception of threat to national security had very real consequences for Muslims in prison. Mohammad Aamir Khan (author of *Framed as a Terrorist: My 14-Year Struggle to Prove My Innocence*), who was picked up by Delhi police in February 1998, was charged in nineteen cases of terrorism, and spent fourteen years in prison being wrongfully accused, has this to say about the changing perception of people around him post-2001:

> I thought I would soon be acquitted in the other cases but two events which occurred at the end of 2001 affected my chances of being free any time soon. I did not immediately realize the impact the two events would have on my life. The attacks on the Twin Towers in New York on 11 September and the attack on the Indian Parliament on 13 December changed the attitude of the jail authorities towards Muslim prisoners, especially those accused in cases of terrorism. Those two events even changed the attitude of other prisoners towards Muslims. (Khan and Haksar 2016, 151)

This narrative is also endorsed by Anjum Habib, the author of *Prisoner No. 100: An Account of My Nights and Days in an Indian Prison*, who was arrested under POTA. Husain, the Urdu-to-English translator of the book, explains that Anjum's life inside prison was "marked by isolation" for being a Kashmiri-Muslim, "almost as though the jail mirrors the outside reality of alienation and discrimination that many suffer" (Habib 2011, xv). Hibib narrates various instances where prisoners mistake her or accuse her of being a Pakistani, and even those in authority conflate the identities of Kashmiri, Muslim, and (alleged) Terrorist when dealing with her. She tells us, "to most of them [the women prisoners] I was known either as a Pakistani, a terrorist or an anti-national person" (Habib 2011, 147). In an interview, Seema Azad (author of *Zindanama*) confirmed this alienation of those carrying the "Muslim" and "alleged Terrorist" identity. During her time in Naini Central Jail in Uttar Pradesh, while she was charged and confined under the UAPA there were two other women charged under the same legislation. They were branded as terrorists by other prisoners, while owing to her seemingly Hindu and upper-caste identity, Azad did not attract any such stigma toward herself.[8]

Habib's book also tells us that through the routinized practices of control, such as search operations, the authorities seek compliance of the body that is Muslim and is also Kashmiri. Her account includes what might seem repetitive and banal descriptions of prison authorities destroying her belongings in surprise raids one day before the 26th of January (Republic Day of India) and the 15th of August (Independence Day of India) each year. This is also

2. Layered Realities 59

followed by a routine and compulsory attendance for the Republic Day and Independence Day celebrations, therefore disciplining to "compose forces in order to obtain an efficient [patriotic and compliant] machine" by "establishing rhythms, imposing particular occupations, regulating cycles of repetition" (Foucault 1977, 146). The details of the search operations allude to the phenomena of the complex and changing nature of time within prison, as well. The book describes each and every instance of the search operations, that is, during all the five years she spent in prison. They repeat like clockwork not only during her prison life, but also as text in the book—almost as a marker of her annual ordeals in prison. The repetitiveness is also indicative in her phrases like "*as usual*, my cell was searched" (Habib 2011, 112). Interestingly, in one instance where Habib speaks about the raids on August 14, she precedes the paragraph with a description of servitude in prison explaining how "our individuality, is merged into that of the 'jail community'" (35). Thus, not only is her oppression based on what she calls the "master-slave relationship" between the jail authorities and prisoners, which is thus common for all prisoners, but also her "non-Indian" identity is utilized as a mechanism of control and persecution as well, differentiating her from other prisoners.

Simultaneously with the repeal of POTA in 2004, an existing law—the UAPA—was amended to pass on the provisions of POTA into this legislation in September 2004: "Specific provisions of POTA percolated into an existing law giving extraordinary provisions a hitherto elusive permanence, and making it a surrogate of POTA" (Singh 2007, 288). Through the promulgation of UAPA, hitherto existing provisions for periodic legislative review were smothered and some of the existing provisions of POTA were siphoned off to UAPA (306). Simultaneous with defining new charges under UAPA, such as terror funding and holding of terror camps, first information reports (FIRs) materialized with patchy details (Sethi 2014, 5). Ferreira, Azad, and Vishwavijai, as noted above, were all arrested under UAPA, and the law continues to exist in Indian statute books.

While theorizing the "state of exception," Agamben states that "any discussion of the structure and meaning of the state of exception first requires an analysis of the legal concept of necessity" (2003, 24). He posits that either "necessity does not recognize any law," or "necessity creates its own law" (9). For him the state of exception is a space "devoid of law" (9); Johns, however, when analyzing the detention of prisoners in Guantánamo Bay, fundamentally disagrees with Agamben to argue that the state of exception is a consequence of "legal representation and classification," instead of being an "outcome of law's suspension" (2005, 614). According to her, contrary to

Agamben's theorization, "Guantánamo Bay may be more cogently read as the jurisdictional outcome of exhaustive attempts to *domesticate* the political possibilities occasioned by the experience of exceptionalism" (615). In similar vein, it has been argued that the Indian nation-state has rendered the state of exception or emergency as the norm (Singh 2007) and through it "hegemonic structures of nation-state are maintained, by externalizing plural, diachronous and contending structures, forms and sites of self-realization as 'extraordinary'" (49).

An exposition of the ease and impunity with which police officials perpetrate violence in the form of extra-judicial torture continuously runs through the discourse presented by the writers. The actions of police officials are not a consequence of ignorance of the law; in fact Ferreira and Khan speak of the mechanisms of torture adopted by police officials that circumvent the law. Physical torture is done in a manner that it does not leave any apparent marks on the body of the prisoner, thus prohibiting judicial authorities from intervening. Even Habib faces humiliation and beatings at the hands of interrogation officers before she is put in prison.

Azad dedicates the first twenty pages of her book to describing the ordeal that the police put her and her husband through when they were taken in illegal detention. The "normal" and correct procedures of law are not even begun until after Azad and Vishwavijai are illegally detained, mentally tortured, and put through excruciating interrogation. During prolonged interrogation sessions one of the interrogators asks Azad the following question: *"Madam, I want to know that when Maoists and terrorists kill, human rights organisations keep mum but when police officers kill, then you all make a lot of noise, why?"* (112). The answer given by Azad here is not as relevant as the fact that the interrogator is the mouthpiece for due process that cannot attend to the complexities of state violence perpetuated through liberal notions of "progress" or "development." Nor is it apparent to the police officer that extrajudicial killings do not fit the landscape of a constitutional democracy and that human rights organizations cannot function from within the apparatus of the state. This is but one example of the carceral liberalism always at work that Pillai details in the introduction to this volume.

The legal and extralegal contexts within which their arrests take place are more than just a heap of facts detailing the background of arrests. Instead, this analysis uncovers the ways in which the political, social, and legal contexts of formulation of extraordinary legislations is embodied by prisoners. The excesses of the law are thus visible in these acts of writing performed by the prisoners; they create a dent in the dominant discourse presented by the state.

Deliberating the Prison Discourse

> The basic objective of the women's prison in British India was to teach the untaught, the stubborn and the defiant. (Sen 2002, 421)

The colonial history of prisons in India is racist and gendered. This history forms a part of the larger British "civilizing and reforming the natives" mission. While the reformatory objective behind imprisoning men in colonial India was to teach political loyalty, "women's punishment was to restructure the criminalized female's relationship with the sexual/reproductive/evacuative aspects of her body" (Sen 2002, 431). Feminine decency was not a concept which organically originated within Indian society but was "constructed by middle-class English 'teachers' like Carpenter[9] in collaboration with elite Indians" (431). While the history of prisons has been problematic and gendered to say the least, Banu Bargu in the context of Turkish political prisoners has alternatively spoken of the "*production* of the prison wards into spaces of freedom within captivity" (2014, 170). Bargu theorizes the "everyday experiences, meanings, and values that *produce* space and condition the practices and perspectives of those who occupy that space" (169). According to her, the "objective marginality" of prison wards "combined with their isolation from the outside world" provides the "conditions of possibility of their [prison wards'] transformation" (169).

Seema Azad places her prison diary *Zindanama* (2017) within a contemporary national politics in which, according to her, social and political workers and writers are being subjected to frequent imprisonment at the behest of the state forces. She begins with an acknowledgment and locating of the self and the prison within the larger social system. In the way she prefaces her diary, the reader becomes aware of the fact that her purpose in recounting her prison narrative is to counter a particular kind of discourse understood about prisons in the popular imaginary. She wishes to contextualize prisons within our imagination to break prejudices about those who dwell inside them, asserting that prisons should not necessarily be associated with fear and suspicion. Therefore, not only do Azad's writing practices and way of life within prison seek to *produce* the space she inhabited into spaces of freedom (albeit limited), but she in fact also indicates that prisons are places full of life, places that should not be characterized with darkness.[10]

I agree with Azad's assessment that prisons are characterized in a specific manner in the popular imagination or the common person's imagination since carceral spaces are visualized as being inextricably linked to coercive control by prison and state authorities.[11] While such depiction is true to a large extent, a careful reading of prison writings indicates that we can also recover prisons within the popular imaginary as places which are *transformed* by prisoners to subvert control and oppression. Without falling prey to romanticizing or idealizing these defiant aspects of prisoners' lives, a perusal of prison writings dispels our hegemonic understanding of surveillance and control in prison characterized by, for instance, Bentham's Panopticon.

Foucault's important work on the birth of prisons and discipline and their connection to power has been criticized for the fact that the effectiveness of the control asserted by prisons as viewed by him often ignores other objectives such as punitiveness (Garland 1986). Foucault's conceptualization regarding constant surveillance and policing of the docile body within prison is elucidated by Habib: "Jail is an altogether different world. Here, the norms that operate are those between master and slave and they have to be followed strictly. In jail, our very existence, our individuality, is merged into that of the 'jail community,' it is no longer our own. Barefoot, with our heads bent in front of the authorities, we have to repeat 'Yes, madam, yes madam' all the time; the master-slave relation is humiliating and eats into whatever little dignity we may preserve once inside the confines of the jail" (Habib 2011, 35). But what the prison writings also depict is that there is more to be said about this apparently totalizing discourse of surveillance and control within the penitentiary. For instance, the following encounter narrated by Vishwavijai is interesting as an argument that, beyond the omnipresent discourse of surveillance and control, "the human subject is placed in power relations which are very complex" (Foucault 1982, 778): "[After being escorted to circle no. 4 inside prison] the *numberdaar* pointed towards barrack no. 6 and the location where food was being distributed. He left after saying 'Eat your food and then when it is time for the barracks to be closed, go get yourself locked inside barrack no. 6' (Vishwavijai 2017, 11).

The experiences described in the prison writings demonstrate that power relations within prison are exemplified through the control of food as well. "Food in prison operates within the institutional paradigm of punishment" (Chatterjee and Chatterjee 2018, 54). Habib writes, "*Problems regarding food*, the lack of physical comfort, and long period of separation from loved ones ... had ruined my world. I could compare this confinement of life inside the jail to a sort of death" (2011, 182, emphasis mine). The lack of good, healthy, and edible food inside prison is a theme consistently running through all the prisoners' accounts. However, Azad reminds us that "given the fact that we live in an extremely poor nation, many women who come to prison are lucky to eat three times a day" (2017, 161). Vishwavijai and Ferreira, on the other hand, detail practices that undermined the prison rules around consumption

2. Layered Realities   63

of food. There was no separate kitchen where prisoners could cook inside of the Naini Central Jail (where Vishwavijai was lodged), and while there was a canteen to procure food, owing to the lack of monetary resources many prisoners violated the regulations and cooked secretly through the minimum resources that could be arranged within prison. If the control of dietary requirements of the prisoners can be characterized as falling within regimes of punishments, then surely, such accounts tell us that subversive practices to protest against such punishment regimes are also prevalent within prisons. And of course, the practice of going on hunger strike to bring the abysmal and unhealthy quality of food inside jails to the attention of the authorities is not uncommon, as is explained by Azad and Ferreira.[12] "The study of food woven into the punishment agenda has a bearing on understanding how inmates experience health and illness in captivity and the dynamics of power that operates in prisons" (Chatterjee and Chatterjee 2018, 56). Both Habib and Vishwavijai describe facing debilitating circumstances when they fell ill within prison.

Bandyopadhyay (2010) in her ethnography observes that within prisons, "notions of private time and space are not allowed to develop." Such control of time is a "legitimate form of the violation of an individual's privacy" (90). The lack of private space and time leads to the curtailment of freedom or the "mortification of self" (Goffman 1962 in Bandyopadhyay 2010, 90). Multiple facets of resistance, such as hunger strikes, petitions to authorities, diary writing, misbehavior with authorities, and even refusing to partake in bribing activities within prison, are indications of practices that "preserve the self" against possible mortification.

For prisoners, "their life outside prison remains 'references in absentia'" (Da Cunha 2008 in Bandyopadhyay 2010, 288) and these "references in absentia" can be found across different registers. It is indicated in all the writings that prisoners continue to view their lives within prison with reference to their past and (possible) future lives outside; they make efforts in grooming themselves for court visits, learn new skills, or specifically in case of women (without any other option) continue to parent their children inside prison: "Many personal habits had to be given up in jail but one that I continued to maintain was to bathe every morning, wear a set of clean clothes and leave for work although this was a fairly neglected practice in jail. It was this habit that became a source of strength and consolation for me as I carried a mountain of hardship in my heart and had buried any desire or aspiration for my early release" (Habib 2011, 160).

At the cross-section of preservation of the self and construction of meaning of prison life in the context of their life outside prison, prisoners' continuance of various forms of resistance within prison can be explained. So, while a theme of state violence and control through "elaborate regulatory efforts" is discernible in the writings of all the prisoners, there are also details of protests undertaken by the prisoners when faced with brutality and oppression. The language used and details provided by Azad and Vishwavijai reveal that they protested their captivity at every step of the way, by *inter alia* refusing to sign blank papers with made-up charges, Azad demanding the presence of female police officers during her interrogation, and showing agility in matters of recognizing police officials who were informers. Sometimes these protests also became violent. Habib relates an incident where all women within her barrack rose in protest against the officials after one female constable caused the death of a prisoner by beating her up over some petty issue (Habib 2011, 47–48). On hearing of the death of the fellow prisoner, women gathered in spontaneous mourning that was prompted by anger and grief. This was followed by a week of protests, hunger strikes, and even ravaging the offices of authorities to bring their attention to the wrongful and negligent death of a fellow prisoner. What we glean from these passages is the clash of ideas of justice held by the prisoners on the one hand and the prison authorities on the other. There is the anger of the prisoners who feel wronged for not being treated as human beings and the sheer negligence and senseless violence of the constables causing the death of their own. And then there is the repetition of attitude of prison authorities in continuing to treat the protesting prisoners as no more than animals. Habib describes the speech of the director general of police, who made a visit to control the situation in prison: "You women are wild beasts . . . You will certainly be punished for this. You should be ashamed that you behaved in this manner *even though you are prisoners*" (Habib 2011, 47, emphasis mine). Thus, what we witness is the collision of an individual's sense of justice, in this case that of all the women prisoners, against "the idea of justice that the state upholds in the interest of the collective good" (Bandyopadhyay 2010, 23). Here of course the collective good requires subversion and control of the prisoners.

A concluding observation which can be made after reading the prisoners' accounts is that even when writing post-facto (after having been released from prison, although Azad wrote most of her diary from within prison) they look back and describe their ordeals as part of ongoing struggles in life, struggles that need to be overcome to emerge on the other side victorious and stronger than before. So, instead of being crushed within a regime that surveils, controls, and oppresses, the writers (or prisoners) respond to the authoritative regimes inside prison (and sometimes in courtrooms) with hope and determination.

2. Layered Realities   65

Conclusion

The accounts presented in the prison writings above are an exposition of social and power relations within prisons. The writings provide extensive details of social organization within prison, the analysis of which can be rooted in relevant socioeconomic and legal environment and practices. Through an analysis of Indian prison writings in this chapter I have tried to discuss the complexity of understanding the categories of politics of anti-terror laws, state security practices, and forms of resistance in India. The layered realities of prisoners' lives are also discernible through these writings when viewed against the backdrop of their political, religious, and caste identity. By rethinking the carceral through the medium of interpretation of prisoners' writings within specific contexts, this chapter has tried to tease out instances of prisoners' resistance to and condemnation of the control of their private lives and ideologies.

Notes

Epigraph: Rao 2010, 99.

1. *Gender* here is defined as "a set of practices and discourses that constitute 'men' and 'women' and masculinities and femininities in particular ways" (Khalili 2011, 1473). Joan Scott's comprehensive definition of gender as a constitutive element of social relationships based on perceived differences between sexes, and as a primary way of signifying relations of power, captures the inclusive character of this concept (Scott 1986 in Roy 2011, 12).

2. People's Union for Civil Liberties is a human rights body formed in India in 1976 by Jayaprakash Narayan as People's Union for Civil Liberties and Democratic Rights (PUCLDR). He had formed the organization to oppose the suppression of civil and political rights during the constitutionally declared emergency in India.

3. In terms of access, the author is able to analyze writings only in English and Hindi languages. Both the works of Seema Azad (2017) and Vishwavijai (2017) have been written in Hindi, and have been roughly translated into English by the author in this chapter for the analysis.

4. At the time of writing this chapter, Arun Ferreira and many other lawyers, writers, and human rights activists have been arrested under the same anti-terror laws cited and discussed here. These arrests are taking place in a political climate where the current right-wing Hindutva government has taken all measures to stifle dissent and brand everyone who questions the current dispensation as "anti-national." See Joanna Slater, September 2018, "India's Government Is Arresting Lawyers and Activists amid Accusations of Plotting to Overthrow Modi," *Washington Post*, https://www.washingtonpost.com/world/.

5. The term *Naxalite* derives from the Naxalbari movement, which originated in a village called Naxalbari in West Bengal in 1967. This was a peasant movement motivated by Maoist ideology and suppressed by state government by 1972. The term *Naxalite* was subsequently used in national vocabulary (it does not have a legal meaning) to describe people who may have radical left opinions, often leading to the conflating of categories of criminality and leftist ideology.

6. While writing about the structure of the book, the translator Sahba Husain explains that it is not in the form of a diary, a journal, or a memoir. The book does not have any particular structure with which to categorize it (Habib 2011). Anjum Habib mentioned to me that she had no particular form or structure for the book.

7. Singh (2007, 28–29) delineates the following as the features of extraordinary laws: "(i) These laws come with objects and intents proclaiming the need to respond to specific problems of extraordinary nature. (ii) It follows from the fact of extraordinariness that these laws are temporary and that their lives are coterminous with the extraordinary events they intend to overturn. (iii) Since they are extraordinary measures in response to extraordinary events/situations, they are constitutive of extraordinary provisions pertaining to arrest, detention, investigation, evidence, trial, and punishment."

8. Not much is available through the accounts of Habib and Azad in terms of comparison of their experiences. An issue worth exploring is the comparison between the experiences of prisoners from upper-caste background and lower-caste or religious minority backgrounds, convicted under similar provisions of the law. However, given whatever analysis is available through the accounts presented here, it can be deduced that the socioeconomic conditions prevalent outside prison would largely be reproduced or mirrored inside prison as well.

9. Reference is being made to Mary Carpenter, who was a social reformer focused on the reformation of juvenile offenders. Her understanding of reformation of women convicts in India was based on the idea of building a stronger Empire, and she looked toward white middle-class women to reform "alien" bodies. For more, see Anne Schwan, 2010, "Dreadful Beyond Description: Mary Carpenter's Prison Reform Writings and Female Convicts in Britain and India," *European Journal of English Studies* 14 (2): 107–20.

10. Azad (2017) writes, "But since the world of prison is far removed from our every day reality, we remain fearful of it. Therefore, in order that we are able to familiarise ourselves with and get rid of prejudices about prisons, there is a need to extensively write and converse about life inside prisons. The objective should be to not only accustom ourselves to talking about prisons, but also speaking up and fighting for the human rights of prisoners. With this intention in mind, I set out to write and publish this diary" (1).

11. This is indicative in, for example, Azad's mother's constant questioning and worrying regarding her well-being, provisions of food, and the general behavior of authorities toward her. Azad also describes the manner in which some of her col-

leagues and friends immediately distanced themselves upon hearing the news of her arrest, since they were scared or apprehensive of consequences that might befall them. Thus, these glimpses from the book *Zindanama* give the reader a taste of the image of prisons in the popular imaginary. It would also be useful to look toward popular representations of prisons in Indian cinema; however, that is beyond the scope of this chapter.

12. Unfortunately, not many details are provided in the accounts of Anjum regarding cooking practices, which could be because Tihar Central Jail is a huge complex that is centrally managed and is known for providing decent food as compared to the rest of the prisons.

References

Agamben, Giorgio. 2003. *The State of Exception*. Translated by Kevin Attell. Chicago: University of Chicago Press.

Azad, Seema. 2017. *Zindanama*. Kolkata: Setu Prakashani.

Bandyopadhyay, Mahuya. 2010. *Everyday Life in a Prison: Confinement, Surveillance, Resistance*. New Delhi: Orient Blackswan.

Banerjee, Sumanta. 1984. *India's Simmering Revolution: The Naxalite Uprising*. London: Zed Books.

Bargu, Banu. 2014. *Starve and Immolate: The Politics of Human Weapons*. Columbia University Press.

Baxi, Upendra. 1982. *The Crisis of the Indian Legal System*. New Delhi: Vikas Publishing House.

Chatterjee, Debolina, and Suhita Chopra Chatterjee. 2018. "Food in Captivity: Experiences of Women in Indian Prisons." *Prison Journal* 98 (1): 40–59.

Chatterjee, Partha. 1993. *The Nation and Its Fragments: Colonial and Postcolonial Histories*. Princeton, NJ: Princeton University Press.

Ferreira, Arun. 2014. *Colours of the Cage: A Prison Memoir*. New Delhi: Aleph Book Company.

Foucault, Michel. 1977. *Discipline and Punish: The Birth of the Prison*. Translated by Alan Sheridan. Middlesex: Penguin Books.

———. 1982. "The Subject and Power." *Critical Inquiry* 8 (4): 777–95.

Garland, David. 1986. "Review: Foucault's 'Discipline and Punish'—An Exposition and Critique." *American Bar Foundation Research Journal* 11 (4): 847–80.

Habib, Anjum Zamarud. 2011. *Prisoner No. 100: An Account of My Nights and Days in an Indian Prison*. Translated by Sahba Husain. New Delhi: Zubaan.

Hussain, Nasser. 2003. *The Jurisprudence of Emergency: Colonialism and the Rule of Law*. Ann Arbor: University of Michigan Press.

Johns, Fleur. 2005. "Guantanamo Bay and the Annihilation of the Exception." *European Journal of International Law* 16 (4): 613–35.

Kalhan, Anil, Gerald Conroy, Mamta Kaushal, Sam Scott Miller, and Jed S. Rakoff.

2006. "Colonial Continuities: Human Rights, Terrorism, and Security Laws in India." *Columbia Journal of Asian Law* 20 (1): 93–234.

Kannabiran, K.G. 2003. *The Wages of Impunity: Power, Justice and Human Rights*. New Delhi: Orient Blackswan.

Kaviraj, Sudipta. 2010. *The Imaginary Institutions of India: Politics and Ideas*. New York: Columbia University Press.

Khalili, Laleh. 2011. "Gendered Practices of Counterinsurgency." *Review of International Studies* 37: 1471–91.

Khan, Mohammad Aamir, and Nandita Haksar. 2016. *Framed as a Terrorist: My 14-Year Struggle to Prove My Innocence*. New Delhi: Speaking Tiger.

Merry, Sally Engle. 1991. "Review: Law and Colonialism." *Law and Society Review* 25 (4): 889–922.

Rao, Varavara. 2010. *Captive Imagination*. New Delhi: Penguin India.

Roy, Mallarika Sinha. 2011. *Gender and Radical Politics in India: Magic Moments of Naxalbari (1967–1975)*. New York: Routledge.

Seminarist. 2002. "Time to End Abuses." Accessed July 14, 2018. http://www.india-seminar.com/2002/512/512%20seminarist.htm.

Sen, Satadru. 2002. "The Female Jails of Colonial India." *The Indian Economic and Social HIstory Review* 39 (4): 417–38.

Sethi, Manisha. 2014. *Kafkaland: Prejudice, Law and Counterterrorism in India*. New Delhi: Three Essays Collective.

Shah, Alpa, and Dhruv Jain. 2017. "Naxalbari at Its Golden Jubilee: Fifty Recent Books on the Maoist Movement in India." *Modern Asian Studies* 51 (4): 1165–219.

Singh, Ujjwal Kumar. 2007. *The State, Democracy and Anti-Terror Laws in India*. New Delhi: Sage Publications India.

Thiong'o, Ngugi Wa. 1981. *Detained: A Writer's Prison Diary*. Berkshire: Heinemann International Literature and Textbooks.

Verma, Preeti, ed. 2004. *The Terror of POTA and Other Security Legislations in India*. New Delhi: Human Rights Law Network.

Vishwavijai. 2017. *Zindanama*. Kolkata: Setu Prakashani.

3

Seeing Orange

Mediatizing the
Prison Empire

SHREEREKHA PILLAI

Piper Kerman's memoir inspires a binge spectacle, vis-à-vis the Netflix-generated productions of Jenji Kohan's seven seasons of *Orange Is the New Black* (2013–19).[1] OITNB attempts to express activist philosophy from the last several decades while giving primacy to entertaining an audience eager to consume the "other" vis-à-vis the carceral subject. Kohan presents women from the margins—Black and Latina women, poor women, women of all shapes and sizes, women of various sexualities, women transitioning, women we cannot see because the scopophilic order grounded in patriarchy dictates otherwise. Kohan's mise-en-scène challenges the normative gaze, as Mulvey taught us in the foundational era of feminist film theory, tethered on fetishism or voyeurism.[2] Instead the pleasure in looking happens with women at the center of the narrative, not merely as the centerfold. Characters with their backstories, secret desires, flaws, and strengths, correctional officers (CO's) included, urge one to review whom we incarcerate, what incarceration means, and how the carceral complex needs radical reimagination. In highlighting how broken lives are further broken by the carceral system, itself broken and run in different directions by broken people, with systemic drives for profit and capital, the show stops short of dismantling the prison as a carceral empire that stretches Jim Crow into the age of late capital; rather it shows how all people of all colors are caught in its labyrinthine chokehold, which is to say, all who enter it suffer its wrath. However, the very successes of the show that drew in such a wide-ranging audience of varying political allegiances also counters the ideological heart of anti-carceral activist projects; in equally attending to all narratives, it sublimates the radical potential of racial injustice that is the fulcrum of the carceral complex.

First Step of Mediatizing:
Disappear the Book

The memoir by Piper Kerman, rendered as Chapman in the serial, is at a remove from its mediatized progeny. The voluntary entry into prison is rendered verbatim. However, from there, the differences are manifold. The point here is not to unpack the differences between the literary text and its televised offspring, but to articulate the ideological shifts. It is a given that the mediatized version will and has to shed light on its many characters, rather than Piper alone; the televised show with omniscient directorial vision infuses all characters with backstory and context, unlike the memoir that remains lodged in Piper's positionality. The memoir is the output of a human rights social activist invested in creating a radical shift in the methods and conditions of incarceration. In the serial's rendering of the characters with operatic dimensions, what is left out is the author's hard-boiled observations on the many women and their struggles to stay connected to dreams and families beyond the prison; instead the mediatized OITNB gives us Red serving Chapman a tampon in a biscuit, Nikki and lover in the bathroom, and Taystee shooing Piper out of the shower. The televised prison is in extremis.

The mediatized OITNB remains grounded in the discursive order of a white girl who has taken the wrong turn into the heart of darkness, the American prison, a discursive order that borrows from the colonial gaze at the contact zone.[3] The memoir accounts for Piper's privileges in the great treasure of books she receives in parcels from family and friends, her many visitations from the same people, as well as her close relationship with Larry (her boyfriend) and her mother. The memoir highlights women's community and their kindness,[4] a resilience counterrepresented in the serial by devious criminality, Piper's growing hardness, and a whole invented subplot of a Piper–Alex Vause love affair sensationalizing prison life to draw an audience.[5] In fact, the show portrays Larry as a writer who makes it at his job by exploiting and publishing on Piper's incarceration, leaving her seething, whereas in the memoir he stays by her side, visiting her weekly as he grows professionally, finally publishing a column in the *New York Times*'s "Modern Love" section declaring his love for Piper to the world. It is as though Kohan's televised vision is in direct opposition to the reality Kerman narrates with her fiancé who stays true to her; in contrast, Kohan has him dallying into a

3. Seeing Orange   71

romantic affair and then a relationship with her dearest friend, one of the reasons for their rift as the fictive Piper falls into the arms of her jailhouse lover and codefendant, Alex Vause. Not only are the racial and social justice impulses of the show suspect, its feminist vision remains tethered on a patriarchal script that has women clawing at each other for the "man."

In the memoir, Piper shares the kindness the women show toward the pregnant inmates in their midst. "Crazy Eyes" is a Latina woman who is known for her intensity and who nurses a bit of a crush toward Piper that fizzles due to Piper's clear disinterest. By turning this character into a dark-skinned Black woman (played expertly by Uzo Aduba), mentally destabilized as the adoptee in a liberal white family, the serial reifies ableist and misogynist anti-blackness prevalent within American culture. Similarly, the white power–preaching, racist, and drug-addled crowd of the serial is, within the book, a group of wannabe Black, cornrow-wearing white women Kerman calls Eminemlettes. The original Pensatucky character, rather than stowed away by a perverse CO with whom she stages a getaway, has a baby with whom she is attempting to reunite based on Piper's sympathetic and well-written letter. The show also does away with one character, Francesca LaRue, who upsets the author due to her extreme disfigurement from plastic surgery gone awry and her overall strange behavior. The deletion would not be an issue were it not for the fact that the one time the actual Piper acts out of character and a bit gruffly is when Francesca is stretching out her arms as she is walking on the track and Piper, on the eleventh round of lapping her, taps her arms down. In the book, this moment makes her question her own humanity and the hardness that prison life has brought her, quite visibly tame and almost sweet, compared to the sort of machinations and metamorphoses presented in the serial.

The memoir does not detail incidents of sex and violence. Once Piper hears a story of a quiet prisoner who has had enough and fills her tube socks with locks to beat up her nemesis. Piper's tensions come around her habit of picking out the good parts such as spinach at the sad excuse for the salad bar at Danbury's cafeteria. All the good and normal and constructive parts that help Piper survive have been wiped off the mediatized version of the narrative, parts where the writer shares of birthday celebrations, daily yoga gatherings, GED celebrations, pedicures, hair repair, Children's Day, holiday decorations, and the countless other similarities the writer points to between the drab life of the prison and her experience at a women's college, Smith—both being women's communities that have more in common than Kerman had first imagined. The pacifists brought into the book are turned into one very unrealistic Asian American character who is out of touch with everybody's reality. Kerman's human rights work informs her narratorial voice: "Our system of 'corrections' is about arm's-length revenge and retribution, all day and all night. Then its overseers wonder why people leave prison more broken than when they went in."[6] Yoga Janet, unlike Yoga Jones of the serial, is an activist and a healer, a powerful figure who helps Piper serve the time with dignity and community, a woman she grieves upon parting.

One imagines that for the writer of this memoir, the show might be as revelatory as for the average binge watcher of the serial. Other than marking the blond central character as a figure who shares her name, little else holds true from the written to the visual text. In prison, the memoirist learns she is good: "Best of all, I had found other women here in prison who could teach me how to be better."[7] Piper Kerman remains steady as a kind and sweet white woman who stays true to herself, does not transform into any sort of prison gangster, and consoles those who are terrified of the worse conditions awaiting them upon release due to poverty, lack of family support, and lack of resources. The serial brings about a narrative arc of evil, since the prison is portrayed as a den of criminality, followed by the serenity found in the arms of her ex-lover, with whom she is wed before being released, all of it a fiction contrasting the imaginative arc of the memoir. The author, Kerman, keeps her privilege front and center as she navigates through the petty rules of a broken system, and survives due to the kindness and community formed with fellow inmates.

What is heartening in the script-performative complex of OITNB is the interactive, agential, and hyperinvolved spectatorial cyberfandom that drives ahead each season of this narrative.[8] In this regard James Lull's observations prove edifying: "Audience interpretations and uses of media imagery also eat away at hegemony. Hegemony fails when dominant ideology is weaker than social resistance."[9] In addressing the exuberance of its song and the diversity of its cast and characters, this chapter reads the show as generated out of a productive potential of carceral liberalism that falls short of addressing the racial and gendered injustices undergirding the heart of the carceral empire. The most significant critique of the show, primarily that it helps us sympathize with incarcerated lives through the gaze of a privileged, educated white woman, is quite significant precisely because it helps to buttress and erase the structural reality of carceral juridicality; historically, two-thirds of the punished are Black and Latino people, who only make up one-third of the nation. The disproportionate meting out of punitive justice on Black and brown lives[10] is somehow sidelined as we think of the "universal" critique of justice and sympathize with the women serving time, never coming close to the more radical criticism that addresses the structural injustice of the

3. Seeing Orange   73

criminal justice system or the urgency for its abolition or radical overhaul. What Angela Davis invokes as a "state of emergency" is a reality that still remains veiled despite the binge-watching of the serial.[11] The spectatorial eye sees most of the women, through circumstances, having committed the crimes that land them the time; the affective order is generated for the misery of the wrongdoers rather than any radical overarching critique of systemic wrongs done to communities of color.

Joy in Closed Spaces: Songs of Incarceration

OITNB's theme song is Regina Spektor's "You've Got Time." The women's faces, in extreme close-up, are mugshot-style, full-frontal shots that do not gloss over pockmarks, uneven teeth, moles, and unmade faces. In time, the spectators are forced to reckon with this arresting montage and come to grips with the hard reality of women's conditions in American prisons and the humanity of the women within the walls. The faces slowly take on recognizable features as the audience begins to connect stories to each face through their personal tics like scars, smiles, furrows, and skin or hair color so that the simple and stark introduction inverts its own institutional structure of mugshot replay one receives in nightly news telecasts. Instead, by stitching face with story, the audience elides the easy habituation of dehumanizing the other. Through the narratives of sorrow, suffering, humor, and fortitude one learns from each character, the opening segment takes on a lesson in humanizing the condition of the "criminal" other who can no longer remain forgotten by the mainstream.

> The animals, the animals
> Trapped, trapped, trapped 'till the cage is full
> The cage is full
> Stay awake
> In the dark, count mistakes
> The light was off but now it's on
> Searching the ground for a bitter song
> The sun is out, the day is new
> And everyone is waiting, waiting on you
> And you've got time
> And you've got time[12]

The song spells out the dehumanization of the carceral state where people are kept caged like animals, often together or, even more cruelly, separate in segregation units that are deemed a violation of human rights. Yet this form of punishment continues in the American prison system as a way to discipline inmates from a minimum period of hours to indefinite periods that can extend into years in the form of solitary confinement. The song also points to the collusion between the state apparatus of the prison with the neoliberal corporate sector that seeks to profit off the prison industry: keeping the "cages" full yields revenue that can be turned into political slogans about community-building during election years even though research points very clearly to the devastation of the prison regime on communities of the working poor and racially marginalized people of the United States.[13] Reform initiatives like rehabilitation and employment programs focus on making "corrections" less punitive. But they maintain the political framework of "redeeming" bad people, rather than dismantling antisocial systems. According to investigative research by American Friends Service Committee (AFSC), the private prison industry is exploiting prison reform efforts by shifting from brick-and-mortar carceral facilities to outsourced social services, moving these operations to the so-called "treatment-industrial complex."[14]

The psychic condition of long-term debilitation is writ large on the prison institution, which continues to function on paper under the aegis of reform and rehabilitation. The individual stays awake counting her mistakes, unable to sleep in spaces that are marked visibly with lack of control. The condition of the female prisoner, condemned behind bars for long periods, is doubly wounding because patriarchy reproduces the structures of submission where the woman, a secondary citizen at best in the free world, is further reduced behind the walls.[15] Inside and outside, she is being required to perform her duties, but she remains confined within "time," a metonym specifically heightened to reflect internally charged prison discourse where "time" takes on temporal and spatial currency that inversely devalues life. "You've got time" comes to means the higher the number, the less time you have to live.

The very failure of the show is in its naïveté and sweet desire—a Benetton-esque corporate nod to multiculturalism—to represent everybody. The portrait-montage's attempt to show all erases the very fact that the carceral liberalism of the state has historically targeted the poor and the vulnerable, mostly people of color, who are disproportionately sentenced, accorded more time, and punished more within the penal sites than white men and women. Regina Spektor's Grammy-nominated score for the show (2013) has an electronic catchy sound that toes the line of mainstream white feminism and attempts to tell the truth of criminalized, incarcerated, and oppressed Black and brown bodies by opening with an analogy of animals trapped in a cage, a ham-fisted and problematic attempt at grappling with the carceral specter

3. Seeing Orange   75

on hand. The show stops short in the gaps between the aspirations of abolition democracy's work and the specificity of Afro-pessimistic theories that address the historic and systematic punishment, erasure, and annihilation of Black bodies within the American landscape and imaginary.

Intersectional Embodied Narratives

Emily Nussbaum sums up the excitement generated by OITNB in the opening of her *New Yorker* article by saying, "Last year, when the women's-prison series 'Orange Is the New Black' débuted, on Netflix, it felt like a blast of raw oxygen. Part of this was baldly algorithmic: here, at last, were all those missing brown faces, black faces, wrinkled faces, butch lesbians, a transgender character played by a transgender actor—an ensemble of electrifying strangers, all of them so good that it seemed as if some hidden valve had been tapped, releasing fresh stories and new talent."[16]

OITNB stages what bell hooks imagines to be a healthy alternative to an earlier era of television that portrayed the poor as normal and likeable as long as they were "movin' on up" so that they were rendered recognizable with "a piece of the pie."[17] On this earlier era of television, bell hooks critiques, "We must also change the way the poor are represented. It is crucial to construct habits of seeing and being that restore an oppositional value system affirming that one can live a life of dignity and integrity in the midst of poverty."[18] For the audience, a TV show devoted entirely to the carceral complex of female bodies, in difference, is remarkable in its conceit—the heteronormative white male is not the benevolent figure of resolution. All the heroes are convicts; the show resolves its own complex of nuances through a parallel moral/ethical order that hinges around the shifting chimera of players, who arrive under the sign of woman. OITNB shows only the deeply fallen and flawed females being offered the reprieve and possibility of redemption, which can come in all sorts of unexpected forms: the scopophilic reordering around female spectatorial desire; Piper gains forgiveness from Red finally by concocting a homemade remedy of lotion made out of hot pepper and other kitchen products; Taystee, well-read and strong in terms of her own moral fortitude, finally stands up to her old mentor and nemesis, Vee.

As Stuart Hall posits, ideology works in mysterious and imperceptible ways.[19] First, it is not one act as such but a chain of meanings that are in constant motion. Second, even though our statements are our own, they are made not in a vacuum but out of a lattice of preexisting ideologies that work unconsciously into language. OITNB, perhaps in its quest to represent the material reality of its cast of characters, reifies much of what it seeks to question: we are given the show through Piper, the white female blond figure, and it is her central "gaze" that authorizes the narrative, a problematic explored in Suzanne Enck and Megan Morrissey's article.[20] The Black characters include a roster that crosses the spectrum from "crazy" to "drug-den" mamas to "belligerent" and reify larger cultural assumptions about Black femininity. Unless one engages in deliberate reflective thinking that engages with the backstories of the show's Black star characters—Poussey's "coming out" narrative with her military father in Germany, Sophia's gender-transitioning with her teenage son, Suzanne's adoption by her liberal white parents—it is easy to reify dominant anti-Black notions with which an average spectator views the subworld of American crime and punishment, as always already Black and criminalized.

Women Inside/Out

OITNB generates a productive assonance between the condition of women inside the prison and women outside in the "free world." Decades of second-wave feminist intellectual labor generate a palpable parallel between the condition of women locked in patriarchy and women within the walls, that is, classical patriarchy as an imprisonment for women. Deniz Kandiyoti most famously categorizes various forms of global systems of gendered oppression, but what the systems have in common is a promise of a carceral lockdown for women. In U.S. discourse arising from scholars of the second wave inaugurated famously by Betty Friedan's *Feminine Mystique*,[21] domesticity presents an invisible golden cage in which women remain shackled within gendered expectations that keep them quarantined within the home, illegitimate in the public sphere. Such a critique cannot be attributed to white feminism alone; in fact, decades before in distinct parts of the globe, a feminist critique of the domestic servitude promised to women through patriarchal structures of matrimony and placement arose, as seen in literature produced by Charlotte Perkins Gilman, "The Yellow Wallpaper" (1892), and Rokeya Sakhawat Hossain, "Sultana's Dream" (1905). Hossain's short, fantastic, and magical realist story, which prefigures a feminist science fiction, imagines a world run by women where men are quarantined at home, functionaries in reproduction and otherwise perceived as useless. The story, humorous and scathing at turns, is inspiring in its invocation of an early twentieth-century South Asian feminist Muslim progressive voice that imagines an alternate structure of gender and power. Patriarchal ontology too represents a structure of state power; to look at women inside the prison system is looking at in-house experts on penality who have been living the experience of being

3. Seeing Orange 77

disciplined and punished long before entering the walls. Even though Kohan's directorial vision encourages a feminist alliance, the social vision mapped here keeps the carceral liberal subject in place.

Framed as a revolving set of case studies, the backstory of each character reveals a familiarity with thematics of disempowerment that begin long before juridicality. A young African-American woman who early on takes the blame for Piper's misplacement of a tool in the toolshed, Janae Watson (Vicky Jeudy), lithe and graceful, is seen running in track pants every chance she is given to go into the outdoors recreational area. The analeptic shot sequences that inform the second and third season show Janae as being raised in a home where the patriarchal figure wields an authority that he attributes to the Nation of Islam. In one shot sequence, we encounter Janae in running clothes sitting at a kitchen table with a mother who is covered and a father who is refusing to allow her to run because it means revealing skin in immodest ways. The mother speaks up for the daughter saying this might be her ticket to a university. The father refuses and bellows out a forceful rejection to which the daughter says, "If this is what we believe in, then maybe I don't need the Nation." This retort is met with a slap on her cheek, with a young Janae reeling from the rage of the father. The diegetic sequence informs us that she ends up being romantically involved with a gang member in high school, and after a burglary of a cash register goes awry, they are both on the lam; she is accused of "showing off" by her boyfriend, who cannot keep up with her stride. In slowing down, she is caught while her boyfriend escapes. Running, as a feat, talent, and ambition, is rejected in effect, reducing her to a figure on the run from the double register: the Law of the Father and state law. Patriarchy keeps the woman stagnant—the juridical order forbids Janae from running toward her freedom.

Mirkin suggests, "In addition to rape, the Law, the family and religion are the major methods through which men have dominated women. Women have internalized the values of the patriarchs. Thus they become willing, cooperative and passive victims."[22] Mirkin's theorization pits the female as the site of the problem, the woman as both subject and object of the problem of patriarchy. The serialized narrative at times provides alibi for this form of victim-blaming, wherein the woman who leads the Latina women in prison, Gloria Mendoza (Selenis Leyva), replaces the Russian kitchen lead, Red (Kate Mulgrew), and acts as mother figure for various younger Latina women; Gloria is shown as going the extra mile to ensure that her son does not stray and end up in lockdown like her. It is only in the last episode of the third season that we are given an insight into the formative period of a young Gloria, who, lying on a nurse's table in a hospital with her friend, shown to be a practitioner of Santeria, is seen wishfully praying for a son. After her friend completes her incantations, the young ultrasound technician exclaims how this has never happened, where the fetus identified as female is now sporting a little penis, bearing out the phallic order and setting everything right in young Gloria's patriarchal imaginary. The plot corroborates that whatever transpires in the "free" world does not bode well for the children who are caught up in the invisible carceral complex. Numbering ten times more than the 2.2 million incarcerated people in the American prison system are their children and families, who, in many ways, suffer an altered version of the sentence outside the walls.[23] On this, Peter Enns writes that families and communities also experience "the carceral state."[24]

Kohan maps a social imagination in her production that does not interrupt the racial, gendered, and sexual historical subjectifications of Black and Latina women exemplified in the figures of Janae, Gloria, and Daya. Dayanara Diaz, the sweet and young initiate in the system, whose mother is serving time in the same prison for drug-related charges, is another figure with a complex backstory. The racial imaginary of OITNB remains limited within dominant stereotypes. In casting the young Latina woman as voluptuous, innocent, and open to the charms of a guard, the frame reifies racialized tropes of Latinx femininity. As Sjoberg and Gentry analyze the "fallen" figures of women within the global order, they note the disempowerment writ large in their pre-stories.[25] From earliest memories, one sees Daya yearning for her mother's affection and approval while also attempting to find her place in the world that denies her privilege, that makes no room for her artistic soul to survive. In prison, she falls in love with a young, white male guard, Bennett. Pregnant, she finds herself alone and distraught attempting to grieve for the sudden excision of her partner from her life. Their stolen moments of love are no longer available, and she is portrayed as being malleable to the provocations and nefarious plans of her mother, who is against all odds trying to mother from prison. Plans to find a stable home for the baby come to naught. While Daya finds peace with her mother, a peace that counterserves her in later seasons, we see her baby being taken into state custody as the child's caretaker is arrested for drug-related charges. Daya offers the historical subject whose life spells out the diffuse script of carceral liberalism.

Love and Marriage, an Antithesis

The institution of marriage continues, hobbled, with the women, often under duress, maintaining their fractured place within the heteronormative order. While most of the marriages depicted in the world outside the prison walls tend to be in a state of advanced decay, and examples proliferate, the decay continues to an extent with those identified most readily with that world, such as the central figure, Piper, and her partner, Larry Bloom. The state of marriages depicted is one of neuroses and psychic lockdown, ironically enough, for the free people.

Prison romances, but without the heart and Black feminist poetics of Asha Bandele's memoir *Prisoner's Wife*, do happen.[26] Dayanara falls for a baby-faced guard who is removed from the unit after she becomes pregnant. Healy begins to fall for the prison's hardened but soft-hearted leader, Red, without reciprocation. Lorna Morello inspires a young man from the outside to visit, and after falling in love through these visits, conduct an in-prison wedding ceremony followed by hot and sweaty connubial bliss in the soda room. Piper finds another love with Stella, a tattooed punk rocker, after her breakup in the fallout from her machinations with her prison company, Felonious Spunk. What remains fixed is the way the pecking order works in terms of domination and subjugation within patriarchy. Deniz Kandiyoti notes that classic patriarchy becomes a system so deeply internalized that women perpetuate the hegemony of power on one another in order to reap its rewards, secure their own positions and posterity, and ingratiate themselves to systems of power that render them powerless. Kandiyoti writes, "In classic patriarchy, subordination to men is offset by the control older women attain over younger women."[27] As Kandiyoti notes the prescriptions of patriarchy enforced through male progeny, prison structure gains from the lessons learned of patriarchy to continue similar gendered hierarchies, a system of prisonarchy or the hegemony of carceral liberalism writ large within the walls.[28] In the racialized figures of female authority, such as Red (white), Vee (Black), and Gloria (Latina), we view a racialized system that continues to remain implicated and complicit in patriarchy.

As Shakur (2013) reminds us, patriarchy's victims and guards are often one and the same. If one is psychically imprisoned in a system of domination from the start, then imprisonment becomes a new site in which to reconcile old habits of subjugation. Darcy K. War Bonnett, an incarcerated woman, shares, "There is little encouragement or positive affirmation here—little incentive to keep trying. If one prisoner breaks the rule, all the women are punished. Morale is at rock-bottom low. Many women choose to quietly give up and give in. I myself sometimes wonder if I should have stayed with my abuser. Even if he had succeeded in killing me, my life sentence would be done."[29] War Bonnett sees little difference in her existence in a less than salutary heteronormative relationship in the "free world" and her condition as an incarcerated inmate in the American prison system. It is suggested in all the voices offered in the same journal issue that punishment is not finite. OITNB provides windows into lives often broken long before incarceration, marked deeply by the symbolic phallic order, lives that continue unto a path of quiet devastation within the walls.[30] The resistance comes in the wild spaces of interiority (creative expressions) and exteriority (alternative community-building) forged by the women who unyoke from patriarchy. The wild space that many second-wave feminists dreamt about outside the confines of patriarchy are constructed in the secret and not so secret, amorous and friendly, border-crossing and gender-crossing sisterhoods of the carceral empire. The show portrays the doubling of the site of oppression also becoming one of resistance; OITNB represents the agency and will of the female subjects of *prisonarchy*.[31]

Imaginative Failures

The cleavage between the women's and African American people's movements is historical, with fault lines leading to the heart of our current carceral state. In the period marked by the law which abolished slavery and recognized the African American man as a human being with the right to vote, the women's movement chose sides. From 1865 onward, what mattered to the women's movement were the desires and aspirations of white women with class privilege.[32] The fork in the path encountered by activists who might have imagined a solidarity in the mid-nineteenth century disappeared during the Reconstruction with the systematic shutdown of all possibilities of Black enfranchisement through the ossification of Jim Crow in the South.[33] In the current moment, white women's ambitions for collective uplift of all women is pitted against the struggle for racial justice, especially the specific movements arising out of Black and brown communities. The show invokes a feminist version of the "All Lives Matter" response to the BLM movement. In unmuting "all" voices, the racialized gendered other once again recedes from the mediatized imaginary.

Season one begins centered on Piper Kerman, a white woman "doing" time for a former drug offense, entering into a system unknown to her and then, criminalized by the system that hardens her, reifying the idiom of the PIC as a site of criminality producing "bad" women. Season six depicts Piper being released and leaving the system and shows her as having evolved with a complicated moral trajectory, wistfully looking back at the women playing softball in the prison field as her brother pulls away in the car and asks her, "So what are you gonna do now?" The serial departs from the memoir in fundamental ways that displaces the political heart of the memoir. Whilst

3. Seeing Orange   81

Kohan's departures allow for a fuller narrative to develop around the many characters proliferating the prison stage, Piper and a white female imaginary continue to inform and propel the narrative forward, diminishing the greater problems around the PIC and racial injustices that inform its operations. Season six even includes an in-prison ad-hoc wedding of Piper with her long-time lover, Alex Vause, the reason for her incarceration, with her posse officiating the ceremony. Within contexts of dissident feminism, the white *homo*narrative ideal is energized within this discursive order at the cost of disappearing Black and brown lives, the poor, the mentally ill, and many others who are housed in the same bloc and frame narrative. The other is left in the long shadow cast by Piper's desire and its fulfillment; she leaves behind a life that includes the slow arc of descent into criminal behavior through illicit businesses she engages in followed by denouement as a prison labor activist: a woman who awaits her beloved and her release from the same unit. The other remains caricaturized or marginal in this homage to a white woman's struggle in the heart of darkness from which she is able to arise, uplifted in light and hope.[34]

Some people express being more free in prison, such as Piper Kerman's friend Pom-Pom, who writes to her about the troubles of surviving once released in poverty, without possibilities, "It's sad to say I miss that place cause it is crazy out here . . . All this freedom, but I still feel like I'm locked up."[35] While most of the white characters such as Piper, Nikki, Pensatucky, Red, and Yoga Jones arrive in the PIC through criminal behaviors or acts in the free world, most of the women of color come due to structural inequalities such as lives mired in poverty, familial abandonment, or oppression and other circumstances of trouble that funnel poor people of color into the PIC, such as Taystee, Burset, and Black Cindy. For the women of color who inhabit the carceral lockdown experienced by the poor, the prison represents a site where one can count on the stability of three meals and a cot, a basic materiality that keeps bringing them into the system in a revolving door; in a political legerdemain, it also blames the poor for their lack of options and inability to lift out of the cycles of poverty and criminalization.[36] Thus, it is not surprising to hear the white protagonist of the show, Piper, declare early in season two to the prison counselor that it is all right for the prison to be run by criminals—such as Figuero, who is in cahoots with the profit-making machinery of the privatizing industry,[37] which is strongly critiqued—because Litchfield houses criminals. The logic is that criminals deserve no better than criminal treatment; in other words, it is okay for the state to act violently upon a population deemed violent by the state. The tautological flaw here mirrors the long-ranging American habit of criminalizing the poor, mostly people of color who have been targets of the state since emancipation, the population marked by the state as criminal, and thus, the liminal category of people for whom the abolishment of slavery as an institution does not apply.[38] For the dominant population, white Americans who support the law-and-order state, criminals are being punished for criminal behavior by the criminal justice system. For the rest, historically disenfranchised poor people of color, the state itself is the site of criminality that rampantly runs roughshod over their lives and marks their vulnerability and disempowerment as criminal, marking their very ontologies as aberrant and punishable. While Kohan's narrative lifts up in its dissident feminist impulse, especially at the conclusion of season three when the women cavort together on the lake as they skip outside the fence, or when they band together to speak of their rights during the ensuing riots for seasons four and five, at one point forming a human chain of Black, white, and brown linking arms waiting for the armed police in riot gear to take them out, it is crucial to note that the BLM icon, Taystee, disappears from the narrative until she reenters the prison at the end of season six just as Piper emerges into the light. The disenfranchised Black protagonist is entombed as the narrative privileges the already privileged.

Ironically, the prison itself is seen as a sterile safe space with good food, safe beds, and comfortable environs. For a global audience accessing Netflix from the global south, OITNB provides a comfortable vantage with which to view American life, where even its prisoners have it better than people in most parts of the world. Even though academics like Anne Schwan argue for the seriousness of the show in shedding light on women in prison, and my initial spectatorship of the show reflected this sentiment, Schwan's point about needing to form an alliance between academic feminism and popular cultural responses to the show's merit needs further interrogation.[39] At issue is a failure of its imaginary; even when the show grapples with the PIC, it points elsewhere, with the profit-making privatizing sector or certain bad apples, so that overall, Litchfield Penitentiary, symbolized by Warden Caputo, is a sensible institution, a logical extension of the democratic state. Caputo is a good white man who is the final reservoir of humanity, the one human being ready to go to bat for Taystee, the Black female icon of BLM in this show. As she speaks powerfully to the misrecognition and erasure of Black women's lives, she does it within the diegetic frame of speaking to a very concerned Caputo who wishes to see her released and run after the corrupt officer who fires the deadly shot for which she is being charged. The Black and brown women remain tokenized in the narrative that begins and ends with Piper's freedom as the denouement.[40]

The women's prison, in Kohan's vision, becomes a site for the possibility of dissident feminist solidarities at the expense of addressing the systematic inequalities that target Black and brown lives at higher rates: what needs to be pushed forward is how these marginalized figures are punished differently, with longer sentences and harsher treatment specifically for people of color with penultimate costs of carcerality being borne the heaviest by Black bodies,[41] with Black women incarcerated at twice the rate of white women. Feminist solidarities appear as women of all colors find one another and playfully enjoy the light and water at the conclusion of season three in a place the director calls "Freedom Lake." In the conclusion of season five, women of all colors stand with arms linked together as a human wall barricaded against the onslaught of patriarchy in the guise of armed riot police with guns descending to the secret hiding place of the women, a literal wild zone of female freedom. Black female power is repeatedly shown as under siege or invisible: Poussey is stomped on and killed in season four, unable to breathe under a guard who holds her down. "Crazy Eyes" Suzanne nearly dies of medications gone awry. Taystee disappears back into the PIC as Piper emerges, the white character contemplating freedom after having had a taste of danger in the dark side. It seems that despite the show's noble aspirations, Black women are sublimated in homage to white female power.

During the insurgent period of hideout in Frieda's (Dale Soules) bunker, Piper reads their secret encampment as an act of resistance and observes, "Maybe some grandma in Kansas will read an article about this and she will see us as people instead of criminals. I mean, isn't that how change really happens?" The imaginative arc that I call carceral liberalist traverses from a young white woman trapped on the wrong side of the tracks to an old white woman of middle America, envisioning change as one that emerges from the mainstream and status quo. Simply put, the show outlaws dissident feminist imaginaries that contend with the full humanity of its most marginalized populations, a vision that Keeanga-Yamahtta Taylor recalls in her interviews with the Combahee writers under the parameter *How We Get Free*.[42] As Taylor observes in the introduction discussing radical Black feminist consciousness, "The Combahee River Collective built on those observations by continuing to analyze the roots of Black women's oppression under capitalism and arguing for the reorganization of society based on the collective needs of the most oppressed."[43] The political knots that arise in OITNB give evidence to an observation by Demita Frazier, summarized by Taylor in her conclusion: "The point of talking about Combahee is not to be nostalgic; rather, we talk about it because Black women are still not free."[44]

84   PILLAI

OITNB remains entrenched in scopophilic cinematic order by unproblematically consuming the body of the desirable white woman. The show's opening sequence stages Piper's "tv titties" as she showers in the prison; after Taystee (Danielle Brooks) compliments her perky breasts, she notes her foolishness in not purchasing shower slippers at the commissary and then bursts into the Staple Singers' famous "I'll Take You There" as Piper stops to peek at her breasts and smile. Piper's entry into the prison itself is aberrant in that she is driven to the prison by her fiancé and surrenders, wondering if the officer who stops them looks surprised to see her. "My mother told her friends I am doing volunteer work in Africa." "I bet they are all appalled that you have gone somewhere so filthy and dangerous." This is not a non sequitur. The discordant placement of "prison" with "Africa" and "filthy and dangerous" is an enjambment of ideas that ties together these sites of othering, and in psychic remapping, equalizes the colonized other (Africa) with the continuing colonizing project in the United States (prison). The binary staged at the opening shows a "happy" Black woman singing contrasted against the introspective white woman, a binary that forms the ideological backbone of racial systems rooted deep in the American psyche.

Racism here comes to stand as code for racial segregation of the prison public spaces, a reluctant articulation of Piper's whiteness that has to match the "whiteness" of any companions or friends she chooses. Piper's howl that ends this opening segment is balanced by Piper's smile as she emerges into freedom by the final segment of season six, the white woman who survives her trek into the heart of darkness and lives to tell her tale. With even "racism" left as code for the suffering of privileged white women, OITNB disrupts the master narrative of the law-and-order state by bringing us closer to attending to the fragmented stories of the many women without being able to pull together a coherent and radical critique of the system of abuses as well as the targeted bodies that it abuses. In fact, the show can be read as a note, albeit a high note, of carceral liberalism.

Pete Brook says of his photography exhibit on prisoners, *Prison Obscura*, "We need to disassemble the notion that prisoners are different. They are us and prisons are ours. It might not seem like prisons are part of our society, but they are. So we need to be conscientious consumers of images."[45] Seeing OITNB aligns along the scopophilic order while also setting up the table for dialogue;[46] it invites the question sutured into its mise-en-scéne: now that we have humanized the other, what do we do if we don't want to just lock 'em up and throw away the key? In addition, now that we have consumed the other, enjoyed the spectatorial pleasure under the sign of feminist communing, how

3. Seeing Orange   85

do we begin the more difficult process of interrogating our own desires? And finally, how do we exit the simulacra long enough to recognize the material and the real episteme of a carcerality that pits state violence at its most vulnerable bodies, that is, the Black, poor, and vulnerable, a fact disappeared in OITNB, where we enter and exit a script mediated by the white gaze?

Notes

1. Kohan produced seven seasons of "Orange Is the New Black," henceforth referred to as OITNB. My chapter references the first six seasons.

2. Mulvey (1975).

3. Pratt (2007) writes about the uneven power politics of the contact zones, the sites where the colonial dominant gaze encounters the other it seeks to colonize, exploit, and oppress. These zones are never spaces of equitable or fair exchanges, but rather imperial power politics and colonial structures of appropriation.

4. Such women's communities are in actuality, in women's narratives emerging from prisons, the very tether to sanity and survival for many. Lora Lempert gathers as much from her interviews of women doing life: "Most of the respondents in this study describe embracing themselves and their life-serving peers as women with social value, who make contributions to individual and social welfare, and whose lives have meaning, a woman named Destiny shares, 'There's something that they have that can get you through. Everybody'" (Lempert 2016, 99).

5. Dawn K. Cecil provides historical context for this particular show in chapter 7 of her book, informing us that it does follow the order of sensationalism seen in previous popular representations of prison in film and television. However, in the sensitivity it accords to its many characters, and the specific attention it gives to structures of race and poverty that bring the very sympathetic character of Taystee back into the penitentiary, the show is given a thumbs-up as an ally in the project of bringing public attention to the large number of incarcerated women because, according to Cecil, "it humanizes the people behind bars" (2015, 137). According to Cecil, a formerly incarcerated reviewer of the Netflix show feels like once audiences have watched the show, they no longer need to explain their experience to others.

6. Kerman (2010), 181.

7. Kerman (2010), 243.

8. Annemarie Navar-Gill's article on the interaction between groups of the show's writers and its fans is quite illuminating. OITNB has such cultural cachet and media savvy that despite minimal tweets from the collaborative of writers in its writers' room, the fans post thousands of tweets championing and heralding the show. It is a profit model of the show's currency and dissemination that comes from the playful repartee and careful exchanges orchestrated between the media-savvy writers' collective and the fans that is "productive for the television industry" (Navar-Gill 2018, 416) and disciplines the fans into behavior that is profitable for the show's repeat seasons. If the vociferous positive fan reception to OITNB's first six seasons is anything to go

by, then the fanbase has a careful engagement with the show's themes and efforts to humanize the other.

9. Lull 2003, 65.

10. "According to a 2009 report by the U.S. Census Bureau, one out of every nine Black men between the ages of twenty and thirty-four is behind bars. This racial disparity is also reflected in the women's prisons in this country. Nearly half of those imprisoned are women of color. Thirty-four percent are Black, despite the fact that Black people make up only 13.6 percent of the general population," write Robin Levi and Ayelet Waldman in the introduction to their powerful anthology *Inside This Place, Not of It: Narratives from Women's Prisons* (2011, 17–18). Each year, the statistics of incarceration, especially for Black, Latina, and Indigenous women, only grow worse as the carceral state stays implacably in place.

11. According to Angela Davis (2007), it is critical to cross-pollinate movements for social justice and connect antiwar and antiprison movements. Many of the young people of color serving the military industrial complex emerge from poor criminalized communities, and their route to staying out of prison is signing up with the military.

12. Spektor (2013). You've Got Time lyrics © Sony/ATV Music Publishing LLC, Warner/Chappell Music, Inc., 2013.

13. Wacquant (2009).

14. Chen (2015).

15. Carol Jacobsen's documentaries charting the lives of incarcerated women in penitentiaries in Michigan, projects she has been engaged in since the 1980s, attest to the reality of dehumanization experienced by women behind bars. Her films *Segregation Unit* (2000) and *Time Like Zeroes* (2010) bring to the fore the subject of the inhumanity of a system that sends women to the special housing unit (SHU) and the overall difficulty of digesting the numbers that overshadow everything else in the women's lives.

16. Nussbaum (2014).

17. Ja'net DuBois's song lyrics to the 1970s television sitcom *The Jeffersons*, which express class mobility specifically for the African-American working class: "Well we're movin' on up / To the east side / To a deluxe apartment in the sky / Movin' on up / To the east side / We finally got a piece of the pie."

18. hooks (1994), 199.

19. Hall (1981).

20. Enck and Morrissey (2015) articulate the problematic of Piper's gaze as central to the show's diegetic movements right after season one and address the issues of reading the "other" women through a white heteronormative privileged gaze that further marginalizes the poor and the women of color and strengthens the PIC in its ideological argument.

21. Frieden, first published in 1963.

22. Mirkin (1984), 44.

23. Elizabeth Hinton (2016) describes a century-long apparatus at work that targets the poor, the Black, the vulnerable, and finally the petty "drug" criminal and leads

to the modern carceral state in her detail-rich historical overview. The structure of the prison, the military apparatus of the state, and the domestic structures of the communities of the vulnerable all form a lattice supporting the carceral state. Hinton offers an example in the continuing practice that once had the FBI causing foment amidst the Black radicals of the 1960s to divide up their groups now being seen in the strategic dissension caused between street gangs that adds to the arrests and rates of incarceration. "The War on Crime and crime itself had always mutually reinforced one another" (329).

24. Enns (2016), 160.

25. They explain, "All of these narratives share one element: they characterize violent women as having been incapable of choosing their violence, and imply that, had they a choice, women would not have chosen the violence" (Sjoberg and Gentry 2007, 190).

26. Bandele (1999).

27. Kandiyoti (1988), 279.

28. Putting together Kandiyoti's (1988) theories of classic patriarchy and Sanyika Shakur's (2013) theories of patriarchy in prison, I propose "prisonarchy," which follows a similar pecking order; the example here is the older women running the various sites of power and privilege in the prison and younger women having to fall in line, the only choice being how far down the line they wish to stand and ingratiate themselves to the senior women in power.

29. War Bonnett (2001), 3.

30. In fact, Marie Gottschalk's politically informed historical point of view is key to understanding how the women's carceral experience is set in place by late nineteenth-century reformatory movements that replaced earlier forms of bodily punishment for errant women by modernizing punishment. A woman was to be kept in seclusion in order to be reformed back into acceptable norms of femininity so that she was no longer viewed as a monster but as an "errant child" in need of instruction (2006, 117).

31. Prisonarchy, as I conceptualize it, speaks to the workings of carceral liberalism on the bodies of female subjects of the PIC, unto whom the structures of late capital, heteropatriarchy, imperialisms, and racisms all conjoin and work simultaneously to reproduce even more rigid and ossified internal hierarchies within sites of state violence, i.e., the prison here.

32. For more on the structures of the old Jim Crow (late nineteenth to early twentieth centuries) and the new Jim Crow (late twentieth to twenty-first century and continuing), read Michelle Alexander (2010).

33. Crumpacker, Russett, and Moynihan (1994).

34. I am referencing the imperial imaginary informing Joseph Conrad's late nineteenth-century novel *Heart of Darkness* (1899), which is prophetic in summarizing alongside its colonial trope a neoliberal gesture of helping the lost "white man"; this affective order informs Piper's gaze as she enters the carceral heart of darkness, finds

her white nemesis who becomes her lover, and then, by marrying her, saves and rescues her much as Livingstone does for Kurtz.

35. Kerman (2010), 247.

36. Wacquant (2009).

37. As early as 1999, Christian Parenti writes about the burgeoning private prison industry, "the drive towards lower costs—that is, the drive towards greater profit—engenders various other problems. Private prisons make money by cutting corners, which means skimping on food, staffing, medicine, education, and other services for convicts" (220–21).

38. These ideas are informed by the works of Saidiya Hartman, Frank Wilderson, and Jared Sexton. Sexton speaks of Black lives lived in a state of social death, not as opposition to social life, but as a structured form of historical erasure that continues to target and punish Black bodies but refuses to see the violent structures that interpellate Black lives, a form of color blindness of the state that becomes an alibi for continuing its practices. For more, read Sexton (2018).

39. Schwan (2016).

40. Christina Belcher's (2016) brilliant analysis of the first season of OITNB highlights the problematic of the show's collusion with neoliberal politics of color blindness that mutes any possibility of radical abolition democracy critiques.

41. Read key works by Talitha LeFlouria, Sarah Haley, Douglas Blackmon, Angela Davis, Ruth Wilson Gilmore, Leith Mullings, and Robert Perkinson.

42. Taylor (2017).

43. Taylor (2017), 5.

44. Taylor (2017), 14.

45. Pete Brook, interviewed in Frank (2015).

46. I am referencing, in an intertextual feminist sense, the artist Judy Chicago's penultimate dinner table installation, *Dinner Party* (1979), about which the preeminent art historian Jane Chin Davidson notes, "The Dinner Party has played a special role as the emblematic artwork produced through collective means" (2011, 34). Chicago's art project inaugurated a sea change in feminist second-wave discourse about women finally being acknowledged and having a seat at the table.

Bibliography

Alexander, Michelle. *The New Jim Crow: Mass Incarceration in the Age of Colorblindness*. 10th anniversary ed. New York: New Press, 2020.

Bandele, Asha. *The Prisoner's Wife: A Memoir*. New York: Scribner, 1999.

Belcher, Christina. "There Is No Such Thing as a Post-Racial Prison: Neoliberal Multiculturalism and the White Savior Complex on Orange Is the New Black." *Television and New Media*, 17, no. 6 (2016): 491–503.

Blackmon, Douglas. *Slavery by Another Name: The Re-Enslavement of Black People in America from the Civil War to World War II*. New York: Doubleday, 2008.

Cecil, Dawn K. *Prison Life in Popular Culture: From The Big House to Orange Is the New Black*. London: Lynne Rienner Publishers, 2015.

Chen, Michelle. "How Prison Reform Could Turn the Prison Industrial Complex into the Treatment-Industrial Complex." *The Nation*, November 20, 2015. http://www.thenation.com/.

Conrad, Joseph. *Heart of Darkness*. New York: Penguin Classic, 2012.

Crumpacker, Laurie, Cynthia Russett, and Ruth Barnes Moynihan. *Second to None: A Documentary History of American Women*. Vol. 2, *From 1865 to the Present*. Lincoln: University of Nebraska Press, 1994.

Davidson, Jane Chin. "Commemorating Feminism: The Graphic Symbol and the Sign." In *Setting the Table: Preparing Judy Chicago's The Dinner Party, 30 Year Anniversary Exhibition at the University of Houston-Clear Lake*, 34–41. Houston: Alfred R. Neumann Library, 2011.

Davis, Angela. "State of Emergency." In *Racializing Justice, Disenfranchising Lives: The Racism, Criminal Justice, and Law Reader*, edited by Manning Marable, Ian Steinberg, and Keesha Middlemass, 323–27. New York: Palgrave Macmillan, 2007.

———. *Are Prisons Obsolete?* New York: Seven Stories Press, 2008.

DuBois, Ja'Net. "Movin' On Up: The Jeffersons Theme Song." Supported by Oren Waters. January 18, 1975. EMI.

Enck, Suzanne, and Megan Morrissey. "If *Orange Is the New Black*, I Must Be Color Blind: Comic Framings of Post-Racism in the Prison-Industrial Complex." *Critical Studies in Media Communication* 32, no. 5 (2015): 303–17.

Enns, Peter K. *Incarceration Nation: How the United States Became the Most Punitive Democracy in the World*. New York: Cambridge University Press, 2016.

Frank, Priscilla. "Photographer Wants to Open Your Eyes to the Brutal Realities of the American Prison Complex." *Huffington Post*, September 3, 2015. https://www.huffpost.com/.

Frieden, Betty. *The Feminine Mystique*. New York: W. W. Norton, 1997.

Gilman, Charlotte Perkins. *The Yellow Wall-paper, Herland, and Selected Writings*. New York: Penguin, 2019.

Gilmore, Ruth Wilson. *Golden Gulag: Prisons, Surplus, Crisis, and Opposition in Globalizing California*. Berkeley: University of California Press, 2007.

Gottschalk, Marie. *The Prison and the Gallows: The Politics of Mass Incarceration in America*. New York: Cambridge University Press, 2006.

Haley, Sarah. *No Mercy Here: Gender, Punishment, and the Making of Jim Crow Modernity*. Chapel Hill: University of North Carolina Press, 2016.

Hall, Stuart. 2021. "The Whites of Their Eyes: Racist Ideologies and the Media." In *Writings on Media: History of the Present*, edited by Charlotte Brunsdon, 177—200. Durham, NC: Duke University Press.

Hinton, Elizabeth. *From the War on Poverty to the War on Crime: The Making of Mass Incarceration in America*. Cambridge: Harvard University Press, 2016.

hooks, bell. *Outlaw Culture*. New York: Routledge, 1994.

Hossain, Rokeya Sakhawat. *Sultana's Dream and Selections from The Secluded Ones*. New York: The Feminist Press at the City University of New York, 1988.

Jacobsen, Carol, dir. 2000. *Segregation Unit*. DVD. Michigan Women's Justice and Clemency Project and Amnesty International. 30 mins.

———, dir. *Time Like Zeros*. 2010. DVD. Michigan Women's Justice and Clemency Project and Amnesty International. 13 min.

Kandiyoti, Deniz. "Bargaining with Patriarchy." In *Gender and Society* 2, no. 3 (Sept. 1988): 274–90.

Kerman, Piper. *Orange Is the New Black: My Year in a Woman's Prison*. New York: Spiegel and Grau, 2010.

LeFlouria, Talitha. *Chained in Silence: Black Women and Convict Labor in the New South*. Chapel Hill: University of North Carolina Press, 2015.

Lempert, Lora Bex. *Women Doing Life: Gender, Punishment, and the Struggle for Identity*. New York: New York University Press, 2016.

Levi, Robin, and Ayelet Waldman. *Inside This Place, Not of It: Narratives from Women's Prisons*. San Francisco: McSweeney's and Voice of Witness, 2011.

Lull, James. "Hegemony." In *Gender, Race, and Class in Media: A Text-Reader*, edited by Gail Dines and Jean Humez, 61–66. London: Sage, 2003.

Mirkin, Harris. "The Passive Female: The Theory of Patriarchy." *American Studies* 25, no. 2 (1984): 39–57.

Mullings, Leith. "Domestic Policy and Human Security in the U.S." *Peace Review* 16, no. 1 (2004): 55–58.

Mulvey, Laura. "Visual Pleasure and Narrative Cinema." In *Feminist Film Theory: A Reader*, ed. Sue Thornham, 58–69. New York: New York University Press, 2006.

Navar-Gill, Annemarie. "From Strategic Retweets to Group Hangs: Writers' Room Twitter Accounts and the Productive Ecosystem of TV Social Media Fans." *Television and News Media* 19, no. 5 (July 2018): 415–30.

Nussbaum, Emily. "Lockdown: The Lessons of 'Orange Is the New Black' and 'Louie.'" *New Yorker*, June 2014.

Orange Is the New Black. Seasons 1–6. Created by Jenji Kohan; directed by Michael Trim et al.,; written by Jenji Kohan et al., Lionsgate Television. 2014–19.

Parenti, Christian. *Lockdown America*. New York: Verso, 1999.

Perkinson, Robert. *Texas Tough: The Rise of America's Prison Empire*. New York: Picador, 2010.

Pratt, Mary Louise. *Imperial Eyes: Travel Writing and Transculturation*. New York: Routledge, 2007.

Schwan, Anne. "Postfeminism Meets the Women in Prison Genre: Privilege and Spectatorship in Orange Is the New Black." *Television and New Media* 17, no. 6 (2016): 473–90.

Sexton, Jared. *Black Men, Black Feminism: Lucifer's Nocturne*. New York: Palgrave Pivot, 2018.

Shakur, Sanyika. "The Pathology of Patriarchy: A Search for Clues at the Scene of the Crime." *Prison Focus* 39, no. 1 (Spring 2013): 1, 4–5.

Sjoberg, Laura, and Caron E. Gentry. *Mothers, Monsters, Whores: Women's Violence in Global Politics*. New York: Zed Books, 2007.

Spektor, Regina. "You've Got Time." Sire Records, 2013. Single.

Taylor, Keeanga-Yamahtta. *How We Get Free: Black Feminism and the Combahee River Collective*. New York: Haymarket Books, 2017.

Wacquant, Loïc. *Punishing the Poor: The Neoliberal Government of Social Insecurity*. Durham, NC: Duke University Press, 2009.

War Bonnett, Darcy K. "Women in Prison Tell It Like It Is." *Off Our Backs* 31, no. 2 (2001): 9–12.

4

Emptied Chairs and Faceless Inmates

A Critical Analysis of the Texas Prison Museum

BETH MATUSOFF MERFISH

Hand-painted billboards along the major highways to Huntsville, Texas, advertise the small city's only major tourist attraction, the Texas Prison Museum, with the logo of a ball and chain. The museum, founded in 1989 and in its current site since 2002, is the only public-facing representation of the prison system in Huntsville, despite the fact that the Holliday Transfer Unit, one of the largest transfer units in Texas, sits on over 1400 acres of land just across the highway from the museum. The museum has largely become attractive to tourists because of its most (in)famous exhibit: an electric chair nicknamed "Old Sparky" (as advertised on the museum's website) that was the tool of execution for three hundred and sixty-one inmates between 1924 and 1964. Through its website, the major tool of written communication between the public and the museum, the museum describes the electric chair as "chilling," "legendary," and "controversial."[1]

In many ways, this vocabulary is not surprising. In popular culture and in language, prisons and their artifacts are often sensationalized. Most of what we see of prisons is crafted for our entertainment and is based on what is eye-catching and attention-grabbing. Dawn K. Cecil chronicles the impact of popular-culture depictions of prisons; more importantly for us, she also points out that the frequency of those depictions means that people often believe they know what a prison looks like without setting foot inside one. This is the effect of distance: "The further a subject is removed from the public eye, the more influential images become in shaping people's perceptions."[2] When those images are sensationalized, they exacerbate the problem of distance by presenting a world that is so idiosyncratic that it is unrelatable, the stuff of scary stories and senseless jokes, ready to thrill and amuse. That the most dramatized and also sanitized aspects of prison life are those that hold the public's attention for the longest is further supported by Robert Perkinson's observation that the electric chair is "what holds visitors' gaze longest" at the Texas Prison Museum.[3]

The terminology the Texas Prison Museum uses for the execution tool also reveals and exemplifies deeper narratives at work in the Texas Prison Museum. The terms are indicative of the museum's engagement in the narratives of dark tourism ("chilling" and "legendary") and of the museum's attempt to display itself as a neutral reporter ("controversial"), documenting rather than commenting on the institutions and systems at the heart of its mission. In this essay, a critical analysis of the Texas Prison Museum and the narratives that it perpetuates regarding the limits and structure of the state carceral system, I will problematize the museum's self-representation of neutrality and instead situate it among other cultural institutions as an arbiter of truth. The dialogues and initial queries in which the museum engages visitors serve as distractions from more profound and impactful lines of questioning and critical analysis. By separating objects from their contexts and reifying tropes in the public perception of prisons, the museum not only reinforces but in fact replicates the process by which the carceral system creates deep rifts in our geographies, families, and society.[4] This recurring motif of removal also perpetuates a sense of "us versus them," "free world versus prison," that serves as justification for the prison system and, in the end, bolsters our own myths of freedom outside of that system.[5]

I first explain the ways in which the museum presents itself as a neutral institution and its narrative as fact before considering its context as a center of dark tourism. Next, I consider several ways in which the themes of removal and separation run through the museum: through a group of objects I am calling "disembodied" or "emptied" objects, through a second group of objects separated from their contexts, and, finally, through the architecture and geography of the museum.[6] My focused study of these displays culminates in a discussion of the ways in which these themes of separation are indicative of much more expansive ways in which we understand the carceral system. The impact of that narrative of the prison system is both broad and deep: it characterizes our relationship with the massive criminal justice system that is both invisible and a major part of our society and also obscures the nature of our own carcerality.

The Texas Prison Museum's Intentional Neutrality

I have already referenced the language used to describe the Texas Prison Museum's most famous exhibit. The terms used to represent the electric chair on the museum's website are in some sense empty signs: each points to a broad range of sensations one might feel when viewing the exhibit without assigning moral value to those sensations. For example, the words "chilling" and "legendary" leave room for those who are impressed by the electrical power of the electric chair itself, those for whom it is a somber reminder of a death penalty often meted out according to deep-seated biases and uneven justice processes, and those for whom the death penalty is the site of government-sponsored murder. "Controversial" is a term that does the same: it allows visitors to the website and the museum to be excited, thrilled, anxious, and/or appalled, without requiring the museum to take a decisive stance regarding the electric chair.

This is not the only instance in which the museum assumes an ostensibly neutral stance. A visit to the museum begins with a short video narrated by the museum's director, Bill Stephens, a former correctional officer who became a prison-system director in the course of a thirty-five-year career, and a series of panels containing complementary texts and photographs. The video begins with a description of the current prison system as "modern and clean" in contrast to hard and inhumane conditions historically found in prisons, setting up a rigid trajectory of linked progress and modernization.[7] The video describes the Convict Lease Period (1871–1912) and the Post-Convict Lease Period (1912–1948) as a time of severe maltreatment of prisoners that ended with the appointment of Dr. George Beto as Director of the Texas Department of Corrections (TDC) in 1948. This, the video and the texts that accompany it proclaim, was a time of major reform, particularly in regard to the mistreatment of inmates at the hands of prison guards. The text ends with a note that, "ironically, two months prior to Beto's retirement, an inmate named David Ruiz filed a lawsuit against TDC, claiming that his Eighth Amendment rights that protect against cruel and unusual punishment were being violated."

The panel describing that lawsuit, *Ruiz v. Estelle*, reveals a fissure in the carefully constructed neutral reporting of the museum. Despite the fact that the case was decided in Ruiz's favor in 1974, the text of the panel specifies any testimony of misconduct or cruelty as "alleged" or describing "practices deemed detrimental." These linguistic cues are important: the Texas Prison Museum was established during the nearly thirty-year period (1974–2002) during which the federal government controlled the TDC in response to *Ruiz*. The text at the museum picks the TDC's side in a case brought by inmates who were nothing short of revolutionaries and whose personal sacrifices revealed such widespread injustices within the TDC that the decision by Federal District Judge William Wayne Justice declared that the "totality of conditions" in the TDC violated the inmates' constitutional rights.[8] That the narrative casts doubt on testimony and the court's ruling provides a sobering glimpse into the biases of the museum.

As the video concludes, those biases are again on display to a careful or informed visitor: the video ends with a reminder of the modernity at work in the current prison system. The narrator makes a quick remark, in the midst of this advertisement of the educational opportunities and cleanliness of the TDC facilities, to indicate that the prisons are not air-conditioned, but does not connect that with inhumane conditions. That gloss is again revelatory: decisions in lawsuits filed by inmates since 2014 have affirmed that it is cruel and unusual punishment to hold inmates in over 100-degree temperatures, and some verdicts have gone even farther, calling the TDC's refusal to pursue climate control a sign that the TDC was in contempt and displaying "negligible interest in ascertaining the breadth of the problem, its likely cause, or the necessary remedies."[9] In other words, even after rulings requiring temperature regulation, the TDC was "deliberately indifferent to the potential harm excessive heat could cause to prisoners."[10] That the prison museum's videos and texts do not even mention what continues to be a drawn-out series of legal battles in which several judges have ruled that the TDC is intentionally avoiding its legal responsibilities reveals the museum's very specific appetite for "controversy."

The Texas Prison Museum and Dark Tourism

It is useful to situate the museum and my analysis of it within the rapidly expanding field of dark tourism studies. "Dark tourism" is the term "branded into an internationally recognized taxonomy to denote travel to sites *of* or sites associated *with* death or 'difficult heritage' within global visitor economies."[11] Those sites are wide-ranging and include but are not limited to memorials, concentration and death camps, plantations, morgues, natural disaster locations, and jails. Scholars of dark tourism such as Tony Seaton have argued for the term "thanatourism," reconceiving of dark tourism as emerging from a universal human need to contemplate and face death.[12] Lucy Lippard has used the term "tragic tourism,"[13] and Laurie Beth Clark prefers "trauma tour-

96   MERFISH

ism."[14] These terms imply that the visitation they describe is characterized by a search for truth about oneself, an understanding of death that teaches a visitor something about their own human status.

Prison tourism does, indeed, teach visitors about their own status, but that learning does not happen through access to that which seems universal. As Sarah Hodgkinson and Diane Urquhart write in their analysis of prison tourism in the UK, those who pursue prison tourism seek "to explore what remains firmly outside our own experience, as the sanitization of punishment provides limited opportunity to witness it directly."[15] What Hodgkinson and Urquhart term "the sanitization of punishment" is what I am calling separation or dislocation. In many ways, Hodgkinson and Urquhart's analysis of prison tourism sites aligns with my understanding of the Texas Prison Museum: it is a space in which sensationalism rules and in which "some compromise between sustainability and historical authenticity is . . . probably inevitable."[16] Like the Texas Prison Museum, the cultural sites Hodgkinson and Urquhart study strike sometimes ineffective balances between entertaining and educating, between thrilling and informing.

What makes the Texas Prison Museum distinct is that it is not a historical site, the reminder of a heavily reformed or obsolete system. There is a substantial difference between a historic venue that is (of course inaccurately) enlivened by reenactment and tourism and a museum constructed for the sole purpose of allowing a visitor to understand themselves as having peeked inside of a working prison system. Those historic venues are fully capable of and often guilty of erasure of their residents, as Jacqueline Z. Wilson has written in her work on decommissioned Australian prisons,[17] but the high stakes seem even higher with the Texas Prison Museum. Despite the emphasis on past prison reforms in the introductory video and the anachronistic ball and chain logo on the signs advertising the Texas Prison Museum, it is not an institution with the luxury of historical distance. Its narratives, including those it encourages in visitors' own imaginations, have the potential to impact a current and active carceral system (or carceral systems) which is an ongoing site of trauma and death. This distinction sets the Texas Prison Museum apart from other destinations of prison tourism, and of dark tourism more generally, and makes my analysis even more important. Regarding the historic prisons they study, Hodgkinson and Urquhart write that "the 'tourist gaze' all too often reifies difference and distance between the 'viewer' and the 'viewed.' The constructed narratives about punishment can also facilitate popular punitivism and an assumption that incarceration is both necessary and uncontested today. Too often the suffering of our past prisoners becomes a source of shallow entertainment or imparts the idea

4. Emptied Chairs and Faceless Inmates   97

that prisons, although once bad, are now somehow unproblematic."[18] Their words ring true with regard to their subject and with regard to mine, where the stakes seem even higher and the effects even more direct. The historic prisons enshrine the separation between us and them and thus affirm a need for a carceral system; the Texas Prison Museum affirms the same narratives without the veil of history.

Emptied Objects

The separation of the objects of the prison system from the experience they represent is a constant motif within the Texas Prison Museum. That motif is made concrete by a number of exhibits containing objects which are not simply removed from the prison environment but are furthermore emptied of the very bodies that typically inhabit those spaces. The absence of the inmates from these spaces, namely the electric chair, prison cell, and inmate uniforms, is so evident that each, in its own way, compels the visitor to fill it. I term these objects "emptied" rather than "empty," because of the way in which they speak to a vacuum and the evidence that those outside of the prison system fill those spaces with their imaginations, bodies, and biases.

The most obvious of these emptied objects is the prison cell recreated in the museum. Situated in a back corner of the main exhibition space, the cell is outfitted with two bunk beds with pillows and blankets, a small table with plates and utensils, and a toilet. A small sign inside the cell describes its set-up as typical in Texas prisons; a much larger sign invites visitors to rent a striped uniform for one dollar from the gift shop and to take photos in the cell behind its gate. The emptied nature of this space is clear, as is the explicit invitation to the museum visitor to fill it with their sensations, imagination, and impressions. It bears mentioning, as obvious as it may seem, that the visitor's feelings of being inside the cell when the (non-locking) gate closes do not in any meaningful manner relate to the inmate's. Nor do the photographer's feelings when snapping the supposedly humorous photo (the example on the sign features a family of four clinging to the bars) in any way echo the feelings of family members separated by prison bars from their relatives. This is an obvious hole in the veil of neutrality otherwise espoused in the museum: the cell functions primarily for entertainment, as further evidenced by the black-and-white-striped garments, which recall cartoon villains and prison escapees for much of the public but are not actually in use in Texas prisons.

The current garments of Texas prison inmates make up another exhibit in which the museum visitor is asked to map preexisting ideas onto an aspect of the prison system. The two mannequins modeling inmate uniforms sit adjacent to four mannequins in varied prison employee uniforms. The latter group is made up of a series of mannequins with relatively life-like faces. Three appear to be Caucasian, and two appear to be women. The mannequins have facial features and hairstyles. Publicity photographs of the museum published with Getty Images in 2002 reveal that the mannequins modeling two different styles of the all-white uniforms worn by Texas prison inmates used to have similarly realistic facial features.[19] Those mannequins formerly on display were both male and light-skinned; they were also exhibited behind bars. The current arrangement has eliminated the bars between the visitor and inmate mannequins, and the mannequins have been replaced by featureless models with smooth, round, and coal-black heads. The contrast between the guard mannequins and these black forms is stark. One wonders what the process of choosing those mannequins must have been: how did the choice of these black male forms not prompt a conversation about race and racism in the prison system? How could the museum staff not anticipate the twin dangers provoked here as the visitor is asked to project any identity onto inmate mannequins and prompted to do so on bodies that are black? These mannequins immediately call to mind Michelle Alexander's deeply impactful text *The New Jim Crow: Mass Incarceration in the Age of Colorblindness*, in which she forcefully argues that the laws that shape the lives of those convicted by the criminal justice system restrict those people, a dramatically disproportionate number of them Black men, to "an *undercaste*—a lower caste of individuals who are permanently barred by law and custom from mainstream society."[20] These mannequins, stripped of every indication of personhood beyond their color, represent at best a particularly malevolent form of disregard and at worst a malicious erasure of the Black men whose lives are severely and permanently restricted by the fact of their prison sentences. That they are faceless means a visitor cannot see them as fully and identifiably human: once again, the visitor is compelled to rely on tropes and on often untested or false ideas about the identities of inmates. That the blankness of the mannequins coincides with their blackness heightens the fact that the museum presents a prison façade emptied of human experience, again perpetuating the us versus them dynamic.[21]

The electric chair provides yet another of these invitations to project. The chair dominates its own space in the museum and is surrounded by walls meant to replicate the room in which inmates were executed. The reverse sides of those walls are home to a moving exhibit by local photographer Barbara Sloan in which she photographed the families of both inmates and crime victims in the aftermath of the administration of the death penalty, pairing their photographs and words with the last statements of the executed inmates to whom they are connected.[22] That exhibit, though, is kept separate from the space of the electric chair, so that the juxtaposition of the chair and the pain it represents is not one of high tension. Indeed, the ability of the visitor to view the electric chair without also considering the way in which the death penalty impacts entire families is verified by the sign on the chair, added since the 2002 stock photographs, prohibiting visitors from jumping the barricades and sitting in the electric chair. That normal barricades are not enough here to keep visitors from using their bodies to fill the space of the electric chair affirms its status as an emptied object, one from which bodies have been removed and one which, displayed in the museum, asks to be filled. Here, the distinction between the inmate and visitor is even more stark than it is in the case of the cell: there is no plausible educational explanation for the visitor who jumps into the chair to be photographed by a relative or friend, replacing the inmate facing execution and asking a companion to replace the families of inmates and victims. The museum may display the moving Sloan photographs, but it also enables visitors to see the chair unencumbered by entreaties to their humanity.

Commerce without Context

The three exhibits I discuss above (the cell, faceless mannequins, and electric chair) are examples of disembodied objects in which the visitor is very clearly asked to insert their own body or project their own ideas onto an aspect of prison culture, but the erasures of the museum are not always as obvious or as open-ended. In several smaller exhibits, the museum separates objects from their contexts and also hides a major and often unknown aspect of the prison system: the way in which it interacts with and drives commerce.

Very few objects created by inmates are credited to those makers in the museum. Exceptions are a few paintings or craft objects that bear the signatures of their makers; far more objects are simply listed as "made by inmates" without any marker of the identities of those craftspeople and workers. When visiting the Texas Prison Museum, a visitor both enters and exits through the gift shop, a series of glass cases containing objects made mostly from wood, metal, and leather. Those objects, signs confirm, are made by inmates in the corrections system. The financial relationship between the museum and the TDC is unclear here: The museum proclaims itself to be a nonprofit institution entirely independent from the TDC, but these objects for sale and those displayed of course indicate a financial relationship between the two entities. What's more, nothing in the gift shop calls the visitor's attention to the financial considerations at play. Texas remains one of very few states in the country in which prisoners are not legally permitted to be paid for their work;[23] the inmates who created these objects do not in any way benefit from their sale. This relationship is simply a microcosm of a much larger system in which prisons depend on unpaid inmate labor to operate and often generate profit.[24] The scale of that profit is staggering: in 2018, the TDC Annual Review reported that the revenue from sales of goods manufactured in TDC facilities by inmates totaled $76.7 million dollars.[25]

The financial system that serves as the foundation of the TDC is also hidden in the exhibits of prisoner-made objects. A case of "contraband," including weapons made from prison objects, contains descriptions of each item, including their use, the location at which they were found, and, for some, the inmate who made or possessed them. The large display of meticulously crafted and highly decorated wooden furniture that sits directly adjacent to the contraband case describes the style of each desk, table, or hutch, names the prison supervisor who used the object, and only sometimes identifies the unit in which the furniture was made. The contrast between the texts is clear: the contraband case emphasizes the inmates' role, while the furniture display deemphasizes the inmates. But that obvious contrast overshadows a much more important and invisible motif of the unpaid labor inmates do to enable the prison system to run and to make the lives of its supervisors comfortable.

This comfort and the role of commerce in the prison system is also made evident in a critical view of a nearby case displaying "service awards" for prison staff. These are items given by the TDC to employees to honor career milestones. The small label explaining these items contains a note that the practice ended in the 1990s due to the "unprecedented levels" of prison employment as a result of the massive expansion of the prison system. The objects given to staff are often obviously and exaggeratedly genteel, as in the floral gold-trimmed Lenox China candlesticks and fluted decorative bowl or a ballpoint pen set awarded for twenty years of employment in the TDC and a silver and glass carousel relish serving dish awarded for fifteen years. Other objects are so overtly connected to commerce that one marvels that they do not seem to be intentionally ironic: clutch purses, leather billfolds, a leather keychain. These objects draw a sharp contrast between the inside of the system, in which money is prohibited and keys are kept under heavy security, and the free world. Their display in the museum as neutral objects, seemingly documenting career service without commentary, further perpetuates the notion that the TDC employees to whom these objects were given are part of the "us," consumers in the free world enjoying cultivated lives.

4. Emptied Chairs and Faceless Inmates   101

Architectures of Separation

Thus far, I have analyzed two sets of exhibits, one in which inmates' bodies are separated from visitors' bodies and one in which the commercial nature of the prison system is disguised to perpetuate the distinctions between the prison and the free world, between the "us" that visits the museum and the "them" that cannot. The last category of display I critique here is the one that represents the most concrete juxtaposition of us and them: the exterior space of the museum and its geography. The construction of the museum building enshrines a false separation between the prison and free world that is written and affirmed by the museum's exhibits.[26] The museum is marked by a fake guard tower identical to those marking the entrances of Texas prisons, absent the layers of barbed wire determined by the security level of the prison. The guard tower of a prison serves as a tangible reminder of the power of the system: the guard is the first person with whom a visitor interacts upon entering the campus of the prison and is a constant reminder to inmates of the limits of their space. A person entering the prison does not meet the guard face to face. When teaching incarcerated students, I often wait outside in the heat, cold, or rain as a guard in the tower lowers a bag into which I place my ID to be raised and checked before it is lowered again, and I am allowed to enter the unit. I am not, of course, powerless in the way that my students are, but the structure of the guard tower, the indirectness of my experience with the guards, and the lack of human interaction has become for me a symbol of the hierarchies of the prison system. That the Texas Prison Museum intentionally constructed a useless guard tower serves as an explicit reinforcement of those hierarchies. I wonder how it might be used: is it a site of nostalgia for the retired guards who seem to gather at the museum for reunions? If so, that is nostalgia for power, for the physical elevation of oneself above all others; the theme of separation of us and them resounds there.

That separation is further enshrined when one leaves the museum and looks out across the parking lot and over Interstate 45 to see the aforementioned Holliday Transfer Facility. As a visitor leaves the objects of the museum behind, ending a brief engagement with the public face of the prison museum (the museum's website states that most visitors spend about 45 minutes in the museum), that visitor sees an institution that is constantly sorting new inmates, executing the task of separating them from their homes and families as they await farther posts in the TDC System. There are then several layers of displacement at work: these inmates are experiencing complete transfer from their communities, and the exiting museum visitors are performing their own separation from a prison system that is massive, ubiquitous, and still invisible.

Conclusion

In this volume, Shreerekha Pillai has rightly defined carceral liberalism as a hyperobject, an idiom so vast and ubiquitous that it is both powerful and invisible. The tropes of prison and penalization are part of and contributors to that idiom. A visitor to the Texas Prison Museum who stands in front of the electric chair, poses in the cell, imagines faces for the faceless inmates, buys a souvenir, or marvels at the objects created by inmates does so without an indication that they are not having an individual experience but are rather buying into a series of ideas about prisons and the people who fill them. For the visitor consumed by those tropes who submits to the persuasive and all-encompassing underlying argument of the museum, the "us vs. them," the museum becomes a perfect series of simulacra, experiences that convince the visitor they are true, authentic, and representative. The visitor leaves the museum convinced of the authenticity of their new "knowledge," feeling affirmed that the "us" represented by the free world is justifiably and rightfully separate from the "them" who occupy the building complex across the highway.

The consequence of the reification of the division is that a visitor and the public at large understand the "free world" to be one entirely independent of the carceral system. This negates what Michelle Alexander has identified as the carceral complex;[27] there is in fact no "us" of the free world, in part because we are not a monolithic community extricable from the community of people who have spent time behind bars. We include their families and community members; the free world and the world behind bars are one inextricable world. The dichotomy is false.

How, then, can we resist these persuasive and all-encompassing narratives that define and distort our understanding of carcerality and our own role in it? There are constantly evolving standards for institutions of public culture that, if followed, would make the museum more transparent and would reposition the museum as a space of community interaction and dialogue. In the case of the Texas Prison Museum, one of the foundational texts of that movement would be highly instructive: in his 1971 lecture "The Museum: A Temple or the Forum," then director of the Brooklyn Museum Duncan Cameron vigorously contested the notion that the highest calling of the museum was to be a temple: to enshrine value, to ritualize viewing, and to instruct.

4. Emptied Chairs and Faceless Inmates   103

Instead, he argued, while some museums would continue to be temples, museum reform was essential: "There must be concurrent creation of forums for confrontation, experimentation, and debate."[28] He continued: "The forum is where battles are fought, the temple is where the victors rest."[29] The Texas Prison Museum is a temple, constructed, scripted, and fixed by those who hold power in the prison system. What if the Texas Prison Museum was, instead, a forum that invited discussion and debate not between "us" and "them" but amongst a broader, intertwined community? Given the current state of the museum, that would be a revolutionary transformation. On an individual level, though, the key to resisting, revealing, and reforming might be as simple as bridging the divide between "us" and "them."

My own experience is representative: I did not understand my own indirect contact with the prison system until I experienced direct contact as an educator in prison classrooms. My incarcerated students have laid bare for me the wrongness and the injustice of "us" versus "them." In my graduate-level humanities classroom, we are one community of thinkers. A lifelong feminist and critic of hierarchical structures, I have felt much more secure interacting with my students than I do when interacting with the prison guards who are the visible representation of strictly enforced systems of power and disempowerment. I was not, of course, a member of the inmates' community in a significant way; I was the educator, possessor of multiple graduate degrees, free to leave once our sessions were over and to return to my home and my family, to access information and texts at will, to be paid for my work. At the same time, I understood myself as having little in common with the guards, whose mission was so different from my own. I was not part of the "us" or the "them," and, in truth, those groups did not exist outside of the imaginations of the unexposed.

Previously I wrote that for a visitor unaware of their consumption of carceral tropes, the Texas Prison Museum reifies the us versus them division. For a visitor for whom that division no longer exists, the museum is a site of deep pain, of erasure of bodies that are absent but are not insignificant. For me, the mannequins are my erased and absented students; for others, they may be family members, friends, loved ones. And so a possibility for a fissure in the hyperobject reveals itself when we write for this volume and others like it, when we speak of our experiences with carcerality, when we make room for the voices of those more directly impacted (as the editor of this volume has done), and when we reject the false dichotomy of us versus them.

Notes

1. Texas Prison Museum, published 2019, http://www.txprisonmuseum.org.

2. Cecil, *Prison Life in Popular Culture*, 7.

3. Perkinson, *Texas Tough*, 17.

4. The pain of this separation is made clear almost immediately by Ruth Wilson Gilmore in *Golden Gulag: Prisons, Surplus, Crisis, and Opposition in Globalizing California*, from the very first words of her prologue, in which she describes a diverse group of families tied together only by their quest for freedom for their incarcerated loved ones (1).

5. The racialized nature of this "us vs. them" must also be acknowledged. As Marie Gottschalk has documented, men and women of color are incarcerated at dramatically disproportionate rates in the United States (*The Prison and the Gallows*, 19). In 2016, she wrote of the United States: "The incarceration rate for black males is several times the rate that South Africa was locking up black men on the eve of the end of apartheid in the early 1990s" (*Caught*, 121). These huge discrepancies further enable a false sense that the "us" of the free world is entirely distinct from the nonrepresentative "them" of the prison world.

6. Despite its relatively small size, the Texas Prison Museum contains a large number of exhibits. I have used a sampling here and have not attempted to address the entire museum.

7. Texas Prison Museum, "Welcome Video," viewed 21 February 2020.

8. Perkinson devotes most of a chapter to documenting David Ruiz's life and the process of his decision to sue the TDC. The trial was a marathon effort, with 349 witnesses and 1,530 exhibits, and its conclusion was decisive, requiring sweeping change in the TDC (*Texas Tough*, 251–85).

9. *Cole v. Collier*, Civil Action No. 4:14-cv-1698, Doc. No. 1449 (S. D. Tex.) (Ellison, J.), August 9, 2019, accessed via https://www.courtlistener.com/.

10. Jodie McCullough, "A Judge Told Texas to Put Some Inmates in Air Conditioning. Lawyers Say Prison Officials Are Violating That Order," *Texas Tribune*, September 5, 2019, accessed 1 March 2020, https://www.texastribune.org/.

11. Philip R. Stone et al., "Dark Tourism Themes, Issues, and Consequences: A Preface," in *The Palgrave Handbook of Dark Tourism Studies* (London: Palgrave Macmillan, 2018), vii.

12. Willis, *Theatricality, Dark Tourism and Ethical Spectatorship*, 6.

13. Lippard, *On the Beaten Track*.

14. Laurie Beth Clark, "Coming to Terms with Trauma Tourism," in *Visions and Revisions: Performance, Memory, Trauma*, edited by Caroline Wake and Briony Trezise (Copenhagen: Museum Tusculanum Press, 1999).

15. Sarah Hodgkinson and Diane Urquhart, "Prison Tourism: Exploring the Spectacle of Punishment in the UK," in *Dark Tourism: Practice and Interpretation*, edited by Glenn Hooper and John J. Lennon (Abingdon-on-Thames, UK: Routledge, 2016), 41.

16. Hodgkinson and Urquhart, 51.

17. Wilson, *Prison: Cultural Memory and Dark Tourism*.

18. Hodgkinson and Urquhart, 52.

19. Paul Buck/AFP, "HUNTSVILLE, UNITED STATES: This photograph is an exhibit showing inmate uniforms on display at the Texas Prison Museum in Huntsville, Texas 07 December 2002. The Texas Prison Museum features numerous exhibits detailing the history of the Texas prison system. Created in 1989, the non-profit charitable corporation, features exhibits from the point of view of the inmates as well as the men and women who worked within the prison walls." December 9, 2002, accessed via Getty Images.

20. Alexander, *The New Jim Crow*, 16.

21. In *Nobody: Casualties of America's War on the Vulnerable, from Ferguson to Flint and Beyond*, Marc Lamont Hill writes compellingly about the ways in which vulnerable, disempowered people are rendered as "nobodies" in American economy and society. The erasure of the men represented by the mannequins in the museum should be understood within that broader context.

22. Many of the images and statements are reproduced in the self-published book by Barbara Sloan, *Last Statement* (Blurb, 2014).

23. Vicky Camarillo, "'The Penal System Today Is Slavery': Lawmakers Finally Start to Talk about Unpaid Labor in Texas Prisons," *Texas Observer*, May 10, 2019, https://www.texasobserver.org/penal-system-slavery-unpaid-labor-texas/.

24. The (unnecessary) degree to which a state's economy and its prison system are entertwined has been forcefully argued by Gilmore in *Golden Gulag*.

25. Texas Department of Criminal Justice, *Texas Department of Criminal Justice Annual Review 2018*, 58, https://www.tdcj.texas.gov/documents/Annual_Review _2018.pdf.

26. Any notion that life within prison is extricable from life outside is dispelled by Amy E. Lerman as she writes about the ways in which anyone who experiences prison life—guards, inmates, families of both—behaves in ways reflecting that experience even outside of the prison. Moreover, she writes, entire communities to which ex-inmates return "display social dynamics that echo the atomized social organization of American's more punitive and violent prisons" (*The Modern Prison Paradox*, 151).

27. In *The New Jim Crow*, Michelle Alexander maps the extent of the carceral system in the United States as well as the ways it impacts life outside of prisons. To name only two that impact society on the massive scale mirroring that of the prison system: family structures are dramatically disrupted, and former inmates are barred from full participation in civic life.

28. The lecture was almost immediately revised and published; it remains essential reading in the field of museum studies. Cameron, "The Museum, a Temple or the Forum," 19.

29. Cameron, 21.

Bibliography

Alexander, Michelle. *The New Jim Crow: Mass Incarceration in the Age of Colorblindness*. 10th anniversary ed. New York: New Press, 2020.

Cameron, Duncan F. "The Museum, a Temple or the Forum." *Curator: The Museum Journal* 14, no. 1 (1971): 11–24.

Cecil, Dawn K. *Prison Life in Popular Culture: From the Big House to Orange Is the New Black*. Boulder, CO: Lynne Rienner Publishers, 2015.

Gilmore, Ruth Wilson. *Golden Gulag: Prisons, Surplus, Crisis, and Opposition in Globalizing California*. Berkeley: University of California Press, 2007.

Gottschalk, Marie. *The Prison and the Gallows: The Politics of Mass Incarceration in America*. Cambridge: Cambridge University Press, 2006.

———. *Caught: The Prison State and the Lockdown of American Politics*. Princeton, NJ: Princeton University Press, 2016.

Hill, Marc Lamont. *Nobody: Casualties of America's War on the Vulnerable, from Ferguson to Flint and Beyond*. New York: Atria Books, 2016.

Hooper, Glenn, and John J. Lennon, eds. *Dark Tourism: Practice and Interpretation*. Abingdon-on-Thames, UK: Routledge, 2016.

Lerman, Amy E. *The Modern Prison Paradox: Politics, Punishment, and Social Community*. Cambridge: Cambridge University Press, 2013.

Lippard, Lucy. *On the Beaten Track: Tourism, Art, and Place*. New York: New Press, 1999.

Perkinson, Robert. *Texas Tough: The Rise of America's Prison Empire*. New York: Picador, 2010.

Sloan, Barbara. *Last Statement*. San Francisco: Blurb, 2014.

Stone, Philip R., ed. *The Palgrave Handbook of Dark Tourism Studies*. London: Palgrave Macmillan, 2018.

Wake, Caroline, and Briony Trezise, eds. *Visions and Revisions: Performance, Memory, Trauma*. Copenhagen: Museum Tusculanum Press, 1999.

Willis, Emma. *Theatricality, Dark Tourism, and Ethical Spectatorship: Absent Others*. London: Palgrave Macmillan, 2014.

Wilson, Jacqueline Z. *Prison: Cultural Memory and Dark Tourism*. New York: Peter Lang, 2008.

AGAINST INNOCENCE
Ravi Shankar

Learned the recipe for how to jam brown rage
into a mayonnaise jar: use two hands to twist
and to tamp down each grievance on the page,
caustic words the occupier can ball in their fist,
shove down, screw the lid. Call it the void zone.
An airtight and antiseptic alternate universe
where the white imaginary shapes the unknown
into fireflies that blink and flit, join and disburse
against the transparent walls of the container.
Such heavy loads might not sag, nor sugar over,
but in time they explode! That's a no-brainer:
pressure = force / area, no matter the enclosure.
Juvenile delinquent and super predator? The cause
is the consequence, the consequence...take pause.

SUNDAY SCHOOL
Ravi Shankar

Heavily indebted
local governments
authorize austerity
measures then over-

police and incarcerate
disproportionately
their citizens based
on color and class

to fill revenue gaps
rather than fund
more social services
and education.

Spare more taxes
on the rich, squeeze
folks on the bottom—
that's John Calvin,

the predestination
of the elect, wealth
accrues as blessing
and shame to those

who don't conform
who won't reform
who will be reborn
better the next life—

5

These Stories Will
Not Be Confined

JOANNA ELEFTHERIOU

I'm driving south toward the Texas state prison where I teach, and the terrain grows pastoral as I get further away from the city. Placid cows stare at my speeding car. Near a bayou, a heron stands on a fence. Palms, oaks, and rose bay sway in the wind. When I near the prison grounds, two signs appear. TOWN OF SUMAC, POPULATION: 319 and then, HITCHIKERS MAY BE ESCAPING INMATES. Then, more fields. Short, leafy stalks emerge from dark soil—soy, maybe, or potatoes. Bright against that dark earth, I spot the white uniforms of incarcerated men working the land on tractors and on foot. Many have wrapped their heads in white cloth to protect them from the sun.

After the fields, I pass rows of low, unremarkable houses where the guards must live, then reach the prison parking lot and draw a deep breath. Every week, before gathering my board markers and books, I prepare myself for the ritual of entry by sitting still for a moment and looking at the vast wall of gleaming concertina wire. Its coiled razors are beautiful. They reflect sunshine even on gloomy days, but when the sun glares, they look wildly bright, almost heavenly, and I am always torn in my admiration; these long, shining coils are instruments not exactly of torture but certainly of control.

When, from the watchtower above, I am seen outside the fence, a gate swings open and I step inside the fencing of a sally port. As the gate swings closed behind me and other staff members, we gather around an aluminum pail, which dangles from a rope. Into the pail we drop our ID cards. The aluminum pail is the size of a child's toy, the kind I once used to build castles in the sandbox of my local park. This pail has a hole in it for the rain. Using a set of pulleys, a guard in the watchtower hoists the pail toward him, checks our IDs, and lowers them back down in that swinging aluminum pail. A guard asks if we've left our weapons in the car. *Yes.* Cell phones? Cash? We nod together *Yes, yes we have.* We remember the rules.

I am more than my crimes, you wrote, and you, B., offered an example to me of what it looks like to be free from self-blame and perfectionism. B., your writing made me cry. Not because you had suffered (you fell from a dangerous machine while working on the prison farm and were hospitalized for weeks), but because you owned up to everything you had done. *I have destroyed many lives with my actions,* you wrote.

And you went on: *I am more than my crimes. I deserve to be loved.*

Built like a mid-distance runner, broad-shouldered and lean, with carefully gelled hair and a baby face, B., you appeared too young to have lived through all that your writing detailed. You said little in class but turned in some of the boldest work. You described your teenage self as the middle-class parent's nightmare, the kid who was given everything but just didn't care. You wrote of joyrides in expensive cars, terrible accidents, and more stupid risk. Somehow, in prison, you made a decision and changed. *I am not the man I was.* You learned what many of us still struggle to believe: that our humanity is sacred, that our very bodies are a gift. That it is our privilege and our responsibility to treat our bodies with generosity, with tenderness, with care. I don't have the wisdom and humility that you displayed in your writing, at least not yet. I crave confirmation. I have a "poor me" problem, an entitlement problem, and unlike you, I have not been able to change.

This semester, in the wake of Hurricane Harvey, you wrote about how the Texas Department of Corrections prioritized your unit's mattresses during the rescue operation. Incarcerated human beings came second, after the mattresses. By the time officers rescued the men, water had begun to seep into their cells. You chose the title "What Is a Life Worth?" Understated and intelligent, a virtuoso exposé of the absurd, your essay asks readers to reckon with their complicity in the prison industrial complex. When your cinderblock cages filled with floodwater, and you were held inside until the mattresses were saved, those of us who are free did nothing to protect you. When we found out later, we did nothing to make it right.

B., you wrote your own story well. I want you to have a voice, and I am sorry I haven't found a way to help you publish it. I, myself, have access to publication, and I've told my story. I claim I don't want to speak for you, yet here I am—telling yours. Like everyone complicit in your suffering—in the humiliation and inhumane treatment of incarcerated Americans—I say that *there's nothing more I can do.* I'm lying. I haven't tried. I don't want to try any harder. I appropriate your story, tell it, sign my name, and reap my reward.

The prison yard is immaculately manicured. Pink roses are well pruned and someone has shaped the hedges beautifully, as if those hedges were his one shot at making art. Someone has raked the leaves. To the left as I enter, there's a little well with a round wall, a bucket and sloping roof. I believe it is fake, there only to make the yard a little pretty. When I approach the first building, usually another white-clad inmate is mopping the steps and, always, he holds the door for me. I enter another sally port, hand over my ID, and wait at the next door. That foyer always smells aggressively clean, antiseptic like an unsanitary hospital desperate to stamp out disease. I have used this smell as an example when I teach the writers about telling sensory detail. What this detail tells us, I explain, is how hard society has tried to purge itself of people like you. After I say something like this, I always apologize. I apologize to my students a lot because I am free and they aren't; I shower alone and they can't; I enjoy the feeling of not being watched and they don't; I will spend many hours this year just being outside in the mild Texas winter air, and they won't.

R., your essays painted a clear picture for me of life as a U.S. sailor and Navy vet. I can see 1990s Miami before me as I recall your work. And I can't shake from my mind your descriptions of the severed limbs you carried in your arms after an explosion—I believe it was during the Gulf War—risking your life so that nobody's body was left behind. You kept going back to carry body parts out of the bomb site to make possible the mourning of the families that would survive. You wrote of spiraling down after that horror, about the nightmares that led you to drink. And then, something else. And here you are. *I am not the same man as I was*, you wrote, and I believed you. You taught me that "rehabilitation" does happen in prison, and that time inside did help you, thus confounding my expectation that prison is only cruel, only a hardship. You are glad to have changed. You accomplished the kind of penance cast by most theologies as necessary but elusive, almost impossible for egotistical man. And for woman—for me.

R., you are a really, really good writer. You are brilliant. If you were my student in "the world," as you called the world outside the prison, I'd urge you to attend readings and I'd send you to Newpages.com to find journals that might publish your work. Instead, in class I did an exercise where groups of students formed a hypothetical journal and solicited work from one another, explaining what merits made them select every piece. In an end-of-semester exercise, you named your imaginary literary journal *Sadness*, and for hypothetical publication, you chose the essay about Hurricane Harvey and the rescued mattresses.

My papers and books are tucked under my arm, and a clear plastic baggie holds my board markers and pens. Bags must always be transparent. I clutch the tools of my trade and hold my faculty ID before me to say, all at once, *I am supposed to be here; it's my job* and also *I don't belong here; I'm only here for the day.* For me, the most frightening thing about prison isn't the people who've done a bad thing, but the revealed precarity of my own freedom.

Before, I used to dismiss the carceral system as an ancillary aspect of society. I was naïve enough even to wonder why the prison was such a big deal for Foucault. Once I passed inside this place, I was changed; I will forever know that captivity is the consequence of making too serious a mistake.

Still clenching my ID, I walk through a sweltering corridor. Enormous, deafening fans do nothing but move around the hot air. Every twenty feet I stop and stand at a gate. It feels like a religious procession. I struggle to hold onto my papers, folders, markers, and books. Inmates walk beside me at a distance of three or four feet, always, because the hallway of the prison looks like a stretched-out, extra-long basketball court with a yellow line indicating the out-of-bounds area to which inmates must be confined. While we wait, together, for a guard with his enormous skeleton key, the men look at me from that distance of three or four feet. They say polite things like "hello," even though the walls bear signs that forbid this: No talking in the halls. I want to be polite and say hello back, but I also want desperately to obey. My students have told me, *You know, Dr. E., those signs are not meant for you.*

The prison walls are painted with many more such instructions and facts. A small black-and-white sign reads "Security is never convenient," in quotation marks, as though the statement were mocking itself. In enormous orange letters, painted right on the cinderblock wall, there is a warning with the words *elimination, silence,* and *rape.* It tells the men every single day that if they keep violence a secret, they are at fault. They are to blame. Since the Prison Rape Elimination Act of 2003, the prisoners must by law be told that they are committing violence if they remain silent after witnessing an assault.

C., the convex glasses you wear for farsightedness make your eyes large and pleading and sad. I feel embarrassed by your need. My answers to your questions all sound like apologies. I am sorry you don't get to sit idly in the sun with a newspaper the way my father did at your age; I'm sorry you won't dote on grandchildren any day of the week you please; I'm sorry something bad happened and so you are here. You wrote essays about your grandparents, who started a farm in Iowa in the nineteenth century, and about your little self, born there a few decades later. You were one child among many, and in that large family you sought attention by pulling stunts. Placed into a body cast after an accident at age three, you dropped pencils and keys into the plaster so that your parents had to turn you upside down to shake out their belongings. Now, you are once again confined, and wearing white.

Unlike the main building, the education unit is air-conditioned and well lit. Its walls speak in a different language. Instead of admonishing the men, here, the walls advocate positive thinking via motivational clichés. Diagrams depict the criminal-addictive cycle and offer simple suggestions for exiting its grip. Here, it is a different, brighter, kind of humiliation.

When I enter the education building I sign my name and the time I entered, so that if "something happens," officials will know I'm in there and get me out. While I am signing the safety roster, my students line up outside the door and stand with their hands clasped over their heads while a guard checks their bodies for contraband.

I sit in my classroom at an enormous wooden desk (although I never sit behind desks in the free world), organize my notes, and wait. The men will stand as close as they can to me, lean over the desk, look me in the eye, and share news. They report what they heard about my own hometown, or some interesting fact from another class, or some writing they are working on in addition to my assignments. I refer to my students as "men" when I talk about the course I teach at the prison, and I'm not sure why. A person's gender seems to matter here, his manliness. My own lack thereof. Maybe it is a question of power.

I fancied myself a writer, you wrote, and it showed. S, your essays were such a pleasure to read I forgot you were a student expecting feedback and a grade. You thought deeply. You seemed upbeat in the way a spiritual leader, a guru or monk, might be happy in the face of suffering. I wonder often where you found such patience, strength, and peace. Maybe you just loved coming to class. You would say "since I got locked up" like it was an accident, a stroke of bad luck. S., you wrote about becoming a father with more insight into your own masculinity than almost anyone I've read.

During your daughter's gestation, you feared that parenthood might make you "square," so you bought a hip, masculine baby-bag that later became a perfect instrument of literary self-deprecation and telling detail. You wrote a collage essay about the four important people in your life—your daughter, your mother, your wife, and your best friend—and did so with an elegant and astoundingly nuanced grasp of feminist thought. You've read everything and everyone, contemporary and classic, and I wonder how.

An incarcerated worker pops in to ask if I need anything. I ask for paper. The students pay tuition for the courses they take toward their Master of Arts

5. These Stories Will Not Be Confined   115

in Literature, but they can't purchase supplies. The worker brings a package of loose-leaf paper for the men. He straightens up classrooms and makes a photocopy or two if the copies I made on my home campus come up short.

The men trickle in slowly, each delayed at different points by security. I peek at their shoes, the only part of their outfits that varies. Most wear white New Balance sneakers, but others sport black work boots or thick-soled, fake-leather shoes. They carry taped-together flip flops sometimes, and these sit on their desks during class. My fear and also my idle curiosity, a voyeurism I can deny but not shake, makes me alert to such objects. In my second year, I learn that they shower all together in groups twice as large as the showers can comfortably fit.

Sometimes, my graduate students spill handfuls of candy onto the desk when they sit down, and share them with one another during class. I remember the commissary cards, and how complicated it is to procure toiletries and snacks, so I guess these sweet tokens are a luxury.

> W., as you handed me the loose-leaf paper I requested for the men, you told me your name a dozen times before I remembered it, even though it's a simple, common Anglo-Saxon name. I remember only the names on my rosters, which I see written down. Yours was printed on a roster years ago, before I became a teacher here, but when administrators realized that after fifteen years inside, you'd only be eligible for parole, they rescinded your loans. After the end of your full thirty-year sentence, you'd be too close to the average age of death to repay the loans. You told me that in a Missouri prison before your transfer to Texas, you made five cents an hour for a job much like what you do here, in the Education Building, fetching paper and mopping the floor. In Texas, you work for nothing, you said, and I didn't believe you until I saw the figures for myself. According to a page called "State and Federal Prison Wage Policies and Sourcing Information" on prisonpolicy.org, "regular (non-industry) labor" in Texas prisons is unpaid.[1] Neither of us knew, at the time of our conversation, what my later internet search revealed: by law, every able-bodied incarcerated Texan must work, and this law is possible because the thirteenth amendment outlawed slavery only for those who had not been convicted of a crime. Workers like you have no legal recourse. According to *The Atlantic*, "By judging the relationship between prisons and incarcerated workers to be of a primarily social or penological nature, the courts have placed wage and working condition protections out of reach for incarcerated workers."[2]
>
> Knowing none of this until I read up on prison policy months after I last saw you, I naively assumed that you, W., were free to either work or stay in your cell. Going off that naïve assumption, I asked you what motivated you to leave your bed to mop floors and make copies without pay. You

said that as a younger man, the choice between flipping burgers inside a greasy fast-food cage versus managing your own drug supply and sale was a no-brainer—of course you'd choose the autonomy and challenge of the drug beat over the brain-crushing monotony of menial jobs. You told me you'd decided to work, in prison, for no money in order to get used to it, so that when you got out you'd be able to resist the lure of a lucrative, autonomous, and intelligence-demanding business that could get you locked back up. In *Prison Legal News*, I read that "complaints about the program center on the long hours worked by prisoners, often in industries that do not translate to marketable job skills, for no pay while under the watchful eye of prison guards and the threat of discipline if they do not work."[3] You made none of these complaints. You didn't even tell me you were forced to work. You just smiled wide, and talked about your hope of returning to college.

I looked for that smile of yours when I returned to the prison in my third year and found you had been transferred to another work assignment. When I asked where you were, your replacement explained knowingly, "They don't let anyone stay in one place very long."

According to the website of the Texas Department of Criminal Justice, Texas Government Code §497.002 states that the objective of inmate labor programs consists of: "providing marketable job skills training to incarcerated offenders" as well as providing an "inexpensive option" for a labor supply.[4] W., I hope that your mopping and photocopying skills do prove marketable, and that you can keep a job you want when you get out. And I hope you can come back to college.

Once our class gets started, the volley of questions and ideas feels like any other graduate creative writing class. I forget I'm in a prison. The men raise their hands, they offer a perspective, and I moderate the discussion in ways that I hope will help them understand how literature is made. One small difference is that incarcerated students have read more than my MA students in town. They make connections that surprise me, and when I speak, they listen closely and take notes. I cut my teeth teaching non-incarcerated students whose attention is divided between the classroom and their outside lives, especially text messages from lovers relayed by their phones. To better hold the attention of my late-teenage students in the free world, I developed a teaching style that drew important principles out of class members rather than stating the ideas myself. At R., this method faltered, as if the students had trouble wrapping their mind around the notion that their fellow inmates were just as much authorities as me. One wrote me a letter after the first semester insisting that because *I* am the professor, I offer more direct, authoritative instruction.

This pattern of heightened deference to me is diametrically opposed to the problem I expected when faced with a class full of mostly older-than-myself men. In the world, men dismiss my arguments and see me mostly as a body. They value me insofar as I am cute, but rarely permit my intelligence to command their respect. The first times I had to tell my incarcerated students to rethink their positions, I trembled a little because a large group of men had never before responded to me without hooting or saying something crass. I'd been a grown woman for over twenty years by the time I arrived on the prison campus, and my experience in a female body suggested that the manlier the man, the more likely he was to deride or sexualize me, or to make displays of power with hoots or with his gaze.

Though more typically masculine in appearance (for reasons ranging from tattoos to hairstyles to musculature to speech patterns and gait) than most of the nerdier, lankier, artsier men I deal with as an academic, my incarcerated students afforded me serious, unconditional respect. They looked at me attentively always, even when their classmates spoke. Perhaps, I thought, no one else permitted them to believe their fellow inmates had anything important to say. When I urged them to listen to one another, a student said *We are listening*. When you live in prison, he explained, to stare at another inmate is to incite danger. *This is why we are always looking at you.*

> T., you wrote a little too allegorically, too philosophically. I told you to give me scene. Your essays were all metaphor and reflection on the problem of right and wrong, the problem of temptation, the problem of love. There was a love scene and no one could figure out if it was part of the story or a symbol. I encouraged you to use more concrete language because your ideas mattered, but abstract reflection is hard to follow. When you wrote me that letter, telling me I am the authority in the class and should be giving more direct instruction, I wrote a response defending my methods. I never sent it. I cried at your graduation. Your peers tell me you are a free man now, and I hope you send your story out to be published and read.

Halfway through, our class is interrupted by an officer who comes in for "count." The officer stands by my desk and counts the men. This occurs once or twice during every class period. She points at each man and in response, they report the place where they sleep. They report their wing and cell number, and either top or bottom bunk. One of the men says "lower" instead of "bottom." Every time, I wonder if it is because of his literary sensibility (he is one of the best) or because of the word's sexual connotation indicating a passive recipient of sex.

I am sorry, I think as I wait for the men to be counted. I am sorry that I fear your fate and I want to get away from you as if your bad luck could stick to me. I know this belief in communicable bad luck is the impulse that makes gay people suffer, this is the impulse that puts lepers on islands by themselves, this is the impulse that makes melanin the mark of half a man. This is what makes rich New York City apartment-dwellers insist that their poorer neighbors enter through the back door; it is the impulse to put distance between ourselves and the people whose fate makes us afraid. Something inside me scrunches up when the men are counted by the guards. I'm taken with horror and I'm trying not to believe what I see.

M., you wrote science fiction, and more *I'm sorries* arose in me when your eager face asked if I'd enjoyed the work, when in fact I could barely follow your prose. I told you to focus on developing scenes and deepening your characters. After our first semester, you came up to my desk to thank me for encouraging you, which made me happy since my critiques had seemed to hurt. You'd sent a story to a magazine and the editor had sent you detailed feedback that matched my own suggestions. I asked how you found the journal's submission guidelines, and you said you'd ordered the most recent *Writer's Market*. You had worked in IT when you were in the world, and your home has closets larger than your prison cell. You really wanted to become a better writer, and when I wrote kind encouraging notes to you, you said be tougher on me, doc, I can take it.

The writers' progress is like that of any other university student—slow, but exciting and important when it happens. They write a little better with each assignment. I hope this growth matters to them. They tell me it does. I've taught poetry, fiction, memoir, and essay here, and the students have learned it all eagerly, although some confessed they had only taken the class because a field they really wanted to study, like psychology, wasn't offered at the MA level. Thankful still for whatever learning they can get, the men memorize the literary terms I teach. Enjambment, narrative tension, the poetic turn. They learn to imply emotion rather than name it, and to employ resonant imagery.

Each semester I focus my instruction on a single genre, but give students freedom to compose some assignments in whatever form they prefer. The men mostly write memoir; they are dogged in their effort to chronicle their lives. Nonfiction genres dominated the early American literary scene: the spiritual autobiography, the homily, the captivity narrative, and later the slave narrative reigned most popular for two centuries until overtaken by the fic-

5. These Stories Will Not Be Confined   119

tion of Irving and Cooper, then Hawthorne and Poe. In colonial times, John Smith, Mary Rowlandson, Cotton Mather, Ben Franklin, Jonathan Edwards, St. John de Crevecoeur, and Olaudah Equiano all wrote out of an expedient need to document the facts of their lived experience. *This is what happened to me*, the Puritans wrote. *I am a man*, the fleeing slaves wrote. As Rowlandson and Equiano wrote down what happened before, during, and after their captivity, so too do incarcerated writing students write down the events that made them who they are. Perhaps when we are extracted from our community, we write down our lives in order to reflect our existence onto the page.

When the state sends us to prison, it deprives us of the people who can mirror us; we lose the people whose love shows us who we are. It may try to suspend our existence, but by making our time in prison into art, we can say *No, I'm still alive*. We can assert that we are still citizens. *Though stripped of many rights*, we can say, *I still contribute to our shared culture of my world*. My students pit their own stories against the forces that would obliterate them. Harriet Jacobs told the truth that way, and reclaimed the time she'd spent hunched in an attic by writing her testimonial. Thoreau wrote "Civil Disobedience" after being taken to jail. From a jail cell, St. Paul wrote an epistle and Reverend King wrote his "Letter from Birmingham Jail."

Nonfiction genres have long been tied to theology. Narratives of conversion, from St. Augustine's written life to the declarations required of every Puritan who joined the early American church, are thought to be the origin of contemporary memoir. A significant change, an epiphany or a decision, forms the narrative's culmination, and after that climax, in the denouement, the narrator is a changed woman or man. *I am not the man I was.*

> V., I remember your clean-shaved smile, fashionable rimless glasses. You struck me as authoritative and professional even in your pajama-white clothes, and it made me sad to learn of all you lost because you were so very, very eager to please. You recounted a fifth marriage in Vegas and intense regret about ignoring your kids. You, too, showed me what it means to say I made mistakes and insist that the present is a new beginning. You forgave the man you once were. You showed me the commissary card prisoners hold as they wait on long lines to buy toothpaste, deodorant, and shoes. You told me what you wanted most was to give your daughter a hug.

Once count clears, the students will be able to get onto the dinner queue. I've heard them call it chow. Count often clears several minutes before class ends, and then the men get restless, shuffle papers, indicate they are eager to leave. I resist the ego-driven impulse to take affront. I remember that I don't know what it means to wait on a long line daily for a chance to eat.

As the men file out and I gather my papers from the large wooden desk in that odd, platitude-plastered classroom, I feel like I, too, am captive inside this cinderblock cage. Our fates merge in that time. They see me eager to leave and I wish I could tell them it's not *them* I want to escape but that feeling they endure daily, the feeling of being contained. I read their work, give feedback, distribute grades, and finally, in May, I leave. I speed on the way home.

I will enter the summer haunted by the shadow of the carceral state, and the guilt of giving to others too little of my good fortune. I will remember that my employer, the state of Texas, fills its coffers by forcing inmates to work. The Texas Department of Corrections website explains that prison labor is an "inexpensive option," as if its practices were driven by the Protestant virtue of thrift. In their writing, the students have a chance to say no, I am not an inexpensive option. *I am a man. A man is more valuable than a mattress.*

I will go abroad on a research trip, and I will remember the men who work without pay when my Greek taxi driver starts a conversation about justice. He lifts both hands above the wheel and cries, *The man who eats caviar has blood on his hands!* He bangs the steering wheel. *You and I have clean hands because we work for the cheap fish we eat.* The rich can't sleep well like we do, he explains. *Their caviar is dripping with innocent blood!*

I'm less confident of my innocence than the taxi driver. My desk chair is soft, teaching injuries are rare, and I make more money than I need to eat. I dare for a moment to let myself believe my work is hard, like the taxi driver's, with its secondary trauma and exhausting hours before the page. I dare to think the work we—my students and I—do together matters. In my class, the men learn how to carve into the culture a space for themselves. They bear witness to their lives. They use words to disrupt the comfortable mythology that casts incarceration as some kind of cleanse, and casts human beings as toxins or parasites of which the social organism must be rid. Once, when W. had brought me some loose-leaf paper, he began telling me about prison rumors, and explained that over the years of his incarceration several female staff members had been fired for sexual activity with the incarcerated men. I must have betrayed an expression of shock because I couldn't fathom the logistics, and because I am a person who assiduously obeys rules, but W. read my face differently and countered, as if in defense, "You know, not everybody in here is trash."

J., you gave me photographs of your children—perhaps as a visual aid for your memoir, I can't recall for sure—and it is too much for me to bear the sight and know that tonight, they will not get to hug their father. It's too intimate, the photos, and in my head I write formal addendums to the

5. These Stories Will Not Be Confined 121

syllabus: *Please do not hand Dr. Eleftheriou anything but your assignment.* Your peers have given me copies of the *New Yorker* to read and return, as well as original drawings they've made, all things they're sure will help me with my work as their professor. It's too much, though. I can't bear to owe you even this, a copy of the *New Yorker* or a handful of photographs. I forget them in my car. I have space in my head only for my task as your professor. I'm not your angel or even your friend. I'm torn apart and *I* need someone to listen to *me*. I need someone who will listen to me tell about how my heart is broken because of your broken lives.

Again I feel the guilt of my unwillingness to fight for better conditions for you, so I want to say *I'm sorry*. I'm sorry your loss is too much for me to contain; I'm sorry there comes a point where I do not want to know; I'm sorry that you have married and yet you live tonight and every night without what we all need, which is human touch.

The depth of need in these students' eyes exhausts me. What they need is compassion and someone to listen to their stories. I am sorry that I am exhausted, depleted, wrung dry of anything kind to say. I am sorry that after three semesters of teaching you, I have no stronger confession, no redemptive or enlightened lesson. I confess only terror, and that I was happier before. I don't know if I will ever overcome the devastation of bearing witness to the cruelty of such punishment for sin, or *hamartia*, or, missing of the mark. I don't know if I will recover from the knowledge that our state is ruthless and unkind, and eager to deprive and humiliate a man who makes a serious mistake.

I am terrified of their lives. I am devastated by their confinement and devastated again each time I learn more about all that they suffer. I long for someone to hold for me the pain of knowing their pain. I feel like I am bursting, like this grief is more than I can contain.

Driving to Sumac isn't just an escape from the concrete that encases my city. It is also an exit from a bubble that long kept the truth of the carceral state comfortably out of view. It was easier to live inside that bubble. It was easier to live with the threat of imprisonment as an abstract shadow-terror. None of us are really free. Prison is a shadow in every heart. We are all sinners, according to most religions, and all pray to be forgiven and—according to the most common faith in Texas—ask God to "forgive us our debts, as we also have forgiven our debtors." In church, I learned that repentance matters, and that God requires everyone to forgive. The state does not forgive.

Here is the hardest thing to say: the penitentiary exists in part to protect privileged people like me from the consequences of pain and loss and confusion and mistakes of people like you. I admire intellectually the prison abolition work, but a tight, scared part of me wants my own security more urgently than it wants the end of your suffering. That scared part of me would rather forget that in America, *this* is *hamartia's* consequence: this hardship, this isolation, this humiliation. You lose the freedom to piss when you need to piss, to earn money for your labor, to touch a person you love.

By documenting caged lives and exposing state cruelty, nonfiction by incarcerated Americans brings more truth into the light. When more readers learn what is happening, they help bear the burden of knowing. And once we are able to *bear* the knowledge, we can face it, and our collective outrage can effect change.

I envision writing as a kind of exposure therapy to increase bit by bit the public tolerance for the truth, and wean them off the comfortable lie that everyone gets what they deserve. Like I was, the populace is more comfortable not knowing what happens to human beings behind the cinderblock walls. Merely by existing, those stories undermine the saccharine platitudes that elide distinctions between virtue and privilege. Because the truth is, there are cruel, unrepentant wrongdoers both inside and outside the prison walls. And on both sides of the concertina wire, there are penitents, too.

Determined to face their *hamartia*, learn from their errors, and create from the rubble of their lives a new and more virtuous self, the men forge on the page their own redemption. They write new selves into existence. Their documented lives provide for me, too, an example of how I might be patient as I face my own *hamartia*, and overcome my failure to be generous and brave. I have not yet learned to love my neighbor as myself. I haven't even learned not to fear him. I seek a redeemed and humble love. If I have not yet been able to change, if humility and open-heartedness elude me still, I can still keep working. I can work to attain humility like my students,' and imitate their effort to make themselves anew.

And if all I've learned so far is to say *I'm trying to have compassion* and *but for the mercy of God go I*, eating cheap fish and hoping by some grace to be washed from my many sins, then that's what I'll say, and I will point to your words, for if we trust and help each other, no legal power can keep your story from being told.

Notes

1. Prison Policy Initiative, "State and Federal Prison Wage Policies."
2. Benns, "American Slavery, Reinvented."
3. "Texas Correctional Industries: Useful Skills or Slave Labor?"
4. Texas Correctional Industries, "About Us."

5. These Stories Will Not Be Confined   123

Bibliography

Benns, Whitney. "American Slavery, Reinvented." *The Atlantic*. September 21, 2015. https://www.theatlantic.com/business/archive/2015/09/prison-labor-in-america/406177/.

Prison Legal News. "Texas Correctional Industries: Providing Useful Work Skills or Slave Labor?" August 7, 2014. https://www.prisonlegalnews.org/news/.

Prison Policy Initiative. "State and Federal Prison Wage Policies and Sourcing Information." April 10, 2017. https://www.prisonpolicy.org/reports/wage_policies.html.

Texas Correctional Industries, Texas Department of Criminal Justice. "About Us." Last updated April 2018. https://tci.tdcj.texas.gov/info/about/default.aspx.

REACHING GUANTÁNAMO
Solmaz Sharif

Dear Salim,

Love, are you well? Do they   you?
I worry so much. Lately, my hair   , even
my skin   . The doctors tell me it's
I believe them. It shouldn't
. Please don't worry.
                 In the year, and moths
have gotten to your mother's
            , remember?
I have enclosed some   —made this
batch just for you. Please eat well. Why
did you   me to remarry? I told
     and he couldn't   it.
I would never   .
Love, I'm singing that   you loved,
remember, the line that went
"   "? I'm holding
the   just for you.

Yours,

PART TWO

Carceral Bodies and Systems

SPACE

Jeremy Eugene

Tell me how much space
a Black body takes up.
How much room
to keep the dead in memory?
I thought it was a small space:
a square inch of the nation
a few minutes—
probably the same size
as that space in your brain
which makes whole lives go missing after a year.

Somebody told us we were wrong last night.
While standing in the last spot where Sandra Bland was a free woman
We, seven students, poised to broadcast
One of Sandy's 5-minute inspirational videos on the side of a church,
because even in her hometown, most people don't know
that Sandra was more than a Black woman who back-talked an officer.
That she was a light who shined every single day.

And a man in a pickup truck drives by
Our ode to the fallen—this woman
reduced to picture frame, roses, and dusty teddy bears
yelling *"White Lives Matter too, Donald Trump for President."*

And you know what needs to happen....
someone needs to teach me how to be omnipresent—
to have all the space, even those that don't exist anymore.
Teach me how to proudly declare war on the already dead.
To see a broken kingdom
as something to break further.
Somebody teach me how to bite a mouth closed.

You said I know how already?
You think a Black mouth can shout a brick wall down?
Yes, we Black activists have podiums, yes, we make all the noise
that never leaves the rally.
It goes in one Black ear, out another Black mouth:
we siphoners of our own shouts—
we bullhorns in a Grand Canyon.

You, teach me, "no."
Teach me "no time for you."
No is the answer. The answer is no.
There is no yours.
There is only mine. It is always mine.
Teach all of me how to always have all the space.

You have figured it out.
You are in life, in passing, in mourning, in resurrection,
you do it all with such ease
I think you've forgotten what embarrassment is.

Did you know I cannot feel entitled to your house?
Did you know if I tried to, shame would evict me?
Teach me how to bury shame
deeper than a Black body goes.

Teach me to snuff out the ghost and the time traveler
in a single statement.
To make mutes of those who can no longer
speak through their own mouths.
Make my entire timeline a roll of black duct tape.

I want to rob the night of itself.
To become a scorched grave policy
disguised as an everlasting light
—a sun so spiteful
I would snarl at a candle I have already blown out.
To learn greed so strong it will take even your absence,
Yes, I want to be the black hole
and its recipient.

Teach me how to make *everything* mine.

To stop raising my own echo.
To dance on the dead
and claim my feet were here first.

The very least you owe me is this lesson.
Pray that I am a bad student.

6

Cornered

Day Laborers, Criminalization, and Legal Rituals of Democracy in Texas

FRANCISCO ARGÜELLES PAZ Y PUENTE, AKA PANCHO

This piece narrates my experience as a plaintiff in the 2012 federal lawsuit of Jornaleros de las Palmas v. League City TX *and its police chief.[1] It is the story of how I accompanied[2] a group of Mayan Indigenous migrant workers who were harassed, arrested, and deported for seeking work in the street, leaving their apartments, or going to buy groceries. They just wanted to work, but the local forces of carceral liberalism cornered them into organizing and becoming Los Jornaleros de las Palmas to defend their dignity and to save their lives. Their efforts culminated in a partial legal victory but not justice in a case that set legal precedent and gave theoretical protection to day laborers all across Texas. Yet the case failed to even acknowledge the root causes of the injustices they constantly face, let alone to repair the damage caused to them or to begin to undo these injustices.*

Fragment One

Wood and leather. This is the image, smell, tactile memory I have of the courtroom as I try to remember the trial. I was impressed at how much wood and leather surrounded us, as if this would add respectability to the legal rituals performed there. Desks, chairs, walls, and a gavel created a black and mahogany illusion of fairness and rationality. If only Black and mahogany bodies could be treated with such consideration. Sitting in that court felt like being in a movie, except there were no cameras or jury. This trial would be decided by a judge, U.S. Magistrate Stephen Wm. Smith, who after months of depositions, testimonies, interrogations, and study of precedents concluded that day laborers' right to solicit work in the street is protected by the First Amendment because it is a form of speech. Thus, the constant harassment, arrests, fines, and other intimidatory actions taken by League City's police had to stop. This was a big victory that the courage of the Jornaleros and the hard work of our lawyers made possible; it stopped the concrete oppression Los Jornaleros de las Palmas were suffering, but also meant harassment of day laborers by any other local or state law enforcement agency throughout Texas had to stop too. The verdict, however, also felt like a hurtful defeat because of the lack of actual consequences for the abusive police chief and his officers and because there was no restitution for the damage they caused or recognition of the racist and xenophobic nature of their actions.

Ten years later as I review my notebooks to tell this story a tidal wave of images starts flooding my head: from the first meetings with the jornaleros in a crowded unit at Las Palmas Apartments to the meetings with police chief Jez at the police station or at the corner where day laborers waited for work to the trial and the long months waiting for a resolution. Then other battles, some older and some more recent, start crowding my head and heart: our decades-long attempts to pass immigration reform, the fight to stop record deportations under the Obama administration, the endless wage theft and workplace abuses day laborers and migrant workers face, especially after disasters like Hurricanes Ike and Harvey,[3] and our very limited success recovering their stolen wages. I recall the organizing efforts by migrants with spinal cord injuries who were denied access to catheters, diapers, and other necessities due to their lack of medical insurance and were forced to start an organization to help one another,[4] the countless stories of workers detained for months and years at for-profit detention centers and then deported, the families searching for their loved ones who disappeared at the Texas-Mexico border, the images of children in cages, toddlers crying separated from their parents, and migrant communities further criminalized and vilified by the Trump administration, the stories of women raped and abused at detention centers, the testimonies of trans women detained and abused when put in the detention centers with the male population, the images of Black men and women executed by the police, the thousands of disappeared Central American migrants crossing Mexico in the past twenty years, the hundreds of thousands of Mexicans killed, disappeared, displaced by the violence linked to the so-called War on Drugs. All for the benefit of a racialized capitalist system that takes pride in performing the rituals of democracy and at the same time wreaks havoc on the lives of our people and profits from this. These are not things I read about or saw on television: these are fights I fought, testimonies I heard, cases and stories of people I know and love.

Suddenly an overwhelming anxiety grips my heart, my heartbeat accelerates, my chest tightens, my hands get sweaty, and that empty pit in my stomach that I have learned to numb becomes my center of gravity and threatens to swallow me whole, so I jump from my chair as if pushed by a spring. I can't sit still, can't concentrate, I can't write anymore! After taking some deep breaths to re-center and slow down enough to ask myself what is happening I realize that I have just stepped on a mine in my heart.

A MINEFIELD CALLED MY HEART[5]

This emerging text,
a weaving of words trying to explain an absurd experience,
legal victory in a battle that we are still losing,
is torn apart as my grief and pain explode in me

I am tired of trying to explain the humanity of my people
to a nation that chooses moral amnesia every day
Sarah Fabian,
DOJ lawyer
dirty work
for Obama and Trump in her CV
arguing in court this time
against toothpaste and soap for children in cages
while corrupt talking heads in omnipresent screens
expect me to debate their loud ignorance
and their louder commitment to ignoring our humanity

Every time I force myself to watch their perverse "debating"
re-baiting
my heart breaks a little more
in Texas
cynical theater where we remember The Alamo
but ignore the Black and brown bodies languishing in cages
while the bright white bones
of my sisters and brothers
lay
unburied
unrecognized
all along the border

6. Cornered   133

I am slowly becoming my rage
and there is not enough
Ritalin,
Xanax
CBD oil
in the world
to make me sit still long enough to continue writing.

I go without writing for days and weeks
fearing this rage made me lose my trust
in the power of words
and then
like a tide
the rage subsides
and I can see what makes
my words run away from me:
is not just rage but shame and guilt
because my brothers and sisters
are still in cages and dying in the desert
and my efforts
our efforts
are not enough to free them
save them
save us
from this cruel Manifest Destiny

It is too hard to write with clenched fists
I hear a toxic voice telling me to shut up
"real men" don't give in to "feelings"
silence
wise sisters knew and taught me a while ago
words find their way to flow through broken hearts
for this is how we heal and find our strength

And so this broken heart attempts to write
for me, for you, for them
this confession
of pain and shame
that I vow to let go
and this memory of our dignity
another root of hope for our cageless future
the one we will create together
where we can freely come and go
in Abya Yala
land of our ancestors

I can sit now in peace
for I can see
the only way to reclaim
this minefield called my heart
Is for my life to become a love letter to my people

Fragment Two: Another Attempt at Weaving the Story as Text

This piece *was supposed to be* a personal narrative and analysis of my experience as a plaintiff in the 2012 federal lawsuit of *Jornaleros de las Palmas v. League City*. I wanted to denounce how the police chief cornered Los Jornaleros de las Palmas into organizing to defend their dignity and protect their lives and how this led to our paths crossing. I was going to describe all the essential jobs jornaleros do in our communities: cleaning and rebuilding after hurricanes and floods, helping us move, painting our homes, fixing our yards.

I wanted to describe that I was working then part-time at the Houston Interfaith Worker Justice Center when the jornaleros reached out after some of them had been arrested, and I and my brave young coworker Laura Boston went to meet with them at a small apartment where the elder Don Celso had taken a leadership role in organizing his community of Indigenous Guatemalan migrants and migrants from Mexico and other parts of Central America. They had organized a mutual aid network to pay the fines they were constantly given for "trespassing."[6] They had to constantly scramble to bail (ransom) each other out of jail before La Migra could come and deport them back to the deadly conditions they left behind, but sometimes there was not enough time or enough money and some compañeros got deported never to be seen again. I wanted to tell the story of how we organized a meeting with Chief Jez, with the help of some local white allies, residents of League City, and how I brought interpretation equipment and surprised the police chief with a group of jornaleros who were there with their earphones, ready to receive simultaneous interpretation from English to Spanish and to speak up for their rights, and how this bilingual space gave way to a shift in power. I wanted to tell the story of how in the days following that meeting the police escalated their criminalization of day laborers with a sting operation, and how this affront galvanized our efforts and led us to seek the support of the National Day Laborer Organizing Network and the Mexican American Legal Defense Fund (MALDEF). But mostly I wanted to tell the story of the legal case and to reflect on the irony of how this battle culminated in a legal victory,[7] but not justice, and how the case makes visible the carceral political system that criminalizes migrants while extracting profit first from their labor and later from their imprisonment and surveillance.[8]

Judge Smith states that the case is about "League City's alleged policy of targeting day laborers and applying (and mis-applying) state laws to prevent them from soliciting employment in the city."[9] His ruling, as reported by the *Houston Chronicle*, established that "a League City police policy banning day laborers from seeking employment in public areas violated the workers' First Amendment free speech rights." Judge Smith found that the 1989 anti-solicitation law in Texas "is itself unconstitutional because it limits speech based on content, and creates 'an unnecessary risk of chilling free speech.'"[10]

Our lawsuit also accused League City and its police department of race and national-origin discrimination in violation of the Fourteenth Amendment, but this charge and our demand for damages were dismissed by the judge. This is one of the reasons the legal victory still tastes so bitter. The judge argued that even if the actions of the police had a discriminatory impact, the intent to discriminate had not been proven, therefore day laborers "were not targeted based on who they were, but on what they did—that is, exercise their right to free speech."[11] In other words, he absurdly argued that they were discriminated against because they are day laborers, not because they are Mayan migrants. The sentence recognized that day laborers suffered damage every time their right to solicit work was denied but concluded that "a monetary award for each violation of a day laborer's First Amendment right to solicit would be speculative because the amount of damage would be difficult or impossible to measure."[12] And just like that allowed the police to keep thousands of dollars in fines obtained illegally.

The outcome of this case seems to be saying, "Jornaleros are persons and have a right to freedom of speech, this is what makes our democracy great. But they are aliens, not fully human, so they will have to continue working without rights, this is what makes our economic system so great too." This acceptance of limited personhood is a serious threat from below to democracy the same way that the personhood of corporations and their right to free speech expressed as millions of dollars financing political campaigns is a threat from above to democracy.[13]

With this article I wanted to denounce how, in the context of a criminalized population in a carceral state, migrant workers are condemned to survive in the American "golden cage" that exploits their labor, steals their money, and denies their humanity. Through this story I wanted to show U.S. democracy as a performance and a ritual to protect and reproduce white supremacy and a capitalist system founded on colonial genocide and exploitation of Indigenous, Black, and working-class people. I wanted to show how these legal rituals in the criminal(izing) justice system are not about justice, but about the self-exoneration of what Pillai aptly conceptualizes in this volume as carceral liberalism. As my work during this past decade has brought me close to a myriad of organizations and activists working for abolition and racial justice across the country, I thought I was ready to use what I had learned from this case and develop a deeper understanding of what we need to do to be free, but I didn't see that in order to denounce this "shining city on a hill" built on top of a post-apocalyptic landscape, I had to journey through this minefield called my heart.

So I declare myself incapable of telling this story at this time. I hope one day I can tell this story of the case and its causes. Maybe if I don't try to do it alone I will be able to do it; I will ask our lawyer, the brilliant Marisa Bono, for her help. I will look for the jornaleros who testified with me at the trial, Amado (a name I imagine the great Toni Morrison would have liked because it literally means "beloved") and Lalo, and will ask them to join me telling the story of this battle. Writing for this collection gives me the freedom to be truthful; I refused to do violence to myself and to the story in order to respond to an intellectual canon that is not designed for us or by us. I also trust the light that the many brilliant contributors to this volume are shining on the nature of the carceral regime we are facing, on the power of our resistance and on the road to our liberation.

As my discourse exploded after I stepped on one of the many mines I carry in my heart, I learned that being denied the peace and time to make sense of our battles turns into this labyrinth of unprocessed stories, loss, grief, pain, and even joy, that end up lying around like unharvested fruits rotting in the soil. What kind of evil cage do we live in where we end up booby-trapped to our memories? How different is this from the cage where the oppressor lives booby-trapped to their fear, their moral amnesia, and their commitment to ignore our humanity? How essential are these internal cages to the production and reproduction of the larger legal-political-economic infrastructure that keeps "la jaula de oro" going? Maybe I did not get to tell the story, but I might have found some good questions and in the process confirmed Los Tigres del Norte were right: *Aunque la Jaula sea de oro, no deja de ser prisión.*[14]

If we are to abolish these internal and external cages we have to acknowledge that colonialism and the carceral state it built have taken away from us the time and space we need to process, retell, and reclaim our stories. This essentially means we lack time in community, for what is community if not a space and time to tell and listen, to see and be seen with respect? And what are colonialism and racialized capitalism if not a violent replacement of communities with factories, markets, and jails? Colonial oppression, capitalist exploitation, and patriarchal isolation exist by robbing us of our place and time to acknowledge one another in dignity and love; this is also the extreme manifestation of the alienating space of carceral liberalism, the construction of a multiplicity of cages where brown and Black bodies are placed beyond our space and time but inside a machinery that produces punishment and profit.

Farewell

In November of 2014 the great African writer and global elder Ngũgĩ Wa Thiong'o spoke at the University of Houston; after the panel I asked him how to avoid becoming bitter or hopeless, and he looked me in the eye with immense kindness and told me: "Never become a problem to yourself, you are only a problem for the colonizer."

Aprendiendo a vivir en este minefield called my heart I wonder if instead of trying to avoid the mines, I can start intentionally stepping on them and just embrace the experience of exploding and then coming back together again and again for love of my people, until there are no more mines, or me, or mine, just us, in community living free.

Notes

1. *Jornaleros de las Palmas v. City of League City, Texas, et al.*, Civil Action H-11-2703.

2. For a description of the concept of accompaniment, its roots in the popular movements in Mexico and Central America, and its connection to theology of liberation, see Argüelles, "We Are Never Alone."

3. The crucial role of jornaleros in disaster recovery and the conditions they face in the context of climate change is described in Theodore, "Recovering from Climate Disasters."

4. I served as executive director of Living Hope Wheelchair Association until August 2021. For detailed discussion of how these migrants work to defend their rights, see Kovic, "Demanding to Be Seen and Heard."

5. This unexpected poem is inspired by the title and spirit of the seminal book edited by Cherríe Moraga and Gloria Anzaldúa, *This Bridge Called My Back* (1981). The courage and clarity of praxis by women of color has been central in my own praxis as a popular educator and organizer. The friendship and accompaniment of my sisters in the movement has been and still is essential to my growth and survival. Working with and learning from compañeras like Maria Jiménez, Alma Maquitico, Eunice Cho, Makani Themba, Margo Okazawa-Rey, Ash-Lee Henderson, Mónica Hernández, Claudia Muñoz, Shreerekha Pillai, Shaw San Liu, and so many others is gift and joy.

6. This use of trespassing charges has been taken to a whole new level by Texas Governor Abbot with Operation Lone Star, which criminalizes immigrants to court right-wing voters for his presidential aspirations. A recent report by the Immigrant Legal Resource Center ("Civil Rights Organizations Allege") analyzes this policy and characterizes it as racist, xenophobic, and discriminatory.

7. Falkenberg, "Case Proves Constitution Works."

8. The growing use of technology as a key element of the prison industrial complex surveilling immigrants and other criminalized populations for profit and social control is analyzed by Puck Lo and Community Justice Exchange from an abolitionist perspective in their recent report "From Data Criminalization to Prison Abolition."

9. *Jornaleros v. League City.*

10. Falkenberg, "Case Proves Constitution Works."

11. *Jornaleros v. League City.*

12. *Jornaleros v. League City.*

13. Corporations are increasingly making, and winning, the claim that they have the rights of persons. See Torres-Spelliscy, "Does 'We the People' Include Corporations?"

14. Los Tigres Del Norte are an internationally known band of the Norteño musical genre and winners of multiple Grammy awards. Their songs describe and lift up the immigrant experience. Their song "La Jaula de Oro" (the Golden Cage) is a common reference among immigrants describing our experience in the United States. "Aunque la Jaula sea de oro, no deja de ser prisión" means "Even if the cage is made of gold, it won't stop being a prison" (my translation). They performed this song live at Folsom Prison on the fiftieth anniversary of Johnny Cash's legendary performance.

Bibliography

Argüelles Paz y Puente, Francisco. "We Are Never Alone: Some Thoughts on Accompaniment." *Comment* (Fall 2019). https://comment.org/we-are-never-alone/.

Falkenberg, Lisa. "Case Proves Constitution Works for Day Laborers, Too." *Houston Chronicle*, May 21, 2013.

Immigrant Legal Resource Center. "Civil Rights Organizations Allege Texas' Operation Lone Star Targets and Punishes Migrants with Discriminatory Shadow Criminal Legal System." December 15, 2021. Accessed May 1, 2022. https://www.ilrc.org/civil-rights-organizations-allege-texas'-operation-lone-star-targets-and-punishes-migrants.

Jornaleros de las Palmas v. City of League City, Texas, et al., Civil Action H-11-2703. May 17, 2013. Accessed May 1, 2022. https://law.justia.com/cases/.

Kovic, Christine. "Demanding to Be Seen and Heard: Latino Immigrant Organizing and the Defense of Human Rights in Houston." *City and Society* 26, no. 1 (2014): 10–28.

Lo, Puck. "From Data Criminalization to Prison Abolition." Community Justice Exchange, 2022. Accessed April 10, 2022. https://abolishdatacrim.org/en/report/introduction.

Los Tigres del Norte Oficial. "Los Tigres Del Norte- La Jaula De Oro (Live at Folsom Prison)." YouTube. October 10, 2019. https://www.youtube.com/.

Moraga, Cherríe, and Gloria Anzaldúa. *This Bridge Called My Back: Writings by Radical Women of Color*. Watertown, MA: Persephone Press, 1981.

Theodore, Nik. "Recovering from Climate Disasters: Immigrant Day Laborers as 'Second Responders.'" National Day Laborer Organizing Network. April 2022. Accessed May 1, 2022. https://ndlon.org/wp-content/uploads/2022/04/Recovering-from-Climate-Disasters-Report-2.26.22.pdf.

Torres-Spelliscy, Ciara. "Does 'We the People' Include Corporations?" *Human Rights* 43, no. 2 (2018). https://www.americanbar.org/groups/crsj/publications/human_rights_magazine_home/we-the-people/we-the-people-corporations/.

7

Resisting Criminalization

Principles, Practicalities, and Possibilities of Alternative Justices beyond the State

AUTUMN ELIZABETH, D COULOMBE, ZARINAH AGNEW

Introduction

"How do we imagine a better world and raise questions that permit us to see beyond the given?"
—Angela Davis

In September of 2015, a small group of people got together in an intentional community in San Francisco, California, to figure out how to solve a problem.[1] One of their community members had sexually assaulted another community member, and no one wanted to involve the police: not the victim/survivor, not the community, not the person who had committed the harm. A year earlier, a different intentional community had experienced the same quandary with a domestic violence situation. These situations raise many questions: questions of the efficacy of state systems, questions of how best to help communities, questions of how to create a better world outside of the looming presence of the seemingly inevitable and unavoidable criminal justice system (CJS). These questions are at the center of the work and creation of alternative justices (Alt-J).

Why Alternative Justices Are Needed

Prison populations in the United States have exploded since the 1980s as a result of "tough on crime" policies enacted to control the working and workless poor in urban cities, manufacturing a demand for a privatized network of detention and imprisonment that continues to expand today. In California alone, "the state prisoner population grew nearly 500 percent between 1982 and 2000, even though the crime rate peaked in 1980."[2] Private prisons are big business. In 2014, the Bureau of Prisons paid $639 million in state funds to private prisons, about $22,159 per prisoner.[3] Angela Davis notes, "The global prison industrial complex is continually expanding. It has come to include not only public and private prisons, but also juvenile facilities, military prisons, and interrogation centers. Moreover, the most profitable sector of the private prison business is immigrant detention centers."[4] It has been well researched that the advent of the prison industrial complex is only the most recent institution of population control in the centuries-long history of structural oppression of black and brown people in the United States.[5] Whereas historically, the role of the black population in U.S. American capitalism was one of surplus labor, late capitalism has ushered in an expanded definition of incarceration that includes the physical containment and control of black bodies,[6] as well as the bodies of immigrants, political activists, and other marginalized people, as an additional apparatus for profit.

The prison industry has boomed as a result of a mainstream discourse of scare tactics, designed to justify an aggressive erosion of civil liberties through an ever-expanding security apparatus and the criminalization and imprisonment of people without due process. CJS grossly misapplies characteristics of extreme outliers of social dysfunction (e.g., serial killers) to a general populace to invent the "criminal" (or, Foucault's "delinquent")[7]—a person who causes harm to their community, regardless of any wider social or structural context, who is therefore undeserving of help, compassion, democratic participation, or basic human rights. The primary objective of the prison is not to rehabilitate criminals nor to enact justice, but to keep criminals separate from society. Since the state defines what constitutes crime, determines who can commit crimes, and enforces who is punished for crimes and to what extent, the prison industrial complex operates as a tool for the state to suppress vulnerable populations, especially those it deems enemies of the state, while also generating new vectors for profit.

In an age of mass incarceration and indefinite detainment disproportionately targeting vulnerable communities, CJS is mobilized by those in power as a tool of oppression that is fundamentally at odds with the communities it claims to serve. As the ever-expanding apparatus of state-sanctioned punishment grows increasingly oppressive, specifically toward communities of color and immigrants,[8] the need to provide alternative systems that prevent, reduce, and respond to harm becomes imperative. To this end, Alt-J resists criminalization of those who cause harm and complicity with state violence, by seeking strategies for addressing harm in community-focused ways.

Through a critique of carceral liberalism as conceptualized by Shreerekha Pillai, which centers the epistemological labor of radical black feminism, it becomes apparent that rather than address the material conditions of daily life and the toxic cultural environments that contribute to crime, the state uses CJS to disappear selected populations into prisons, disrupting communities and often perpetuating the conditions that support crime to keep the machine running. "Imprisonment is the punitive solution to a whole range of social problems that are not being addressed by those social institutions that might help people lead better, more satisfying lives."[9] Additionally, taxpayer money that should be used to bolster social programs and provide support to communities is instead diverted to these private prisons to subdue the same populations for profit. Critical human services, such as education and healthcare, have also become increasingly privatized and commodified, subsidized by public funds, allowing capitalists to profit off exploited communities that do not have the same access to resources as more privileged communities. The profitability of these privatized social services, as well as prisons and CJS more broadly, is demonstrative of interlocking systems of oppression upon which capitalism is dependent.[10]

Punitive state-run systems of imprisonment and disenfranchisement reproduce conditions that exacerbate social problems. Once one enters CJS, every aspect of life is regulated and monitored by the state, often for life, and any form of resistance or disobedience becomes grounds for further punishment. Once this cycle of state surveillance and regulation is started, it becomes nearly impossible to reintegrate back into a previous community due to legal discrimination that may deny housing, employment, education, public benefits, and civic engagement.[11] When incarceration is utilized as a one-size-fits-all response to harm, there is no care taken to ensure that the institution itself does not reproduce harm. Prisons are made to house those designated as "criminals," and "criminals" are undeserving of social support and require punishment. However, punishment does not address the material conditions that led to harm being caused, nor does it consider the victim/survivors' needs or wants, nor the impact on the wider community by removing a person who caused harm. Instead, incarceration makes reintegration nearly impossible, even after the period of imprisonment has ended.

The harms that come from both hiding social problems in prisons and from imprisonment itself can be addressed with alternative justices. Alt-

7. Resisting Criminalization   143

J strategies allow communities to resolve conflicts without replicating the harm of the state systems and without ignoring the larger social issues that contributed to harm in the first place. Through the involvement and integration of those who have been punished by state systems of incarceration, Alt-J works to retroactively transform the harm these systems create. Furthermore, Alt-J seeks to provide alternatives that undermine the ubiquity and expansion of carceral liberalism, which masquerades as a tool of empowerment while promoting oppression that serves a neoliberal elite. The tenets and practices of Alt-J promote liberation and support for all people by rejecting criminalization and state imprisonment in favor of community-driven strategies.

Sexual/Gender Violence

"It is critical for us to develop responses to gender
violence that do not depend on a sexist, racist, classist,
and homophobic criminal justice system."
—*Critical Resistance and INCITE!*

The prison industrial complex and CJS are but two complex social systems that both entrench and codify ancillary cultural conditions that lead to harm by selectively defining and punishing criminality. Rape, as one example, is sexism codified into a violent criminal act; selectively defined and punished, essentially along lines of gender[12] and often along lines of race and class. However, in the prejudicial punishment of rapists, CJS fails to address the prevalence of rape culture—the sociological environment that normalizes and trivializes acts of sexual assault—allowing the state to selectively punish specifically men of color for acts that are treated as normal in other, privileged, white communities. In fact, historical characterizations and definitions of sexual violence have been a key mechanism of controlling and policing marginalized communities (see Patricia Hill Collins's *Black Sexual Politics* for further analysis of rape and lynching as tools of social control in the post-emancipation South and the impact of this legacy in the 1991 testimony of Anita Hill against Clarence Thomas).[13] On this issue Coker suggests, "It is inaccurate to describe the state's response to domestic violence as a unified refusal to intervene in 'private' family matters. Race and class mark the history of the state's relationship to families."[14] In the absence of dissolving prejudices codified and reproduced by CJS, alternatives are fundamental to addressing and remedying these issues when responding to cases of sexual assault as well as other harms, whether they are the gendered assumptions made about victims or the gendered treatment of perpetrators compounded by race, economic status, and other vectors of oppression.

For these types of harm that hit so close to home, the need for community-based responses, as opposed to state systems, is even more clear. Due to the fact that a range of mental health issues are associated with sexual assault, ranging from post-traumatic stress to depression and sleep disorders, recovery is slower for sexual than non-sexual assault victims, and crucial factors influencing recovery are emotional support from friends, relatives, and other community supports. A true justice system must involve whole communities, and calls into question the use of CJS.[15]

Ultimately, the ways CJS is used to deal with sexual/gender harm illuminates that system's biggest failings. CJS takes cultural norms for which society as a whole holds collective responsibility, unevenly punishes the most vulnerable actor/perpetrators, delegitimizes victim/survivors, and hinders the healing process of victim/survivors by refusing to allow them agency in the process.[16]

Existing Alternatives

"The relinquishing of community power to a state government is unnecessary because there is no reason to believe the state can perform better than the community could."
—Coy McKinney, "An Anarchist Theory of Criminal Justice," 14.

Much if not all the work on Alt-J relies heavily on the often unacknowledged brilliance of Indigenous communities,[17] queer communities,[18] communities of color,[19] comunidades latines, and others, who were working on these systems long before white academia supposedly discovered them. Additionally, Alt-J encompasses a number of existing alternatives to current methodologies of criminalization and relies on several of these methodologies and theories for its foundation. Alternatives to CJS such as restorative justice (RJ), transformative justice (TJ), and anarchist criminology are among the most pertinent for the work of Alt-J, but other alternatives to criminal proceedings such as civil actions for damages, criminal injuries compensation, human rights complaints, and compensation packages can factor in as well.[20] With a focus on continual iteration and learning from failure, Alt-J seeks to use what is beneficial and learn from what is limited about these systems to build a concept and practice of alternative justices that allows for adaptability, creativity, and broader applications of existing alternatives.

Restorative Justice

Historically, there have always been multiple models of justice and ways to deal with harm. In the 1970s in the United States, thinkers, activists, and religious leaders began to take some of these forms of justice not used by the dominant culture and tried to incorporate them into forms of justice that would foster peace. Ultimately, RJ came out of these attempts, a history which is perhaps best summarized by Anthony J. Nocella: "The most well-known theory within the field of peacemaking criminology is Restorative Justice (RJ), co-founded by Howard Zehr (1995). Zehr working with others, developed RJ out of aboriginal and Native American practices in North America and New Zealand, which use community circles to bring victims and offenders together to heal, forgive, and take accountability."[21]

Zehr and other RJ scholars have created a variety of frames and principles for RJ over the years,[22] but the main principles of RJ can be summarized as:

- Crime presents dangers and opportunities for learning
- Early intervention is highly desirable
- Crime is primarily a harm to individuals and communities
- Repairing harm as much as possible is the primary goal of justice
- Harm creates obligations to individuals and communities
- Healing harm requires accountability from offenders and communities
- Processes and tools should be cooperative and collaborative
- The government has its place in the justice process as enforcers for offenders who do not wish to cooperate
- Community and religious institutions have a place in the justice process as teachers of the community's moral standards[23]

Although many are used in conjunction with CJS, the RJ movement has developed numerous harm-restoration tools and processes that are part of the Alt-J toolbox. One of these tools is Victim-Offender Conferencing (VOC). Zehr says that VOC "consists of a face-to-face encounter between the victim and the offender. In these meetings emphasis is upon three elements: facts, feelings, and agreements. The meeting is facilitated and chaired by a trained mediator, preferably a community volunteer."[24]

Despite the frequent use of RJ within the carceral state, it is used in other contexts as an alternative to prison and punishment. Sandhya Jha notes, "Restorative justice really is being used in school and neighborhood groups as well as prisons. It can be a powerful way of practicing a different form of justice that honors everyone's humanity or capacity."[25] It is worthwhile to consider that by implementing RJ strategies in schools, young people are exposed to ways of handling conflict that may preclude more harmful outcomes later in life and allow for stronger communities that need not rely so heavily on the state to handle justice.

Transformative Justice

As academics in the west began to think about and develop theories of RJ, people like Ruth Morris, Anthony J. Nocella, and others noted that material conditions of systematic oppression and inequality were not considered in RJ and began the formulation of TJ. TJ theory, tools, and practices place "issues of inequality, oppression, and domination at the forefront."[26] Unlike RJ's more interpersonal approach, TJ "takes a systems approach to conflict, recognizing that we are all interconnected: the offender and the victim, one's choices and one's situation, the community and its social structures, power differentials among all involved in a crime."[27]

While RJ and TJ share a number of similarities, the differences in viewpoints can be seen through the distinctions in the main principles. As with RJ there is variety among TJ theorists, but the main principles of TJ can be summarized as:

- Many types of harm, including but not only crimes, are conflicts that can be transformed
- Crime presents an opportunity for change and healing for individuals and the community
- Mediation, empathetic listening, negotiation, and community circles are crucial tools
- Responding to needs of victims and offenders is vital for transformation
- Systems of oppression must be considered in harms and must also be transformed[28]

While TJ focuses on systemic oppression, it is not necessarily envisioned as a replacement for the state justice system, but rather as a way to transform state systems.

Nocella, arguably one of the main theorists and advocates of TJ, says, "Transformative justice is not about destroying and building anew," and goes on to say, "Everyone needs to be involved in a voluntary, safe, constructive, and critical dialogue about accountability, responsibility, and the initiative to heal" and that "both activists and oppressors, as well as law enforcement, lawyers, judges, prisoners, community members, teachers, students, politicians, spiritual leaders, and others, must come together."[29]

TJ's cooperation and complicity with state systems echoes the current and past use of RJ in prisons. While TJ and RJ may not be the exclusive domain of CJS, they are meant to be compatible with, and even integrated into, these state institutions, and as such are limited in their capacity to generate alternatives.

Anarchist Criminology

While anarchist criminology can be traced back to anarchist thought from the 1800s,[30] more contemporary anarchist criminology, which has also been called "peacemaking criminology," saw a resurgence in the late 1970s and again in the early 2010s. Anarchist criminology critiques state systems of law and crime, as well as mainstream criminology, creating space to imagine possibilities beyond criminalization and state authority. Anarchist theory rejects a centralized authority and asserts self-sovereignty; thus anarchist criminology challenges CJS by creating "a theory of criminology which does not require a central authority for its operation."[31]

While most anarchist criminology is not process-based, there are similarities between anarchist criminology and the main principles of RJ/TJ. Anarchist criminology addresses "the fact that 'justice' is determined by the state, and not the individuals involved. Worsening this is the fact that the origin of the state was built on discriminatory ideals. This has resulted in a criminal justice system that does not serve the people, but works to maintain oppressive and discriminatory, governmental authority."[32] This critique both echoes and confronts RJ/TJ. Anarchist criminology cites the failure of the state to include the individuals involved when carrying out justice, but also asserts that CJS is an oppressive authoritarian tool that bolsters a centralized state power that unnecessarily causes harm.[33]

Generalizing the long history of anarchist criminology[34] and the work of numerous scholars, the main principles of anarchist criminology can be defined as:

- Self-sovereignty is paramount in both deterring harm and healing it
- Communities and individuals, not the state, hold the power to implement justice
- Theory of crime and crime control come from communities, not just from academics
- Centralized legal authority is destructive
- Harms create needs and responsibilities for individuals, collectives, and communities

While anarchist criminology often does not offer tools or systems for creating alternatives to CJS, it does offer a critical view of the state and generates a discourse for developing community-based alternatives that resist criminality and oppression. Some anarchist criminologists advocate for RJ or TJ as methods for implementing anarchist criminology, while others call for the envisioning of new systems to support anarchist goals.

Critiques and New Directions

Although RJ, TJ, and anarchist criminology offer alternatives to CJS, there are several critiques to their systems that are part of what inspired the creation of Alt-J. RJ, and to some extent TJ, are still entangled with state systems of punishment, and while they may focus on fulfilling victims' needs better than the state, they are still being primarily used as add-ons to state-run legal systems.[35] The connection with CJS and the state that RJ/TJ sometimes have can disempower communities and victim/survivors, as well as implicate RJ/TJ in the biases and problems of the state system, such as: prejudicial treatment of both actor/perpetrators and victim/survivors along lines of race, class, gender, and citizenship; reproduction of harm and perpetuation of disadvantageous social conditions; and isolation from community.

Additionally, RJ and TJ do not intentionally analyze and develop their practices to learn from their mistakes, and they do not pay sufficient attention to the need to evolve with changing sociocultural conditions, all of which limit their ability to address and transform harm.

Anarchist criminology, while bolstering the need for anti-state systems, does not offer many methodologies or practices for dealing with harm. This absence of praxis instead thrusts the burden of creating tools and systems of alternatives onto the communities already most affected by the flaws in CJS that anarchist theorists set out to critique. Anarchist criminology does not articulate adequately the need for decentralization, and often ignores the fact that the state is not the only authority that can generate conditions of inequality. Oppressive structures of power can be reproduced in even small communities, especially if decentralization is not made imperative.

Finally, none of the aforementioned alternatives offer ways to work retroactively. While they critique CJS to various degrees, they do not look to transform the harm already done by the state. This failure allows harms caused by CJS to continually affect communities and those already harmed by CJS. Any strategy that is only preventative cannot be viewed as a holistic approach to addressing all harms.

Defining Alt-J

Analytics from a variety of political perspectives examine
more than two centuries of interlocking prison and legal
reforms and ask what role activists of many kinds—such as
benevolent liberals or women fighting domestic and sexual
violence—play, first in normalizing prison and then enabling
its perpetually expanding use as an all-purpose remedy for the
thwarted rights of both prisoners and harmed free persons.
—Ruth Wilson Gilmore, *Golden Gulag*, 23.

Reflecting on the limitations and detriments of state-run justice systems and
the systems that work within them, as well as the pressing need to disavow
systems that further entrench racism, sexism, classism, and other intersections of oppression, Alt-J posits a need to create ways for addressing harm
that exist entirely outside the bounds of the state. Alt-J practices are decentralized in order to shift power away from the state and prevent power from
consolidating amongst a few within the creation and application of Alt-J
strategies. Alt-J seeks to address harms caused by the state by being both
backward-healing and future-imagining, by working to heal harms done by
CJS, by using knowledge gained from that work to build future strategies,
and by sharing these strategies with others. Alt-J is not static and uses the
anarchist value of failure to build entire systems by being continuously it-
erative, critical, and reflective. Cultural norms and conditions are not static,
and solutions to cultural ills and social problems that lead to harm must not
be static either. Responses to harm must be flexible to change with shifting community needs, whether due to changes in the community members
themselves, changes in wider social or political circumstances, or emergent
new strategies.[36] Alt-J prioritizes praxis and asserts that praxis must be representative of the community it serves.

It is possible to envision Alt-J as a toolbox, where these key elements
and the following shared critiques make up the box itself and tools from a
plethora of sources are held inside.

Communities are encouraged to use the tools to create their own systems
of justice that fit the needs of their particular community at any given time,
as well as share their successes and failures in an effort to add more tools to
the box.

Shared Critiques

Alt-J theories advance from positions of shared critiques as opposed to affirmative principles. While primary proponents of Alt-J theory use shared critiques at this time, asserting affirmative principles may work better for other communities and in other times. Many groups working to advance Alt-J focus on the following shared critiques as starting points. It is possible to formulate many versions of RJ, TJ, and anarchist criminology under these shared critiques.

Alt-J primarily critiques the following:

- Punitive measures and retribution as effective or ethical methods of addressing harm
- Systems that maintain dominant and oppressive power structures, including the prison system, the police, the criminal justice system, and any alternative justice systems that do not actively dismantle their own biases, conscious and unconscious, and consistently work to create ever more equitable systems
- Individualizing responsibility by scapegoating a single actor/perpetrator of harm as solely responsible, while ignoring the community's complicity in the factors that may have led to that harm
- Failure to acknowledge that harms to individuals extend beyond the individual victim/survivor such that the harms to the community are ignored, self-harm to the actor/perpetrator is ignored, and the community focuses accountability solely on victim/survivors, thus ignoring their responsibility to actor/perpetrators, the community as a whole, and the larger communities in which they exist
- The idea that any single action, system, or solution will work to transform all harms, negating the plurality and complexities of humanity and the distinct needs and desires of different communities
- Delaying action in order to achieve perfection, professionalism, or authority; harms will not wait for the perfect solution, and professionalism and authority undermine transformation
- Refusal to both acknowledge failure and share the learnings derived from such failures; centralizing knowledge this way limits possible solutions and privatizes transformation
- The false reality that actor/perpetrators of harm only exist outside communities/in other communities and the perpetuation of the idea that people who commit harms, even exceedingly violent ones, are irredeemable individuals[37]

These shared critiques center around anti-oppression and intersectional analyses of current systems like CJS as well as RJ, TJ, and anarchist criminology and have an underlying insistence on praxis, self-critique, iteration, and decentralization that help keep Alt-J positioned as a continually evolving, radical, ever-improving philosophy of action.

In addition to the overarching shared critiques, Alt-J specifically critiques the following with regards to sexual/gender violence:

- Rape culture, as it passively and actively normalizes rape and treats rape as something necessarily distinct from other forms of violence and harms
- Victim-blaming and how it holds victim/survivors responsible for the harm they experience and also, paradoxically, for resolving that harm
- Revictimization that occurs through disbelief of victim/survivors, emotional reactions on behalf of victim/survivors, and revictimization caused by the social idea that rape must be traumatizing to be "real"
- Increased policing of each other's actions, thoughts, and touch as an effective solution for ending rape culture[38]

These additional critiques around issues of sexual/gender violence serve to show both how sexual/gender violence is a unique case of the application of Alt-J and how sexual/gender violence is still part of larger issues of violence and harm that can be treated with Alt-J systems.

Creating and Using Alternative Justices Systems

One of the central tenets of Alt-J praxis is a focus on community-generated solutions, and as such, systems developed using the Alt-J lens must inherently come out of a specific community or set of communities. In order to explore what some of these systems can look like, what follows is an in-depth analysis of the Alt-J systems at the Embassy Network (EN).[39] Since many state systems often perpetuate a cis-hetero-normative, imperialist, white supremacist, capitalist patriarchy[40] and are informed by rape culture, the examination and exploration of Alt-J in community contexts is particularly important for elucidating means of addressing harm that are not complicit with state violence.

EN is a collective of intentional communities in which each house within the collective is autonomous and self-governing. The Alt-J strategies developed by the EN communities studied in this chapter mainly focused on dealing with sexual/gender violence in a community living situation. A challenge for EN was to allow each house to determine their own values and processes around sexual assault in the community, while also protecting the community from multiple harms by the same person and ensuring that those repeat offenders got the care they needed when they wished to transform their behavior. While the goals and other aspects of EN-created Alt-J systems were applied to EN locations across the globe, the Record Keeper System was only tested at two locations, a large home called the Red Victorian, with more than thirty people, and the first location of EN, called Embassy SF, which housed about twenty people, both of which were located in San Francisco, California, about 1 mile apart. In 2018, these EN locations were the closest in physical proximity, had the most overlap in members, and had the strongest interest in Alt-J.

At the time of this case study in 2018, Alt-J systems seeking to address the root causes of sexual assault and domestic violence, while also addressing the harm caused to all parties and to the larger connected communities by these incidents, had been in development for three years at EN. The authors of this case study occupy two separate positions with regards to EN and this project. Agnew and Elizabeth were members of EN, each living at one of the test locations for the Record Keeper System during its implementation. While they were part of the core team that developed the Record Keeper System at EN, they did not participate as Record Keepers. Coulombe was not associated with EN during the time of the Record Keeper test, and was invited to collaborate on this paper as an activist, outside observer, and scholar with critical theory expertise in this area.

Case Study

Drawing on the decentralized and flexible nature of Alt-J theory, some systems created for addressing sexual/gender violence borrow from RJ/TJ, such as victim-offender mediation, conflict transformation, and a focus on harms as opposed to crimes. The Alt-J systems at EN were designed to align with EN core values of experimentation, openness, consensual engagement, and learning and unlearning. Thus, the systems were implemented as experiments, with transparent processes while also being opt-in and modular. These systems also work in conjunction with the Embassy Network Accountable Space Policy, so named to explicitly recognize that fully safe spaces cannot be guaranteed, but that all who enter can be made aware of the community norms and held accountable to upholding those norms.[41]

EN began by creating these goals for their Alt-J systems through community conversations:

1. Empower actors to take responsibility
2. Take the burden off victim/survivors
3. Uphold the Accountable Space Policy

EN prioritized the goals in this order because they saw empowering actor/perpetrators as a way to both take the burden off victim/survivors and uphold the Accountable Space Policy.

Record Keeper System

The first system created was a community incident tracking system called the Record Keeper System. This system involved designated Record Keepers at each test location/house, and one "floating" Record Keeper, as well as community mediators. It relied heavily on a loose group of people to push forward the goals of the project for the community. Record Keepers were apprised of consent violations in person and each maintained a list of these violations. With permission of the person reporting the violation, the incident could be referred to an Alt-J mediator, professional therapist, community member, or any other form of support and harm transformation to which the community subscribed. In terms of the lists the Record Keepers maintained, the community decided the level of confidentiality required. The three options presented to the community were High Privacy, Name-Ping, and Shared List options.[42] The EN communities chose the Shared List option, which allowed them to share information about harms across houses. Reports to the Record Keeper could be anonymous on the part of the victim/survivor, who would then only be known to the Record Keeper.

Additionally, with permission from the victim/survivor, anyone could make a report to the Record Keeper on the victim/survivor's behalf, allowing them to opt into whichever aspects of the Alt-J process with which they were comfortable, as opposed to feeling that they must disclose their identity. In fact, although it was not intentionally designed this way, a person could report their own experience of violation to a Record Keeper in third person. This unintentional loophole allowed more space for victim/survivors to share experiences in person without outing themselves as the target of harm.

Individuals who participated in any type of community mediation or harm transformation were contacted at 3, 6, 9, and 12 months to offer support and follow-up, and those who experienced harm or harmed someone and left the community were contacted at 6- and 9-month intervals to offer options for support and community mediation. In the design of this system, the responsibility for maintaining this contact was unintentionally unassigned.

In accordance with the goals formed by EN, every aspect of the system strongly encouraged those who committed harm to initiate a process of healing and transformation by informing the Record Keeper of their actions, especially in cases where it was not clear to either or both parties if a violation had taken place. This encouragement existed in both the system design and in information delivered to the communities about the Alt-J system. One such example was the community's attempt to use language that would empower actors to come forward. The frequent use of the terms *victim/survivor* or *target* instead of *victim* and *actor/perpetrator* as opposed to *offender* were efforts to lessen stigmatization for all parties and denote that these systems were not about establishing factual guilt or innocence but about transforming harms.

Record Keepers were empowered to be the starting point for all Alt-J processes, but were not responsible for filling all those roles. They were empowered to reach out to community members with mediation skills for victim/offender mediation, if that is what the victim/survivor wanted. They could also provide access to a collective therapy fund for actors and victim/survivors. They were also responsible for starting the process of addressing community harm caused by folks who had created more than two instances of harm across the network of communities.

Two-Strike Policy

The lists Record Keepers maintained were part of a community-initiated Two-Strike Policy. Prior to creating Alt-J systems, certain community members knew of repeat violations by the same actor/perpetrator happening across the network of houses, but felt unable to share this information in the absence of a system for reporting such things. EN had also seen other communities use expulsion from the community as the only consequence of causing harm, which thrust the responsibility of one community onto whatever community the expelled actor/perpetrator went to next. These factors were the main impetus for the creation of the Two-Strike Policy. Since each EN house is self-governing, the Two-Strike Policy was designed and implemented with the explicit goal of prioritizing the autonomy of each individual house, while also protecting the wider community from nomadic actors committing repeated harms.

Record Keepers met quarterly and shared their lists to compare actor/perpetrator names. If a name appeared on any of their lists twice or more, this was viewed as an escalated harm, meaning that even if victim/survivors did not want an Alt-J process, the harm of having hurt members of the community more than once was considered a harm against the community as a whole, and a transformative process was initiated on behalf of the community at large.

Failures and Successes of the Record Keeper System

The Record Keeper System had a number of successes for the EN community. The privacy of the Record Keeper lists was maintained, and the names of actor/perpetrators were not shared with any external community backlists that are often used as tools of isolation and punishment. The Record Keeper System also helped to unburden those individuals who were unofficially holding information about harms in the EN community. The implementation of the Record Keeper System did decrease unnoticed/undocumented recidivism across the network and raised the level of awareness around the issue of consent in EN houses. Finally, members of the EN reported that they found the community mediation and various RJ/TJ tools very effective.

Despite these successes, there were many failures of the Record Keeper System as determined by EN. One example is the lack of any structure for maintaining communications with actor/perpetrators and victim/survivors. While leaving this labor unassigned could have resulted in a decentralized method of accountability for follow-up contact, allowing mediators, community members, or Record Keepers to follow up according to what fit the community best, in the EN case this ambiguity instead resulted in all follow-up communication being left to a handful of the most ardent supporters of Alt-J ideas and thus concentrated both power and labor upon these few individuals. Additional failures of the implementation of the Record Keeper System as identified by the EN were:

- When all involved parties left the EN houses, follow-up became difficult
- Overly complex systems were hard to follow and lowered participation
- Large turnover led to Record Keepers being unknown to new members of the EN
- Record Keepers were unaware of the time commitment required for their role and were unable or unwilling to contribute necessary time and effort
- Record Keepers saw their role as separate and individual, which caused confusion and deviated from the goals of the Record Keeper System across the communities

- The system was absolutely reliant on Record Keepers, so failure of one Record Keeper to engage or understand the project as a whole led the whole system to collapse

While the Record Keeper System may be an effective system for smaller, less transient communities, where the Record Keepers are more dedicated to the goals of Alt-J, the Record Keeper System did not work for EN. The lack of involvement of the Record Keepers led to some members of one of the houses to step back from Alt-J systems and methods and, in one case, actively work against the Alt-J goals at EN. Additionally, despite efforts to be decentralized, the Record Keeper System, as enacted in the EN experiment, centralized power in two ways: by being reliant only on Record Keepers to initiate a process and by leaving the control and labor of actor/perpetrator and victim/survivor contact to only a few individuals. One potential site for iteration on the Record Keeper System is to explore ways to deconstruct these two sites of centralized power.

In speaking with members of EN in 2018 during the examination of this case study, it is clear that EN learned a great deal about maintaining a connection to a project and set of values across autonomous houses and collectives through their Record Keeper and other Alt-J experiments. A primary learning was that the cultural work of these types of projects is as important as work on larger logistics and individual instances, and a project is more likely to succeed if all aspects of the project are supported and integrated.

Furthermore, EN identified the lack of integration of formerly incarcerated individuals in this system as a major flaw. The support and knowledge of folks who had directly experienced incarceration could have made them excellent Record Keepers, or accountability partners for the Record Keepers in ways that would have vastly improved this system.

Stewards System

After the failure of the Record Keeper System, EN moved to a more decentralized model. Community members were invited to be "Stewards" of Alt-J processes in regards to instances of gender/sexual harm. To become a Steward, individuals fill out an application based on the shared critiques of Alt-J. That application is then evaluated by all existing Stewards within that community. Alt-J Stewards serve three main functions:

1. Support victim/survivors of sexual, partner, and gender violence
2. Monitor the Alt-J email and text messages for reports of sexual, gender, and partner violence in the community

3. Reach out to both actor/perpetrators and victim/survivors at established intervals for follow-up and mediation

Stewards help support transformative experiences for those harmed by sexual and partner violence by supporting both the victim/survivor and the actor/perpetrator. The main goal is for Stewards to offer support according to what both parties feel is needed for behavioral transformation. Activities for Stewards are varied because each situation is different, and people often want different things. Activities have included: helping victim/survivors feel heard, sending messages to communities or actors on behalf of victim/survivors, and longer-term mediation between the involved parties and their communities.

Stewards are accountable for checking in regularly with actor/perpetrators and working with them to understand how they came to harm someone. This involves regular check-ins, helping create pathways to therapy by finding appropriate therapy venues, and helping them access the Collective Therapy Fund, and/or inviting them to attend consent events, such as a Consent Confessional event or an Alternative Justices Transformation Pod group. By interacting with actor/perpetrators, Stewards give victim/survivors space to heal themselves, assuring them that someone is working with the actor/perpetrators to minimize the risk of repeat offences.

Stewards also support one another and act as an ethics/advice resource for one another, particularly when difficult or complex situations arise. Through these shared actions and constant communication, one Steward is not acting in isolation, and their power can be checked and balanced by other Stewards. Additionally, Stewards are not permanent; they do not belong to any one house or location, and their application answers are available to be reevaluated by other Stewards.

Other Aspects of EN Alternative Justices Systems

Some aspects of Alt-J systems implemented at EN exist in both the Record Keeper and Steward Systems. During the seven years EN has been experimenting with Alt-J so far, from 2015 to 2022, these and many other aspects of the Alt-J systems have evolved across the EN.

Mediation

In 2018, three years into their Alt-J experimentation, EN employed numerous tools from RJ/TJ to provide community and individual mediation. As is the case in many communities, most mediators only had informal training. The mediation provided was not strictly VOC, but often borrowed heavily from that standard.[43] Many victim/survivors in the community did not want to be in contact with the person who caused them harm, so Stewards often acted as intermediaries. In 2022, the stewards collectively decided to shift away from mediation, except at the community level to mediate instances of harm when the entire community feels harmed, such as when there has been a violation of the Two-Strike Policy. In the years since 2015, numerous Alt-J-aligned trained mediation options have come to exist outside the EN community, and being that EN Stewards were still limited in number, they felt their labor was best used to achieve the EN Alt-J goals in other ways and rely on the expertise of outside systems for true individual meditation when that was desired.

Cultural Shifts

To increase awareness of rape culture and consent culture, and to start dialogues toward transformation, EN offers events, talks, lectures, and workshops to generate discourse around Alt-J topics.[44] Accountable Space documents and flyers were created for use within EN, so community norms are clear and to provide passive education of those who use EN community spaces. EN also started a Consent Confessional event series, which specifically aimed to create a trusted space to share stories of how people had violated consent, how they felt about it, and what could be done.[45] These events focused on creating dialogues around the struggles that exist within a society that often values and rewards dominance. A Post-Gender Men's Group was created in order to address issues around masculinity and harm, borne out of a public and very heavily attended discussion of how patriarchy hurts men.

Closing the Loop: Formerly Incarcerated Communities and Alt-J Systems

As a way to both allow for full representation in Alt-J systems and to transform harms done by CJS and the state, EN started to build community with individuals who served long sentences in the U.S. prison system.[46] These new community members revealed that finding ways to change the CJS and build alternative systems was vital to their recovery and empowerment. Since 2018, EN Alt-J experiments have been shaped by the contributions, expertise, and experiences of those who have been directly harmed by the CJS. EN has facilitated anti-violence training by formerly incarcerated individuals and encouraged dialogues between these experts and those who have caused harm but have not yet entered CJS.[47] Initially, these members were nonresidents due to the oppressive restrictions placed on formerly incarcerated individuals by the CJS, including parole requirements.[48] However, in January of 2019, EN launched its first transformational house where formerly incarcerated people live alongside community members who have not been incarcerated, and residents support community and individual transformation.

The Alternative Justices Project

Born out of initial conversations about Alt-J at EN in 2015, the Alternative Justices Project has become a hub for theory, praxis, and education about alternative justices.[49] The Alternative Justices Project now exists as part of District Commons, a community nonprofit, and supports individuals and communities across the world in creating, experimenting with, and developing alternative justices. Their work includes the creation of a transformation pod syllabus and tools created by those who have gone through Alt-J processes.

Future Objectives for EN

Based on their experimentation thus far, EN has begun working toward a number of further objectives. In 2022, alongside The Second Life Project, which grew from EN community-building with formerly incarcerated folks, EN is trying to launch its third transformational, parole-compliant residence. EN is also working toward finding a technical solution to make the Two-Strike Policy work for larger groups and is working to increase the number of Alt-J Stewards. As community members come and go, enthusiasm for Alt-J experimentation within EN has fluctuated, although Alt-J values and theory are generally accepted by most EN members and are often unprompted topics of conversation at several EN locations.

Conclusion

"The work to be done and the countless issues that this work
represents merely reflect the pervasiveness of our oppression."
—The Combahee River Collective Statement

Alt-J grew from explicit requests from communities who were unable to find sufficient alternatives to address harms that did not require police involvement or beginning a process of criminal justice. Alt-J can and does represent a fully autonomous alternative to CJS that refuses to be co-opted or incorporated by state systems, thus creating space for a plethora of independent justice systems to be created. Simultaneously, Alt-J allows for systems that work with or within current state systems to continue their transformation of those entities. Working in parallel, these approaches undermine harmful systems and work to dismantle the seemingly monolithic sociopolitical institutions operating within a larger framework of carceral liberalism. Alt-J alternatives not only provide ways of addressing specific harms and offering transformation and healing on an interpersonal level, but also provide material ways to resist the state's push for criminalization. To fully achieve these goals, Alt-J requires the dedicated labor of communities and individuals against the forces of capitalism, sexism, and white supremacy, both within and beyond themselves, alongside a commitment to decentralized, community-specific experiments and theories of harm transformation that explicitly seek to resist every form of criminalization and punishment.

Notes

Epigraph: Davis, *Abolition Democracy*, 20.

1. Broadly speaking, intentional communities are groups of people who seek to achieve a shared goal, often living together in a shared dwelling. Intentional communities can be synonymous with ecovillages and communes. For more, see the Foundation for Intentional Community (https://www.ic.org/) and Shenker, *Intentional Communities: Ideology and Alienation in Communal Societies*.

2. Gilmore, *Golden Gulag*, 7.

3. Office of the Inspector General, "Review of Federal Bureau of Prisons' Monitoring."

4. Davis, *Freedom Is a Constant Struggle*, 6.

5. Alexander, *The New Jim Crow*.

6. Wacquant, "From Slavery to Mass Incarceration."

7. Foucault, *Discipline and Punish*, 301.

8. Stanford SPARQ, "SPARQ Scientists Release Oakland Police Findings."

9. Davis, *Abolition Democracy*.

10. Combahee River Collective, "Combahee River Collective Statement," 264.

11. Gilmore, "What Is to Be Done?," 258.

12. Stemple and Meyer, "Sexual Victimization of Men in America."

13. Collins, *Black Sexual Politics*, chap. 7.

14. Coker, "Transformative Justice," 131.

15. Sarkar and Sarkar, "Sexual Assault on Woman."

16. Fischel, *Sex and Harm*; Armatta, "Ending Sexual Violence."

17. Sierra, "Las Mujeres Indígenas."

18. GSA Network, "GSA Statement in Support of Restorative Approaches."

19. Combahee River Collective, "Combahee River Collective Statement"; Movement for Black Lives, "Vision for Black Lives."

20. British Columbia Law Institute Project Committee, "Civil Remedies for Sexual Assault."

21. Nocella, "Overview of History and Theory."

22. Zehr, *Changing Lenses*; Zehr, *Little Book of Restorative Justice*; Claassen, "Restorative Justice Principles."

23. Nocella, "Overview of History and Theory"; Derby, *Restorative Justice*, "Section 1: What Is Restorative Justice?"

24. Zehr, *Changing Lenses*, 161.

25. Jha, *Transforming Communities*, 46.

26. Nocella, "Transforming Justice and Hip Hop," 216.

27. Nocella, 216.

28. Nocella, "Overview of History and Theory"; Nocella, "Transforming Justice and Hip Hop"; Coker, "Transformative Justice"; Generation Five, "Transformative Justice"; Morris, *Stories of Transformative Justice*.

29. Nocella, "Transforming Justice and Hip Hop," 216.

30. Ferrell, "Against the Law."

31. Ruth-Heffelbower, "Anarchist Criminology," 2.

32. McKinney, "Anarchist Theory of Criminal Justice," 4.

33. McKinney.

34. Ruth-Heffelbower, "Anarchist Criminology"; Ferrell, "Against the Law"; McKinney, "Anarchist Theory of Criminal Justice."

35. Walgrave, "La Justice Restaurative."

36. Brown, "Emergent Strategy."

37. Brown, "We Will Not Cancel Us."

38. Agnew, "Alternative Justices: Shared Critiques."

39. https://embassynetwork.com.

40. hooks, *Feminist Theory*; Cox, "Actually its cisnormative"; Combahee River Collective, "Combahee River Collective Statement."

41. Red Victorian, "Vision and Mission"; Embassy SF, "Our Accountable Space Policy."

42. Elizabeth, "Community Information Sharing."

43. Elizabeth, "Alternative Justice Procedures for Conflict."

44. Embassy Network, "Consent Culture Salon."

45. Embassy Network, "Consent Confessional."

46. Agnew, "Second Life at the Embassy."

47. Embassy Network, "Mindful Communication and Conflict Resolution Workshop."

48. Division of Adult Parole Operations, "Parole Conditions."

49. https://www.alternativejustices.com.

Bibliography

Agnew, Zarinah. "Second Life at the Embassy." Medium. 2017. https://medium.com/embassy-network/second-life-e862ad6ae519.

———. "Alternative Justices: Shared Critiques." Medium. January 19, 2018. https://medium.com/the-alternative-justices-project/.

Alexander, Michelle. *The New Jim Crow: Mass Incarceration in the Age of Colorblindness.* New York: New Press, 2012.

Armatta, Judith. "Ending Sexual Violence through Transformative Justice." *Interdisciplinary Journal of Partnership Studies* 5, no. 1 (2018), article 4.

British Columbia Law Institute Project Committee on Civil Remedies for Sexual Assault. "Civil Remedies for Sexual Assault." BCLI report no. 14. June 2001. https://www.bcli.org/project/civil-remedies-sexual-assault/.

Brown, Adrienne. *Emergent Strategy.* Edinburgh: AK Press, 2017.

———. *We Will Not Cancel Us: And Other Dreams of Transformative Justice.* Edinburgh: AK Press, 2020.

Claassen, Ron. "Restorative Justice Principles and Evaluation Continuums." Paper presented at National Center for Peacemaking and Conflict Resolution, Fresno Pacific College, May 1995.

Coker, Donna. "Transformative Justice: Anti-Subordination Processes in Cases of Domestic Violence." In *Restorative Justice and Family Violence*, edited by Heather Strang and John Braithwaite, 128–52. Cambridge: Cambridge University Press, 2002.

Collins, Patricia Hill. *Black Sexual Politics.* New York: Routledge, 2004.

Combahee River Collective. "The Combahee River Collective Statement." In *Home Girls: A Black Feminist Anthology*, edited by Barbara Smith, 264–65. New Brunswick, NJ: Rutgers University Press, 2000.

Cox, Laverne. "Actually its cisnormative heteronormative imperialist white supremacist capitalist patriarchy my spin on @bellhooks." Twitter, November 14, 2015, 10:21 a.m. Accessed August 9, 2016. https://twitter.com/Lavernecox/status/665595357288640513.

Critical Resistance and Incite! "Critical Resistance-INCITE! Statement on Gender Violence and the Prison-Industrial Complex." *Social Justice* 30, no. 3 (2003): 141–51.

Davis, Angela Y. *Abolition Democracy: Beyond Empire, Prisons, and Torture.* New York: Seven Stories Press, 2005.

———. *Freedom Is a Constant Struggle: Ferguson, Palestine, and the Foundations of a Movement.* Chicago: Haymarket Books, 2016.

Derby, Jonathan. *Restorative Justice: Principles and Practice.* Prison Fellowship International, 2021. https://restorativejustice.org/resources/restorative-justice-handbook/.

Division of Adult Parole Operations. "Parole Conditions." California Department of Corrections and Rehabilitation. Accessed September 9, 2018. https://www.cdcr.ca.gov/parole/parole-conditions/.

Elizabeth, Autumn. "An Alternative Justice Procedures for Community Conflict Transformation." Medium. July 28, 2017. https://medium.com/the-alternative-justices-project/.

———. "Community Information Sharing and the Issue of Privacy." Medium. July 19, 2018. https://medium.com/the-alternative-justices-project/.

Embassy Network. "Consent Culture Salon." 2015. https://zarinahagnew.gitbooks.io/transformative-justice-and-accountable-spaces/content/altj-events/consent-culture-salon.html.

———. "Consent Confessional." 2018. https://zarinahagnew.gitbooks.io/transformative-justice-and-accountable-spaces/content/altj-events/consent-confessional.html.

———. "Mindful Communication and Conflict Resolution Workshop (Run by Formerly Incarcerated Community)." 2018. https://zarinahagnew.gitbooks.io/transformative-justice-and-accountable-spaces/content/altj-events/antiviolence-training.html.

Embassy SF. "Our Accountable Space Policy." Embassy Network. Accessed July 10, 2018. https://embassynetwork.com/locations/embassysf/accountablespace/.

Ferrell, Jeff. "Against the Law: Anarchist Criminology." *Social Anarchism* no. 25 (1998): 5–15.

Fischel, Joseph J. *Sex and Harm in the Age of Consent*. Minneapolis: University of Minnesota Press, 2016.

Foucault, Michel. *Discipline and Punish: The Birth of the Prison*. Second ed. New York: Vintage Books, 1995.

Generation Five. "Transformative Justice." Accessed April 15, 2018. http://www.generationfive.org/the-issue/transformative-justice/.

Gilmore, Ruth Wilson. *Golden Gulag: Prisons, Surplus, Crisis, and Opposition in Globalizing California*. Berkeley: University of California Press, 2007.

———. "What Is to Be Done?" *American Quarterly* 63, no. 2 (2011): 245–65.

GSA Network. "GSA Network Statement in Support of Restorative Approaches to School Discipline." 2013. https://gsanetwork.org/news/gsa-network-statement-support-restorative-approaches-school-discipline/100213.

hooks, bell. *Feminist Theory: From Margin to Center*. Boston: South End Press, 1984.

Jha, Sandhya Rani. *Transforming Communities*. Saint Louis: Chalice Press, 2017.

McKinney, Coy. "An Anarchist Theory of Criminal Justice." Anarchist Library. May 2012. https://theanarchistlibrary.org/library/coy-mckinney-an-anarchist-theory-of-criminal-justice.

Morris, Ruth. *Stories of Transformative Justice*. Toronto: Canadian Scholars' Press, 2000.

Movement for Black Lives. "A Vision for Black Lives." August 2016. https://m4bl.org/policy-platforms/.

Nocella, Anthony J., II. "An Overview of the History and Theory of Transformative Justice." *Peace and Conflict Review* 6, no. 1 (2011): 1–10.

———. "Transforming Justice and Hip Hop Activism in Action." *Counterpoints* 453,

From Education to Incarceration: Dismantling the School-to-Prison Pipeline (2014): 210–23.

Office of the Inspector General. "Review of the Federal Bureau of Prisons' Monitoring of Contract Prisons." U.S. Department of Justice. August 2016. https://oig.justice.gov/reports/2016/e1606.pdf.

Red Victorian. "Vision and Mission." Embassy Network. Accessed January 5, 2018. http://embassynetwork.com/locations/redvic/vision/.

Ruth-Heffelbower, Duane. "Anarchist Criminology: A New Way to Understand a Set of Proven Practices." Paper presented at the annual meeting of the Academy of Criminal Justice Sciences, Toronto, March 2011.

Sarkar, N. N., and Rina Sarkar. "Sexual Assault on Woman: Its Impact on Her Life and Living in Society." *Sexual and Relationship Therapy* 20, no. 4 (2005): 407–19.

Shenker, Barry. *Intentional Communities: Ideology and Alienation in Communal Societies*. London: Taylor and Francis, 2011.

Sierra, María Teresa. "Las Mujeres Indígenas Ante La Justicia Comunitaria: Perspectivas Desde La Interculturalidad y Los Derechos." *Desacatos* 31 (2009): 73–96.

Stanford SPARQ. "SPARQ Scientists Release Oakland Police Findings." Stanford University. June 15, 2016. https://sparq.stanford.edu/opd-reports.

Stemple, Lara, and Ilan H. Meyer. "The Sexual Victimization of Men in America: New Data Challenges Old Assumptions." *American Journal of Public Health* 104, no. 6 (2014): 19–26.

Wacquant, Loïc. "From Slavery to Mass Incarceration: Rethinking the 'Race Question' in the US." *New Left Review* 13 (Jan/Feb 2002): 41–60.

Walgrave, Lode. "La Justice Restaurative: À La Recherche d'une Théorie et d'un Programme." *Criminologie* 32, no. 1 (1999): 7.

Zehr, Howard. *Changing Lenses: Restorative Justice for Our Times*. Herald Press, 2015.

———. *The Little Book of Restorative Justice: Revised and Updated*. Skyhorse Publishing, 2015.

8

Going Carceral

Analyzing Written and Visual Representations of Prison Yoga Programs

TRIA BLU WAKPA AND JENNIFER MUSIAL

Introduction

Yoga is a popular but often exclusionary practice, especially when taught in studios or retreats. Convinced that yoga offers physical, psychological, and spiritual benefits, some teachers have sought to make the practice more accessible by offering classes in alternate spaces like parks, community centers, and retirement homes. In this chapter, we examine prison yoga programs, which bring yoga to another underserved group. Since U.S. prisons are frequently located in remote areas and regulate outsider access and/or information about their operations, mainstream narratives about prison, such as the ones under examination here, shape public opinion about the carceral system and those within it. The authors ask, what politics undergird representations of prison yoga programs?

To answer this, we examine a 2011 three-part series about prison yoga that ran on *Elephant Journal*, a popular digital media site dedicated to mindfulness. This series features articles titled "Do Prisoners Deserve Yoga?," "Know about Yoga and Meditation for Incarcerated and At-Risk Youth?," and "Yoga at San Quentin: Prisoner Interviews and Photos." All of the articles were written by Anneke Lucas, the founder of Liberation Prison Yoga, and the first and third articles mentioned include images of incarcerated men doing yoga by celebrated photographer Robert Sturman.

Building on Shari Huhndorf's framework of "going native,"[1] we offer the term "going carceral" to describe how mainstream prison yoga programs reaffirm dominant racial, gender, and class hierarchies. In *Going Native: Indians in the American Cultural Imagination* (2001), Huhndorf highlights how European American/White settlers in the United States have constructed racial and gender identities in relationship to non-Native representations of Indigenous peoples in a way that supports U.S. settler colonialism. In the book, "going native" can refer to a fantasy in which a colonizer (frequently a European American male) is granted insider access to an Indigenous society, which allows him to interact with, perform, and surpass the Native Other, thereby conveying White supremacy. The fantasy is frequently short-lived as a result of Indigenous people's supposedly inevitable and self-inflicted demise caused by their inability to adapt to modernity. In contrast, the protagonist—now well-versed in Native and White worlds—has no option but to return to European American society, which, unlike Indigenous peoples and nations, is equated with modernity and futurity. The imagined absence of Native peoples allows the European American/White male to become the beneficiary of the Indigenous land without acknowledging his complicity in Native genocide, which supports U.S. settler desires.

Huhndorf's "going native" is a useful framework to understand some narratives written by outsiders about U.S. carceral institutions. Such institutions are a product of settler colonialism and disproportionately imprison Indigenous peoples and people of color. In conversation with Huhndorf's "going native," we offer "going carceral" as a way to understand the encounter between an outsider, colonizing figure (often depicted as a European American/White person) and an incarcerated figure within the prison. Articles on prison yoga programs illustrate the connections between "going native" and "going carceral." In these articles and the photographs that accompany them, European American or White-coded outsiders—writers, photographers, and teachers—enter the racialized environment of the prison and emerge as heroic and benevolent individuals. Historically and contemporarily, the heteronormative—read White, male—photographic gaze, often misinterpreted as objective "truth," has been integral to promoting the project of U.S. settler colonialism.[2] Written and visual outsider representations have often detrimentally affected Indigenous people, people of color, and incarcerated people.[3] By focusing on the imprisoned individual and his need for reformation—in part through the "civilizing" project of yoga and *not* addressing the system of the prison industrial complex or questions of yoga access and depictions—these representations reify the exclusion, invisibilization, and/or typecasting of people who are imprisoned and conceal the ways that the outsiders are implicated in and profit from carceral violence. As Shreerekha Pillai underscores in the introduction to this book with her concept of "carceral liberalism," "in so many ways, liberal notions of carcerality flow from the colonial logic of imperial machinery institutionalized under the cloak of civilizing missions that include uplift, education, conversion, and other 'liberal' tasks that act as alibi for the violence of the colonial apparatus."[4] "Going carceral" describes how these mainstream narratives about prison yoga programs attempt to rectify the injustices of imprisonment but end up obscuring and fortifying the violence that the carceral system enacts.

In the prison yoga program narratives that we examine, "going carceral" may stem from mainstream concerns about the inefficiency, ineffectiveness, and injustice of the carceral system. Settler colonialism attempts to eclipse imprisoned people and their circumstances like it tries to obscure Native peoples and issues, so that these peoples and topics do not constitute a crisis. Scholars call the neglect of populations like people who are incarcerated and Indigenous peoples "social death," which requires imagining these populations are "out of sight" and therefore "out of mind."[5] Settler colonialism creates the conditions for social death in part because the situations—or crises—of incarcerated and Indigenous peoples can undermine "American exceptionalism" and U.S. authority. Yet, historically and contemporarily, social death and social control vis-à-vis detention centers are fundamental to the ongoing project of U.S. settler colonialism. As Pillai argues, "Carceral liberalism, unlike the more prevalent and commonly invoked idioms of western life, freedom, liberty, and justice, undergirds the union in the United States."[6]

Settler colonial narratives sometimes invoke Indigenous and incarcerated peoples, but in a stereotypical manner and/or for outsider interests and/or identities. For example, in the carceral context, Dylan Rodriguez articulates that in response to mass incarceration, liberals and right-wingers alike have championed reform agendas aimed at fixing the unjust carceral system.[7] This is also evidenced by Lucas's prison yoga program articles, which offer yoga as a solution to the overrepresentation of people of color in carceral facilities as well as their economic strain on society. However, the problem with this logic is that the prison industrial complex is itself a symptom of an unjust system.[8]

"Going native" and "going carceral" reinforce dominant structures of power. In a contemporary context, "going native" positions Native peoples as superior to European Americans.[9] For example, the New Age movement romanticizes Native peoples and hence "goes native in its quest for solutions" to social crises such as "environmental destruction, spiritual bankruptcy, and rampant health problems," which arise out of settler colonialism to begin with.[10] New Agers likewise appropriate yoga as the antidote to modern

168   BLU WAKPA AND MUSIAL

Western problems. In contrast to the ways that New Agers frequently romanticize Native peoples, cultures, and yoga, we find that in "going carceral" the White writers, photographers, and teachers do not perceive that incarcerated people can offer answers to societal problems. This is likely because without a structural analysis, imprisoned people are viewed as flawed and fallen with few redeeming qualities. When a structural critique is absent, incarcerated people emerge as "spiritually bankrupt" and, because of their race, class, and social location, are more likely to experience "rampant health problems" and hail from areas of "environmental destruction," caused by settler colonialism.[11] In this misguided framing, the incarcerated person purportedly cannot offer "solutions" to modern Western crises. Yet Whitewashed yoga—a practice with Indigenous roots from another continent—can supposedly save the West and its institutions, particularly when benevolently offered by European American instructors. Because in these articles yoga is codified as White and imprisoned people as non-White, while claiming to (re)solve injustice, "going carceral" actually (re)settles the system.

Like Lucas, we, the authors—as scholars, activists, and yoga teachers—are also complicit in the interlocking settler colonial, capitalist, and carceral systems and benefit economically, socially, and culturally from our engagement with the prison and yoga industrial complexes, as evidenced in part by the publication of this article. We have also completed yoga trainings aimed at teaching yoga in carceral contexts and combined have over a decade of experience teaching yoga to people who are imprisoned. Although as a form of "carceral liberalism," yoga programs for incarcerated people can extend the longevity of prisons by making institutions that perpetuate social death appear to be humane, even benevolent, we also cannot overlook the material benefits that these yoga programs provide. For example, as Demita Frazier articulates in this book's foreword, programming inside prisons can offer people who are incarcerated opportunities for "creative expression" and "mitigate [their] isolation."[12] We live these tensions and contradictions—even as we grapple with them—which also allow the violences of settler colonialism and its institutions to thrive.

Settler Colonial Crises and the Convergence of the Prison and Yoga Industrial Complexes

According to Huhndorf, "going native" narratives serve two primary aims: to "resolve widespread ambivalence about modernity as well as anxieties about the terrible violence marking the nation's origins."[13] In both the Native and carceral contexts, dominant discourses imagine state-sanctioned violence as relegated to the past. As Michel Foucault famously articulates, the prison enhances state power by ending public torture and/or execution.[14] Foucault underscores that these public performances of state power have the potential to garner the people's sympathy for the convicted and hence turn them against the state.[15] He emphasizes that regardless of the rhetoric, the creation of prisons does not result from the people's desire for more humane forms of punishment; rather, the sovereign's concern was that their participation might lead to "disorder."[16] Likewise, today, mainstream narratives often overlook the ongoing violence that the carceral system inflicts, including torture (for example, solitary confinement), premature death, and genocide. Prisons largely disappear the incarcerated people who inhabit them and severely curtail their voices, hallmarks of social death, because they have the power to illuminate the injustices of settler colonialism, thereby challenging "American exceptionalism" and, by extension, U.S. authority. In terms of human rights, the carceral crisis—again, like that of Indigenous peoples—largely disappears before it is articulated.[17]

Settler colonialism, intertwined with capitalism, creates crises that impact humans, other animals, and our environment, all of which Indigenous epistemologies understand as interrelated.[18] Yet because settler colonialism creates racial, gender, and class hierarchies, vulnerable groups are often more detrimentally impacted by such crises. Tracing the ways that "certain kinds of people, land, capital, and state capacity became idle," thereby contributing to the rise of mass incarceration in California, Ruth Wilson Gilmore writes, "Crisis means instability that can be fixed only through radical measures, which include developing new relationships and new or renovated institutions out of what already exists."[19] The prison industrial complex constitutes one such "radical measure." According to Angela Y. Davis, the term *prison-industrial complex,* has been strategic, designed precisely to resonate with the term *military-industrial complex* to highlight how these interconnected complexes profit from inflicting violence while draining social resources.[20] Davis cites the overrepresentation of young people of color in the military to escape the structural oppression that frequently leads to incarceration as evidence of the "symbiotic relationship of the military and the prison."[21] Given the ways that settler colonialism oppresses all non-dominant groups, but in particular seeks to annihilate Indigenous peoples,[22] it is perhaps no surprise that Native peoples are per capita the largest ethnic group in the U.S. military[23] and represent a rising prison population disproportionate to the total U.S. population.[24]

While Native and incarcerated people endure ongoing and often unacknowledged crises caused by settler colonialism, outsider portrayals also construct them in complicated and contradictory ways that support settler colonial aims, complexes, and institutions on structural and individual levels. Luana Ross writes that "crucial to understanding Native criminality is knowledge of the disruptive events brought about by assimilationist, racist policy and prohibitive legislation mandated by federal, state, and municipal governments. These policies and accompanying criminal statutes were concerned with cultural genocide and control" of Indigenous peoples and nations.[25] The abolitionist organization Critical Resistance specifies that dominant typecasts are integral to the prison industrial complex because they mark people as nonnormative, "criminal, delinquent, or deviant," and therefore perpetuate the notion that incarceration is necessary for societal safety.[26] In the prison yoga program portrayals that we examine, incarcerated people are typecast in similar ways but possess at least some redeemable qualities, which, with the right/White coaching, can be sublimated into yoga—again, a practice that is problematically conceived of in this context as White. Appropriated and subsumed into Whiteness, the philosophy and practice of yoga can supposedly solve the inefficiency and ineffectiveness of the carceral system and, moreover, solidify White supremacy and individual identities configured in contradistinction to imprisoned people.

Yoga is also an "industrial complex," which interconnects with the prison industrial complex and, in doing so, helps to extend the prison industrial complex's "life or scope."[27] The yoga industrial complex emerges out of the intersections between capitalism, cultural appropriation, healthism, White supremacy, gentrification, and gendered sizeism.[28] Like "going native" stories, the yoga industrial complex arose to resolve anxieties about modernity—the stress of global capitalism is eased by *asana*; fear of multiculturalism is solved through cultural appropriation and gentrification under the guise of cultural "appreciation"; declining participation in organized religion is settled through panspiritual practices; neoliberal expectations to be healthy are ironed out through a disciplined wellness regime, and so on. In this way, yoga functions as a panacea.

Scholars argue that yoga is an intersection of heterogeneous South Asian spiritual practices and Indigenous knowledges that were prohibited by the British before being modified to suit postcolonial Indian nation-building.[29] Yoga's complicated cultural history is forsaken through the yoga industrial complex where it is distilled into a postural practice.[30] While ancestral practices are winnowed into *asana*, South Asian bodies are "invisible and yet hyper visible" in yoga spaces, leading to microaggressional racism.[31] Lakshmi Nair explains, "When my Indian body entered a yoga space, I was either greeted with googly eyes as if I were the Goddess Lakshmi Herself descended from the heavens and any words I uttered were instantly magical or profound OR I was greeted with defensiveness as if my presence made people feel they had to prove their knowledge of Sanskrit, yoga, and all things Indian."[32] Likewise, when Punam Mehta shared her childhood experience of Jain camp during yoga teacher-training, "The teacher responded quite negatively by rolling her eyes and totally ignoring my experience, which made me feel awkward and uncomfortable in my own brown skin."[33] These examples show how "whiteness spreads tentacles into yoga so as to absorb, own, and feed off of it."[34] White supremacy and colonial appropriation make it possible to dehistoricize, depoliticize, and deracialize yoga while at the same time remaining uncomfortable with actual brown bodies.

Huhndorf's "going native" offers insight into how a practice once lambasted as charlatan mysticism is recuperated as India's export to the West, where it is taken up by privileged White people who can then "offer" it to mostly non-White incarcerated peoples. Here, privileged subjects dive into yoga through *asana* practice and/or a teacher training; they may even seek out an "authentic" teacher by traveling to India to encounter the Native informant. Now minimally trained, they become yoga teachers who can build their empire by branding their approach to *asana* and opening yoga schools of their own: they become experts who proclaim their brand can heal twenty-first-century bodies that are afflicted with problems "old-fashioned" yogis could not have foreseen. Traditional South Asian models of yoga teaching involve a guru and a sannyasin, with the sannyasin devoting their lifetime to studying with a guru: the student might never become a teacher, might teach only after the death of their guru, or might teach only if their guru calls them to do so. The yoga industrial complex speeds this up significantly, sometimes even forgoing an expectation that teacher trainees have a required number of practice hours before embarking on a teacher training program. This is how the yoga industrial complex "ultimately replicates exploitative colonial relationships and perpetuates spiritual neocolonization of the practice"[35] while participating in late capitalism. When put through the sieve of White supremacy and colonial domination, yoga becomes a decontextualized gift that teachers can inherit and give back through *seva* (oft-translated as "selfless service"). Incarcerated peoples are one example of *seva* recipients.

Researching Prison Yoga
Program Representations

This chapter analyzes representations of prison yoga through a three-part series for *Elephant Journal*. We chose articles written by Anneke Lucas, creator of Liberation Prison Yoga. Two of the three articles were paired with photographs by Robert Sturman, a reputable artist known for capturing the beauty of *asana*. Lucas and Sturman purport to counter stereotypes about incarcerated people by finding beauty in prison. Knowing their benevolent intentions, we conduct a close reading of the articles and images. Foucauldian discourse analysis serves as our research method because there is no neutral "truth" about incarcerated people; rather, meaning is constructed through individualized factors (that is, the social locations of the authors, prison yoga teachers, and incarcerated yoga practitioners) and structural forces (that is, the prison industrial complex, histories of representation, White supremacy, colonial knowledge practices, and so forth). Therefore, we are attentive to the historical context underpinning this series. In the tradition of Foucauldian inquiry, we ask "whom does the discourse [about prison yoga] serve?"[36] We chose not to include Sturman's images in this essay. We were concerned that replicating the photographs might invite the same fetishizing gaze that we critique. The images are freely available online for those who wish to view them.

The site of study informs how prison yoga is framed and reveals a lot about the intended audience. The series was published by *Elephant Journal*, a website that produces content that "helps us to live a good life that also happens to be good for others, and our planet."[37] *Elephant Journal* is a fitting publication for these articles because they appeal to readers who are interested in cultivating and curating good karma. These stories may be received as a passive "feel good story" or readers may actively donate to existing programs; they may even participate in a prison yoga teacher training. However, readers of the prison yoga series are encouraged to feel rather than critically think or reflect despite the website's advertising as a space devoted to contemplation. Readers' feelings are mediated by their social location and access to privilege: a White, thin, upper middle class, cisgender woman reader, the average yoga lifestyle consumer,[38] is more likely to relate to the yoga teachers and photographer quoted in these stories than the incarcerated men and boys depicted, most of whom are tattooed, strong-looking, and/or non-White. Thus, as we argue next, the series invites a fetishizing gaze of Othered bodies.

Dylan Rodriguez contends that early prison regimes were designed to teach White men how to reintegrate into an emerging capitalist society as a "productive law-abiding citizen."[39] Later, nineteenth-century reformers theorized that a conscious choice to engage in criminality was the real problem, not ignorance of correct legal behavior. Reformers set out to remedy the souls of incarcerated individuals through a moral education.[40] Yoga is like prison in this respect: both are designed to discipline one into healthier choices based

8. Going Carceral   173

on virtue rather than vice. Placed within the history of prison philanthropy, outlined by Rodriguez, prison yoga operates as a civilizing apparatus where privileged yoga teachers (most of whom are White) enter the racialized space of the prison to preach the gospel of mindfulness to reorient unruly bodies to control themselves. The *Elephant Journal* series ends up reifying stereotypes about prisoners as deviant, bad choice-makers while depicting prison yoga teachers as heroic saviors. It is through prison yoga that prisoners can find redemption, moving from deviant to noble savage. Indeed, as Gayatri Spivak illuminates, the white savior trope functions as the colonizer's attempt to justify colonial intervention, often by purporting to rescue Indigenous peoples and people of color from themselves.[41] Little attention to how systemic oppression sustains carcerality results in a three-part series that parrots some of the same discourses used by the prison industrial complex.

Encountering and Typecasting Imprisoned People

The encounter narrative is present in writings about prison yoga. Sturman's comments portray the photographer as a brave figure who enters the violent, even deadly prison environment but is surprised to find enthusiastic students. Setting the tone for Sturman's supposedly courageous expedition in "Do Prisoners Deserve Yoga?," Lucas writes, "When photographer/artist Robert Sturman received an invitation to come and take photos by warden Ms. Salinas of Deuel Vocational Institution, DVI, a reception center in Tracy, California, he felt ready." The statement that Sturman "felt ready" implies that the photographer faces a challenge. Lucas continues,

> Judgment at a distance translates to fear up close. Inside the cage, Robert Sturman was briefly confronted with his own fears when he had each prisoner sign a release form. "As I was squatting down and talking and giving them the pen to sign," he says, "I realized that every time I'm giving someone a pen I'm giving them a weapon that they can jab in my throat. But after that I thought: 'Okay, no more *Oz!* No more *Dexter!* Too much television!' I took a few breaths, and got over that stuff."[42]

Sturman acknowledges that his fears about the encounter are framed by media. Left unacknowledged is the fact that prisons are highly regulated environments—perhaps even more so in spaces and situations that allow volunteers to interact with people who are incarcerated—and Sturman has gained cultural, economic, and social capital from the photographs he has captured there.[43]

Assumptions about individual men parallel Sturman's fear about the violence of prison environments. For example, Sturman says,

> I was a little startled when I came face to face with someone who had eight teardrops tattooed on his face. In the gang world each teardrop represents a murder, and that threw me, but it passed quickly. He was actually the most responsive student, and spoke eloquently about how peaceful he felt from doing yoga. It was a beautiful experience. I realized that these men went astray for whatever reason, let their anger elevate to an uncontrollable level that is punishable and not okay in our world, but it's the same kind of warrior energy and intelligence that, if directed properly, produces something entirely respectable and productive.[44]

In this passage, Sturman recognizes then rejects the vilification of incarcerated people, which the prison industrial complex perpetuates through its creation and circulation of stereotypical representations. Although Sturman can "[take] a few breaths, and [get] over"[45] the violent images that he conjured, people who are currently and formerly imprisoned often cannot easily escape such stereotyping. Though likely unintended, Sturman's fantasy about the prison reads people—the majority of whom are non-White—in scripted ways informed by colonial histories. This typecasting—which reinforces damaging stereotypes about incarcerated people as violent, frightening, and in need of rescue—is a common feature of the *Elephant Journal* series. Sturman also positions people who are imprisoned as diametrically opposed to humans who are "respectable and productive" and assumes that their incarceration is a result of their "anger."[46] Further, by linking "respectable" with "productive," Sturman implies that successful participation in the capitalist system is the primary metric by which he deems a person "respectable."[47]

Lucas's narratives typecast imprisoned people as violent, childish, and/or nonnormative. Representing Indigenous people, people of color, and in this case, people who are imprisoned as nonnormative is a settler colonial strategy that attempts to justify state-sanctioned intervention. "Yoga at San Quentin" opens with three men confessing to their role in homicide. This narrative hook not only perpetuates stereotypes of people who are incarcerated, but also is irrelevant and unnecessary to discussing the prison yoga program. Likewise, "Know about Yoga and Meditation for Incarcerated and At-Risk Youth?" begins with an excerpt from a film in which a young man states, "Personally, I'm a little violent."[48] In "Do Prisoners Deserve Yoga?," Lucas pathologizes and infantilizes people who are incarcerated in a muddled, generalized, and unfounded claim about the relationships between them and their parents. She writes, "Inmates are finely attuned to all nuances of vilification. Possibly, this kind of transference is at the root of the psychological problems that landed them in jail in the first place. 'Being bad' may be a childish way to protect a parent's skewed perception of them."[49] Indeed, with very little proof, Lucas reinforces the notion that the deviant individual is entirely to blame for their imprisonment. Since many do not question carcerality and may even believe that incarcerated people should experience prison as a cruel, austere environment, the article's title is troubling. When posed as a question, "Do Prisoners Deserve Yoga?," *Elephant Journal* fortifies the idea that yoga is a luxury, which invites the critique that incarcerated peoples are not worthy of the privilege of practice.

Children are also depicted as potentially deviant in "Know about Yoga and Meditation for Incarcerated and At-Risk Youth?"[50] Writing about Black and Latino young men, Victor Rios argues that terms such as "at-risk" are problematic because such labels "stigmatize [the youth], and, in turn, their delinquency persists or increases. In the era of mass incarceration, labeling is also a process by which agencies of social control further stigmatize and mark the boys in response to their original label."[51] Under settler colonialism and capitalism, what counts as deviant is not only socially constructed, but also more likely to be configured as non-White by the settler colonial state and its institutions such as schools and prisons. Lucas states, "An increasing number of yoga teachers are going into secure detention centers and organizations for at-risk youth all around the country to try and teach these kids yoga and meditation, to help them respond calmly to situations that might otherwise end in violence."[52] This statement suggests an implicit racial bias because "at-risk" is frequently coded as non-White, and Lucas implies that the youths' families have not taught them to behave in a socially appropriate manner, which a yoga teacher (frequently depicted as European American/White) can supposedly remedy. Further evidence of pathologizing families appears in Lucas's writing about Bart Van Melik, a yoga and meditation teacher to youth in detention centers, who says, "Whatever brought them there has so much to do with their condition and environment."[53] In this passage, Van Melik highlights the way conditions that are outside of youths' control led to their imprisonment. However, he blames the youths' "condition and environment" rather than recognizing how structures of oppression have not only shaped those "condition[s] and environment[s]" in the first place, but also "severely restrict people's options and decision-making abilities," what Tria Blu Wakpa has termed "social confinement."[54]

Like the term "at-risk," the reference to a nonnormative "condition and environment" is frequently coded as non-White and often not contextualized within systems of power. Conversely, Patricia Hill Collins refers to Black youth as "at risk" because of the ways that dominant discourses problematically portray them as "problems to their nation, to their local environments, to Black communities, and to themselves."[55] Collins notably attributes the supposed deficiencies in Black families' "condition[s] and environment[s]" to "new variations of the negative effects of colonialism, slavery, and traditional forms of racial rule."[56] Likewise, the concept of "social confinement" centers axes of oppression that limit individual agency, therefore critiquing post-racial and post-gender narratives and choice paradigms, which assume that incarcerated people have simply made "bad" choices without accounting for a lack of "good" options.[57]

Prison Yoga as a Civilizing Apparatus

Yoga complements the rehabilitative promise of incarceration, including offering important benefits for people who are imprisoned. Through *asana* and meditation, people who are incarcerated are invited to change their "destructive" behavior in favor of a more peaceful outlook. Interviews with prison yoga participants demonstrate the transformative nature of yoga practice. Kayla, who is framed as "at-risk" in the article "Know about Yoga and Meditation for Incarcerated and At-Risk Youth?," exalts the program: "Before learning yoga if I got angry I would hurt someone. So not only is my life saved but their life is saved from me."[58] This high praise is mirrored by men who practice yoga at San Quentin. Like Kayla, Ke reports that yoga helps with reactivity. He says, "13 years ago, I couldn't walk away from an argument without being violent. And I was afraid about change, and so wasn't open to it. Also, thinking about my actions, you know, like what I did, wasn't high on my list, but thinking about it helps me breathe, you know, like yoga does."[59] Nearly all of the incarcerated men say that yoga enhances mindfulness leading to nonattachment and, in turn, a sense of calm. Bilal says that he appreciates "the peace of mind and the serenity I get out of it. The serenity is very important and I started to utilize that. I started to really calm myself in different situations, just through the breathing that I learned from James [Fox, founder of the Prison Yoga Project]."[60] There are other affective benefits too: Robert says that yoga opened him up to compassion and empathy, while Stefan feels that yoga has helped him to process shame and guilt associated with criminalized behavior. We do not wish to diminish incarcerated people's positive experiences with yoga. An anti–prison industrial complex position supports people who are incarcerated in their efforts to survive this dehumanizing environment. After all, we want incarcerated people to feel ease and well-being in their daily lives. For these men, yoga is an essential tool for behavior modification, which simultaneously fits with the supposed goal of incarceration.

Carceral yoga is framed as a way to find liberation behind prison walls, but liberation is defined in secular-psycho-spiritual terms. From the prison yoga program articles alone, it is impossible to know what facilitators actually teach their students; there is no discussion of using yoga to reach the spiritual state of enlightenment in the *Elephant Journal* articles. The reason for this may be two-fold: first, as we have argued, the yoga industrial complex decouples yoga from its South Asian history and spiritual practice. Instead, what may be offered to prison yoga students emerges from a secular (deracialized as brown and reracialized as White and dehistoricized) perspective. Second, it is possible that prison yoga teachers think yoga philosophy and spirituality is too esoteric for their students, perhaps underestimating their intelligence.

Within this *Elephant Journal* series, yoga—again, often equated with Whiteness—offers the means to civilize even the most savage individuals. Sturman's "beautiful experience" photographing men who have "warrior energy and intelligence"[51] is reminiscent of the "noble savage" present in many colonial narratives. As Huhndorf articulates, "noble" and "savage" are "in many respects, two sides of the same coin. Each one serves as a means of defining Western identities (either individual or collective) against an other, figured alternatively as superior or inferior to oneself."[62] In contrast to the "going native" trope, in "going carceral," the portrayals of people who are imprisoned do not configure them as superior to yoga photographers or teachers. Instead, the people who are imprisoned achieve "nobility" through the practice of yoga provided to them through prison yoga, which prefigures the program facilitator as a benevolent hero or savior figure.

The Superior Yoga Photographer/Teacher in the Carceral Context

The prison yoga series positions the typically male photographer or teacher as the heroic protagonist while obfuscating unequal power dynamics between those who are incarcerated and those who are not, which reinforces the superiority of the European American or White-coded outsider. In supposedly "fixing" the carceral crisis by offering yoga, the yoga teacher emerges as a savior of sorts. Blu Wakpa proposes the framework of "fixing"—drawing on denotations of the word itself—to describe the ways that settler colonial strategies have attempted to control, repair, and sterilize Native bodies, and conversely, Indigenous people's reconfiguring of these projects to perpetuate and innovate their Native cultural and national identities.[63] Similarly, by "going carceral," yoga programs and teachers in settler colonial institutions purport to "fix" the inadequate care and training that people who are incarcerated have received from their families and communities, while people who are imprisoned "fix" the meanings of the practice to meet their own interests. Because the embodied and visual realms are fluid, the written narratives about prison yoga programs help to situate the photographs and the practice, but for what purposes?

A return to Bart Van Melik's statements illustrates the troubling savior complex at work. Van Melik tells Lucas that his "greatest challenge in his job is that sometimes what the kids share about their lives is so hard he wishes he could take them home with him."[64] Here, Van Melik assumes that by removing young people from their families and communities, he can improve their lives. With this comment, Van Melik configures his own identity as a benevolent teacher and superior caregiver by portraying himself in contradistinction to the youths' environment and, by proxy, their familial guardians. Based upon dominant depictions and the racial and class demographics of yoga practitioners and incarcerated youth, the underlying subtext is that Van Melik—as a yoga teacher—is White and middle class and therefore has access to a stable and healthy home, and the imprisoned youth are Indigenous people and people of color from economically impoverished areas. Furthermore, as history has revealed, removing Indigenous young people and young people of color from their communities and bringing them to live in assimilative environments is often not a kind gesture, but a violent, settler colonial strategy.

The final article in the series, "Yoga at San Quentin: Prisoner Interviews and Photos," strengthens the trope of the exceptional yoga teacher. Of the fifteen photographs, five include James Fox, founder of the largest training program, called the Prison Yoga Project.[65] In the first image, Fox practices alongside his students, suggesting that he is their equal. However, in the next photograph, Fox poses beside a student who is incarcerated; Fox embraces the man's shoulder and shakes his hand, which creates the impression that Fox is the figure of authority. In the third image depicting Fox, the men practice standing backbends; though pictured in the background of the photograph, Fox's black shirt contrasts with the white shirts that the incarcerated men wear. The final two images of Fox portray him kneeling while his students take Corpse Pose; again, the photograph suggests that Fox holds power that the other men do not. In Lucas's narrative and the accompanying images, Fox emerges as a benevolent teacher, mentor, and even spiritual leader. As Bilal Chatman states, "James is, I don't know how to really put James in words because I've never known anybody who's influenced me as he has. He's like

8. Going Carceral   179

my Iman [*sic*], like a preacher or a rabbi. I look at him as someone like that, because he's soothing and his voice is really good and he's very helpful."[66] Yet again, this narrative neglects the unequal power dynamics between those who are incarcerated and those who are not, teacher and student, and how the teacher/protagonist benefits from his participation in the prison industrial complex.

Building on bell hooks's concept of "eating the other," Amara Miller describes the ways that yoga reifies systems of privilege and oppression as "eating the other yogi." Miller writes, "In this way, the taker is able to engage in the politics of self-serving distinction, utilizing the appropriated culture to garner higher prestige or status unavailable to members of the non-dominant group."[67] The prison yoga photographer and/or teacher gains social, economic, and cultural capital from their supposedly selfless service to those whom dominant discourses represent as savage, forgotten, and disappeared. This is perhaps particularly true at a time when people depict their activism and volunteerism in online publications and on social media platforms for self-promotion. Demonstrating how one can profit from prison yoga programs, Lucas concludes "Know about Yoga and Meditation for Incarcerated and At-Risk Youth?" with this call to action: "If you are frustrated by the high rates of youth incarceration and the disproportionate confinement of racial minorities from low-income neighborhoods, consider a Teacher Training."[68] By surmising that the solution to imprisonment is to train more yoga teachers to offer yoga to economically impoverished, Indigenous youth, and youth of color, this statement again fails to address how systemic structures contribute to incarceration while bolstering the yoga industrial complex. Although yoga does possess the potential to alleviate some of the stresses that oppression and imprisonment produce, the practice alone—which again, is often not accessible to Indigenous people and people of color—cannot combat pervasive, systemic discrimination and other forms of violence.

In the prison yoga program articles, the (White or White-coded) yoga teacher is framed as a benevolent figure who understands carceral conditions, making them the ideal teacher for this population. The White or White-coded teacher stands out as special, unlike other White people, which supports a common refrain that not all White people are bad. For instance, the incarcerated men who participate in the yoga prison program rave about James Fox. Stefan Liebb, who Lucas describes as "the Jewish prisoner incarcerated for stabbing a man to death," states,

> Occasionally we have guest teachers, and maybe they're wonderful athletes in the way they do these asanas, but James is a wonderful teacher;

he teaches from his heart without ego. . [H]e is so patient and gentle in his approach, it guides me to what I need, so I feel really, really fortunate to have this teacher and have him teach me still. He's an example of yoga in the way he conducts himself. I feel like if he had been someone else I wouldn't have taken to yoga the way I have.[69]

In this excerpt, Liebb compliments James by comparing him to the guest teachers, whom Liebb views as less skilled. This creates the impression that there are good and bad yoga teachers—read White people—working within detention centers, and Fox is one of the good ones. One should question, how and what does Fox gain from his prison yoga programs and workshops? How might power structures and the carceral context (such as an upcoming parole hearing or a desire to maintain the yoga prison programming) influence how people who are incarcerated speak about him? And how might the construction of Fox's superior portrayal—particularly in comparison to Lucas's swift and stereotypical description of Liebb—bolster the prison and yoga industrial complexes, both of which uphold White privilege?

Neglect of a Systemic Analysis

There is little analysis of the carceral regime in the *Elephant Journal* series. Although Lucas includes information in the articles that evidences the material consequences of structural inequities, she either draws non-sequitur conclusions or offers no analysis whatsoever. For example, in "Know about Yoga and Meditation for Incarcerated and At-Risk Youth?" Lucas writes, "In the U.S., where black youth are four times as likely as their white peers to be incarcerated, this boy was lucky to be on the streets, merely at-risk. In New York, the only state in the nation that incarcerates 16-year-olds as adults, minors end up in the city's jail at Riker's Island awaiting adjudication for any offense, including misdemeanors."[70] Rikers Island is infamous for its "barbaric abuses," including gang and guard violence committed against youth and the implementation of solitary confinement for minors until 2014[71]—in some cases for up to 23 hours a day.[72] As previously discussed, "at-risk" is a term that connotes deviance; Black youth are not "lucky" to be racialized in this way. Racialization may lead to criminalization and imprisonment, and incarceration can have devastating and even deadly consequences, as illustrated by the death of Kalief Browder. Incarcerated at the age of sixteen for three years while awaiting trial, Browder endured approximately two of those years in solitary confinement, which caused enduring psychological trauma and led him to die by suicide in 2015.[73] Lucas does not comment on the violence of incarceration and in particular, the drawbacks of imprisoning young people with adults. Other missed opportunities to talk about injustice include one man serving a life sentence under California's Three Strikes sentencing law for three "drug related" offenses and another man earning eleven cents an hour while incarcerated.[74] As Robert Perkinson clarifies, the three strikes "statute's broad wording mandated protracted imprisonment for thousands of individuals convicted of relatively minor third felonies."[75] Furthermore, critical prison studies discourses often understand prison labor as a loophole to the Thirteenth Amendment's prohibition of slavery and involuntary servitude.[76]

A closer look at prison yoga advocacy in these articles uncovers a discourse that ultimately supports the prison industrial complex. When responding to whether prisoners deserve yoga, Sturman defends, "We are not trying to shorten this inmate's sentence."[77] He maintains that prison yoga offers personal transformation rather than a change to the material conditions of incarceration or large-scale sociopolitical change. Prison therapist and yoga teacher Swapan Munshi's comments further bolster Sturman's assertion, again revealing how yoga can strengthen the prison industrial complex. As Munshi tells Lucas, "I feel yoga can be even more powerful than any psychological approach. *Prison yoga offers solutions to a broken system.* It can reduce medical costs of prisoners, decrease violence, reduce recidivism, [70% in California—the highest in the nation] and transform individuals and society."[78] When Munshi references a "broken system," he is not speaking of injustices that settler colonialism and capitalism inflict, but instead common concerns regarding the efficacy of the carceral system, which yoga can purportedly help solve. Prison yoga is not about dismantling the prison industrial complex as a system that perpetuates social death; for Munshi, yoga actually makes for a more efficient and cheaper carceral regime. A peaceful, more mindful, prisoner is often considered a more docile one, which makes the job of incarceration easier. Thus, these prison yoga advocates are not interested in actual liberation in the form of dismantling the prison industrial complex or releasing incarcerated peoples. Instead, they reinforce, perhaps inadvertently, the mission of the carceral system. Furthermore, Munshi does not consider imprisonment as a form of social control, whereas many activists and scholars have recognized that the system—the interlocking structures of settler colonialism and capitalism—is not "broken," but instead functioning as it is intended: to perpetuate European American/White wealth and political power.

Unfortunately, the voices of the people who are imprisoned further contribute to the notion that yoga is the solution to a "broken system," and individuals are entirely to blame for their incarceration. This may point to the unequal power dynamics that render people who are imprisoned vulnerable, and therefore there can be immense pressure for them to speak highly of carceral institutions and authority figures. This also may highlight the discourse of rehabilitative programming in detention centers, which is often premised on neoliberal logics that place the onus for decision-making entirely on the individual while overlooking "social confinement" or how social structures shape "choice."[79] In "Yoga at San Quentin," Bilal Chatman states, "There are no victims in this case except that I'm a victim of my own stupidity and drug use."[80] Similarly, Liebb says, "I have taken full responsibility."[81] These statements contrast with central findings in critical prison studies that show that incarceration helps to alleviate "political economic crises,"[82] which cannot be attributed to an individual problem. Underscoring themes of internalized oppression, the supposed necessity of prisons, and yoga as a civilizing project, Chatman underscores, "There's a whole bunch of idiots in here! We do need prisons. It's really easy to find problems here if you look for them, but I've learned to walk away, and the peace and serenity I've found through the yoga help with that."[83] By focusing on the supposed deficiencies of the individual who is imprisoned, these descriptions justify the need for prison and by extension, prison yoga programs.

Conclusion

Foregrounding incarceration as a settler colonial method of social control, this chapter demonstrates the racialized and gendered trope of "going carceral" as it operates in representations of prison yoga programs. Settler colonial narratives and strategies often disappear Indigenous and/or incarcerated peoples and/or invoke them in a stereotypical way that reifies White supremacy. As we have shown, yoga is complicit in settler colonialism too. Illustrating this point, Enoch Page writes, "The yoga we pass on to others today began evolving in a Western way during the colonial era so it now comes to us with commercial baggage and colonial fears. As a result, we no longer can offer the gift of yoga without the baggage of its promises serving as bait. When others accept our invitation to enjoy the gift of yoga, they do not realize that they have bitten into the bait that we may not have intended to offer them."[84] Lucas's portrayals of incarcerated people in the three articles that we have discussed highlight the "commercial baggage and colonial fears" at the convergence of prison and yoga, as does our critique from a critical abolitionist standpoint. Indeed, as Edward W. Said has famously stated, "The act of representing others almost always involves violence to the subject of representation."[85] How might we move beyond this violence?

Although the censorship of the carceral context can create many challenges, one possibility might be to illuminate and circulate the voices and visuals about prison yoga programs produced by people who are currently and formerly imprisoned. Would their self-representations be any different from Lucas and Sturman's depictions? They might. In Lucas's "Do Prisoners Deserve Yoga?" one third of Sturman's photographs of incarcerated people portray the individual practitioner literally behind bars, which functions to foreground their status as imprisoned and alone. In contrast, Nicole R. Fleetwood writes about incarcerated people's self-representations within and despite carceral regimes: studio portraits of imprisoned people and their relatives, which incarcerated people typically take and create the backdrops for. Fleetwood notes that these insider portrayals are "striking" in their "absence of obvious signs of incarceration"[86] and argues these photographs can produce "intimacy, kinship, and futurity that circulate between imprisoned people and their loved ones and through the porous boundaries of the U.S. carceral system."[87] Colonization and confinement, central to settler colonial strategies, have longed targeted the "intimacy, kinship, and futurity" of Indigenous people and people of color in horrific ways. This is why structural changes that reassert their humanity, such as the abolition of the prison industrial complex, and counternarratives that support these aims are so vital.

Notes

1. Huhndorf, *Going Native*.
2. Rickard, "Occupation of Indigenous Space," 57.
3. Fleetwood, "Posing in Prison," 493.
4. Pillai, introduction to this volume, 19.
5. Cacho, *Social Death*, 6. People with disabilities, people with substance use disorder, people who are not White, people who are poor, people who are undocumented, incapacitated senior citizens, refugees living in camps, displaced peoples, etc., also fall under "social death" because they are "ineligible for personhood" due to a suspension of, or failure to recognize, fundamental human rights (7). Unsurprisingly, some of these populations are also most likely to be criminalized.
6. Pillai, introduction to this volume, 6.
7. Critical Resistance, "Dylan Rodriguez."
8. Critical Resistance.
9. Huhndorf, *Going Native*, 162.
10. Huhndorf, 162.
11. Huhndorf, 162.
12. Frazier, foreword to this volume.
13. Huhndorf, *Going Native*, 2.

14. Foucault, Discipline and Punish, 57.

15. Foucault, 57–59.

16. Foucault, 57.

17. Interestingly, narratives about prison yoga may contradictorily portray yoga as both a mechanism of punishment and the antidote to imprisonment and its inhumanity. Yoga philosophies may also present the practice as a way to achieve liberation; however, we posit that it is vital to contextualize prison yoga programs politically, historically, and contemporarily because liberation discourses can obscure structural oppression and other forms of violence.

18. Tinker, "Stones Shall Cry Out," 108.

19. Gilmore, Golden Gulag, 26–27.

20. Davis, Abolition Democracy, 39.

21. Davis, 39.

22. Tuck and Yang, "Decolonization Is Not a Metaphor," 6.

23. Gover, "American Indians Serve."

24. Flanigan, "Native Americans Are the Unseen Victims."

25.-Ross, Inventing the Savage, 17.

26. Critical Resistance, "What Is the PIC?"

27. Critical Resistance, "About."

28. For our purposes, healthism refers to an expectation that individuals will take responsibility for their own health and well-being, which neglects to acknowledge the ways in which institutions and structures of oppression impact an individual's health. Gentrification is a term used to describe the pushing out of local residents from their communities due to rising housing costs, zoning decisions, and land appropriation in the service of attracting a more "desirable" (often White, able-bodied, class-aspirational) resident. Finally, gendered sizeism denotes the cultural message that there is a normative body weight dictated by one's gender.

29. Kaushik-Brown, "Toward Yoga as Property"; Page, "Gender, Race, and Class Barriers"; Patankar, "Ghosts of Yogas Past and Present"; Sood, "Cultivating a Yogic Theology."

30. Kaushik-Brown, "Toward Yoga as Property"; Mehta, "Embodiment through Purusha and Prakriti"; Nair, "Whose Yoga Is It Anyway?"; Shroff, "Finding My Yoga Home"; Sood, "Cultivating a Yogic Theology."

31. Nair, "Whose Yoga Is It Anyway?," 158.

32. Nair, 156.

33. Mehta, "Embodiment through Purusha and Prakriti," 228.

34. Kaushik-Brown, "Toward Yoga as Property," 69.

35. Miller, "Yoga R/Evolution," 52.

36. Foucault, Power/Knowledge, 115.

37. Elephant Journal, "About Elephant Journal."

38. Berila, "Introduction," 2.

39. Rodriguez, Forced Passages, 89.

40. Rodriguez, 89.

41. Spivak, "Can the Subaltern Speak?" 92.

42. Lucas, "Do Prisoners Deserve Yoga?"

43. Lucas.

44. Lucas.

45. Lucas.

46. Lucas.

47. Lucas.

48. Lucas, "Know about Yoga?"

49. Lucas, "Do Prisoners Deserve Yoga?"

50. Lucas, "Know about Yoga?"

51. Rios, *Punished*, 45.

52. Lucas, "Know about Yoga?"

53. Lucas.

54. Blu Wakpa, "Constellation of Confinement," 163.

55. Collins, *Black Sexual Politics*, 54.

56. Collins, 55.

57. Blu Wakpa, "Constellation of Confinement," 163.

58. Lucas, "Know about Yoga?"

59. Lucas, "Yoga at San Quentin."

60. Lucas.

61. Lucas, "Do Prisoners Deserve Yoga?"

62. Huhndorf, *Going Native*, 6.

63. Blu Wakpa, "Native American Embodiment," x.

64. Lucas, "Know about Yoga?"

65. The Prison Yoga Project was created in 2002. The organization has claimed, "We have trained more than 1700 volunteers, many in major prison-intensive cities, how to teach yoga in prison and how to work with prison administrators. Those teachers are now going into 185 prisons and jails and countless related facilities in 25 states and several countries outside the US. We have printed and shipped over 17,000 copies of our yoga instruction manual, 'Yoga, A Practice for Healing and Recovery' free of charge to prisoners who request it" (Prison Yoga Project—San Diego, 2022).

66. Lucas, "Yoga at San Quentin."

67. Miller, "Yoga R/Evolution," 11.

68. Lucas, "Know about Yoga?"

69. Lucas, "Yoga at San Quentin."

70. Lucas, "Know about Yoga?"

71. New York Times Editorial Board, "Rikers Island."

72. Schwirtz and Winerip, "Kalief Browder."

73. New York Times Editorial Board, "Rikers Island."

74. Lucas, "Yoga at San Quentin."

75. Perkinson, *Texas Tough*, 331.

76. Alexander, *New Jim Crow*, 31–32.

77. Lucas, "Do Prisoners Deserve Yoga?"

78. Lucas, emphasis added.

79. Blu Wakpa, "Constellation of Confinement," 163.

80. Lucas, "Yoga at San Quentin."

81. Lucas.

82. Gilmore, *Golden Gulag*, 26.

83. Lucas, "Yoga at San Quentin."

84. Page, "Gender, Race, and Class Barriers," 41.

85. Said, "In the Shadow of the West," 4.

86. Fleetwood, "Posing in Prison," 495.

87. Fleetwood, 491.

Bibliography

Alexander, Michelle. *The New Jim Crow: Mass Incarceration in the Age of Colorblindness.* New York: New Press, 2010.

Berila, Beth. "Introduction." In *Yoga, the Body, and Embodied Social Change: An Intersectional Feminist Analysis,* edited by Beth Berila, Melanie Klein, and Chelsea Jackson Roberts, 1–12. Lanham, MD: Lexington Books, 2016.

Blu Wakpa, Tria. "A Constellation of Confinement: *The Jailing of Cecelia Capture* and the Deaths of Sarah Lee Circle Bear and Sandra Bland, 1895–2015." *American Indian Culture and Research Journal* 40, no. 1 (January 2016): 161–83.

———. "Native American Embodiment in Educational and Carceral Contexts: Fixing, Eclipsing, and Liberating." PhD diss., University of California, Berkeley, 2017.

Cacho, Lisa Marie. *Social Death: Racialized Rightlessness and the Criminalization of the Unprotected.* New York: New York University Press, 2012.

Collins, Patricia Hill. *Black Sexual Politics: African Americans, Gender, and the New Racism.* New York: Routledge, 2004.

Critical Resistance. "Dylan Rodriguez, 'Shifting Responses to the Prison Industrial Complex.'" YouTube. September 15, 2017. https://www.youtube.com/.

———. "About." Accessed 2018. http://criticalresistance.org/about/.

———. "What Is the PIC? What Is Abolitionism?" Accessed 2018. http://critical resistance.org/about/not-so-common-language/.

Davis, Angela Y. *Abolition Democracy: Beyond Empire, Prisons, and Torture.* New York: Seven Stories Press, 2005.

Elephant Journal. "About Elephant Journal." Accessed 2016. https://www.elephant journal.com/about/.

Flanigan, Jake. "Native Americans Are the Unseen Victims of a Broken US Justice System." *Quartz,* April 27, 2015. https://qz.com/392342/native-americans-are-the -unseen-victims-of-a-broken-us-justice-system/.

Fleetwood, Nicole R. "Posing in Prison: Family Photographs, Emotional Labor, and Carceral Intimacy." *Public Culture* 27, no. 3 (2015): 487–511.

Foucault, Michel. *Discipline and Punish: The Birth of the Prison.* Translated by A. Sheridan. New York: Pantheon, 1977.

————. *Power/Knowledge: Selected Interviews and Other Writings 1972–1977*. New York: Pantheon Books, 1980.

Gilmore, Ruth Wilson. *Golden Gulag: Prisons, Surplus, Crisis, and Opposition in Globalizing California*. Berkeley: University of California Press, 2007.

Gover, Kevin. "American Indians Serve in the U.S. Military in Greater Numbers Than Any Ethnic Group and Have Since the Revolution." *HuffPost*, May 22, 2015, updated December 6, 2017. https://www.huffpost.com/.

Huhndorf, Shari Michelle. *Going Native: Indians in the American Cultural Imagination*. Ithaca, NY: Cornell University Press, 2001.

Kaushik-Brown, Roopa. "Toward Yoga as Property." In *Yoga, the Body, and Embodied Social Change: An Intersectional Feminist Analysis*, edited by Beth Berila, Melanie Klein, and Chelsea Jackson Roberts, 67–89. Lanham, MD: Lexington Books, 2016.

Lucas, Anneke. "Do Prisoners Deserve Yoga?" *Elephant Journal*, March 12, 2011. https://www.elephantjournal.com/2011/03/139550/.

————. "Know about Yoga and Meditation for Incarcerated and At-Risk Youth?" *Elephant Journal*, March 24, 2011. https://www.elephantjournal.com/2011/03/serve-where-it-matters-teach-yoga-and-meditation-to-incarcerated-and-at-risk-youth/.

————. "Yoga at San Quentin: Prisoner Interviews and Photos." *Elephant Journal*, May 6, 2011. https://www.elephantjournal.com/2011/05/do-prisoners-deserve-compassion/.

Mehta, Punam. "Embodiment through Purusha and Prakriti: Feminist Yoga as a Revolution from Within." In *Yoga, the Body, and Embodied Social Change: An Intersectional Feminist Analysis*, edited by Beth Berila, Melanie Klein, and Chelsea Jackson Roberts, 227–41. Lanham, MD: Lexington Books, 2016.

Miller, Amara. "Yoga R/Evolution: Deconstructing the Authentic Yoga Body." PhD diss., University of California, Davis, 2018.

Nair, Lakshmi. "Whose Yoga Is It Anyway? An Indian American's Adventures in Yoga-Land." In *Yoga Rising: 30 Empowering Stories from Yoga Renegades for Every Body*, edited by Melanie Klein, 153–62. Woodbury, MN: Llewellyn Publications, 2018.

New York Times Editorial Board. "Rikers Island and the Death of Kalief Browder." *New York Times*, June 9, 2015. https://www.nytimes.com/.

Page, Enoch. "The Gender, Race, and Class Barriers: Enclosing Yoga as White Public Space." In *Yoga, the Body, and Embodied Social Change: An Intersectional Feminist Analysis*, edited by Beth Berila, Melanie Klein, and Chelsea Jackson Roberts, 41–57. Lanham, MD: Lexington Books, 2016.

Patankar, Prachi. "Ghosts of Yogas Past and Present." *Jadaliyya*, February 26, 2014. http://www.jadaliyya.com/pages/index/16632/ghosts-of-yogas-past-and-present.

Perkinson, Robert. *Texas Tough: The Rise of America's Prison Empire*. New York: Metropolitan Books, 2010.

Prison Yoga Project—San Diego. "About." 2022. https://www.facebook.com/pypsd/.

Rickard, Jolene. "The Occupation of Indigenous Space as 'Photograph.'" In *Native

Nations: Journeys in American Photography, edited by Jane Alison, 57–71. London: Barbican Art Gallery, 1998.

Rios, Victor M. *Punished: Policing the Lives of Black and Latino Boys*. New York: New York University Press, 2011.

Rodriguez, Dylan. *Forced Passages: Imprisoned Radical Intellectuals and the U.S. Prison Regime*. Minneapolis: University of Minnesota Press, 2006.

Ross, Luana. *Inventing the Savage: The Social Construction of Native American Criminality*. Austin: University of Texas Press, 1998.

Said, Edward W. "In the Shadow of the West." *Wedge* 7–8 (Winter-Spring 1985): 4–11.

Schwirtz, Michael, and Michael Winerip. "Kalief Browder, Held at Rikers Island for 3 Years Without Trial, Commits Suicide." *New York Times*, June 8, 2015. https://www.nytimes.com/.

Shroff, Zubin. "Finding My Yoga Home." In *Yoga Rising: 30 Empowering Stories from Yoga Renegades for Every Body*, edited by Melanie Klein, 283–90. Woodbury, MN: Llewellyn Publications, 2018.

Sood, Sheena. "Cultivating a Yogic Theology of Collective Healing: A Yogini's Journey Disrupting White Supremacy, Hindu Fundamentalism, and Casteism." *Race and Yoga* 3, no. 1 (2018): 12–20.

Spivak, Gayatri Chakravorty. "Can the Subaltern Speak?" In *Colonial Discourse and Post-Colonial Theory: A Reader*, edited by Patrick Williams and Laura Chrisman, 66–111. New York: Columbia University Press, 1994.

Tinker, George "Tink." "The Stones Shall Cry Out: Consciousness, Rocks, and Indians." *Wicazo Sa Review* 19, no. 2 (2004): 105–25.

Tuck, Eve, and K. Wayne Yang. "Decolonization Is Not a Metaphor." *Decolonization: Indigeneity, Education and Society* 1, no. 1 (2012): 1–40.

9

Vacant Refuge, Unfinished Resettlement

Ambivalence among Syrian and Iraqi Refugee Women and Children in Houston, Texas

MARIA F. CURTIS

Introduction

This chapter focuses on the lived experiences of Syrian and Iraqi refugee women and children during the transition in policy between the Obama and Trump administrations.[1] In the wake of the Muslim Ban,[2] resettlement in the United States for refugees from the Arab world edged toward the criminalization of those fleeing violence and death in their home countries, recasting them as the agents of persecution from which they fled.[3] Muslim women have experienced an ever-increasing level of precarity risking abuse and exploitation during the journey after displacement which continues to impact them in resettlement.[4] This tenuous state of refuge promised against a 9/11 backdrop, "a new subscript for 'freedom'" (as Pillai puts it in the introduction), produces and reproduces moments of anxiety, feelings of being betwixt and between amid a dystopic nativism born of carceral liberalism that distorts belonging and liberty beyond recognition. I aim to connect the everyday experiences of refugee women and children to larger institutional forces that shape and restrict their ability to feel "at home" as they encounter resettlement in the United States. Houston is a sanctuary city with a long history of offering refuge located in a state that turned away federal funding for resettlement,[5] and it offers an opportunity to understand deep impacts to resettlement after the implementation of the Muslim Ban.

Houston, Texas, as a Site of Refuge

In America's most ethnically diverse city, Houston's schools and neighborhoods bear witness to global experiences of war and displacement.[6] Despite metropolitan Houston's progressive City Hall leadership, politics in the state capital in Austin have leaned to the right.[7] Before Trump's Executive Order No. 13769, which banned immigration from a long list of primarily Arab nations, "The Muslim Ban," Texas politicians rebuffed Obama's efforts to fund resettlement organizations and increase immigration caps to allow more Syrians asylum. Texas is a state of roughly 26 million people, with regional politics that are largely shaped by its rural constituents coupled with consequences of a large bloc of nonvoting citizens, and its anti-Muslim sentiment is perhaps older than we can fully realize. Even when it was still Spanish territory, Spanish towns that now straddle the U.S.-Mexico border bear testimony to the Spanish Inquisitions that took place on North American soil, prompting Muslims and Jews who came to this "new world" after the Reconquista to flee or hide yet again. The town *Matamoros*, named after a celebrated "Moor killer,"[8] is now an entry point for Latin American immigrants who live in fear of deportation and racial profiling whether they are undocumented or not. Underneath contemporary Texas, identity politics are vestiges of earlier histories of exile and refuge. The Trump administration created fear of the migrant caravan along the Texas-Mexico border, claiming it consisted of dangerous migrants and "Islamic terrorists."[9] Texas immigration politics are a strange and ironic accumulation of welcome and exile, and its recent iterations of anti-immigrant and anti-Muslim rhetoric dominated the 2016 Presidential elections. Texas Senator Cruz and then–Presidential hopeful Trump sparred in election debates, but Cruz's influence can be tracked in "Make America Great Again" slogans. This was a platform built on the cross-criminalization of people of color, and what began as political campaign fodder has manifested in the resettlement landscape.

To Be or Not to Be a Sanctuary City:
When Sanctuary Is Criminalized

Houston is a city of nearly 5 million souls where one in ten people are born outside the United States.[10] The city is an anomaly in the field of Texas politics, yet in spite of its being designated America's most ethnically diverse city it must comply with state policies that seem contradictory in spirit.[11] Whilst Houston Mayor Sylvester Turner welcomed refugees publicly, Texas Governor Greg Abbott withdrew the option to obtain Obama-era funding that would support nonprofit resettlement groups already working on a shoestring budget to assist in the monumental task of resettling Syrians and Iraqis across the city.[12] Before the national Muslim Ban, Texas enacted its own version by refusing that funding.[13] This later informed Trump's restriction of refugees from predominantly Arab or Muslim countries.[14] Amid current deportations and the separation of children from their families, Syrian and Iraqi refugees look on as their Latino neighbors fear the worst. The disintegration of a feeling of safety is felt by all under a shared fear of policeability, regardless of legal status.[15] In this mixed field of welcome and open hostility, Syrian and Iraqi refugees arrived in Houston to find a place they hoped would be their new home. Resettlement is a conceptual misnomer; "home" is not mere shelter, but a feeling of being part of a community.[16] Because less than 1 percent of the world's refugees are resettled in their home country, to become a refugee is in essence to become an exilee from one's home, to be extracted and removed from the ebb and flow of one's home culture and society. This exilic condition produces a carcerality of the mind from which most people never fully recover.[17]

While Houston celebrates the real and felt presence of diversity in a myriad of festivals, ethnic neighborhoods, restaurants, and markets, its diversity is also the result of economic stagnation in the 1970s and 80s when migrants from around the globe arrived and made it their home and helped build it as the economic powerhouse it is today.[18] Refugees who arrive in the United States are required to move through resettlement with thin support, yet those who arrived at the end of the Obama administration occupy a more cruel social space. U.S. rates of admission for refugees had been consistently 68,000 per annum, Obama petitioned to have it increased to 75,000 as he left office, and Trump reduced that number to 48,000 per year, the lowest since the Vietnam era. In Houston we see an up-close example of the "burden of irreconcilable meanings" of refugee identity, a kind of "double vision,"[19] a lived ambiguity between resettlement and forced exile, and ever-shifting boundaries between authentic hospitality and tenuous legal protections.[20]

The Burden of Proof: Becoming a Refugee and the Surrender of Privacy

Given this volume's meditation on multiple forms and experiences of carcerality and institutional violence, I describe what the Combahee River Collective (CRC) has characterized as "interlocking and simultaneous measures of oppression and inequality"[21] by examining the lived experiences of Syrian and Iraqi families resettled in Houston's urban poor neighborhoods. The modern

192   CURTIS

state as panopticon remains firmly intact across a wide spectrum of local, state, regional, national, and international institutions.[22] Refugees enter the United States only after rigorous vetting, screenings, and hearings conducted by various agencies on multiple continents. The official bureaucracy and its required documentation and evidence of events leading to displacement reinforce an internal expectation that one must be ready to prove, perpetually re-explain, and justify one's identity, to demonstrate one's right to request refugee status and be "deserving enough"[23] of basic human rights earned through great loss and suffering.[24] The protracted process of submitting paperwork, collecting required documents, securing approvals, undergoing repeated interviews and testimonies, calling witnesses and references, and providing official identification and birth certificates requires one to be ready to answer any and all questions, leaving little room for privacy, not to mention the considerable resources needed to assemble such documents.[25] Families must often decide how to move forward once they are granted refugee status, making difficult decisions about which family members will migrate first. Perhaps it is only in the virtual lockdown of a global pandemic that non-migrants and those who have never experienced displacement can finally understand feelings of abrupt separation, the never-ending up-endedness of one's life against the monotony of waiting it out until things settle.

The external process of the state in establishing one's legal status, one's actual statelessness, and the vulnerability of existing between and across states[26] in the post-9/11 environment yields to a more internalized form of surveillance of the self, a "drone poetics"[27] wherein one's cumulative identities create a dense web of otherness from which one may never fully break free. These entangled struggles, accumulated traumas, cultural barriers, and social prejudice create feelings of inescapable carcerality, a sense of being stuck somewhere between older memories of displacement and new fears of exclusion in the "home" of resettlement. Refugee status becomes the "hyperobject," as Pillai observes, that dims one's own sense of self and value. The apparatus of power that created displacement is never far from one's mind and lingers there; the panopticon of the prison yard is no longer a fixed geographic space but hovers, drone-like, in the mind of the person building a resettled home. Ubiquitous markers of power create intersections of difference where one may never "feel" free at all. The CRC statement is a potent frame, and Keeanga-Yamahtta Taylor's *How We Get Free* offers a critical lens through which to read and understand the politics of everyday life for refugees.

The in-between gray zones of the city where new refugees are resettled among America's working poor creates of a "state of exception" where "the *possibility* of suspending the law allows the elimination of entire categories of citizens who for some reason cannot be integrated into the political system."[28] In these urban refugee resettlement zones, refugee bodies are not confined in a camp, but they become part of tightly knit yet precarious immigrant neighborhoods. These neighborhoods are sites of economic and social struggle attesting to Houston's title as America's most ethnically diverse city and to the efforts of generations of those who worked their way to homeownership in other parts of the city. Although free from the physical or political dangers they once left behind, refugees often arrive in the United States in a state of deep exhaustion and in debt for their resettlement expenses, in this fog that is recognized by medical professionals as PTSD.[29]

Microaggressions, Islamophobia, and Rationalizing Carceral Violence

The cumulative effects of September 11 may never be measurable, neither for Americans nor for the Arab and Muslim Americans who were scapegoated as targets of hostility. It is now a taken-for-granted assumption in introductory textbooks on international relations of the Middle East that the American invasion of Iraq after 9/11 marks a significant turning point in American diplomacy in the Arab world.[30] The pre-9/11 context of ethnic prejudice against Arab Americans shifted to a wholesale conflation of Arabs with terrorists, people with a supposed propensity for violence.[31] The post-9/11 environment created multiple forms of hypervisibilty for Muslim women, with misplaced pity on the one hand for women presumed to be without rights and with physical assault and in some instances murder on the other.[32] From furtive stares and insinuations and verbal comments to full-blown fear of deportation, or the "lawfare"[33] of sending people "back to where they came from," the post-9/11 environment has presented great challenges. Newly arriving refugees enter into an already complex cultural scene where even Arabs and Muslims born in the United States suffer daily challenges. Microaggressions in apartment complexes where refugees resettle, in public schools serving refugee children who may have never set foot in a school, and among and between neighbors and employers reinforces a sort of self-imposed house arrest, which keeps refugee women and children inside and "at home," both exiled and surveilled. It is this exilic condition that produces a carcerality of the mind, carceral circuits, and carceral geographies.[34]

Having survived displacement and violence in their homelands, and possible multiple micro-exiles in their journey to resettle in the United States, they have encountered state-level violence at multiple junctures and learned to live alongside regimes of profiling; once they leave home, they are in essence

194   CURTIS

trading in old carceralities for new ones.[35] *Refugee,* a term once synonymous with one who must be given shelter, has become a word largely synonymous with *terrorist* in the post-9/11 context, and has further deteriorated in the wake of the Muslim Ban.[36] Mustafa Bayoumi's notion that Muslims are the "new Blacks"[37] has been a theoretical model through which we can track the coming together of different circles of American activists who were the principal organizers of the Women's March, such as Linda Sarsour.[38] Leaders of the Women's March and the Black Lives Matter movement have made significant gains in the political polls, seeing support of candidates who might never before have been political candidates.[39]

Women and Children First: The Politics of Vulnerability

My contact with Syrian and Iraqi refugee women began in the fall of 2015 in Houston, Texas, when I joined a group of volunteer English teachers. Many of the newly arriving children had never really known regular schooling in their homelands as their parents or grandparents had; some were quite literally born in hospitals as they were being bombed.[40] I met large extended families, and as time passed, my would-be English students were more often women, babies and preschool children, the chronically ill, and the elderly. The men in the families were tasked with earning income, while women managed home life. Women and children may be the first to receive sympathy as *refugees,* but in their daily struggles they articulated feeling left out in all spheres of their lives, homebound and stranded.

As the situation of war and political unrest drags on in Syria and Iraq, and stretches and unfolds across the MENA region (Middle East and North Africa) in unexpected ways, we continue to see an increase in the numbers of women and children moving across borders as refugees and uprooted in their home countries as internally displaced.[41] Narrowly defining the qualifications of who is "worthy" of protection and marked as vulnerable creates increasingly dangerous circumstances for women and children refugees, adding risks for human trafficking, assault, and extortion. Underestimating them as potential agents of social change and not recognizing their abilities to act as autonomous actors renders an incomplete understanding of their true potentiality. We should more fully examine the reasons that place them in the position of need in the first place, and how need is in effect delivered if we are to comprehend the larger systemic consequences and impacts of forced migration.[42]

In a 2017 UNHCR report, vulnerabilities of women and children are presented along with measures to interrupt cycles of violence. The idea that ar-

9. Vacant Refuge, Unfinished Resettlement   195

riving at a reception center or an official UNHCR site means one has found refuge is far from true,[43] and the UNHCR has ongoing sexual harassment trainings that are mandatory for its personnel.[44] Stories are circulating from different refugee centers globally, and the #MeTooUN hashtag has been a site for new concerns. In the first nine months of 2018, some 78 cases of abuse were reported involving UNHCR personnel. Is there another example of the validity of Agamben's claims that the power of the body politic renders the refugee body *homo sacer*?[45] The discourse of resettlement is rooted in older neocolonial foreign policy in the Arab world. Trauma and abuse continue to cast long shadows over the lives of migrant and refugee women that they must later reckon with in resettlement contexts.

The Carceral Logic of Support

Conventional programs, "support services," often include ESL courses for "newcomers" focusing on language mastery, immunization and medical screenings, and medical and wellness services often ill-equipped for the needs of large extended families and women who have experienced trauma.[46] During the Trump era, refugees were left with much less support than they would have had just a few years earlier.[47] American policy has impacted even those not entering the United States because elements of the Muslim Ban have been implemented in similar measure elsewhere, criminalizing Arabic-speaking Muslim refugees and migrants globally.[48] Lack of consistent and coherent policies across institutions creates a sense of utter immobility, a sort of carcerality of the mind that paralyzes movement and progress in day-to-day life and future decision-making. Although women and children are most likely to receive more immediate empathy in the public sphere, their needs are complex given the forms of trauma likely encountered before arriving in the United States. If they arrive without a male family member, the mother will be required to work and will then be faced with the challenge of how to provide financially and caregive in the absence of family networks. Privately funded agencies dedicated to supporting refugee women and children, like Amaanah Refugee Services in Houston, Texas, operate with more flexibility as they are not custodians of state or federal funding. They fill in needed gaps where other agency resources run thin, and there is a cooperative network and communication between different types of agencies. Each institution has its own bureaucratic logic, which may or may not operate as other institutions' logic does. Juggling school administrations, working with Medicaid and seeking medical attention in routine and emergency cases, managing health benefits, working, learning to pay taxes and manage a household,

196   CURTIS

shuttling children in multiple schools, is overwhelming, and no single agency is equipped to meet all of these needs.

Registering for Medicaid is often confusing, and status updates are required. I met many people who were unable to manage their status, resulting in significant lapses in coverage. Insurance approvals for doctor visits and prescriptions add layers of complexity that operate in counterintuitive ways vis-à-vis being able to secure treatment directly from a pharmacist as is possible in many countries. An area of great need is around delivering culturally sensitive gynecology and birth-control support. Amber Jar, a pharmacy run by former refugees from Iraq and other regions, provides phone consultations, home delivery, and a range of products that are not widely available elsewhere. They run a space for refugee artists to display their work and a neatly decorated salon where women can practice English together in a comfortable setting. During a visit I came across a product called Rosa Virginity Soap featured prominently beside the cash register. The staff explained that refugee women, many of whom had experienced sexual assault during displacement, often used the soap with the understanding that it "repaired" the physical damage from rape as it claimed to "whiten and tighten vaginal muscle." Many women use these types of products because they are afraid and ashamed to discuss these topics in the United States, and they are uncomfortable culturally with physical exams, fearing they will do more damage.

The most extreme case I witnessed was that of an elderly Iraqi woman who had fibroids and needed surgery. Her insurance coverage had lapsed because she had forgotten to submit a form, and she could not afford the procedure out of pocket. She did not have a car and did not feel comfortable asking her son for help, so she relied on other women to introduce her to a Muslim woman doctor. After trying to get assistance with the help of resourceful volunteers, she eventually decided to return to Iraq to her own neighborhood clinic. Returning meant risking her refugee status and possible danger in her neighborhood, frequently a site of militia bombings. She had the procedure and returned to Houston. How can it be easier for an elderly Iraqi refugee woman to return to Iraq for medical treatment she could not access in Houston's Medical Center, the largest medical center in the world? Having access to resources along with thoughtful, culturally appropriate delivery is necessary if refugee programs are to be truly successful and restorative.

Homesick/Homebound Resettlement

Working outside the household may present a new set of fears or anxieties about safety for both a mother and her children. The family power dynamic within the household changes in the American context. Even when men acknowledge the families' economic need for two working parents, socially they may be unable to adapt to this economic reality. Older children or elderly family members may become stand-in parents. A young Iraqi mother whose husband left her suddenly found herself the head of her household. She and her family had to move to a smaller and cheaper apartment complex, and she accepted a higher-paying job in a large retail chain but had to work nights, leaving her children and mother alone. The location where she worked at night stocking inventory locked its employees in for "safety." While she was locked in at work, her mother and children were locked in their apartment in a neighborhood where they felt unsafe. They communicated via smart phones during her long shifts to comfort each other. This family received ongoing personal donations of money and food from mosques and several agencies. They secured housing, learned English quickly, landed employment, and established deep friendships, and the children were successful in their schools. Even with all of this support, life remained precarious with little time for leisure or visits with friends or the comforts of the home and their extended family they had left behind. Finding work, managing gainful employment, having a home, these are the things that are the milestones of success in resettlement, yet they are often not enough to replace the life one once had, nor are they enough to undo extended periods of trauma.

Reenactments of Home

During an interview with an Iraqi resettlement case manager who had been in the United States for more than ten years, when I asked him where he went in the city to experience something of Iraqi culture, he said he could not find such a place. He said that even if we went back to Iraq, the home he knew and loved no longer existed. He explained that what had once been one of the Arab world's most developed economies, where people had access to advanced education, where women once enjoyed some of the highest rates of professional freedom and educational opportunities, Iraq had morphed into something completely different, a ghost of its previous self. To feel "home," he said, he made himself a pot of tea, turned off his phone, and read poetry to himself in Arabic. The lines of poetry of Nazik Al-Mala'ika[49] offered a sense of home, a place erased by decades of war, occupation, and sectarianism that eclipsed once-flourishing intellectual traditions.

TO A GIRL SLEEPING IN THE STREET

In Karrada at night, wind and rain before dawn,
when the dark is a roof or a drape never drawn,

when the night's at its peak and the dark's full of rain,
and the wet silence roils a fierce hurricane,

the lament of the wind fills the deserted street,
the arcades groan in pain, and the lamps softly weep.
—Nazik Al-Mala'ika, 1923–2007[50]

When I asked an elderly Iraqi woman what types of food she and her family prepared for Eid celebrations, she invited me over to see for myself. Her grandchildren, she said, had never experienced traditions like she had. They had no idea what it meant to bask in the glow of a family celebration, to eat and laugh into the late hours and share in collective fasting, to sit down to a meal together hearing the call to prayer over the television and from the neighborhood mosque; these are memories her grandchildren do not have. In her family in Houston, adult children worked several jobs to make ends meet while she minded the kids. She assembled food for Iftar, the fast-breaking meal, as her grandchildren played on devices at home indoors, learning to fast and observe Ramadan in their new home in Texas. She claimed that no one under the age of thirty could really remember what it might have felt like to celebrate Ramadan and Eid without fear of danger. She recounted this as we sipped banana milk while eating foods from her childhood. She reserved the most comfortable chair for me, instructing her grandchildren to dote on me, reenacting ancient patterns of hospitality embedded in Islamic traditions of giving and sharing. I had read an article that week that discussed how Iraq offered sanctuary to a great number of Syrians, those who chose not to move toward Europe, but moved into areas of Iraq once they were displaced. Despite Iraq's own internal displacements and years of political upheaval, they offered sanctuary to Syrians fleeing ISIS and Assad's regime in numbers that dwarf refugee resettlement numbers of western countries.[51] I took all this in, as the kids brought me their favorite foods, happy to share this Eid day. So much of the most important and enduring resettlement work is done by refugees themselves in these types of settings, whether through offering simple meals to one's own family or in inviting others to share in exchanges of hospitality.

9. Vacant Refuge, Unfinished Resettlement   199

Truancy, Surveillance, and Exclusionary Discipline: Drone Parenting and Interrupted Schooling

Many refugee children who come to the United States have experienced interrupted schooling due to political unrest and war.[52] They enter the ESL classroom with children from other contexts with increasingly high needs.[53] In 2016, Houston received in excess of 11,000 "newcomer" students distributed across America's fourth-largest public school system.[54] Before they can enter school, students are assessed for fluency, given medical screenings, and immunized. After Trump took office, such medical screenings and services once performed by the State of Texas stopped due to funding shortages. These initial health screenings must occur to place kids in school, yet the process happens in fits and starts, often dependent on the availability of mobile health units working with resettlement agencies that visit the homebound. Children may have to miss school to get immunized, ironically in order to qualify for entry into school, creating attendance problems. Refugee moms who are required to have children immunized or lose health benefits are threatened with stiff penalties when their children miss school for medical visits. Some school districts have begun issuing excessive fees in the hundreds of dollars for unexcused absences, though such policies were fiercely debated in the Texas State legislature.[55] Though other states also have penalties in place to prevent chronic absenteeism, only two states, Texas and Wyoming, prosecuted children in adult court with misdemeanor C violations. According to recent studies, Texas has charged some 100,000 students a year for truancy, more than double all of the other states combined. Nearly all of the children who are chronically absent from school are facing extreme hardships beyond their control at home, and when they enter courts they cannot afford legal representation and rarely understand the legal ramifications of the proceedings. Although Texas claims to have relaxed elements of its truancy policies, parents with students with high absenteeism are still sent warning letters reminding them of their responsibilities and legal consequences.[56]

Prosecution for chronic absenteeism leads to higher dropout rates. Children are left to obtain a high school diploma through GED courses, further limiting their ability to attend college. We can track the likelihood of incarceration with school dropout rates, and refugee children like others who suffer economic and social hardships at home that prevent them from attending school are at risk.[57] Kids between the ages of twelve and seventeen can be fined, along with their parents. Younger children do not accrue fines, but their parents can along with being charged with class C misdemeanors. Refugee children arrive with a disproportionately larger chance of health problems requiring regular medical attention.[58] The Texas Appleseed Project has studied the phenomenon of "exclusionary discipline" in Texas schools, finding a disproportionate number of children of color and children from lower socioeconomic status among those who have higher absentee rates, who drop out, or who are more frequently incarcerated, connecting the dots between the school to prison pipeline.[59]

Refugee children who are offered free and reduced lunches may have *halal* dietary restrictions that make the food inedible.[60] They may also be bullied for their different appearance, for wearing the hijab, for example.[61] Refugee parents may not understand the importance of turning in a doctor's note when they return after an absence in a state that severely penalizes absenteeism. Refugee children are often placed in ESL learning environments where the staff can never hope to meet the sheer volume of children and needs, keeping them unintentionally on a track of subpar education. Parents may also not understand the concept of risk when kids roam freely in their neighborhoods, where playing unattended may be perceived as parental negligence. When children ride bikes alone in parking lots or to the neighborhood store, they may be picked up by police and returned home to their mothers, who are instructed to watch their children lest they be taken in by child protective services. The concepts of kidnapping and sex trafficking are synonymous with what happens in war zones, not in residential American neighborhoods. Some working refugee parents are so frightened to let their children play outside that they forbid them from leaving their apartments at all. Changes in food, diet, and physical activity create new health concerns that seem to defy straightforward resolution.[62] For many, the experience of resettlement in America is utterly *unsettling*, often triggering traumatic experiences from flight and displacement.[63]

As a means of creating safety nets,[64] refugee parents purchase cell phones for each member of the family to track and monitor movement and location. Phones are also portals back to relatives and places from which they fled, which sometimes feel safer than their new American homes. They live next door to neighbors from other cities whom they also may fear for a number of reasons. They may be unable to attend language courses regularly because the family's livelihood depends on their being on call for kids around the clock. They are entitled to more forms of support for their children if they arrive at school not able to speak English. Though eager to shed the legal status of "refugee," they are forced to leverage it to maximize when they can count on more resources. Women and children are often alone as husbands and fathers more readily move into the workforce taking on jobs deemed inappropriate for women. Because large numbers of women who have been displaced report sexual violence and assault at some point of displacement, some remain fearful of being out on their own.[65] Men who once held positions of rank and formal education are forced to accept whatever work they can, and the pain and humiliation are felt by all members of the family until employment and income levels begin to resemble the lifestyles they left behind in their home countries.

Conclusion

Amid diminished resettlement services, shifting sands of public support, and political restrictions, refugees can count on little predictability during the resettlement process. Those waiting for extended family members must reimagine lives on their own. Resettlement agencies do what they can with what they have, yet they are obliged to follow state guidelines and funding protocols if they are public institutions on federal funding. The strain on formal institutions has forced individuals and religious communities to take on larger roles and costs. The increase in actual needs and the scale of trauma are also important factors to take into consideration given that some generations of refugees have not seen or witnessed a day without fear or violence; their "normal" has never been without trauma. In the post-9/11 context, most Americans consume media about the Arab world through the prism of homeland insecurity and terrorism. Millennials have only ever experienced a U.S. foreign policy that is engaged in long-standing conflicts in the Arab world and may have family members or friends who served tours in Iraq and Afghanistan with their own experiences of PTSD.

Gaps in much-needed support render the prospect of refuge in the United States vacant, not a home in the fullest sense, but rather a hollow shell that offers few comforts, what Agamben has described as "bare life." "Women and children first"[66] has long been a rallying cry for those dark moments when a greater sense of humanity is called upon to meet catastrophe with mercy.

Although women and children are most likely to receive more immediate sympathy in the public sphere, their needs are complex and long-standing. Despite the support a refugee receives, even the more fortunate ones, each institution offering need-based services has its own bureaucratic logic. The institutions once relied on for meeting needs are so diminished in the current political climate that new forms of networks and social ties are beginning to emerge.[67] The wide range of psychological, economic, social, and religious layers of misunderstanding and discrimination have made navigating the physical world more difficult. The use of smart phones and social groups managed through apps helps put those in need with people from their religious and virtual communities in productive ways. Resettlement remains an unfinished and unfulfilled promise, and only time will tell what the impact of today's broken refugee resettlement process will mean for those who are left to move through it. Still, individuals continue to help each other as they may with what resources they have at their disposal. Immigrant women assist refugee women in private groups via WhatsApp chat groups where their voices are heard and needs are met through resource-sharing, bartering, and exchange. It is here that the informal economic caregiving economy overcomes current barriers. It is often here under the private digital shelter built through their shared dialogue and experiences that emotional, spiritual, and practical needs are met, and a sense of emotional refuge may take root.

Notes

1. Martin, *Refugee Women*, chap. 3; Schwartz, "Issues Impacting Migrant Women," 263.

2. Ayoub and Beydoun, "Executive Disorder," 223.

3. Morrison, "Dark-Side of Globalisation," 71; Naimou, "Double Vision," 230.

4. Hynes, "On the Battlefield of Women's Bodies," 433; Gökariksel, "Body Politics of Trump's 'Muslim Ban,'" 469; Akram, "Millennium Development Goals," 286; Parker, "Hidden Crisis," 2341–42; Gerdau, Kizilhan, and Noll-Hussong, "Posttraumatic Stress Disorder and Related Disorders."

5. Barbash and Schmidt, "Texas Gov. Abbott Springs Surprise."

6. Mejia, "How Houston Has Become Most Diverse."

7. Jentleson, "Global Governance," 147.

8. Spellberg, "Inventing Matamoras," 150.

9. Sacchetti and Stanley-Becker, "Blow to Trump's Immigration Agenda."

10. Emerson et al., "Houston Region Grows More Diverse"; Karson, "Confronting Houston's Demographic Shift," 210.

11. Capps, Fix, and Nwosu, "Profile of Immigrants in Houston."

12. Chemerinsky, "Constitutionality of Withholding Federal Funds," 60.

13. Subcommittee on Immigration and Border Security, "Sanctuary Cities: A Threat to Public Safety"; Huetteman and Flegenheimer, "Ted Cruz Challenges President Obama."

14. Filindra and Kovács, "Analysing State Legislative Resolutions," 33–37.

15. Rosas, "Managed Violences of the Borderlands," 401.

16. Malkki, "Refugees and Exiles."

17. Gill et al., "Carceral Circuitry."

18. Kragie, "Greater Houston Resettles More Refugees."

19. Naimou, "Double Vision," 227–29.

20. Houston and Morse, "Ordinary and Extraordinary," 30–37; Bauder, "Sanctuary Cities," 178.

21. Taylor, *How We Get Free*, 4.

22. Betts, "Institutional Proliferation," 56.

23. Fairchild, "US Immigration," 604–5.

24. Norman, "Assessing the Credibility," 276.

25. Clutterbuck et al., "Establishing Legal Identity."

26. Edkins, "Missing Migrants," 362–63.

27. Brady, "Drone Poetics," 120.

28. Ross, "Introduction," 12, emphasis added.

29. Riber, "Trauma Complexity and Child Abuse," 861; Kira et al., "Psychometric Assessment"; Heptinstall, Sethna, and Taylor, "PTSD and Depression in Refugee Children."

30. Fawcett, *International Relations of the Middle East*.

31. Naff, *Becoming American*; Curtis, "Discrimination."

32. Abu-Lughod, "Do Muslim Women Need Saving?"; Mishra, "'Saving' Muslim Women."

33. Richter-Montpetit, "Beyond the Erotics."

34. Gill et al., "Carceral Circuitry," 204.

35. Sheth, "Unruly Muslim Women," 460.

36. Kerwin, "Faltering US Refugee Protection System."

37. Bayoumi, *How Does It Feel?*

38. Hogue, "Performing, Translating, Fashioning"; Sarsour, "My Take: My Hijab"; Sarsour, *Not Here to Be Bystanders*.

39. McLaren, "Muslim Innovations," 147–50.

40. Gangamma and Shipman, "Transnational Intersectionality in Family Therapy," 206–10.

41. Zavratnik and Krilić, "Addressing Intersectional Vulnerabilities," 89.

42. Smith, "Ethical and Effective Research Methods."

43. Hyndman, *Managing Displacement*; Ramadan, "Spatialising the Refugee Camp," 65–70.

44. UN High Commissioner for Refugees, "Tackling Sexual Exploitation."

45. Ross, "Introduction," 11.

46. Tomlinson and Egan, "From Marginalization to (Dis)Empowerment," 1025; McBrien, "Educational Needs and Barriers," 330; Terasaki, Ahrenholz, and Haider, "Care of Adult Refugees," 1039; Wanigaratne et al., "Influence of Refugee Status," 625.

47. Scribner, "You Are Not Welcome Here," 274.

48. Houghton, "Learning from the 'Muslim Ban.'"

49. Creswell, "Nazik Al-Mala'ika and Pan-Arabism"; Al-Khamisi, "Al-Malaika and Identity Crisis."

50. Nazik Al-Mala'ika, in Drumsta, "Revolt against the Sun," 98–99.

51. Durable Solutions Platform, "Far From Home."

52. Jaffe-Walter, Walsh, and Lee, "This Issue."

53. West, "Social Capital and Refugee Mothers."

54. Personal communication during interviews with personnel from the Houston Independent School District, 2016 and 2017.

55. Feldman, "Truancy Bill Will Be Hotly Debated."

56. Texas Association of School Boards, "Compulsory Attendance and Truancy."

57. Evans and Fitzgerald, "Economic and Social Outcomes."

58. Yun et al., "Health Profiles of Newly Arrived Children," 128–30.

59. Craven, "Suspended Childhood."

60. Stokes, "Conceptualizing and Measuring Food Security."

61. Hussein, "Prejudice against Muslim Students."

62. Bettmann et al., "Resettlement Experiences of Children."

63. Shannon, O'Dougherty, and Mehta, "Refugees' Perspectives on Barriers," 47–50.

64. Liamputtong et al., "Peer Support Groups," 715.

65. Freedman, "Sexual and Gender-Based Violence."

66. Coomaraswamy, "Women and Children."

67. Houghton, "Learning from the 'Muslim Ban.'"

Bibliography

Abu-Lughod, Lila. "Do Muslim Women Really Need Saving? Anthropological Reflections on Cultural Relativism and Its Others." *American Anthropologist* 104, no. 3 (September 2002): 783–90. https://doi.org/10.1525/aa.2002.104.3.783.

Al-Khamisi, Fatima Ali. "Al-Malaika and the Identity Crisis of an Arab Woman." *American International Journal of Contemporary Research* 7, no. 1 (March 2017): 73–78. http://www.aijcrnet.com/journals/Vol_7_No_1_March_2017/9.pdf.

Akram, Susan. "Millennium Development Goals and the Protection of Displaced and Refugee Women and Girls." *Laws* 2, no. 3 (September 2013): 283–313. https://doi.org/10.3390/laws2030283.

Ayoub, Abed, and Khaled Beydoun. "Executive Disorder: The Muslim Ban, Emergency Advocacy, and the Fires Next Time." *Michigan Journal of Race and Law* 22, no. 2 (March 2017): 215–41. https://doi.org/10.36643/mjrl.22.2.executive.

Barbash, Fred, and Samantha Schmidt. "Texas Gov. Abbott Springs Surprise on Critics, with Unannounced Facebook Live Signing of Sanctuary Cities Ban." *Washington Post*, May 8, 2017. Gale.

Bauder, Harald. "Sanctuary Cities: Policies and Practices in International Perspective." *International Migration* 55: no. 2 (2017): 174–87. https://doi.org/10.1111/imig.12308.

Bayoumi, Moustafa. *How Does It Feel to Be a Problem? Being Young and Arab in America*. New York: Penguin Books, 2008.

Bettmann, Joanna E., Mary Jane Taylor, Elizabeth Gamarra, Rachel L. Wright, and Trinh Mai. "Resettlement Experiences of Children Who Entered the United States as Refugees." *Social Development Issues* 39, no. 3 (2017): 1–18.

Betts, Alexander. "Institutional Proliferation and the Global Refugee Regime."

Perspectives on Politics 7, no. 1 (March 2009): 53–58. https://doi.org/10.1017/S1537592709090082.

Brady, Andrea. "Drone Poetics." *New Formations: A Journal of Culture/Theory/Politics* 89, no. 89 (January 2017): 116–36. https://doi.org/10.3898/NewF:89/90.07.2016.

Capps, Randy, Michael Fix, and Chiamaka Nwosu. "A Profile of Immigrants in Houston, the Nation's Most Diverse Metropolitan Area." Migration Policy Institute. March 2015. http://www.migrationpolicy.org/research/profile-immigrants-houston-nations-most-diverse-metropolitan-area.

Chemerinsky, Erwin. "The Constitutionality of Withholding Federal Funds from Sanctuary Cities." *Los Angeles Lawyer* 40, no. 2 (April 2017): 60.

Clutterbuck, Martin, Laura Cunial, Paola Barsanti, and Tina Gewis. "Establishing Legal Identity for Displaced Syrians." *Forced Migration Review* 57 (February 2018): 59–61. www.fmreview.org/syria2018.

Coomaraswamy, Radhika. "Women and Children: The Cutting Edge of International Law." *Proceedings of the ASIL Annual Meeting* 108 (2014): 43–65.

Craven, Morgan. "Suspended Childhood: An Analysis of Exclusionary Discipline of Texas' Pre-K and Elementary Schools." August 2016. Updated April 2017. https://report.texasappleseed.org/suspended-childhood-updated.

Creswell, Robyn. "Nazik Al-Mala'ika and the Poetics of Pan-Arabism." *Critical Inquiry* 46, no. 1 (September 2019): 71–96. https://doi.org/10.1086/705300.

Curtis, Maria F. "Discrimination." In *Encyclopedia of Muslim-American History*, 2-volume set, edited by Edward E. Curtis, 150–53. New York: Infobase Learning, 2010.

Drumsta, Emily, ed. *Revolt against the Sun: The Selected Poetry of Nazik Al-Mala'ika: A Bilingual Reader*. London: Saqi Books, 2020.

Durable Solutions Platform. "Far from Home: Future Prospects for Syrian Refugees in Iraq." ACAPS. January 2019. https://www.acaps.org/country/iraq/crisis/country-level.

Edkins, Jenny. "Missing Migrants and the Politics of Naming: Names without Bodies, Bodies without Names." *Social Research* 83, no. 2 (June 2016): 359–89.

Emerson, Michael O., Jenifer Bratter, Junia Howell, P. Wilner Jeanty, and Mike Cline. "Houston Region Grows More Racially/Ethnically Diverse, With Small Declines in Segregation: A Joint Report Analyzing Census Data from 1990, 2000, and 2010." Kinder Institute for Urban Research and the Hobby Center for the Study of Texas. 2012. https://kinder.rice.edu/sites/default/files/documents/Houston%20Region%20Grows%20More%20Ethnically%20Diverse%204-9.pdf.

Evans, William, and Daniel Fitzgerald. "The Economic and Social Outcomes of Refugees in the United States: Evidence from the ACS." National Bureau of Economic Research. NBER Working Paper Series. June 2017. https://doi.org/10.3386/w23498.

Fairchild, Al. "US Immigration: A Shrinking Vision of Belonging and Deserving." *American Journal of Public Health* 108, no. 5 (2018): 604–5.

Fawcett, Louise. *International Relations of the Middle East*. 5th ed. Oxford, UK: Oxford University Press, 2019.

Feldman, Claud. "Truancy Bill Will Be Hotly Debated in the Texas Legislative Session." *Houston Chronicle*, January 18, 2015. https://www.houstonchronicle.com/life/article/Truancy-bill-will-be-hotly-debated-during-the-6012827.php.

Filindra, A., and Kovács, M. "Analysing US State Legislative Resolutions on Immigrants and Immigration: The Role of Immigration Federalism." *International Migration* 50, no. 4 (January 2012): 33–50. https://doi.org/10.1111/j.1468-2435.2010.00658.x.

Freedman, Jane. "Sexual and Gender-Based Violence against Refugee Women: A Hidden Aspect of the Refugee 'Crisis.'" *Reproductive Health Matters* 24, no. 47 (June 2016): 18–26. https://doi.org/10.1016/j.rhm.2016.05.003.

Gangamma, Rashmi, and Daran Shipman. "Transnational Intersectionality in Family Therapy with Resettled Refugees." *Journal of Marital and Family Therapy* 44, no. 2 (April 2018): 206–19. https://doi.org/10.1111/jmft.12267.

Gerdau, I., J. I. Kizilhan, and M. Noll-Hussong. "Posttraumatic Stress Disorder and Related Disorders among Female Yazidi Refugees Following Islamic State of Iraq and Syria Attacks—A Case Series and Mini-Review." *Frontiers in Psychiatry* 8 (December 2017). https://doi.org/10.3389/fpsyt.2017.00282.

Gill, Nick, Deirdre Conlon, Dominique Moran, and Andrew Burridge. "Carceral Circuitry: New Directions in Carceral Geography." *Progress in Human Geography* 42, no. 2 (April 2018): 183–204. https://doi.org/10.1177/0309132516671823.

Gökariksel, Banu. "The Body Politics of Trump's 'Muslim Ban.'" *Journal of Middle East Women's Studies* 13, no. 3 (2017): 469–71. https://doi.org/10.1215/15525864-4179133.

Heptinstall, Ellen, Vaheshta Sethna, and Eric Taylor. "PTSD and Depression in Refugee Children: Associations with Pre-Migration Trauma and Post-Migration Stress." *European Child and Adolescent Psychiatry* 13, no. 6 (December 2004): 373–80. https://doi.org/10.1007/s00787-004-0422-y.

Hogue, Simon. "Performing, Translating, Fashioning: Spectatorship in the Surveillant World." *Surveillance and Society* 14, no. 2 (April 2016): 168–83. https://doi.org/10.24908/ss.v14i2.6016.

Houghton, Frank. "Learning from the 'Muslim Ban': Implications of the Trump Presidency for International Public Health." *The New Zealand Medical Journal* 130, no. 1451 (2017): 75–77.

Houston, Serin D., and Charlotte Morse. "The Ordinary and Extraordinary: Producing Migrant Inclusion and Exclusion in US Sanctuary Movements." *Studies in Social Justice* 11, no. 1 (February 2017): 27–47. https://doi.org/10.26522/ssj.v11i1.1081.

Huetteman, Emmarie, and Matt Flegenheimer. "Ted Cruz Challenges President Obama to Debate on Syrian Refugees." *New York Times*, November 18, 2015. https://www.nytimes.com/politics/first-draft/2015/11/18/ted-cruz-challenges-president-obama-to-debate-on-syrian-refugees/.

Hussein, Tarek. "Prejudice against Muslim Students in Public Schools (Houston, Texas)." Master's Thesis, University of Houston–Clear Lake, 2015. ProQuest.

Hyndman, Jennifer. *Managing Displacement: Refugees and the Politics of Humanitarianism.* New ed. Barrows Lectures 16. Minneapolis: University of Minnesota Press, 2000.

Hynes, H. P. "On the Battlefield of Women's Bodies: An Overview of the Harm of War to Women." *Women's Studies International Forum* 27, no. 5–6 (2004): 431–45.

Jaffe-Walter, R., D. Walsh, and S. J. Lee. "This Issue: Imagining Sites of Possibility in Immigrant and Refugee Education." *Theory into Practice* 57, no. 2 (June 2018): 79–81. https://doi.org/10.1080/00405841.2018.1425818.

Jentleson, B. W. "Global Governance, the United Nations, and the Challenge of Trumping Trump." *Global Governance* 23, no. 2 (2017): 143–49.

Karson, Tom. "Confronting Houston's Demographic Shift: The Harris County AFL-CIO." *WorkingUSA* 8, no. 2 (December 2004): 207–27. https://doi.org/10.1111/j.1743-4580.2004.00012.x.

Kerwin, Donald. "The Faltering US Refugee Protection System: Legal and Policy Responses to Refugees, Asylum-Seekers, and Others in Need of Protection." *Refugee Survey Quarterly* 31, no. 1 (January 2012): 1–33. https://doi.org/10.1093/rsq/hdr019.

Kira, Ibrahim A., Vidya Ramaswamy, Linda Lewandowski, Jamal Mohanesh, and Husam Abdul-Khalek. "Psychometric Assessment of the Arabic Version of the Internalized Stigma of Mental Illness (ISMI) Measure in a Refugee Population." *Transcultural Psychiatry* 52, no. 5 (2015): 636–58. https://doi.org/10.1177/1363461515569755.

Kragie, Andrew. "Greater Houston Resettles More Refugees Than Any Other City." *Houston Chronicle*, September 13, 2015. Updated December 22, 2017. https://www.houstonchronicle.com/news/houston-texas/houston/article/Greater-Houston-resettles-more-refugees-than-any-6502351.php.

Liamputtong, Pranee, Lee Koh, Dennis Wollersheim, and Rae Walker. "Peer Support Groups, Mobile Phones and Refugee Women in Melbourne." *Health Promotion International* 31, no. 3 (September 2016): 715–24. https://doi.org/10.1093/heapro/dav015.

Malkki, Liisa H. "Refugees and Exile: From 'Refugee Studies' to the National Order of Things." *Annual Review of Anthropology* 24, no. 1 (1995): 495–523. https://doi.org/10.1146/annurev.an.24.100195.002431.

Martin, Susan Forbes. *Refugee Women.* 2nd ed. Atlantic Highlands, NJ: Zed Books, 2003.

McBrien, J. Lynn. "Educational Needs and Barriers for Refugee Students in the United States: A Review of the Literature." *Review of Educational Research* 75, no. 3 (Fall 2005): 329–64.

McLaren, Kristin. "Muslim Innovations in American Exceptionalist Rhetoric: Linda Sarsour's American Jeremiad." *Journal of Religion and Popular Culture* 29, no. 2 (July 2017): 147–61. https://doi.org/10.3138/jrpc.29.2.4085.

Mejia, Brittny. "How Houston Has Become the Most Diverse Place in America." *Los Angeles Times.* May 9, 2017. https://www.latimes.com/nation/la-na-houston-diversity-2017-htmlstory.html.

Mishra, Smeeta. "'Saving' Muslim Women and Fighting Muslim Men: Analysis of Representations in *The New York Times.*" *Global Media Journal* 6, no. 11 (October 2007): https://www.globalmediajournal.com/open-access/saving-muslim-women-and-fighting-muslim-menanalysis-of-representations-in-the-new-york-times.php?aid=35266.

Morrison, John. "'The Dark-Side of Globalisation': The Criminalisation of Refugees." *Race and Class* 43, no. 1 (July 2001): 71–74.

Naff, Alixa. *Becoming American: The Early Arab Immigrant Experience*. Carbondale: Southern Illinois University Press, 1985.

Naimou, Angela. "Double Vision: Refugee Crises and the Afterimages of Endless War." *College Literature* 43, no. 1 (Winter 2016): 226–33.

Norman, Steve. "Assessing the Credibility of Refugee Applicants: A Judicial Perspective." *International Journal of Refugee Law* 19, no. 2 (July 2007): 273–92. https://doi.org/10.1093/ijrl/eem015.

Parker, Stephanie. "Hidden Crisis: Violence against Syrian Female Refugees." *The Lancet* (UK Edition) 385, no. 9985 (2015): 2341-42. https://doi.org/10.1016/S0140-6736(15)61091-1.

Ramadan, Adam. "Spatialising the Refugee Camp." *Transactions of the Institute of British Geographers* 38, no. 1 (January 2013): 65–77. https://doi.org/10.1111/j.1475-5661.2012.00509.x.

Riber, Karin. "Trauma Complexity and Child Abuse: A Qualitative Study of Attachment Narratives in Adult Refugees with PTSD." *Transcultural Psychiatry* 54, no. 5–6 (2017): 840–69. https://doi.org/10.1177/1363461517737198.

Richter-Montpetit, Melanie. "Beyond the Erotics of Orientalism: Lawfare, Torture and the Racial-Sexual Grammars of Legitimate Suffering." *Security Dialogue* 45, no. 1 (January 2014): 43–62. https://doi.org/10.1177/0967010613515016.

Rosas, Gilberto. "The Managed Violences of the Borderlands: Treacherous Geographies, Policeability, and the Politics of Race." *Latino Studies* 4, no. 4 (December 2006): 401–18. https://doi.org/10.1057/palgrave.lst.8600221.

Ross, Alison. "Introduction (Homo Sacer: Sovereign Power and Bare Life, Giorgio Agamben)." *South Atlantic Quarterly* 107, no. 1 (December 2008): 1–13. https://doi.org/10.1215/00382876-2007-052.

Sacchetti, Maria, and Isaac Stanley-Becker. "In Blow to Trump's Immigration Agenda, Federal Judge Blocks Asylum Ban for Migrants Who Enter Illegally from Mexico." *Washington Post*, November 20, 2018.

Sarsour, Linda. "My Take: My Hijab Is My Hoodie." CNN Belief. April 5, 2012. http://religion.blogs.cnn.com/2012/04/05/my-take-my-hijab-is-my-hoodie/.

———. *We Are Not Here to Be Bystanders: A Memoir of Love and Resistance*. New York: Simon and Schuster, 2020.

Schwartz, Eric P. "Issues Impacting Migrant Women." *Proceedings of the ASIL Annual Meeting* 108 (2014): 262–65. https://doi.org/10.5305/procannmeetasil.108.0262.

Scribner, Todd. "You Are Not Welcome Here Anymore: Restoring Support for Refugee Resettlement in the Age of Trump." *Journal on Migration and Human Security* 5, no. 2 (2017): 263–84. https://doi.org/10.1177/233150241700500203.

Shannon, Patricia, Maureen O'Dougherty, and Erin Mehta. "Refugees' Perspectives on Barriers to Communication about Trauma Histories in Primary Care." *Mental Health in Family Medicine* 9, no. 1 (January 2012): 47–55.

Sheth, Falguni. "Unruly Muslim Women and Threats to Liberal Culture." *Peace Review* 18, no. 4 (October 2006): 455–63. https://doi.org/10.1080/10402650601030328.

Smith, Valerie J. "Ethical and Effective Ethnographic Research Methods: A Case Study with Afghan Refugees in California." *Journal of Empirical Research on Human Research Ethics* 4, no. 3 (September 2009): 59–72. https://doi.org/10.1525/jer.2009.4.3.59.

Spellberg, Denise A. "Inventing Matamoras: Gender and the Forgotten Islamic Past in the United States of America." *Frontiers: A Journal of Women Studies* 25, no. 1 (2004): 148–64. https://doi.org/10.1353/fro.2004.0042.

Stokes, Hannah. "Conceptualizing and Measuring Food Security among Resettled Refugees Living in the United States." Master's thesis, University of Vermont, 2017. ProQuest.

Subcommittee on Immigration and Border Security, Committee on the Judiciary, United States House of Representatives. "Sanctuary Cities: A Threat to Public Safety." Hearing. 114th Congress, 1st Session (July 23, 2015). Serial No. 114–36. Washington: U.S. Government Publishing Office, 2015. https://www.govinfo.gov/.

Taylor, Keeanga-Yamahtta. *How We Get Free: Black Feminism and the Combahee River Collective.* Chicago: Haymarket Books, 2017.

Terasaki, Genji, Nicole C. Ahrenholz, and Mahri Z. Haider. "Care of Adult Refugees with Chronic Conditions." *Medical Clinics of North America* 99, no. 5 (July 2015): 1039–58. https://doi.org/10.1016/j.mcna.2015.05.006.

Texas Association of School Boards. "Compulsory Attendance and Truancy." TASB School Law eSource. Updated February 2022. https://www.tasb.org/services/legal-services/tasb-school-law-esource/students/documents/compulsory_attendance_and_truancy.aspx.

Tomlinson, Frances, and Sue Egan. "From Marginalization to (Dis)Empowerment: Organizing Training and Employment Services for Refugees." *Human Relations* 55, no. 8 (August 2002): 1019–43. https://doi.org/10.1177/0018726702055008182.

United Nations High Commissioner for Refugees. "Tackling Sexual Exploitation and Abuse and Sexual Harassment: 2020–2022 Strategy and Action Plan." UNHCR. https://www.unhcr.org/5f3cfec44.

Wanigaratne, Susitha, Donald C. Cole, Kate Bassil, Ilene Hyman, Rahim Moineddin, and Marcelo L. Urquia. "The Influence of Refugee Status and Secondary Migration on Preterm Birth." *Journal of Epidemiology and Community Health* 70, no. 6 (June 2016): 622–28. https://doi.org/10.1136/jech-2015-206529.

West, Lauren Thomas. "Social Capital and Refugee Mothers." Master's thesis, International Institute of Social Studies, Erasmus University, 2019.

Yun, Katherine, Jasmine Matheson, Colleen Payton, Kevin C. Scott, Barbara L. Stone, Lihai Song, William M. Stauffer, Kailey Urban, Janine Young, and Blain Mamo. "Health Profiles of Newly Arrived Refugee Children in the United States, 2006–2012." *American Journal of Public Health* 106, no. 1 (January 2016): 128–35. https://doi.org/10.2105/AJPH.2015.302873.

Zavratnik, Simona, and Sanja Cukut Krilić. "Addressing Intersectional Vulnerabilities in Contemporary Refugee Movements in Europe." *Druzboslovne Razprave* 34, no. 87 (April 2018): 85–106.

10

Social Control, Punishment, and Gender

Silenced Memories of Peruvian Women in Wartime

MARTA ROMERO-DELGADO

Introduction

The Peruvian Armed Conflict (1980 to 2000)[1] confronted the government with two armed organizations/groups, the Peruvian Communist Party-Shining Path (*Partido Comunista del Perú-Sendero Luminoso, PCP-SL* in Spanish)[2] and Tupac Amaru Revolutionary Movement (*Movimiento Revolucionario Tupac Amaru, MRTA* in Spanish),[3] leaving the Andean country in an internal war for two decades. In 2001, the Peruvian Truth and Reconciliation Commission (in Spanish: *Comisión de la Verdad y Reconciliación—CVR*) was established in order to analyze the causes, responsibilities, and costs, both human and material, of the violence that ended with the defeat of both armed groups. According to the Final Report of the Truth Commission (2003) there were approximately 69,280 casualties; 79% of the dead lived in rural areas, 60% had a primary education, and 75% had Quechua or another native language as their mother tongue. Thousands of cases of torture were reported, and there was a mass exodus. The Peruvian state determined the economic cost of this war that spanned 1980–1992 to be an estimated $21 billion. The development of this armed conflict aggravated existing social, ethnic, and gender inequalities in Peru (CVR 2003).[4] In this period of political violence, there is an abrupt change in the existing social roles. Female participation in the conflict was widespread and unexpected. In this conflict many women were communal leaders, "ronderas,"[5] commanders, and fighters. The women who joined the Shining Path group were significant in number.[6]

In a global context, war is still perceived as being the prerogative of men alone. Women are generally excluded from the debate on belligerence except as passive victims of the brutality inflicted on them by their masculine contemporaries (Fernández Villanueva 2000; Blair, Londoño, and Nieto 2003; Scott 2008). However, history has shown that women played a role in armed hostilities, sometimes even being the main protagonists (Bennett, Bexley, and Warnock 1995; Cockburn 2007; Romero-Delgado 2017). But still the general idea is to consider women as victims and not as fighters, making their direct involvement in political violence seem anecdotal. The main reason for this is due to the social construction of violence, which is very masculine, and despite the information available women appear in war marginally, unless the fighters are a regular army. Nevertheless this certainly dominant pattern of violence where mostly perpetrators are male and the victims female, feminist scholarship has not moved much beyond the dichotomy between agency/victimhood and does not take into account another kind of politics that involves giving importance to female perpetrators (Sjoberg and Gentry 2007, Glynn 2009, Parashar 2011, Roy 2012).

The majority of the fieldwork for this chapter was carried out in Peru from 2007 to 2009. I collected data using a variety of qualitative and quantitative methods of analysis. The study population was made up of women who were involved in one of the two armed groups: PCP-SL and MRTA. Some of them were already out of prison but others were still serving their sentences.[7] In addition, I contacted members of the Truth Commission, scholars, family connections, and NGOs familiar with the subject. I also interviewed men from both armed groups who had recently been released from prison.

My investigation emphasizes the social and political factors that influence the presence of women in wars. It reconstructs the memory of women in both Peruvian armed groups to analyze the structural and psychosocial reasons for the involvement of women as agents of political violence. The reasons for becoming involved in armed groups are similar for both men and women: political ideology, current personal situation, and the influence or pressure from the group. Due to space limitations, in this chapter I focus on prison experiences of these women. The central argument is how power relationships act in order to entrench discrimination against those who do not have privileges in society. But it is inside prisons where we can clearly see how systems of oppression work at the coming together of racism, patriarchy, and political order. The Peruvian case is another example that prisons and the punitive system "reveal the dangerous intersections of racism, male domination, and state strategies of political repression" (Davis 2003, 61).

Peruvian Punitive System: Continuum of Violence, Racism, and Patriarchy

According to the CVR (2003), between 1980 and 2000 approximately 20,000 men and women were imprisoned. In 1995, the National Coordinator of Human Rights of Peru—CNDDHH in Spanish—stated in its report that only 20% of the total population incarcerated had been sentenced, the remaining 80% had only been accused (CNDDHH 1995). Out of that 80%, 66% were sent in during Alberto Fujimori's government (1991–1996, his first term). Rita,[8] (a leader in an association of relatives of political prisoners, missing people, and victims of genocide), said in an interview in 2009, "During the hardest time, there were 800 female detainees, so that gives you an idea of the number of women, 800 women, and that was only between 1994 and 1995."

In Peru, the Report of the Ombudsman conducted in 2011 states the following: out of the 3015 interned women scattered throughout Peru, only 74 were still imprisoned for the crime of terrorism, which is currently incorporated among the crimes classified as "against public tranquility" (Defensoría del Pueblo del Perú 2011). As we can see from these figures, even though the number of women incarcerated for the crime of terrorism and "treason against the homeland" has always been lower than that of men, as it is among the rest of the total prison population, their sentences have been longer. According to Chavez (1989) women had a more active part in the execution of acts of terrorism than men, and their responsibility is also greater, if we judge by the penalties imposed on them. This situation is confirmed when we observe that 76.7% of these women were sentenced to between five and twenty years of custody, while only 54.9% of men were given sentences of the same length. This data raises several questions, including how real it is that women played a more active role and had greater responsibility in armed groups compared to their male counterparts, and whether the number of years imposed could be due to the perception the judges had of the "mandatory nature" of female identity and to the generalised social representation of the women who belonged to these groups. Here is Marina's testimony. Below is her answer to the question of whether she believes there is any type of discrimination in the prison sentences for being a woman:

> I was detained when I was 23 years old. I was arrested along with my boyfriend. They pressed more charges against him than me, but I got 23 years and him and another male comrade got 15 years. My lawyer told me that at the trial he found the prosecutor in the loo. He asked him about my sentence of 23 years in comparison with the 15 that the other two men

got. "At least, she should have gotten 15 years too," he said. "But she's a woman!" the prosecutor said. So yes, I do believe there is discrimination, they give us longer prison sentences for being women." (Marina, MRTA)

By transgressing traditional gender roles, women of the PCP-SL and the MRTA received greater "social punishment" than their male counterparts, even when they were accused of the same or less serious actions. And the fact that women were taxed as "more cruel," an assertion repeated again and again, might be due to the application of these same traditional gender stereotypes in the functioning of the criminal justice system, which considered crimes to be more serious when perpetrated by women.

As Davis (2003, 2005) and Gilmore (2007) maintain, in order to reinforce the current prison industrial system, it is necessary to reproduce disposable, undesirable, and dangerous people according to the dominant discourse. Prisons around the world have become not only opaque places to "store" those who are not socially "useful," but a lucrative business and a fruitful source of income. The case of the United States of America is paradigmatic, as Wacquant (2009) argues. The United States is the country with the second-highest number of incarcerated people in the world, behind Russia, where the percentage of prisoners has doubled since the collapse of the Soviet state. That increase is due to the new approach to regulate the poverty level, which has been shifted from the social welfare to the criminal justice apparatus. In fact, the strategy of criminalizing poverty has spread throughout the globe. It has already had a strong impact on political debates about crime and punishment in all countries where neoliberal ideology has contributed to the deregulation of the economy and the collapse of the social protection network (Christie 1993, Sudbury 2005, Wacquant 2009). The social exclusion, marginalization, and criminalization of the poor and vulnerable people, mostly racialized, means that their lives and bodies belong to the System. This large tradition of white supremacy, heteropatriarchy, and neoliberal capitalism gave rise to the implementation of punitive measures by the governments to address social problems, mainly with prison-expansion business. As Shreerekha Pillai argues in this edited volume, carceral liberalism points to a clear relationship between "the colonial state that historically carried out its violent machinations under the sign of benevolence and civilization, whilst marauding and violating native bodies, knowledge, and industries" (21). And this is how one understands a comprehensive continuum of a "lattice fortifying structures of oppression within and beyond prison walls."

The female subject is punished in a more subtle way than her male counterparts, due to the structural nature of patriarchy. Feminicide is the dominant form of punishment for women, which also explains the smaller number of female prisoners. Men are punished mainly in the public sphere, while women continue to be disciplined and punished in public and also in private through other, invisible ways. This reality explains the transfer between state violence and sexist violence. It should be noted that women have traditionally been institutionalized in mental institutions more often than men. Males considered worthless or surplus are being perceived as "delinquent" whereas their female counterparts are seen as "degenerate" and "mentally unbalanced." Prisons are considering the continuation of slavery (Davis 2005, Gilmore 2007). They are places where even the basic human rights are violated, like reproductive rights, especially if the prisoners are "racialized" people, women, poor, and political prisoners (Shakur 2001, Ocen 2012).

We should not forget that the criminal justice system reflects social reality and at the same time contributes to its reproduction, and consequently prison, like every social institution, is built with an androcentric conception (Antony 2000, Larrauri 2000). As one of the interviewees noted, she considers that her other crime, besides being a leader of her organization/group, was being a woman: "I thought that being a woman in that type of prison designed to 'take revenge from man to man'—because it is possible to admit that a man would rebel, but it is absurd and illogical for a weak woman to do it—made me feel the double oppression of the regime. I suffered not only the same as the others [male comrades], but also the humiliations, derogatory, arrogant, morbid, lustful attitudes that one feels with the looks or the gestures and attitudes of the male prison warden" (Laura, MRTA). In other words, the symbolic elements of the social structure, such as male and female roles, condition the material elements of the criminal justice system, by varying the length of sentences according to the gender of those condemned (Baratta 2000, Juliano 2009).

Prisons became an extension of the ideological, military, and symbolic battle being fought at that time in the country, while the PCP-SL's ideological and moral strength became evident (Rénique 2003). Here is a clear example of how prisons played an important role within the conflict. Everything that happened outside was reflected inside and vice versa: "Before President Gonzalo and the other comrades fell down, the wardens did not touch us. We were treated with respect and fear at the same time. The wardens were fearful in case the Party rose to power and took reprisals against them, as happened in China with Mao" (Lola, PCP-SL).

Many of the women in this research experienced drastic changes in the prison regime, from the first decade of armed conflict—1980 to 1990, with the Belaúnde and García governments, up until the coming to power of the

Fujimori government. The measures taken by Alberto Fujimori and his government, in power from 1990 to 2000, were a turning point for the criminal justice system, but also for public discourse and action. The advent of Fujimori's government meant worse changes still in the political, penitentiary, and living conditions of women interviewed, but in this case their experiences varied considerably and were influenced by multiple factors.

Those who had joined the PCP-SL or the MRTA as a result of political and social convictions had been arrested, imprisoned, and tortured on several occasions. But with changes in anti-terrorism laws, sentences were at minimum ten to twenty years—whether they were innocent or simply suspects, with or without judicial process, with evidence that confirmed the sentence or not. Once again, it is important to point out how they joined their organization, as it was a decisive factor in how they later handled their long prison sentences and how these extreme experiences affected their subjectivity. This was the hardest and most difficult stage to handle for all the prisoners interviewed. They told me that they had to stay in this cellular or closed regime for eight years, with four to six women sharing a cell, locked up for twenty-three and a half and sometimes even twenty-four hours a day. They could only receive visits from direct relatives once a month, for thirty minutes, talking through a mesh that prevented any physical contact. They understood that they had to occupy their time somehow, so as not to "let themselves die" because at first they were not allowed to have anything.

Until 1992, they were allowed to weave, sew, and even read books, although even the Old Testament was considered subversive. For some years, all kinds of books were banned; actually anything that gave them a distraction wasn't allowed. The reason behind this was the power some prisoners had inside, especially the ones from PCP-SL. In prison, they lived in "*a commune style.*" They self-financed by making handicrafts, like tapestries, that were sold outside. The prison officers did not know anything about these activities, or if they did know, they did not say anything. After 1992, when the leadership of both organizations/groups was captured, according to the interviewees "*the regime simply existed to annihilate*" (Aurora, PCP-SL). That statement has been corroborated by Human Rights agencies. "It is obvious that the treatment provided had no rehabilitative objective. According to the mentors of the regime, it was not enough to suppress their freedom; they also had to be punished to the limit of their resistance. This system violated the Standard Minimum Rules for the Treatment of Prisoners given by the United Nations Organization" (CVR 2003, V, 463–64). "There, in that place, in prison, you could not control the time. You were punished because they did not want you to read, they did not want you to knit, they did not want you to control your own time; survival was already a luxury" (Lola, PCP-SL). The loss of control over their existences, the torture, the humiliation and constant vexations during detention and later in prison were a recurring theme in almost all the narratives of women interviewed.

Thus prison marked a turning point in their lives, not only because of the stress that comes from being enclosed in a confined space without intimacy and at the mercy of others, but also because within these spaces their rights were systematically violated, with total impunity and with the full knowledge of successive governments and of the rest of the social institutions.

Due to gender socialization, women and men regard family relationships in completely different ways. Women keep contact with their children even in the worst times of war, even clandestinely while in prison. Men are able to separate war from family. Because of that, motherhood in prison was used by Peruvian authorities as a means of both formal and informal control of PCP-SL and MRTA prisoners and constituted another clear example of punishment based on gender.

The leaders of both these movements had the strictest and most inhospitable prison conditions, if only because their cases had more media coverage and visibility. For the Peruvian government, it was another opportunity to show who had won the war; so some were even imprisoned in military prisons with extreme security. It should be recalled that although it was difficult to survive almost twenty-four hours a day in a cell, most of the women—and men—shared a cell with other "comrades" in the same situation, which meant that they were able to support each other and thus minimize the psychosocial effects that in conditions of total isolation were even more difficult to face (Shalev 2008). At the time of the interview in 2009 within the prison, Laura had been imprisoned for sixteen years. She was in a leadership role in MRTA and had been arrested four times, two of them leading to imprisonment. She assures me that she had always been tortured when detained. At the Naval Base of the Callao, she spent five years in total isolation. She wasn't the only one; there were other prisoners also isolated. After that, she spent another three years in Yanamayo's prison (Puno Region). It was located 3,800 meters above sea level. She tells me about her transfer to the Naval Base of Callao in 1993 by members of the Army Intelligence Service (SIE):

> "I was informed by a Major about the routine in the prison of Callao. I would be locked up 24 hours in a cell 2 X 2.5 m and 2.5 m high, with a metal door 8 cm thick; with three huge locks whose keys were kept by three different people; one of them was Vladimiro Montesinos,[9] to prevent the doors from being opened without his knowledge." (Laura, MRTA)

Extreme Prison Experiences:
Torture and Punishment Based on Gender

Regardless of their rank or function within the organization, virtually all women and men both from the PCP-SL and from the MRTA, whether they were members or suspects, were subjected to physical and psychological torture after being detained. The places where police and military agents performed these systematic practices were at different locations belonging to the Interior and Defense Ministries. Torture was part of the strategy of both the state and of insurgent groups, although the Peruvian state torture was more "sophisticated" because they had greater resources and logistics.

Davis (2005) observes, "We tend to think about torture as an aberrant event. Torture is extraordinary and can be clearly distinguished from other regimes of punishment. But if we consider the various form of violence linked to the practice of imprisonment—circuits of violence linked to one another—then we begin to see that the extraordinary has some connection to the ordinary. Within the radical movement in defense of women prisoners' rights, the routine strip and cavity search is recognized as a form of sexual assault" (43). The last time that women from PCP-SL were forced to undergo strip searches and cavity searches in their vaginas was in 2010. As many irregularities were discovered in that process, several associations, journalists, and scholars condemned that violation of human rights.

As Hamilton (2007) suggests, it is important to consider the ways in which "the very process of arrest and torture constructs sexual difference through the actions of the torturers." In recounting their experiences of police abuse, the women "attributed the specificity of their experience 'as women' not to their own prior gender identities or biological difference, but to the words and actions of the officers." By "targeting certain parts of their body (for example, breasts and buttocks), using explicitly sexual language, taunts and threats, and even accusing arrestees of undermining conventional gender roles through their activism, the police emphasized the femaleness of detainees from the outset" (135). The clearest example of this is rape and other forms of sexual violence used as practices of torture which, for some authors, seen through the patriarchal lens, could be interpreted as a penalisation of gender intended to "feminize" the victim—whether it was a woman or a man, considering the feminine as that which can be penetrated and subdued (Nordstrom 1996, Taylor 1997, D'Antonio 2009). Through these penetrative acts of violence, we see a systematic feminization of the incarcerated subject, and a method to feminize their vulnerability.

The use of sexual violence as part of the military strategy to humiliate, eliminate, and defeat the enemy was a systematic practice in the Peruvian conflict, especially in rural areas of Ayacucho where barracks and military bases were built after the state of emergency was declared in 1982 (Mantilla 2005, Boesten 2014).[10] In addition, rape, abuse, and other forms of torture were accompanied by humiliating insults and racist discrimination in reference to ethnicity, demonstrating the close relationship between authoritarian discourse and practices like sexism, racism, exclusion, and discrimination. This process of disgust and "symbolic trashing" (*basurización simbólica*, so called by Silva Santisteban 2008) made those physical practices allowable by demeaning, devalorising, and dehumanising Indigenous and *mestiza/o* peoples involved either as victims of state violence or as perpetrators from the PCP-SL and the MRTA.

The women interviewed argue that everything is shared in prison, not just the few material things they had, but the emotions and sensations both good and bad. Emotions should be considered a collective instead of an individual issue because they are built and signified in social relationships (Ahmed 2004). Usually prisoners became one big family. Raquel told me that on one occasion when a special commando of DINCOTE (National Directorate Against Terrorism, of the National Police of Peru) came to the prison to torture them, she was pregnant, and therefore a cellmate asked for her to be excused. When the prisoners were ordered to come out of the cell to receive the torture, the rest of Raquel's cellmates defended her belly with their bodies in order to protect the baby. "I could imagine what they would do to my friend, right? Then they all said: 'No, you're not going to leave here, first they have to beat us all.' And they did. They opened the bars, ah, they hit us hard, hard, hard, me, my head, the body, the girls protected my belly, they covered my belly and they got beaten their bodies" (Raquel, PCP-SL).

Clara reports, "In prison, I met many people, people very valuable to me, people, for example, who died. As we have been together inside so many years, we have gone through many things together. Anyway, in general there is an atmosphere, you could say, as a family, a big family, where you share everything, right? Including joy, sorrow, sadness, pain, suffering, right?" (Clara, MRTA). For Clara, these extreme experiences are what have made it so that even outside today they continue to see each other, sharing their time and activities. They consider that although the majority of them have already left prison, the mutual support that began as something imposed on them turned into a "*very deep friendship*" as time passed by with all the hard experiences lived. "The cohabitation has made you generate another family, a big family, where we shared everything. If they brought you a plate of food, you could not eat it alone, you had to share it . . . Eh, they are your sisters, you had to look after them, sometimes even wash their clothes. It was a solidarity support among all of us. I believe that unity has also let us overcome all the difficult and hard situations we have gone through" (Clara, MRTA).

During the period of imprisonment two types of links or ties were constantly intermingling: the political (vertical) and the human (horizontal). On one hand were the structured ties that framed the decisions considered as vital, taken by the political organizations. On the other hand were the human ties, corresponding to the transversal links that encouraged general cooperation irrespective of political affiliation (D'Antonio 2009). Of course, these bonds were not exempt from tensions and interference with each other. As many of these women spent years in prison and some are still inside, the time in jail became a highly influential agent of socialization, in some cases resulting in an authentic process of resocialization. Under these conditions and serving an average sentence of fifteen years, women who experience these exceptional and complex situations alter or transform their identities in different ways. Some of the ways in which this process happened were: (1) to reaffirm their identity as activists and fighters—considering themselves today as political prisoners or prisoners of war; (2) to remain independent but become acclimated to the conditions of prison life; (3) to dissociate themselves completely, either by being repentant or by breaking their links with the groups they were affiliated with; or (4) to claim they were innocent. We should clarify that this classification is not rigid and that a single woman could take several of these positions during the years of prison. According to Felices-Luna (2007), through this classification and its corresponding benefit/punishment, the Peruvian state managed to destroy the identity of many political prisoners, women and men, transforming them from active political subjects into passive and obedient persons.

Many women who didn't belong to any of the armed groups were arrested and imprisoned. That happened more often after Fujimori's "self-coup d'état" in 1992.[11] Some of these women were just members of legitimate leftist groups, neighbourhood associations and social movements. Some of them were not activists or did not have a defined political conviction. However, having to face many years of imprisonment, these women came in contact with a reality completely unknown to them until then. Gabriela was "an innocent released"; she states that her time in prison transformed her. Although she never identified herself with the PCP-SL—of which she was accused of being a member—she admits that knowing a different reality made her leave prison completely changed. Now she identifies herself as a political person, but in the broadest sense of the word, as a political subject, with choice and ability to influence society but not as an affiliate to either of the two organizations/groups. She has always maintained her innocence and political independence: "Living 8 years in a political prison means you have already learned many things. I did not enter as a political person but left as one. I had to live with people who I spoke with. Somehow, consciously and unconsciously, I am a woman who entered into prison as a housewife and got out different, transformed because I met many important people" (Gabriela, innocent released).

During the Peruvian armed conflict, as happened outside, prisons became the territories of a dispute about symbols and power that pitted the PCP-SL against the MRTA. This means that both groups battled not only against the state but also with anyone who did not belong to their own organization, especially in the 1990s, when the climate of violence was more intense and the repression more severe. Within the prisons for women and men, there were a number of agreements and both formal and informal rules that the prisoners themselves established and which depended on the prisoners' "status." Hence, this prison hierarchy is structured in the form of a pyramid, putting at the apex of it the members of the PCP-SL; then those of the MRTA; after that the independent prisoners; and at the bottom, the unaffiliated or politically detached, the repentant, and the innocent. Bea talks about it:

> Now I think that sometimes we fought each other in vain because the other prisoners were not the enemy, although Shining Path's [PCP-Shining Path] way did not seem the right and clear way to us. They were many more, so we did not exist. We went on hunger strikes. We did until the end even if they had to take us out on a wheelchair. We wanted to be listened to by any means. All we asked for was recognition; it was fair. We wanted a prison ward just for us alone [female from MRTA], to have our own things, get everything separated, even the people who served the food should be "Tupacamarista" [from Tupac Amaru Revolutionary Movement, MRTA] too. (Bea, MRTA)

The activity of the two groups was drastically reduced as a result of the arrests of its principal leaders and as a result of the enactment of the Repentance Law in 1993. This control mechanism has also been used in other similar contexts where there were political prisoners, and in all cases these rules are intended to cause a split in groups according to their degree of collaboration with power.

Consequently, the state divided the prisoners between the "good" ones (politically detached, repentant, and innocent) and the "bad" ones (who still belonged to PCP-SL or MRTA). However, self-definition and the decision to fit into one or the other category created by the authorities was not as "free" as it appeared, since there were pressures of all kinds, both from the state authorities and from both armed groups. The directors of the prison used all the means at their disposal to get the prisoners to repent, to provide information on the movements of those who remained politically active, and to get them to identify the roles they each had in prison.

Ideology helped many women—and men—survive in prisons, but understanding ideology as something beyond the political convictions of a particular organization, rather as a cognitive universe considered as desirable and to which one belonged. In other words, ideologies are belief systems that are socially shared and need collective understanding of a particular human issue, with which a person has been socialized and which they have subsequently appropriated for themselves. Thus, an ideology is a collection of beliefs that are necessary either at an individual, group, or society level (Billig 1991, Van Dijk 1995, Fernández Villanueva et al., 1998). In this light, the Peruvian prison institution in its entirety faced two major ideological blocks and was the battleground of two competing ideologies: on one hand, armed organizations who already had a political narrative elaborated before and during the conflict; and on the other, the Peruvian state's narrative, whose aim was to reinstill citizenship in those who had repented for their actions. This latter ideology included the concept of "hegemonic Peruvian citizenship" symbolised by the Peruvian flag and national anthem, coupled with a strong religious element through Catholic—and to a lesser extent Protestant—liturgical acts and activities inside the prison.

The symbolic use of the national anthem is not an isolated case or a random component. As Manrique pointed out (2014), among the multiple practices that "demonstrated" the innocence or guilt of a person in prison was their relationship with the Peruvian flag and the national anthem; hence who deserves to be punished and who doesn't. In effect, one of the fundamental goals in the ideology of both PCP-SL and MRTA was to defeat the Old State and build a new nation. Therefore, the patriotic symbols became more than methods of punishment but accessories in a performance in which the entire "cast" participated. Both the national flag and the national anthem were used to project an identity out of oneself, the ward, or the entire prison. The ultimate goal of these symbols was to impose on the inmates a model of Peru as the hegemonic discourse dictated: "He [the military warden] shouted at me to sing the national anthem while he groped me, and every time he shouted louder. As I did not want to sing or speak, then they began to beat me up with a stick all over my body, and they did the same thing to the other comrades, some of them were also beaten with an electrical stick. We all screamed in pain and many cried, it was horrible" (Bea, MRTA).

In order to overcome this violence and feel empowered in this system of oppression, many interviewed women told me that Marxist ideology helped them face prison life, especially those who previously had a strong political socialization. This is what Mercedes says: "The DINCOTE tortured me to break me. What helps is the ideology, the conviction. I was humiliated as a woman. I am transferred to Yanamayo prison, in Puno, and I remain there for 10 years. It was an isolated system. I could not see my relatives. In the trial of 'Megaprocess' I got sentenced life imprisonment that could not be implemented, but for being a leader they condemned me to 18 years, which I already served" (Mercedes, PCP-SL).

Conclusion

Wars reveal the discrimination of some, the privileges of others, and the inequalities that generally preexisted in those societies. Peruvian armed conflict polarized society, particularly in rural areas where the violence was more intense. The groups most discriminated against historically—women and Indigenous peoples—have been frequently considered by the media, governments, and many academics as lacking in agency, bereft of the capacity to be subjects of history with regard to politics or action.

Prison represents one of the hardest experiences for all of the women of the investigation. Their experiences in jail are interesting in terms of how they have faced the long imprisonment and how the following "democratic" governments have legitimized their power through humiliations and physical and psychological torture. Also, it is noticeable that the punishments have depended on gender and racial connotations.

The situations of women from the study population are diverse and depend on their life paths so far, but definitely their time in prison is a decisive factor. All of them, after they went into the jail, have had to face transformations in their identities. Some of them, with more political conviction than before, become "political prisoners" (but not in a legal way, only symbolic). Others, however, disassociated themselves from the group and no longer tried to involve themselves in any political activity. So as far I could see, prison was an important agent of resocialization in different ways. Political ideology helps some with long sentences survive inside prison. Many women, both in and out of jail, still have a firm commitment to their beliefs. They truly consider it all worth it. I have also observed that the stronger the ideological and political conviction, the stronger is this feeling. And this feeling is more obvious in women who have life sentences. We could argue that these women hold this view because they have lost too much—at the material and symbolic levels, deaths, torture, humiliations—and the only thing they cannot "afford" to lose, and that which no one can take away from them, is their ideals. It might explain why in some cases they continue to defend them so vehemently. They believe that since they have had to face such extreme and negative experiences, nothing can stand up to them. Although some of the women in this research continue in prison, they prefer not to look back with bitterness or any sort of negativity at the past, but envision the future with the accumulated experience and the lessons learned through everything they have lived through.

Notes

1. The conflict could be summarized through the following historical moments: the PCP-SL began the armed conflict in Ayacucho—one of the poorest regions in Peru—in 1980; the government declared a state of emergency in 1982; in 1984 MRTA rose up against the Peruvian state; the violence was at its height at the end of the 1980s; self-coup by Fujimori in 1992; capture of both insurgent groups/organizations at the end of 1992 and decrease in the violence; end of Fujimori government in 2000; work of the Truth and Reconciliation Commission (CVR) from 2001 to 2003; public presentation of Final Report of the CVR in 2003; from then until now, post-conflict period. The literature on Peruvian armed conflict is wide, although it usually focuses on the PCP-SL. Among other works see: David Scott Palmer, ed., 1992, *The Shining Path of Peru* (New York: St. Martin's Press); Cynthia McClintock, 1998, *Revolutionary Movements in Latin America: El Salvador's FMLN and Peru's Shining Path* (Washington, DC: United States Institute of Peace Press); Steve J. Stern, ed., 1998, *Shining and Other Paths: War and Society in Peru, 1980–1995* (Durham, NC: Duke University Press); Gustavo Gorriti, 1999, *The Shining Path: A History of the Millenarian War in Peru* (Chapel Hill: University of North Carolina Press); Carlos Ivan Degregori, 2012, *How Difficult It Is to Be God: Shining Path's Politics of War in Peru, 1980–1999* (Madison: University of Wisconsin Press).

2. The PCP-SL defined themselves as following Marxist-Leninist-Maoist-Gonzalo Thought, a Peruvian adaptation referring to their leader, Abimael Guzman (President Gonzalo was his pseudonym). PCP-SL is one of the many divisions of the Communist Party of Peru since its founding in 1928 by José Carlos Mariátegui, a Peruvian communist and socialist author who influenced the entirety of Latin America. The name of this group comes from a statement by Mariátegui: "Marxism and Leninism is the shining path of the future." The highlight of PCP-Shining Path was its strict organization and ideology, creating "generated organisms," defined as "separate movements, organizations generated by the proletariat on different work fronts." One example was the Popular Women's Movement, founded in 1965 for mobilizing women.

3. This group was also born of several previous political efforts. In the late 1950s, it emerged from the Movement of the Revolutionary Left (MIR), which later disintegrated, creating in 1982 the MRTA. This movement also follows the ideas of Mariátegui but with influences from the Cuban Revolution, Vietnamese guerrillas, and South American guerrillas from the 1960s and 1970s. They acted separately from the PCP-SL. During the conflict the two groups fought each other to control different areas of the country. The MRTA did not have specific political work for women as PCP-SL did. This is one of the reasons why this group had fewer women.

4. It must be emphasized that despite Peruvian ethnic and cultural diversity, citizenship has been built by homogenizing a type of ideal minority identity through a *mestizo/a* discourse of racial, cultural, and social integration that has led Indigenous peoples to reject their own languages, clothing, and customs in order to exercise their basic rights (López 1997). These rights certainly have their origin in the "conquest/invasion of America" by the Spanish Empire, which resulted in a break with everything previously known to these native people. They were stripped of their lands, knowledge, and wisdom and were segregated and discriminated against at all levels, while the conquerors founded and built societies based on those colonial and imperial values (Dussel 2000; Quijano 2000; Mignolo 2003). To be more precise, we could say that today in Latin America, there exists a modern-colonial gender system or, to put it in another way, a Westernization and patriarchalization of gender systems (Rivera-Cusicanqui 1996; Lugones 2008; Segato 2011).

5. Peasant patrols (*rondas campesinas*) or self-defense commands (*comandos de autodefensa*) were organized during the armed conflict to defend communities from external attacks, especially those perpetrated by Shining Path. Their alliance with and support of the state in the final years of the war was a key factor in the defeat of both armed groups. Women participated as *ronderas* in several tasks, including as fighters, but their experiences have been invisible and relegated to a peripheral role by official history (Theidon 2007).

6. In PCP-SL the second in command after the leader Abimael Guzman has always been a woman. Of the nineteen members of the Central Committee of the guerrilla group, at least eight were women (Jiménez 2000). Shining Path literature asserted that 40 percent of its guerrillas were women (Theidon 2007). That is the most interesting fact. Women reach positions of power even in the party structure, something unusual in Peruvian political parties, both legal and illegal.

7. In 1992 leaders of the PCP-SL and the MRTA were all condemned to life imprisonment. After "megatrials" in 2006 only Abimael Guzmán (who died in a maximum-security prison on September 11, 2021, at age eighty-six) and Elena Yparraguirre from the PCP-SL were given life sentences. The rest of the members of these two organizations were given prison sentences of twenty to thirty-five years, which they are continuing to serve. Today some members of the MRTA and the PCP-SL still have court cases pending against them regarding requests for life imprisonment. Some have already served their sentences but remain in prison, and on several occasions

preventive jail has been requested to stop militants from going free even though they have served their statutory sentences.

8. In order to protect the privacy of women interviewed, all personal names have been changed.

9. Montesinos was the main presidential advisor to Fujimori in both terms in office (1990–2000). He also was the chief of the National Intelligence Service of Peru (SIN) and government security advisor. Since 2001 he is serving his sentence in the Peruvian Naval Base of Callao, accused of corruption, drug trafficking, leading paramilitary groups, and crimes against humanity, among other things.

10. Sexual assaults on men were also reported (Dador 2007), but most often women were the victims. According to the Truth and Reconciliation Commission 83% of cases were perpetrated by state agents and 11% by armed groups (CVR 2003).

11. On April 5, 1992, President Alberto Fujimori made the so-called "Autogolpe" (self-coup d'état) with the support of the armed forces unilaterally and with opposition from all of parliament. He dissolved the Congress, appropriated judicial power, and suspended the Constitution. According to Fujimori, the exceptional measures were justified by the armed conflict as well as by terrorism, corruption, and drug trafficking.

References

Ahmed, Sara. 2004. *The Cultural Politics of Emotion*. Edinburgh: Edinburgh University Press.

Antony, Carmen. 2000. *Las mujeres confinadas. Estudio criminológico sobre el rol genérico en la ejecución de la pena en Chile y América Latina* [Women confined: Criminological study on the generic role in the enforcement of a sentence in Chile and Latin America]. Santiago de Chile: Editorial Jurídica de Chile.

Baratta, Alessandro. 2000. "El Paradigma del género. De la cuestión criminal a la cuestión humana" [The paradigm of gender: From the criminal issue to the human issue]. In *Las trampas del poder punitivo. El género del derecho penal*, edited by Haydée Birgin, 39–83. Buenos Aires: Biblios.

Bennett, Olivia, Jo Bexley, and Kitty Warnock. 1995. *Arms to Fight, Arms to Protect: Women Speak Out about Conflict*. London: Panos Publications.

Billig, Michael. 1991. *Ideology and Opinions: Studies in Rhetorical Psychology*. London: Sage.

Blair, Elsa, Luz María Londoño, and Yoana Nieto. 2003. *Mujeres en tiempos de guerra. Informe de investigación* [Women in war times: Research report]. Medellín: Universidad de Antioquia.

Boesten, Jelke. 2014. *Sexual Violence during War and Peace: Gender, Power, and Post-Conflict Justice in Peru*. New York: Palgrave Macmillan.

Chávez, Dennis. 1989. *Juventud y Terrorismo. Características sociales de los condenados por terrorismo y otros delitos* [Youth and terrorism: Social characteristics of those convicted of terrorism and other crimes]. Lima: IEP.

Christie, Nils. 1993. *Crime Control as Industry: Towards Gulags, Western Style.* New York: Routledge.

CNDDHH (Coordinadora Nacional de Derechos Humanos del Perú [National Coordinator of Human Rights of Peru]). 1995. *Informe Anual sobre la situación de los Derechos Humanos en el Perú* [Annual report on the situation of human rights in Peru]. Accessed May 28, 2018. www.derechos.net/cnddhh/inf-anua.htm.

Cockburn, Cynthia. 2007. *From Where We Stand: War, Women's Activism and Feminist Analysis.* London: Zed Books.

Comisión de la Verdad y Reconciliación del Perú. 2003. *Informe Final* [Final Report of the Peruvian Truth and Reconciliation Commission]. Lima: CVR.

Dador, María Jennie. 2007. *El otro lado de la historia. Violencia sexual contra hombres.* [The other side of the story: Sexual violence against men]. Lima: Consejería en Proyectos.

D'Antonio, Débora. 2009. "Rejas, gritos, cadenas, ruidos, ollas. La agencia política en las cárceles del Estado terrorista en Argentina, 1974–1983" [Bars, screams, chains, noise, pots: The political agency in the prisons of the terrorist state in Argentina, 1974–1983]. In *De minifaldas, militancias y revoluciones: exploraciones sobre los 70 en la Argentina*, edited by Andrea Andújar, Débora D'Antonio, Fernanda Gil, Karin Grammático, María Laura Rosa, 89–108. Buenos Aires: Luxemburg.

Davis, Angela Yvonne. 2003. *Are Prisons Obsolete?* New York: Seven Stories Press.

———. 2005. *Abolition Democracy: Beyond Empire, Prisons, and Torture.* New York: Seven Stories Press.

Defensoría del Pueblo del Perú [Office of the Ombudsman of Peru]. 2011. *Informe Defensorial No 154–2011/DP: El sistema penitenciario: componente clave de la seguridad y la política criminal. Problemas, retos y perspectivas* [Ombudsman Report No. 154-2011/DP: The prison system: A key component of security and criminal policy: Problems, challenges and perspectives]. Lima, Ombudsman's Office.

Dussel, Enrique. 2000. "Europa, modernidad y eurocentrismo" [Europe, Modernity and Eurocentrism]. In *La colonialidad del saber: eurocentrismo y ciencias sociales. Perspectivas Latinoamericanas*, edited by Edgardo Lander, 41–53. Buenos Aires: CLACSO.

Felices-Luna, Maritza. 2007. "Neutralization, Rehabilitation or Responsibilization of Dissidents, Subversives and Terrorists." Le pénal aujourd'hui: pérennité ou mutations. Équipe de recherche sur la pénalité y Centre International de Criminologie Comparée, Montreal, Canada, December 2007. Accessed June 17, 2018. https://www.erudit.org/livre/penal/2008/000262co.pdf.

Fernández Villanueva, Concepción. 2000. "Sexo, rasgos y contextos: una visión crítica de la agresividad y su relación con el género" [Sex, traits and contexts: A critical vision of aggressiveness and its relationship with gender]. In *La construcción de la subjetividad femenina*, edited by Almudena Hernando, 143–86. Madrid: Universidad Complutense de Madrid.

Fernández Villanueva, Concepción, Roberto Domínguez, Juan Carlos Revilla, Leonor Gimeno. 1998. *Jóvenes violentos. Causas psicosociológicas de la violencia en grupo* [Violent youth: Psychosociological causes of group violence]. Barcelona: Icaria.

Gilmore, Ruth. 2007. *The Golden Gulag: Prisons, Surplus, Crisis and Opposition in Globalizing California*. Berkeley: University of California Press.

Glynn, Ruth. 2009. "Writing the 'Terrorist' Self: The Unspeakable Alterity of Italy's Female Perpetrators." *Feminist Review* 92:1–18.

Hamilton, Carrie. 2007. *Women and ETA: The Gender Politics of Radical Basque Nationalism*. Manchester: Manchester University Press.

Jiménez, Benedicto. 2000. *Inicio, desarrollo y ocaso del terrorismo en el Perú: el ABC de Sendero Luminoso y el MRTA* [Beginning, development and decline of terrorism in Peru: The ABC of Shining Path and MRTA]. Lima: Sanki.

Juliano, María Dolores. 2009. "Delito y pecado: la transgresión en femenino" [Crime and sin: Transgression in feminine]. *Política y sociedad* 46 (1–2): 79–95.

Larrauri, Elena. 2000. *La herencia de la criminología crítica* [The heritage of critical criminology]. Madrid: Siglo XXI.

López, Sinesio. 1997. *Ciudadanos Reales e Imaginarios. Concepciones, Desarrollo y Mapa de la Ciudadanía en el Perú* [Real and imaginary citizens: Conceptions, development and map of citizenship in Peru]. Lima: Instituto de Diálogo y Propuestas.

Lugones, María. 2008. "Colonialidad y género" [Coloniality and Gender]. *Tabula Rasa* 9:73–101.

Manrique, Marie. 2014. "Generando la inocencia: creación, uso e implicaciones de la identidad de 'inocente' en los periodos de conflicto y posconflicto en el Perú" [Generating innocence: Creation, use and implications of the identity of 'innocent' in the periods of conflict and post-conflict in Peru]. *Bulletin de l'Institut Français d'Études Andines* 43 (1): 53–73.

Mantilla, Julissa. 2005. "The Peruvian Truth and Reconciliation Commission's Treatment of Sexual Violence against Women." *Human Rights Brief* 12 (2): 1–4.

Mignolo, Walter. 2003. *Historias locales/diseños globales: Colonialidad, conocimientos subalternos y pensamiento fronterizo* [Local histories/global designs: Coloniality, subaltern knowledge, and border thinking]. Madrid: Akal.

Nordstrom, Carolyn. 1996. "Rape: Politics and Theory in War and Peace." *Australian Feminist Studies* 11 (23): 147–62.

Ocen, Priscilla A. 2012. "Punishing Pregnancy: Race, Incarceration, and the Shackling of Pregnant Prisoners." *California Law Review* 100 (5): 1239. Accessed June 20, 2018. http://scholarship.law.berkeley.edu/californialawreview/vol100/iss5/9.

Parashar, Swati. 2011. "Women in Militant Movements: (Un)comfortable Silences and Discursive Strategies." In *Making Gender, Making War: Violence, Military and Peacekeeping Practices*, edited by Annica Kronsell and Erika Svedberg, 166–82. Lund: Routledge.

Quijano, Aníbal. 2000. "Colonialidad del poder, eurocentrismo y América Latina" [Coloniality of Power, Eurocentrism and Latin America]. In *La colonialidad del saber: eurocentrismo y ciencias sociales. Perspectivas Latinoamericanas*, ed. Edgardo Lander, 201–42. Buenos Aires: CLACSO.

Rénique, José Luis. 2003. *La Voluntad encarcelada. Las 'luminosas trincheras de combate' de Sendero Luminoso del Perú* [The imprisoned will: The "bright combat trenches" of Peruvian Shining Path]. Lima: IEP.

Rivera-Cusicanqui, Silvia, ed. 1996. *Ser mujer indígena, chola o birlocha en la Bolivia postcolonial de los 90* [Being an indigenous, *chola* or *birlocha* woman in postcolonial Bolivia in the 1990s]. La Paz: Ministerio de Desarrollo Humano, Secretaría Nacional de Asuntos Étnicos, de Género y Generacionales.

Romero-Delgado, Marta. 2017. *Identidades (im)pertinentes: Analizando la Guerra desde la Teoría Feminista. El caso de las mujeres del Partido Comunista del Perú-Sendero Luminoso y del Movimiento Revolucionario Tupac Amaru* [(Im)pertinent identities: Analyzing war from the feminist theory perspective: The case of female members of the Peruvian Communist Party-Shining Path and of the Tupac Amaru Revolutionary Movement]. International PhD diss., Universidad Complutense de Madrid.

Roy, Srila. 2012. *Remembering Revolution: Gender, Violence and Subjectivity in India's Naxalbari Movement*. New Delhi: Oxford University Press.

Scott, Joan. 2008. *Género e Historia* [Gender and History]. Ciudad de México: Fondo de Cultura Económica, Universidad Autónoma de la Ciudad de México.

Segato, Rita. 2011. "Género y colonialidad: en busca de claves de lectura y de un vocabulario estratégico descolonial" [Gender and coloniality: In search of reading keys and a decolonial strategic vocabulary]. In *Feminismos y poscolonialidad. Descolonizando el feminismo desde y en América Latina*, edited by Karina Bidaseca and Vanesa Vazquez, 17–47. Buenos Aires: Ediciones Godot.

Shakur, Assata. 2001. *Assata: An Autobiography*. New York: Lawrence Hill Books.

Shalev, Sharon. 2008. *A Sourcebook on Solitary Confinement*. London: Mannheim Centre for Criminology, London School of Economics. Accessed May 23, 2018. www.solitaryconfinement.org/sourcebook.

Silva Santisteban, Rocío. 2008. *El factor asco. Basurización simbólica y discursos autoritarios en el Perú contemporáneo* [The disgust factor: Symbolic trashification and authoritarian discourses in contemporary Peru]. Lima: Red para el Desarrollo de las Ciencias Sociales en el Perú.

Sjoberg, Laura, and Caron Gentry. 2007. *Mothers, Monsters, Whores: Women's Violence in Global Politics*. London: Zed Books.

Sudbury, Julia, ed. 2005. *Global Lockdown: Race, Gender, and the Prison-Industrial Complex*. New York: Routledge.

Taylor, Diana. 1997. *Disappearing Acts: Spectacles of Gender and Nationalism in Argentina's Dirty War*. Durham, NC: Duke University Press.

Theidon, Kimberly. 2007. "Gender in Transition: Common Sense, Women and War." *Journal of Human Rights* 6 (4): 453–78.

Van Dijk, Teun A. 1995. "Discourse Semantics and Ideology." *Discourse and Society* 6 (2): 243–89.

Wacquant, Loïc. 2009. *Prisons of Poverty*. Minneapolis: University of Minnesota Press.

11

Bad Girls of Pinjra Tod

ALKA KURIAN

Soon, it was time to head back to the four walls of my hostel. Having being able to manage only a late-night permission from my hostel, I headed back to the locked doors leaving behind those surreal open streets. These were the streets where tonight, women were free to imagine a street littered with as many women as men. Where women were out of cages, curfews, walls, barbed fences, cameras and time keeping registers at their warden's tables. I slept with a heavy head and heart within the confines of my "safe" hostel. The safety offered to me at the cost of my autonomy, my decision, my freedom. When I could have been on the street with the bunch of women, reclaiming my space. I wake up in the morning and see my Facebook account flooded with pictures of angry women from Kolkata to Pune, Patiala to Darjeeling wanting to break out of their shackles. I am hopeful. I will question my cages. My December 16 will be reclaimed.

—Memoir of a young Pinjra Tod activist

Imagine an Indian city with street corners full of women: chatting, laughing, breast-feeding, exchanging corporate notes, or planning protest meetings. Imagine footpaths spilling over with old and young women watching the world go by as they sip tea, and discuss love, cricket and the latest blockbuster. Imagine women in saris, jeans, salwars and skirts sitting at the nukkad reflecting on world politics and dissecting the rising sensex. If you can imagine this, you're imagining a radically different city. It's different because women don't loiter.

—Phadke, Khan, and Ranade, *Why Loiter?*, vii

Introduction

Pinjra Tod is an autonomous feminist movement against sexist university policies in India seeking respect, independence, and freedom for women residents of university hostels (halls) and paying guest (PG) accommodation. It demands an end to the ways in which in the name of their "safety," adult women are infantilized by means of sexist curfews, regressive dress codes, moral policing, and other restrictions that limit their mobility and access to university resources (libraries, labs, and sports fields) and interfere with their growth and agency as responsible individuals. Women in university hostels had long felt frustrated with being caged, controlled, monitored, and branded as good/bad women at the hands of hostel authorities. What lit fire to their simmering discontent was Delhi's Jamia Millia university's cancellation in 2015 of a two-day "night-out" provision that was already highly policed and restricted. It began as an expression of outrage and triggered a wave of protests on university campuses across the country as it emerged that this kind of gender-discriminatory practice was far more widespread than in "minority institutions" such as Jamia with a substantial Muslim population. It galvanized women residents into launching an agitation that combined awareness-raising through social media and street demonstrations, placards and graffiti, songs and sit-ins, and letters and speeches to institutions and state representatives. Over time, the protests that started as an anti-curfew revolt snowballed into a larger movement against systemic sexism in universities, unaffordable housing for women, especially for minority women and those with disabilities, and ineffective anti–sexual harassment policies and procedures that unraveled the ways in which curfew rules were more about controlling women's bodies than ensuring their safety.

At the core of Pinjra Tod's struggle is a collective refusal to normalize women's infantilization and securitization as the only response to a pervasive, socially sanctioned culture of sexual violence. It's a rejection of the discourse of safety, which in itself is a kind of violence in a country that denies women control over their own bodies, where the simple act of their presence in public places is considered suspect, and for which they are held to account not only by the civic society but also by law enforcement bodies. In light of the rise of Hindutva (Hindu supremacy)—the far-right majoritarian ideology—which is at the epicenter of this phenomenon, "carceral liberalism" as conceptualized by Pillai in this edited volume is at work in a particularly virulent localized iteration within India that is specific in its ideological antipathies and is entrenched in policies and practices that are anti-woman, anti-Dalit, and anti-minority.

It operates through a nexus between patriarchy, nationalism, and casteism that is obsessed with controlling women's sexuality and reproduction as the only way to maintain caste and—by extension—ethnic and national purity. Women form a majority of the student body in Indian universities today, despite being historically shamed as promiscuous merely for seeking education. Gender policing that has continued in twenty-first-century India is in fact a strategy to deny or minimize women's access to education as a portal to freedom. This form of policing stems from modern patriarchal anxieties (Krishnan 2019) over the weakening of caste boundaries resulting from the fear of women's agency to marry for choice, which might potentially result in the intermingling of caste. Controlling young women's bodies on university campuses—and nipping the problem in the bud—becomes even more of an urgent task for a casteist and patriarchal nation-state. On the one hand, caste purity is maintained by the Hindu right violently terrorizing inter-caste and interfaith intermingling, associations, and marriages. On the other, the discourse of caste purity is structurally upheld by policy makers, government bodies, and institutions including university authorities. This societal and institutional control is at its strongest in being openly endorsed by India's current political regime. Its use of the discourse of safety is at the heart of the carceral liberalism that empties out the meaning of safety by, in fact, saving women from their own autonomy and comes to stand as the hegemonic and authoritarian ruling establishment acting to confine, immobilize, and dispossess women. And yet, this phenomenon is also going through its weakest moment, as never before have young women (and men) resisted this kind of societal, civic, state, and institutional bullying (Krishnan 2019). Since the original research and writing of this chapter, the situation in India has taken a dire turn. Two of the leaders of the movement were arrested under the Lawful Activities (Prevention) Act and subsequently released on bail in 2020. Pinjra Tod movement has taken a hit as a result of the state's repressive measures and gone underground. The movement's resistance is an ongoing continuum of feminist struggle against state violence.

Pinjra Tod is also a call for a meaningful overhaul of social and sexual mores in India, underlining a radical rupture from past discursive feminist iterations. The gruesome 2012 Jyoti Singh rape and murder that unleashed mass protests across India foregrounded sexual violence as a political issue in liberal democracy (Kapur 2014). If the 2012 protests outlined concerns about the "continuum of violence against women" at home or in public spaces, those concerns have persisted unabated: women must constantly negotiate misogyny, especially everyday sexual harassment, where walking the streets is a sexually hazardous activity for them, normalized as an inevitable part of the culture. However, rather than addressing the cause of misogyny, campus safety policies lead instead to women's securitization. University campuses therefore have come to represent symbols of Brahminical patriarchy that cage women, refuse to address instances of sexual harassment in a meaningful way, victim-blame, and shield sexual offenders.

Needless to say, Pinjra Tod's single-minded and earnest rejection of the status quo does not constitute a wholesale contempt for security concerns, which the activists agree are very real. Rather than reject accusations of moral depravity, the activists demand a culture of accountability, freedom, and personal growth. Theirs is a brave, exhilarating, and liberating rebellion, a meditation on which leads us to ask the following questions: In what ways does it stem from the changing sociocultural mores of post-1990s neoliberal India? Would it be fair to assume this movement is a chastising of the mainstream Indian Women's Movement's failure to effectively confront the socially sanctioned culture of sexism in the country? How do we understand the centering of freedom, rights, and citizenship by the movement? Does it pave the way for an intersectional fourth-wave feminist movement?

State Response to Agitating Women

At a 2015 Women's Summit in Delhi, the Human Resource Minister Smriti Irani stated that women in India were free to do and dress as they pleased. This prompted a group of Pinjra Tod activists to educate the minister about the reality of women's lives in Indian university accommodation by presenting her with a package of hostel rulebooks of eleven Delhi-based colleges. On being denied access to Irani, they climbed the gates of the ministry, gave speeches, raised slogans, sang songs, and left the rulebook package for the minister to explore in her private time. They also sent a charter of demands to the Delhi Commission for Women, challenging women's unequal treatment on university campuses. A year later, on December 16, 2015, to mark the third anniversary of the 2012 Delhi rape and murder incident, and inspired by the #WhyLoiter campaign,[1] Pinjra Tod activists from across a number of Indian cities boarded public transport buses at night, sang songs, and raised slogans, holding up placards for gender-just residential rules, challenging women's caging and infantilizing in the name of their protection.

In an act of complete disregard for the demands of Pinjra Tod activists, India's Union Minister for Women and Child Development Maneka Gandhi justified the need for stringent curfew rules, comparing them with the "Lakshman Rekha."[2] Speaking on the eve of the 2017 International Working Women's Day, Gandhi claimed that this boundary line was crucial to protect women from their "hormonal outbursts," as the said hormonally challenged women could not be safeguarded by a couple of Bihari security guards who are usually stationed outside women's hostels.

There evidently is a major disconnect on the part of the authorities who refuse to engage with the issues and live in complete denial of the frustrations and humiliations that ordinary women negotiate on a daily basis. Given the general inadequacy of women's accommodation in universities, getting into a hostel in itself is a hard-won battle. Furthermore, failure to abide by the curfew rules results in women's temporary loss of access to accommodation. For many women the hostel room is the only space they have in an unknown city. This is especially the case for those coming from rural, Dalit, or working-class backgrounds, many of whom are first-time learners in their families. Not being able to access the hostel spells disaster for them. It therefore is not so much women's protection from sexual harassment as it is the control of their bodies, behavior, and mobility which drives hostel policies. Critics refer to this as a politically motivated oppression of women whose mere presence in public spaces is perceived by patriarchy as an act of provocation (Baxi 2001). Institutional strategies of women's surveillance, policing, shaming, naming, and humiliation further promote sexual harassment rather than curb it. Women both inside and outside hostel spaces are therefore victims of sexual harassment for which there is no foolproof system of curtailment.

Following the 2012 Delhi incident that constituted a critical moment in the country's discourse on women's mobility and safety in public places, the government responded with precautionary and protectionist measures: an increased number of CCTVs, women-only public transport, development of safety apps on cell phones, smart jewelry with GPS tracking, and so forth. Quite apart from their elitist nature, given the massively uneven internet affordance across class and geography, the trouble with this technologically enabled politics of surveillance is that it puts the burden of safety on women's shoulders. In addition, it ignores the crucial question of culturally sanctioned masculinist hegemony in public places where women are required to justify their presence for "legitimate" reasons such as work or school. Further, such measures are premised on the idea of sexual violence as an exclusively public phenomenon, undermining the different ways in which women are most vulnerable in private places that are often inhospitable to and endanger the integrity of their bodies both physical and sexual in a country where marital rape is not criminalized. Finally, they promote the idea of negative liberty instead of positive liberty, which, according to Isaiah Berlin (1969), allows for "the possibility of acting—or the fact of acting—in such a way so as to take control of one's life and realise one's fundamental purpose" (quoted in Soni 2016, 2).

Not surprisingly, Gandhi's comments triggered a massive outcry from women students from the country's cities small and big. They slammed her arrogant and patronizing attitude and her code of moral conduct that burdens women with regressive notions of respectability and family honor. They demanded that the minister apologize for her stance, which reeked of a Brahminical patriarchal ideology aimed at caging women's minds and bodies and undermining their fundamental right to mobility. They also condemned her casteist and classist views that promoted race purity and divided students and workers into castes and classes. Their rage was triggered by discriminatory and sexist university policies and not women's hormones, they said. They challenged the privilege of people in positions of power who were in fact trapped in cages of narrow thinking.

Within a short space of time, the Pinjra Tod movement prompted waves of opposition against gendered discrimination on university campuses across the country. It now self-identifies as a nationwide, autonomous women's collective (Moraes and Sahasranaman 2018, 409) resisting the different ways in which patriarchy continues to flourish in the country through institutions such as family, schools, and universities that control women's bodies and choices through processes of infantilization, threats, and violence.

Affective Microrebellions

Among a large number of artifacts that emerged from the Pinjra Tod movement were three subversive images of Indian women. One shows a pair of women pulling apart barbed wires, bracketing the slogan "Break the Hostel Locks." The second one portrays an Indian warrior woman in a sari, bandana, and red tilak and holding a baton juxtaposed with a slogan in Hindi that says: "We Can Take Care of Ourselves." Commemorating the March 8th International Women's Day 2017, the third reproduces the image of the 1957 classic movie *Mother India* with the heroine (Nargis) weighed down by a plough emblematic of tradition. Slogans across these posters claim: "We Won't Mother India," "Nationalism Cages Women," and "Women Fight this Brahmanical, Patriarchal Nation State." None of these artifacts represent the image of the eponymous Pinjra—the "cage"—that has animated the "break the cage" movement. Instead, the images foreshadow the metaphorical idea of the Pinjra understood as the process of cultural and institutional confining and constraining. This caging that results from being coerced into staying in the controlled environment of home or hostels is how they understand their situation as representing, using Monika Fludernik's carceral imaginary, a patriarchal prison, "hell, tomb or live burial" (2007, 3, 4).

I draw on Zakia Salime (2014) to refer to these posters as acts of "microrebellion" that turn the collective cultural memory of Indian femininity on its head and insert them into the visual archive of the movement. The women forcing themselves through barbed wires are shown in black—representing universal radical femininity—as they push their way through the chains of subservience. The warrior woman is the fearless, defiant face of this feminist struggle that claims agency by purporting to wrench the rescue narrative from Brahminical patriarchy. The captions on the *Mother India* poster publicly challenge the constructed image of Indian femininity as eternally victimized and subservient, always giving and self-sacrificing. It also debunks the forceful revival by the Hindu Right of a saffron flag–bearing Bharat Mata, aggressively challenging the patriotism of others, ready to birth a hundred Hindu sons, and promoting a Hindu nation that stretches beyond India's official territory.

This resurgence of the Bharat Mata image is not arbitrary, as Mary E. John claimed in her 2016 lecture on nationalism to Jawaharlal Nehru University students. Far from a compassionate figure of feminist empowerment, this deified Bharat Mata forcefully shuts down all feminist conversation for change. Women constituting nearly half of the university student body, their post-2012 assertion for freedom, and their leadership in a number of other struggles (Dalit, Muslim, Queer), have given a hypervisibility to women and their struggles. "All of this makes feminism and its modes of dissent something dangerous to the powers that be. And universities are seen as harbingers of this danger along with the left and anti-caste movements" (John 2016). Faced with a Brahminical patriarchal backlash, India's "unruly daughters" (Menon 2017) oppose women's subordination by turning the collective cultural memory of the originary 1957 *Mother India*—eternally suffering and oppressed—on its head. They reject this constructed image of a Brahmin, North Indian, and Aryan imagination of motherhood that is only a nominal head of the family and whose authority stems from a wholesale endorsement of patriarchy, caste purity, and gender hierarchy (Menon 2017).

Rise of Fourth-Wave Feminism

While not denying the reality of women's inadequate safety in public places, Pinjra Tod activists are trying to "empty out the security rhetoric which is actually done by the securitization of women," claiming a model that is different from locking women up (Wire 2016). Until recently, there has been inadequate research on the different ways in which women have historically been victims of patriarchal oppression on university campuses. The 2012 anti-rape movement in India, however, launched a new feminist politics that embodied a rights-based discourse of gender—in particular, against everyday, generalized misogyny, and sexual harassment and violence—in a way that had not been seriously taken up by the mainstream Indian Women's Movement (IWM). Asserting their right to be treated as equal fellow citizens, the movement saw young women challenging the subordination of their political identity to moral identity, and demanding that the state criminalize sexual harassment, something that it had ignored to do in the sixty-five years of the country's independence. This has become particularly aggravated since the 1990s, a decade that opened up massive job opportunities for women in urban India, as growing financial independence and consumer power have changed their expectations from life and traditional gender roles.

Furthermore, I claim that this feminist discourse was connected to a global vocabulary of rights facilitated, to a large extent, by means of the Internet. Central to this rights-bearing discourse of gender is a focus on the issues of freedom, choice, and desire, which is to say, elements that in the past were viewed with suspicion by those who were committed to the idea of developmental nationalism. The developmental state was too quick to dismiss these elements that came out of modernity because of its own postcolonial legacies marked by conservative gender binaries. The mainstream IWM, in its turn, also had a narrower set of restrictive and protectionist concerns by placing a limit on what women could ask for or do. Moreover, gender in the public sphere was seen by the IWM only through the lens of the developmental state, focusing on employment, wages, education, housing, health, or food. Its examination of gender in the private sphere, on the other hand, concerned itself with issues of maternal health, reproduction, female feticide/infanticide, the girl child, child marriage, dowry, or domestic abuse. A protectionist and paternalistic mainstream IWM has historically disregarded women's sexual autonomy and dealt with the question of their safety by monitoring and policing their behavior in public spaces, promoting instead the culture of moral-policing and victim-blaming. Sexuality was strictly a private matter for the developmental state; it saw its public manifestation only in terms of sexual violence against which women needed to be protected through controlling and disciplining their sexual behavior and policing their access to public places.

The access by means of the Internet to a global vocabulary of rights enabled India's youth to bring gender out of the shadows of this developmental framework. It also challenged the regressive nationalistic register by turning the tide from protection to women's autonomy at home and in public spaces. One can scorn these changes as an upper-class, elitist, and Western phenomenon, or leave it fragmented. But to do that would amount to saying that the rights-based logic is not part of the global conversation. The protectionist zeal of the state and the IWM had failed in eliminating women's sexual vulnerability in public places, especially since the watershed decade of the 1990s, which had brought more and more women out into the public space, unleashing a massive backlash from the conservative sections of the society.

11. Bad Girls of Pinjra Tod   237

Feeling betrayed by the state and spurned by the society, young women didn't wait to be rescued by the mainstream IWM and used what resources they had at their disposal.

Unlike the global success of #MeToo, young Indian millennials have long been leading social media–based campaigns against the culture of sexism and misogyny in public places. Online campaigns such as "Pink Chaddi," "Occupy the Night," "Why Loiter," "Blank Noise," and so forth constitute the earliest manifestations of this collective spirit against everyday sexism. Together they represent a powerful counterculture for women's freedom and agency. The 2012 anti-rape movement provided a trigger for the need to shift from a developmental to a new rights-based state where women had absolute right to their sexual bodies and to public spaces. By bringing the discourse of freedom and sexuality into the public realm—in the streets and through social media—and by insisting on the autonomy of women's political identity, this discourse helped the Indian feminist movement to emerge into modernity. I have elsewhere discussed this feminist resurgence signaling the rise of fourth-wave feminism (Kurian 2017, 2018, 2020). While the third-wave IWM relied on the law and the state for women's safety and disregarded women's sexuality by telling them how to be feminist, fourth-wavers have radically turned the discourse on women's safety and freedom on its head, basing arguments on principles of pleasure and rights, seeking women's unconditional freedom so as to access public spaces without apology or fear.

The Pinjra Tod movement stands at the crossroads of this conversation between tradition and modernity and takes forward the baton for freedom launched at the 2012 moment. It argues that it's counterproductive to constrain women for their safety, that normalizing their presence in public places is the only way to increase their safety, and that the state should be addressing the root cause of misogyny, rather than locking women up in homes or hostels, places from which to police and monitor their clothes and behavior. Didn't one know that given the rising rates of intimate-partner domestic and sexual violence, women often felt safer in public places than at home? Clearly, what was at play were societal anxieties about women's sexuality (and not their safety) and the different ways in which they were perceived to be bringing dishonor to the families and communities which lay at the core of ideological browbeating of women into morally and culturally acceptable notions of femininity. Such anxieties are further manifested in conspiracy theories such as "love jihad" that underline manufactured Hindu anxieties about racial purity, charging Muslim men with hoodwinking vulnerable Hindu girls into marriage with the intention of converting them to Islam.

For Phadke, Khan, and Ranade, rather than raising awareness of street sexual harassment and changing the society's deep-seated belief system that was too complicated and long-winded, women should take things in their hands and deliberately indulge in risky behavior such as loitering the streets purposelessly. As they claim,

> Turning the safety on its head, we now propose that what women need in order to maximize their access to public space as citizens is not greater surveillance or protectionism (however well meaning) but the right to take risks. For we believe that it is only by claiming the right to take risk, that women can truly claim citizenship. To do this, we need to redefine our understanding of violence in relation to public space—to see not sexual assault, but the denial of access to public space as the worst possible outcome for women. (2011, 60)

Pinjra Tod surfaces the psychological damage caused by the politics around women's safety and refuses to exchange their freedom for safety. Curfew rules and moral policing of women reinforce the regime of surveillance and restrictions and "close off numerous possibilities and experiences that a woman student can explore on campus and in the city [and reproduce] patriarchal norms and practices [that] prevent students from enjoying freedom to form friendships and relationships" (Krishnan 2018, 76).

Lieder (2018) characterizes Pinjra Tod as a form of performative protests where women assert their right to public spaces by taking to the streets at any time of day or night. Campaigns such as "Why Loiter" or "Meet to Sleep," aimed at normalizing the sight of female presence in public spaces by women purposelessly wandering the streets or sleeping in public parks of India's neoliberal cities, perform their protest without making an explicit declaration of their intent to protest. By normalizing the act of women simply hanging out for fun and doing nothing in the public space, their goal is to encourage other women to do the same. When loitering is associated with purposelessness at best or criminality at worst in a society "committed to the neoliberal values of production and consumption above all" (Lieder 2018, 154), one can gauge the highly political intention of these campaigns that center fun. These are seen as deeply problematic concepts as they threaten societal understanding of propriety strictly maintained through controlling women's choices related to their dress, intimate partners, marriage, or motherhood. As Phadke, Khan, and Ranade argue, pleasure or fun question the idea that "women's presence in public space is only acceptable when they have a purpose" (2011, 113). "Why Loiter" and other such campaigns challenge the normative discourse in a society where "being respectable, for women, means demonstrating linkages to private space even when they are in the public space [so that] women who are inadequately able to demonstrate this privacy are seen to be the opposite of 'private' women, that is 'public women' or 'prostitutes'" (24). In order to escape the "false binary of visibility/invisibility" (Lieder 2018, 150), women "manufacture purpose through the carrying of large bags, by walking in goal-oriented ways and by waiting in appropriate spaces where their presence cannot be misread" (Phadke, Khan, Ranade 2011, 34)

While Pinjra Tod replicates these protests, it is different in its modality and language of dissent. While the protesting women highlight the "purpose" of their deliberate intrusion into gendered public spaces through singing and raising political slogans and placards, they simultaneously disrupt the patriarchal expectations about how women should be spending their time in cities. In a country whose protectionist ethos defines normative gendered ways of disallowing women a meaningful engagement with public spaces, the only way out is an audacious taking of the risk by occupying public spaces as "an embodied argument for the feminist stakes involved in this right [and] a willingness to encounter others of diverse class and caste backgrounds" (Lieder 2018, 152, 157).

What animates Pinjra Tod is this consciousness for making structural connections, to see the systemic nature of misogyny, to develop an analysis that goes beyond the individual, and to imagine a space that does not reproduce the familial patriarchal model. At its core is the urgency to ensure that in the name of their safety, women are not denied access to university resources and a chance to grow as adults navigating both intellectual and social spaces outside the protectionist rescue logic. More importantly, Pinjra Tod challenges university administrations so that they create an environment going "beyond the formalistic equality notion and substantively demand some kind of equality to reiterate that it's not just about curfew, it's for us to recognize this parental, state, police nexus, this complex which keeps us in cages despite the cages having been broken or tweaked around" (Wire, 2017).

I draw on Mitra-Kahn's (2012) analysis to reflect on the transformations within the mainstream IWM from its earlier "non-autobiographical" formation to its present-day incarnation of cyberfeminism. I claim that the passionate engagement of the millennials with the politics of misogyny and control of women's bodies challenged the perceived sense of political apathy, conservatism, and consumerism among younger women and helped inject a new life into the IWM, whose NGO-zation since the 1990s had blunted its edge (Menon 2004) and weakened and fragmented its feminist politics. Moreover, as discussed earlier, the IWM has historically focused on institutional forms of women's oppression related to sati, widow oppression, dowry persecution, custodial rape, or female infanticide/feticide. The IWM's focus, therefore, has tended to be on specific forms of gender oppression that impact mostly socially and economically backward and mostly rural layers of the Indian society. Without undermining IWM's significant contribution to these major "issue-specific conceptual frameworks," the class differentiation between "activists/theorist middle class feminists" and their disenfranchised "objects of activism and inquiry" (Mitra-Kahn 2012, 110–11) has created an unbridgeable solidarity gap between their self and the other. The privileged members of the IWM understood the pain of the socioeconomically oppressed: it happened elsewhere and to other women, that is, the laborer, the cleaner, the destitute, or the Dalit. But operating from the comfort of its middle-class home or workplace, this "split subject" (John 1998) of the IWM juggled the privilege of the self and the oppression of the other by inadvertently emulating what I claim is a homegrown "Feminist-as-Tourist" model (Mohanty 2003), causing in the process alienation between the two and fundamentally damaging the IWM.

The country, however, has long been in the grip of a silent revolution. On the one hand, due to the 1990s "watershed decade" creating massive expansion of jobs for women in urban India and owing to the unprecedented increase in the number of women students in higher education over the past decade, more and more women from across the class system are getting out of domestic and into public space. As a result, the dominant feminist discourse post-1990s has shifted from the other to the self and the concerns of the erstwhile IWM have become youth concerns. At the same time the greater accessibility of the automobile, the cell phone, and the Internet, the proliferation of nightclubs, pubs, and multiplexes, and the multiplication of dating sites have created unbounded freedom (Menon and Nigam 2007, 92). Added to this is the phenomenon of unprecedented population mobility. Together these factors have liberated urban spaces from traditional mores and conservatism. The resulting shift in the gender dynamic in the public sphere is causing major anxieties for the conservative sections of the society that has not been keeping pace with a growing number of educated and professionally skilled women whose financial independence has opened untold opportunities for them, fundamentally transforming their expectations from the society. Gender-based violence is one of the symptoms of this anxiety. In a situation like this, by neglecting to theorize everyday street sexual harassment, considering it to be exclusively a class issue (Phadke, Khan, and Ranade 2011) that was far too incidental and sporadic in nature to merit its intervention, the ideological feminism of the postcolonial Indian Women's Movement, with its focus on developmental issues, projected itself as exclusionary and too out of touch with the needs of contemporary feminism. It is this activism gap, located between the new and the old order, that Pinjra Tod activists are attempting to close, boldly challenging traditional mores and seeking freedom and not protection from the "Indian capitalist-casteist-feudal-landlordist ruling class" (Sawant 2017) that wishes to preserve the old ways of being.

A regressive and conservative ideology can offer the same old protectionist solution to complaints about sexual harassment, rather than seeing it as symptomatic of a misogynistic culture that denies women the right to their bodies, including their sexuality. Since a disregard of this protectionist discourse is met with the threat or reality of sexual violence, women are raised to practice self-censorship, forever exercising caution with their dress, speech, demeanor, and behavior, living up to the patriarchal expectations of femininity, and fully participating in a discourse that only "good girls" deserve to be rescued and safeguarded by the state.

The Pinjra Tod movement is articulated through a combination of cross-media online, offline, and hybrid methods to subvert masculinized gender relations and spaces in ways that promote collective accountability. The extensive web-based political activism that has emerged in the process can be understood to be stemming from a unique and contradictory situation of modernity and conservatism that Indian middle-class femininity saw itself caught up in at the turn of the century. One can hardly overestimate the impact of the safe/private space offered in this context for women to make sense of and think through these incongruous and incompatible sets of positionalities.

Personal Is Political

It would be wrong to make assumptions about a universal success of Pinjra Tod, for there is still a long way to go. One cannot invite women and expect them all to come on board given the different vantage points of class, ethnicity, sexuality, ableism, and location that determine their engagement with this evolving feminist moment. Coming from a variety of backgrounds and experiencing and negotiating patriarchy differently in their locations, women have different levels of expectations from higher education institutions. For some, having access to the university in itself is too emancipatory an act and the fear of safety concerns too real for them to meddle with Pinjra Tod issues. If they accept hostel rules, it's not because they are fundamentally in agreement with them, but because of their disciplining and internalizing of the ideology of the good, rule-abiding women and bad, rule-breaking women. Women hostelers from some of the "progressive" colleges (such as

St. Stephens or Miranda House) are happy with the relatively liberal curfew rules of 10:00 pm. And then there are those for whom, given the competing demands made on their lives, Pinjra Tod is too small, radical, urban, privileged, and distracting of a phenomenon.

Without undermining the political agency of those who choose not to engage with the movement and recognizing that not all choices stem from internalized misogyny, Pinjra Tod activists are animated by the wish to develop strategies for extending solidarity to collectively explore with everyone the connections between various forms of control and policing of women's bodies that may not immediately be apparent. At the base of this coalition-building is an awareness that it is important for our survival and that it forces us to confront our own attitudes and ignorance that get in the way of coalition-building (Combahee River Collective 1977). It's only when one looks within the nooks and crevices of a system—no matter how small or how well they are packaged—that one understands the contradictions between disparate things, the cracks in structures that seem indissoluble, and the ways in which the system works as a whole. A deeper exploration of the meaning of curfew hours, ostensibly enacted for women's safety, would help us understand the very different ways in which misogyny operates and how systemic and pervasive it is.

Working toward abolishing curfew rules helps us understand how public and institutional violence reproduces violence that is personal and private, for what happens to women at a personal level in hostels is also deeply political. The institutional violence of hostels replicates and reinforces the violence of the family, and the private violence of sexual battery and assault (Davis 2013), so that imprisoning women for their safety perpetuates the same violence, allowing the problem to endure and puts an end to all discussions of eradicating sexism.

Moreover, there is profit in secluding women. Engels explains how "men's control over economy made them control the household which in turn made them dominate their wives and children" (Engels 2001, 34). So, more than the question of honor, a materialistic analysis of gender relations helps us understand how women's oppression is rooted in capitalism that operates by means of creating false notions of a natural division of labor between private (home) and public (economy) spheres. Women's domestication/securitization within domestic/institutional spaces stems from a gendered division of labor in which women are manipulated by patriarchy for its survival. All one needs to do is use the ideological pretense that women are safer inside than out so as to discipline women (especially minority women), pressing them into the service of patriarchal capitalism.

This helps us recognize why patriarchy uses terror as a strategy to control women, a strategy that reaches across and connects family, state, police, and institutions. Further, the terror that controls women's sexual bodies is the same that discriminates against minority women and which gets replicated across the lines of caste, class, and geography. Terror has a longer history and is central to sexism, casteism, communalism, and regionalism (Krishnan 2019). Once we understand this, we begin to see the connection between curfew rules and gender policing by hostel authorities and the epistemic violence that undergirds their blatant disregard for women's safety if they happen to transgress curfew rules. More than women's safety, hostel curfews are about patriarchal feudalistic ideology that follows the logic of domesticating women and coercing their economic, social, and cultural labor. It is thus that we understand the disjunction between the rhetoric of safety and the absence of gender-sensitization workshops, anti–sexual harassment procedures, or women-friendly internal complaints committees. Drawing on Davis's understanding of the prison system, one could argue that hotel curfews consolidate the university and even the "state's inability and refusal to address the most pressing social problem of this era," that is, misogyny (2016, 25).

Moreover, going beyond the politics of gender equality, "feminism must involve a consciousness of capitalism" (Davis 2013) to see the ways in which the control that animates sexist misogyny ensures that university accommodation is far more expensive for women students. Since women's hostels were never a priority for universities and are being built now to meet the massive growth in women student numbers, they are more expensive than housing for men. Apart from the prohibitive hostel cost becoming a barrier to higher education, the system is geared against women, who are penalized for coming into universities later than men, at times being more than one or two generations removed. In addition, run by the same terror of sexism, private sector accommodation is financially unregulated, often sexually exploitative, and discriminatory toward minority students such as those from the North East, Kashmir, or Dalit backgrounds. Women's multiple marginalization due to class, caste, and geography further raises the stakes so that more than being an intersectional analysis about "bodies and experiences," what we are face to face with is an "intersectionality of struggles" that helps us understand the "triple jeopardy" (Davis 2016, 18–19) of class, caste, and geography that women's lives are constrained by. How do we mobilize an analysis that explores the meaning of various social justice struggles on a single platform?

If critics call Pinjra Tod activists too elitist, they forget the groundswell of support they have been able to garner from marginalized women with whom they have proactively been working. Rather than rank oppression in some order, Pinjra Tod calls for a collective struggle against caste, class, and location for, as advocated by the Combahee River Collective (CRC), an integrated analysis alone helps us understand the ways in which oppressive structures are interlocking in nature, how various types of oppression combine to organize and shape our lives, and that marginalized women's oppression is "manifold and simultaneous." Dalit, Muslim, or queer women are simultaneously hurt by structures of caste, religion, and homophobia. It is only by means of this awareness that marginalized women make sense of their oppression.

At the end of the day, the Pinjra Tod movement represents a historical struggle to bring about and expand freedom for all irrespective of people's class or caste locations. Their agitation is not simply about formalistic rights or institutional change but about a social transformation as well as a plea for self-interrogation and-reinvention so that we think through the kind of choices we make as individuals and collectivities. It is only thus that we will stop replicating the patriarchal control of women's bodies that many of us, including women, having internalized its mores, perform, albeit at times inadvertently. And when we reenact such control, we demonstrate our capacity to help the "political [to] reproduce itself through the personal [and reproduce] the relations that enable" (Davis 2016, 106) oppressive conditions for women on college campuses. Without the implicit consent of women—for example as articulated by Smriti Irani and Maneka Gandhi—the regressive hostel policies would not survive. Further, we need also to unlearn the assumption that sexism results from the individual, whose actions can be mitigated through education and training. Until the time we dismantle systemic and structural sexism, despite attempts at gender sensitization in private and state institutions, women will continue to be raped and killed—Jyoti Singh, Kathua, to reference only two. The authoritarian regime of carceral liberalism hounds, demonizes, and brutally suppresses the Pinjra Tod activists, perpetrating a sustained witch hunt of those engaged in genuine and legitimate protest. However, the widespread outcry against the unlawful arrest of key Pinjra Tod activists Natasha Narwal and Devangana Kalita at the height of the coronavirus pandemic in February 2020, triggering their eventual release, speaks to the strength of the movement and its activists' belief in their democratic right to dissent, demand accountability from the state, and their ability to move, have agency, and experience pleasure.

Notes

1. Launched in 2011, the #WhyLoiter campaign encourages women to claim the public space in India that has historically been denied to them. Other than educational, familial, medical, or professional usage, women have experienced little to no possibility of leisure or pleasure in public cityscapes.

2. Lakshman Rekha, whose origins go back to Ramayana, an Indic epic from antiquity, is understood as a culturally upheld boundary, rule, or convention curtailing women's rights to mobility within patriarchal parameters.

References

Baxi, Pratiksha. 2001. "Sexual Harassment." *South Asia Citizens' Wire*. December 19, 2001.

Berlin, Isaiah. 1969. *Four Essays on Liberty*. London: Oxford University Press.

Combahee River Collective. 1986. *The Combahee River Collective Statement: Black Feminist Organizing in the Seventies and Eighties*. Albany, NY: Kitchen Table: Women of Color Press.

Davis, Angela. 2013. "Feminism and Abolition: Theories and Practices for the 21st Century." Lecture at the University of Chicago, Chicago, IL, May 3, 2013.

———. 2016. *Freedom Is a Constant Struggle: Ferguson, Palestine, and the Foundations of a Movement*. Chicago: Haymarket Books.

Engels, Frederich. 2001. *The Origin of the Family, Private Property and the State*. London: Electric Books.

Fludernik, Monika. 2007. "Metaphoric (Im)Prison(ment) and the Constitution of a Carceral Imaginary." *Journal of English Philosophy* 123 (1): 1–25.

John, Mary E. 1996. *Discrepant Dislocations: Feminism, Theory, and Postcolonial Histories*. Berkeley: University of California Press.

John, Mary E. 2016. "Feminism, Freedom, and Bharat Mata." Presentation at the lecture series "Azaadi: The Many Meanings of Freedom," Jawaharlal Nehru University, New Delhi, April 3, 2016.

Kapur, Ratna. 2014. "Brutalized Bodies and Sexy Dressing on the Indian Street." *Signs: Journal of Women in Culture and Society* 40 (1): 9–14.

Krishnan, Kavita. 2018. "Gendered Discipline in Globalising India." *Feminist Review Collective* 119:72–88.

———. 2019. *Fearless Freedom*. New Delhi: Penguin.

Kurian, Alka. 2017. "Decolonizing the Body: Theoretical Imaginings on the Fourth-Wave Feminism in India." In *New Feminisms in South Asia*, edited by Alka Kurian and Sonora Jha, 15–41. New York: Routledge.

———. 2018. "#MeToo Is Riding a New Wave of Feminism in India." *Conversation*, February 1, 2018.

———. 2020. "Indian Women Protest New Citizenship Laws, Joining a Global 'Fourth Wave' Feminist Movement." *The Conversation*, Ed. Beth Daley. https://theconversation

.com/indian-women-protest-new-citizenship-laws-joining-a-global-fourth-wave
-feminist-movement-129602 February 24, 2020.

Lieder, Frances K. 2018. "Performing Loitering: Feminist Protest in the Indian City." *The Drama Review* 62 (3): 145–61.

Menon, Nivedita. 2004. *Recovering Subversion: Feminist Politics beyond the Law*. Delhi: Permanent Black.

———. 2017. "Bharat Mata and Her Unruly Daughters." *Kafila.Online*, July 18, 2017.

Menon, Nivedita, and Aditya Nigam. 2007. *Power and Contestation: India Since 1989*. London: Zed Books.

Mitra-Kahn, Trishima. 2012. "Offline Issues, Online Lives? The Emerging Cyberlife of Feminist Politics in Urban India." In *New South Feminisms: Paradoxes and Possibilities*, edited by Srila Roy, 108–30. London: Zed Books.

Mohanty, Chandra Talpade. 2003. *Feminism without Borders: Decolonizing Theory, Practicing Solidarity*. Durham, NC: Duke University Press.

Moraes, Esther, and Vinita Sahasranaman. 2018. "Reclaim, Resist, Reframe: Re-Imagining Feminist Movements in the 2010s." *Gender and Development* 26 (3): 403–21.

Phadke, Shilpa, Sameera Khan, and Shilpa Ranade. 2011. *Why Loiter? Women and Risk on Mumbai Streets*. New Delhi: Penguin Books.

Salime, Zakia. 2014. "New Feminism as 'Personal Revolutions': Microrebellious Bodies." *Signs: Journal of Women in Culture and Society* 40 (1): 14–20.

Sawant, Kshama. 2017. "The New Anti-Rape Movement Compared to the Erstwhile Women's Movements in India, and the Question of Class in Relation to Women's Oppression." Unpublished manuscript.

Soni, Meher. 2016. "Rethinking the Challenge of Women's Safety in India's Cities." *Observer Research Foundation Issue Brief*, no. 159 (October 2016).

The Wire. 2016. "Watch: Pinjra Tod and Differential Hostel Policies in India." May 12, 2016. Accessed on October 20, 2018. https://thewire.in/gender/watch-pinjra -tod-and-differential-hostel-policies-in-india.

CITIZENSHIP
Javier Zamora

it was clear they were hungry
with their carts empty the clothes inside their empty hands

they were hungry because their hands
were empty their hands in trashcans

the trashcans on the street
the asphalt street on the red dirt the dirt taxpayers pay for

up to that invisible line visible think white paint
visible booths visible with the fence starting from the booths

booth road booth road booth road office building then the fence
fence fence fence

it started from a corner with an iron pole
always an iron pole at the beginning

those men those women could walk between booths
say hi to white or brown officers no problem

the problem I think were carts belts jackets
we didn't have any

or maybe not *the* problem
our skin sunburned all of us spoke Spanish

we didn't know how they had ended up that way
on *that* side

we didn't know how we had ended up here
we didn't know but we understood why they walk

the opposite direction to buy food on this side
this side we all know is hunger

Contributors

ZARINAH AGNEW has degrees from Imperial College London and the University of Manchester and is a contributor to the Alternative Justices Project, launched in 2015, which is run by a decentralized collective of activists and scholars. Their work has been presented at multiple NWSA conferences, the Imagining Abolition 2021 conference, the Emergent Communities conference in 2018, and numerous community venues around the world.

FRANCISCO ARGÜELLES PAZ Y PUENTE, a.k.a. Pancho, was born in Mexico City and has lived in the United States since 1997. For more than thirty-five years he has worked on human rights issues in Mexico, Central America, and the United States: as a rural teacher in Chiapas, supporting Guatemalan refugees, cofounding Universidad Campesina in Nicaragua, and with rural cooperatives in Central Mexico. Once in the United States he cofounded Fe y Justicia Worker Center in Houston and served on the board of the National Network for Immigrant and Refugee Rights, where he coauthored the popular education curriculum BRIDGE: Building a Race and Immigration Dialogue on the Global Economy. He still lives in Houston, TX, where he just finished serving as the executive director of Living Hope Wheelchair Association, a community-based organization of migrants with spinal cord injuries and other disabilities, where he collaborated for the past twelve years. Through PazyPuente LLC he provides training and consulting services to social and racial justice organizations across the country. He also serves on the board of the Highlander Research and Education Center and holds a BA in education from Universidad Nacional Autónoma de México and a masters in multicultural education from University of Houston—Clear Lake. He is currently a Building Community Power fellow with Community Justice Exchange, where he is using popular education methodology to document and advance the radical healing dimensions and potential of abolitionist work around the country.

TRIA BLU WAKPA is an assistant professor in the Department of World Arts and Cultures/Dance at the University of California, Los Angeles. She is a scholar, poet, and practitioner of Indigenous dance, Indigenous sign language, martial arts, and yoga. Her first book project historically and politically contextualizes movement practices at four sites of confinement on Lakota lands: a former Indian boarding school, a tribal juvenile hall, and both a men's prison and women's prison. Her published writings appear in *The American Indian Culture and Research Journal, Critical Stages/Scènes, Dance Research Journal, Practicing Yoga as Resistance: Voices of Color in Search of Freedom, The International Journal of Screendance*, and *Urdimento*. She has taught at public, private, tribal, and carceral institutions and cofounded *Race and Yoga*, the first peer-reviewed and open-access journal in the emerging field of critical yoga studies, for which she serves as editor-in-chief.

D COULOMBE has a degree in sociology from UC Irvine and is a contributor to the Alternative Justices Project, launched in 2015, which is run by a decentralized collective of activists and scholars. Their work has been presented at multiple NWSA conferences, the Imagining Abolition 2021 conference, the Emergent Communities conference in 2018, and numerous community venues around the world.

MARIA F. CURTIS is an associate professor of anthropology and cross-cultural and global studies at the University of Houston–Clear Lake, where she has been teaching since 2007. Her research has focused on Arab and Muslim American communities and on women and cultural production. She has worked with the Arab American National Museum on projects that seek to tell the story of recent Arab immigration to the United States and on increasing awareness about archival collections. She has conducted research in Morocco, Turkey, Oman, and in the United States on Arab American and American Muslims. Her work focuses on diversity within the greater Muslim American community and the ways this community challenges post-9/11 stereotypes and creates multifaith spaces of public dialogue.

JOANNA ELEFTHERIOU is author of the essay collection *This Way Back*. Her poems, essays, and translations appear in *Bellingham Review, Arts and Letters*, and *Sweeter Voices Still: An LGBTQ Anthology from Middle America*. A

252   Contributors

contributing editor at *Assay: A Journal of Nonfiction Studies*, Joanna teaches at Christopher Newport University and the Writing Workshops in Greece.

AUTUMN ELIZABETH has an M.A. from Université Paris Diderot and the University of Bamberg and is a contributor to the Alternative Justices Project, launched in 2015, which is run by a decentralized collective of activists and scholars. Their work has been presented at multiple NWSA conferences, the Imagining Abolition 2021 conference, the Emergent Communities conference in 2018, and numerous community venues around the world.

JEREMY EUGENE is a poet and educator currently teaching high school English. He is of Trinidadian heritage; grew up in East Brunswick, New Jersey; and currently resides in Houston. As a youth poet, he was a member of the 2012 Meta-Four Houston slam team, which competed at the international festival Brave New Voices. He is also a two-time member of the nationally acclaimed Houston VIP Poetry Slam team, and his work has appeared in *The Griot: The Journal of African American Studies.* He hopes to inspire and motivate social change with all of his work.

DEMITA FRAZIER, JD, is an activist, independent scholar, thought leader, writer, and educator. She is a co-founder of the Combahee River Collective, a radical Black feminist organization active in Boston from 1975 to 1981, and a co-author of the Combahee River Collective Statement, a foundational Black feminist primer. She received her Juris Doctorate from Northeastern University School of Law in 1986. Since 1991, she has worked as an external change agent, with a substantive focus on cultural competency education curriculum development, anti-racism and anti-oppression organizational development, executive coaching, and long-range strategic initiative development. She has managed large-scale engagements with significant non- and for-profit organizations, government agencies, colleges and universities, community-based organizations, and many others, locally and nationally.

She remains fully committed to the destruction of the illusion and effects of white supremacy, misogyny, and other forms of oppression, and to the creation of a democratic socialist society. A native of Chicago, she is a proud Black child of the Black South Side.

HONORÉE FANONNE JEFFERS is a poet, essay, novelist, and Professor of English at the University of Oklahoma. Her books of poetry include *Red Clay Suite* and *The Glory Gets.* Her most recent poetry volume, *The Age of Phillis*, was longlisted for the National Book Award and a finalist for the PEN/Volcker Award and Los Angeles Times Book Prize in Poetry. She has won fellowships from the Bread Loaf Writers Conference, the National Endowment of the Arts, and many other organizations.

ALKA KURIAN is an associate teaching professor at the University of Washington Bothell and a recipient of the 2020–2021 Fulbright U.S. Scholar award to Morocco. She is the author of *Narratives of Gendered Dissent in South Asian Cinemas* and a coeditor of *New Feminisms in South Asia: Disrupting the Discourse through Social Media, Film and Literature*. She is currently working on her third book, *Transnational Fourth Wave Feminisms: A Postcolonial Backlash*. She has published extensively on South Asian film and feminism and was the founder-coeditor of the peer-reviewed journal *Studies in South Asian Film and Media*. Alka Kurian is the board president of Tasveer, director of the Tasveer South Asian Literary Festival, and host of the podcast *South Asian Films and Books*.

CASSANDRA D. LITTLE is an independent scholar and an adjunct instructor at Fresno State University and the CEO of Fresno Metro Black Chamber of Commerce. She has her Master's in social work and completed a doctorate in counseling educational psychology from the University of Nevada Reno in 2003. Her past publications focused on counseling skills development and practice. In 2013 the trajectory of her life changed when she was indicted and incarcerated for 23 months at a federal prison camp in Victorville, California. Currently, her teaching and research cut across the disciplines of social work and the carceral state. She is a de-carceration fellow for Progressive Leadership Alliance Nevada (2017) and a communication fellow with the Center for Community Change (2017).

BETH MATUSOFF MERFISH is an associate professor of art history and department chair of liberal arts at the University of Houston–Clear Lake. Her research and previous publications center on Mexico City as a site of global anti-fascism and fascism during the Second World War. Her teaching interests are broad, encompassing art history and museum studies, with a focus on the intersections of privilege and access with cultural production. Her current book-length project considers the ways in which instructors can responsibly and actively engage historically marginalized student populations in the study of art history.

JENNIFER MUSIAL is an associate professor of women's and gender studies at New Jersey City University. She earned her PhD in women's studies. She publishes in three fields: (1) reproductive justice and gender-based violence; (2) critical yoga studies; and (3) women's and gender studies field formation. Recent work has been published in *Social and Legal Studies, Journal of*

Feminist Scholarship, and *Feminist Formations*. She has forthcoming chapters in *Rethinking Women's and Gender Studies*, volume two, and the *Routledge Companion on Gender, Media and Violence*. She is the managing editor for *Race and Yoga*.

SHREEREKHA PILLAI, previously publishing as SHREEREKHA SUBRAMA-NIAN, is Associate Dean of the College of Human Sciences and Humanities and professor of humanities at University of Houston–Clear Lake, where she teaches undergraduate and graduate students on campus and in prison for the "Transforming Lives by Degrees" program. Her research focuses on postcolonial, critical race, feminist, film, and carceral studies. She was the first recipient of the Marilyn Mieszkuc Professorship in Women's Studies at University of Houston–Clear Lake (2008), and she has published her monograph *Women Writing Violence: The Novel and Radical Feminist Imaginaries* (Sage, 2013). Her recent work includes articles on her pedagogy and analysis of South Asian and world cinema focused on spectacles of carcerality.

MARTA ROMERO-DELGADO is a researcher at the department of social anthropology and social psychology of the Complutense University of Madrid. She holds an international PhD in sociology and social anthropology, an MPhil in social psychology, and an MA in social exclusion and citizenship. She has several years of experience in research and sociological intervention in different contexts and countries. Previously, she was visiting researcher fellow at the University of Helsinki (Finland), at the University of Roehampton, London (United Kingdom), and at the National University of San Marcos (Peru). Her research interests are focused on feminism, violence, social movements, critical theory, and human rights.

RAVI SHANKAR is a Pushcart prize–winning poet, translator, and professor who has published fifteen books, including W.W. Norton's *Language for a New Century: Contemporary Poetry from the Middle East, Asia, and Beyond*. He has appeared in print, on radio, and on TV in such venues as the *New York Times*, NPR, BBC, and the *PBS NewsHour*. Chairman of Asia Pacific Writers & Translators (APWT), he founded an electronic journal of arts, *Drunken Boat*, and received his PhD from the University of Sydney. His memoir *Correctional* was published in 2022 by University of Wisconsin Press, and he currently teaches creative writing at Tufts University.

SOLMAZ SHAIF is an Assistant Professor in Creative Writing at Arizona State University and holds degrees from the University of California, Berkeley, and New York University. Shaif's poetry book *Look* was a finalist for the National Book Award. She is also the author of *Customs*. Her awards include the "Discovery"/Boston Review Poetry Prize, the Rona Jaffe Foundation Writers' Award, and the Holmes National Poetry Prize.

SHAILZA SHARMA is a lawyer and is pursuing her PhD at the University of Exeter's College of Social Sciences and International Studies researching women in the Maoist movement in India. Her research is informed by feminist methodology and activist practice. Her research and academic interests lie at the intersection of gender and women's rights, carceral studies, social movements, and contemporary Indian politics. Shailza is also a cofounder and editor at Detention Solidarity, an online space to critically engage with the structures and experiences of detention that constitute the carceral state in India.

JAVIER ZAMORA is the author of the *New York Times* bestseller *SOLITO: A Memoir* and the poetry collection *Unaccompanied*. A 2018–2019 Radcliffe Fellow at Harvard University, Zamora has won fellowships from Yaddo, the National Endowment of the Arts, Macondo, and other organizations. Zamora's awards include the Lannan Literary Fellowship, the Narrative Prize, and the Barnes & Noble Writer for Writers Award.

Index

abolition democracy, 13, 14, 16, 75–76
activism. *See* resistance/activism
Aduba, Uzo, 72
African Americans: Black Lives Matter (BLM) movement, 7, 10, 21n1, 81, 195; Central Park jogger case (1989, New York City), 2; Civil Rights Movement, 1, 7, 20; extent of Black male imprisonment, 87n10; Howard Beach incident (1986, New York City), 1–2; impact of carceral state on, 47–49; Jim Crow/New Jim Crow and, 7, 10, 19, 20, 70, 81, 88n32, 99, 106n27; in *Orange Is the New Black* (television series), 72, 73–74, 78, 80, 82–85; queer communities of color in Nevada and, 38–49; role in U.S. American capitalism, 142; settler colonialism and prison yoga programs, 167–72, 175–84; sexual violation of Black women, 19, 144; as undercaste in Texas prisons, 99; in the U.S. military, 170; women's movement and rights movement of, 81–86. *See also* radical Black feminism
"Against Innocence" (Shankar), 12, 13, 109
Agamben, Giorgio, 53, 60–61, 196, 202
agency. *See* resistance/activism
Agnew, Zarinah, 15–16, 19, 141–65
alcohol use/abuse, 36–37
Alexander, Michelle, 9, 10, 88n32, 99, 103, 106n27
Al-Mala'ika, Nazik, 198–99
alternative justices (Alt-J), 15–16, 141–62;

anarchist criminology, 145, 148–49; critiques and new directions for, 149; critiques of the criminal justice system, 151–52; defining, 150; Embassy Network (intentional communities) case study, 16, 152–60; need for, 141–45; restorative justice (RJ), 145, 146–47; sexual/gender violence and, 141, 144–45; transformative justice (TJ), 145, 147–48
American Dream, 2, 3, 37
anarchist criminology, 145, 148–49; critiques and new directions for, 149; critiques of the criminal justice system, 151–52; no central authority in, 148–49; principles of, 148
Argüelles Paz y Puente, Francisco (Pancho), 13, 15, 23n16, 131–40
armed conflict: military-industrial complex and, 87n11, 170, 202; in Peru (*see* Peruvian Armed Conflict [1980–2000]); refugees from (*see* Syrian and Iraqi refugee women in Houston, Texas)
Australia, decommissioned prisons in, 97
Azad, Seema, 14, 54, 59–63, 65, 66n3, 67n8, 67–68nn10–11

Baldwin, James, 38, 44, 49
Bandele, Asha, 80
Bandyopadhyay, Mahuya, 64, 65
Bargu, Banu, 53–54, 62
Baxi, Pratiksha, 234
Bayoumi, Mustafa, 195

Beccaria, Cesare, 9
Belcher, Christina, 89n40
Beloved (Morrison), 3–4, 137
Benson, Sara, 9
Bentham, Jeremy, Panopticon of, 9, 63, 192–94
Berlin, Isaiah, 234
Bernstein, Elizabeth, 8
Beto, George, 95–96
Black Lives Matter (BLM), 7, 10, 21n1, 81, 195
Black Panther Party, 11
Black Sexual Politics (Collins), 144, 176–77
Bland, Sandra, 10, 13, 15, 18, 129–30
Bloom, Larry, 71–72, 80
Blu Wakpa, Tria, 16, 18, 166–89, 176, 178
Bono, Marisa, 137
Boston, Laura, 135
Brady, Andrea, 193
"Broken Windows" policing, 22–23n15, 24n38
Brook, Pete, 85
Brooks, Danielle, 85
Browder, Kalief, 181
Burton, Susan, 47

California: Embassy Network (intentional communities), 16, 152–60; Folsom State Prison, 139n14; growth of prison population, 142, 143, 170; private prisons and, 142, 143; recidivism rate of prisoners, 182; San Quentin State Prison, 36, 166, 175, 177, 179–80, 183; Three Strikes sentencing law, 182; Victorville prison camp, 42–45
Cameron, Duncan, 103–4
Camp, Jordan T., 10
capitalism: African American role in, 142; patriarchy in India and, 243–44; privatization of prisons, x, 75, 82–83, 89n37, 141–43. *See also* neoliberalism; slavery/enslaved people
Captive Genders (Stanley and N. Smith), 20–21
Carceral Capitalism (Wang), 9, 24n30
carceral democracy (Benson), 9
carceral feminism (Bernstein), 8
carcerality: banality of the carceral, 3; carcerality of the mind and Syrian/Iraqi refugee women, 16, 192, 194–97, 201, 202; colonial logic of imperial machinery and, 19–20; of domesticity, 1, 77–78,

243, 244; in forming the unconscious of lived experiences, 3; intersections with imperialism and patriarchy, 6–8, 10; in public education, 2–3, 22n7, 200–201; Scared Straight field trips and, 3, 22n9; women and (*see* women's incarceration)
carceral liberalism, 1–25; alternative justices and, 15–16, 143, 144, 161 (*see also* alternative justices [Alt-J]); in color-blind systems of justice, 8, 99; critique of, 142–44; dissident feminism projects of liberation and, 4–5, 11–13; Indian prison writings and, 13–14, 61 (*see also* Indian prison writings); Mayan day laborers and, 15, 131, 137–38 (*see also* Mayan Indigenous day laborers); nature of, 2, 5–11, 56, 103; new Jim Crow and, 7, 10, 99, 106n27; *Orange Is the New Black* and, 14, 73–74, 75, 77–79, 84–85 (*see also Orange Is the New Black* [television series, 2013–19]); patriarchy/prisonarchy and (*see* patriarchy); Peruvian Armed Conflict and, 17, 214 (*see also* Peruvian Armed Conflict [1980–2000]); Pinjra Tod movement and, 17, 231, 232, 245 (*see also* Pinjra Tod/Break the Cage movement [India]); prison yoga programs and, 16, 168, 169 (*see also* prison yoga programs); racial and gendered injustices in, 73–76; resistance theories, 18–21 (*see also* resistance/activism); role in fortifying structures of oppression, 17–18; as secret formula of neoliberalism, 2, 6–11, 75 (*see also* neoliberalism); settler colonialism and (*see* colonialism); Syrian and Iraqi refugees and, 16–17, 190 (*see also* Syrian and Iraqi refugee women in Houston, Texas); as term, 2, 5–11, 19; Texas Prison Museum and, 14, 99, 103 (*see also* Texas Prison Museum [Huntsville]); trauma and (*see* trauma); writing and, 14–15 (*see also* writing/creative writing)
carceral state: carceral liberalism and, 56 (*see also* carceral liberalism); dehumanization of, 18, 44, 48–49, 74–75, 87n15, 95–96, 98–99; impact on children of incarcerated parents, 35–40, 44–49, 78–79; nature of, 41–42; role in criminalizing individuals and communities, 53; as site of criminality, 82–83
Carpenter, Mary, 62, 67n9

258   Index

Carruthers, Charlene, 4
Cash, Johnny, 139n14
Cecil, Dawn K., 86n5, 93–94
Central Park jogger case (1989, New York City), 2
Chatman, Bilal, 179–80, 183
Chauvin, Derek, 7
Chicago, Judy, 89n46
Childhelp USA, 37–38
children and youth: "at risk" label and, 166, 175, 176–77, 180, 181; Bureau of Prisons policy for location of incarceration of parents, 44–46; foster care and, 13, 39–42, 44; as immigrants and refugees, 12, 195–98, 200–202; impact of drug and alcohol use/abuse by family members, 36–38, 46; Indian anti-terror laws and, 54–55; invisible carceral complex and, 78–79; minors incarcerated as adults, 181–82; Scared Straight field trips and, 3, 22n9; traumatic impacts of parents in prison and, 35–40, 44–49, 78–79
"Citizenship" (Zamora), 12, 13, 249
Civil Rights Movement, 1, 7, 20
class. See social class/caste systems
Coker, Donna, 144
Collins, Patricia Hill, 144, 176–77
colonialism: American Revolutionary War and, 34n; of Britain in India, 57–58, 62–65; logic of imperial machinery and, 19–20; nature of, 6; prison industrial complex parallels with, 21; settler colonialism and prison yoga programs, 167–72, 175–84; Spanish invasion of the Americas and, 191, 225n4
Colours of the Cage (Ferreira), 14, 54–55, 60, 61, 63–64, 66n4
Combahee River Collective (CRC): coalition building by, 1–2, 8, 15, 18–19, 21, 84, 243, 245; CRC Statement (1977), ix, 1–2, 160, 192, 193; "Forty Years after Combahee" (NWSA panel, 2017), ix–x, 4–5; members of, ix–xi, 4–5, 11–12, 84; origins of name, 4. See also radical Black feminism
Communist Party-Shining Path (PCP-SL, Peru), 17, 211–23, 224–25nn1–3, 225–26nn5–7
community-based justice practices. See alternative justices (Alt-J); Embassy Network (intentional communities)
Conklin, Philip, 24n38

Conrad, Joseph, 88–89n34
contraband/contraband searches, 43, 101, 115, 218
Cooper, Brittney, 9
Correctional (Shankar), 12
Coulombe, D, 15–16, 19, 141–65
Cox, Laverne, 20
Crenshaw, Kimberlé, 4
criminal-addictive cycle, 115
criminal justice system (CJS): alternatives to (see alternative justices [Alt-J]); critiques of, 151–52; formerly incarcerated and, 160; privatization in, x, 75, 82–83, 89n37, 141–43; as reflection of local social realities, 215–17; reform initiatives for, 18, 75, 95–96, 173–74; role of disappearing selected populations into prisons, 142–44; sexual/gender violence and (see sexual/gender violence); treatment industrial complex and, 75. See also prison (generally); prison industrial complex (PIC)
Critical Resistance (organization), 171
Cuba, Guantánamo Bay Detention Camp, 12, 60–61
Curtis, Maria F., 13, 16–17, 19, 190–210

Davis, Angela, 8, 44, 141; on capitalism and the criminal justice system, 11; opposition to the prison industrial complex, 47, 74, 87n11, 142, 170, 214, 215, 243–45; released from prison, 39–40; on torture, 218
day laborers. See Mayan Indigenous day laborers
death: death penalty and the electric chair, 93, 94, 99–100, 103; female feticide/infanticide in India, 237, 240–41; feminicide in Peruvian prisons, 214–15; in prison, 10, 170, 181, 214–15; social death and, 25n46, 89n38, 168–70, 184n5; suicide and, 40, 42, 181; victims of police violence, 7
Dillon, Stephen, 20–21
Dinner Party (Chicago), 89n46
Doing Time on the Outside (Maidment), 19, 25n52
domesticity: carcerality of, 1, 77–78, 243, 244; of Syrian and Iraqi refugee women, 197–99
domestic violence: alternative justices and, 141, 144, 153; in India, 234, 238
drone poetics (Brady), 193

Index   259

drug use/abuse, 6, 36–39, 40, 46, 116–17, 132–33
DuBois, Ja'net, 87n17
DuVernay, Ava, 25n46

education/educators, 20, 111–23; architectures of separation in prisons, 102, 104, 111–15; bachelor's and master's degree programs in prisons, 3–4, 111–23; carcerality of public education, 2–3, 22n7, 200–201; educator interactions with prison guards vs. inmates, 102, 104; educator relationship and marriage to inmate, 80; educator responses to prison conditions, 122–23; educator responses to writing of inmates, 112–22; educator rituals for prison entry, 102, 104, 111–15; in rehabilitative programming in prisons, 16, 18, 75, 113, 142, 177, 183 (*see also* prison yoga programs); restrictions on Indian university women (*see* Pinjra Tod/Break the Cage movement [India]); Scared Straight initiatives in public schools, 3, 22n9; school dropout rates compared with incarceration rates, 200–201; for Syrian and Iraqi refugee children and youth, 195–98, 200–202; university-based protests of gender policing in India (*see* Pinjra Tod/Break the Cage movement [India]); women and gender studies, 18–19; yoga and (*see* prison yoga programs)
Eighth Amendment cruel and unusual punishment protection, 95–96, 105n8
Eleftheriou, Joanna, 13, 14–15, 20, 111–24
Elephant Journal, 166, 168–69, 172–84
Elizabeth, Autumn, 5, 15–16, 19, 141–65
Embassy Network (intentional communities), 16, 152–60; Alternative Justices Project and, 160; cultural shifts and, 159; formerly incarcerated and, 159–60; future objectives, 160; mediation, 158–59; nature of intentional communities, 161n1; Record Keeper System, 153, 154–57; Second Life Project, 160; Stewards System, 157–58, 159; Two-Strike Policy, 155–56, 159
employment restrictions: post-incarceration, 47–49; prison work details as slavery, 21, 44, 100–101, 116–17, 121, 182, 214, 215; for Syrian and Iraqi refugee women,

197–99. *See also* Mayan Indigenous day laborers
Enck, Suzanne, 77, 87n20
Engels, Friedrich, 243
Enns, Peter, 79
Equal Employment Opportunity Commission (EEOC), 47
Espada, Martin, 10
Eugene, Jeremy, 10, 12, 13, 15, 18, 129–30

Federal Bureau of Prisons: policy for location of incarceration, 44–46; self-surrender to, 45, 49–50n11; U.S. Marshals Service (USMS), 49–50n11, 50n17
Felices-Luna, Maritza, 220
Feminine Mystique, The (Friedan), 77
feminism: Black feminist identity and (*see* radical Black feminism); carceral feminism (Bernstein), 8; carcerality of domesticity and, 1, 77–78, 243, 244; fourth-wave resurgence in India, 17, 233, 236–42 (*see also* Pinjra Tod/Break the Cage movement [India]); mainstream Indian Women's Movement (IWM) and, 233, 236–42; second-wave, 77, 81, 89n46; Women's March and, 195; women's movement and African American rights movement, 81–86. *See also* resistance/activism
Ferreira, Arun, 14, 54–55, 60, 61, 63–64, 66n4
First Amendment free speech rights, 131–32, 136
Fleetwood, Nicole R., 184
Floyd, George, 7
Fludernick, Monika, 235
Folsom State Prison (California), 139n14
food: in prisons, 44, 63–64, 67–68n11, 120–21; of Syrian and Iraqi refugees, 199, 201
Fort, Douglass James, 37
foster-care system, 13, 39–42, 44
Foucault, Michel, 8, 53, 54, 60, 63, 114, 142, 170, 173
Fox, James, 177, 179–81, 186n65
Framed as a Terrorist (M. Khan), 14, 55, 59, 61
Frazier, Demita, ix-xi, 4–5, 11–12, 84
Freire, Paolo, 3
Friedan, Betty, 77
Fujimori, Alberto, 213, 215–16, 220, 224n1, 226n9

260   Index

Gandhi, Maneka, 233, 234
gender: anti-queer stance in India, 236, 245; defining, 66n1; dimensions of imprisonment in India and, 52–55, 59–62, 66n1, 67n9 (*see also* Indian prison writings); domesticity of women as carceral position, 1, 77–78, 243, 244; Latinx femininity, 78–79; masculinity/manliness and, 115, 118, 121, 159, 212, 218, 234, 242, 243; in the Peruvian Armed Conflict, 212, 213–24 (*see also* Peruvian Armed Conflict [1980–2000]); queer communities of color in Nevada, 38–49; of refugees (*see* Syrian and Iraqi refugee women in Houston, Texas); transfigures and women's incarceration, 20, 76–77; trans women in immigration detention centers, 132; university-based protests of gender policing in India (*see* Pinjra Tod/Break the Cage movement [India]). *See also* patriarchy; women's incarceration
Gentry, Caron E., 79
Gilman, Charlotte Perkins, 77
Gilmore, Craig, 20
Gilmore, Ruth Wilson, 19, 20, 105n4, 150, 170, 214, 215
Global Lockdown (Sudbury), 9, 17, 18, 19
Going Native (Huhndorf), 167–69, 171, 172, 178
Gottschalk, Marie, 88n30, 105n5
Griffiths, Michael, 1–2
Guantánamo Bay Detention Camp (Cuba), 12, 60–61
Guzman, Abimael (Gonzalo), 215, 224n2, 225–26nn6–7

Habib, Anjum Zamarud, 14, 55, 59–61, 63–65, 67n8, 68n12
Haiven, Max, 17–18
Haley, Sarah, 19
Hall, Stuart, 76
Hamilton, Carrie, 218
Hardt, Guy, 7
Heart of Darkness (Conrad), 88–89n34
Heatherton, Christina, 10
Hill, Anita, 144
Hinton, Elizabeth, 9, 87–88n23
Hodgkinson, Sarah, 97
hooks, bell, 76, 180
Hooks, Mary, 4

Hope, Dennis, 9
Hossain, Rokeya Sakhawat, 77
Houston Interfaith Worker Justice Center, 135
Howard Beach incident (1986, New York City), 1–2
How We Get Free (Taylor), 21n1, 84, 193
Huhndorf, Shari, 167–69, 171, 172, 178
human rights: refugee surrender of privacy and, 192–94; solitary confinement as violation of, 9, 74–75; violations in Peruvian prisons, 216–17. *See also* slavery/enslaved people; torture
Hussain, Nasser, 57
Hylton, Donna, 47

IMD Exclusion Act (1965), 25n45
immigrants and immigration: criminalization of immigrants in Texas, 23n16, 131–39, 191–92; Fourteenth Amendment rights, 136–37; impact in New York City, 22n5; Los Tigres Del Norte and, 137, 139n14. *See also* Mayan Indigenous day laborers; Syrian and Iraqi refugee women in Houston, Texas
imperialism: colonial logic of imperial machinery and, 19–20; intersections with carcerality and patriarchy, 6–8, 10; new form of imperial sovereignty and, 7. *See also* colonialism
India: anti-Dalit (rural/workingclass) stance, 231, 234, 236, 241, 244, 245; anti-Muslim stance, 54, 55, 58–63, 231, 236, 238, 245; anti-queer stance, 236, 245; British colonial legacy of, 57–58, 62–65; fourth-wave feminist resurgence, 17, 233, 236–42; Government of India Act (1935), 58; mainstream Indian Women's Movement (IWM), 233, 236–42; Naxalites/Naxalbari movement, 54–55, 67n5; Pinjra Tod (*see* Pinjra Tod/Break the Cage movement [India]); Prevention of Terrorism Act (POTA, 2002), 55, 56, 58–59, 60; prison memoirs (*see* Indian prison writings); Terrorist and Disruptive Activities (Prevention) Act (TADA, 1985), 56, 58; Unlawful Activities (Prevention) Act (UAPA, 1967), 54–55, 56, 60, 232
Indian prison writings, 52–68; anti-terrorism laws in supporting imprisonment,

Index   261

Indian prison writings, (*continued*)
53, 54–61, 66n4; Seema Azad, *Zindan-ama*, 14, 54, 59–63, 65, 66n3, 67n8, 67–68nn10–11; Arun Ferreira, *Colours of the Cage*, 14, 54–55, 60, 63–64, 66n4; food and power relations in prisons, 63–64, 65; as form of resistance, 21, 53–54, 64–65; gendered dimensions of imprisonment and, 52–55, 59–62, 66n1, 67n9; Anjum Zamarud Habib, *Prisoner No. 100*, 14, 55, 59–61, 63–65, 67n8, 68n12; Mohammad Aamir Khan, *Framed as a Terrorist*, 14, 55, 59, 61; Muslims and, 54, 55, 59–63, 65; Vishwavijai, *Zindanama*, 54, 60, 61, 63–64, 65, 66n3
Indigenous peoples: as day laborers in Texas (*see* Mayan Indigenous day laborers); "going native/going carceral" and, 16, 167–69, 171, 172, 178–79, 183–84; origins of alternative justices (Alt-J) with, 145, 146; in the Peruvian Armed Conflict, 211, 214, 219, 223, 225n4 (*see also* Peruvian Armed Conflict [1980–2000]); in the U.S. military, 170. *See also* colonialism
intentional communities. *See* Embassy Network (intentional communities)
intersectionality, 2, 24n36, 38, 76–77, 150, 244
Irani, Smriti, 233
Iraqi refugees. *See* Syrian and Iraqi refugee women in Houston, Texas

Jacobsen, Carol, 87n15
James, Joy, 8
Jay, Mark, 24n38
Jeffers, Honorée Fanonne, 10, 12–13, 33–34
Jeffersons, The (television sitcom), 76, 87n17
Jeudy, Vicky, 78
Jha, Sandhya, 146–47
Jim Crow: carceral liberalism and, 7; New Jim Crow (Alexander), 7, 10, 88n32, 99, 106n27; professional policing and, 20; Reconstruction and, 81; sexual violation of Black women and, 19
John, Mary E., 236
Johns, Fleur, 60–61
Jordan, June, 38
Jornaleros de las Palmas v. City of League City, Texas, 15, 131–32, 135–39. *See also* Mayan Indigenous day laborers

Justice, William Wayne, 96

Kalita, Devangana, 245
Kandiyoti, Deniz, 77, 80, 88n28
Kapur, Ratna, 232
Kaviraj, Sudipta, 57
Kerman, Piper, 14, 43, 70–86
Keve, Paul, 24n31
Khan, Mohammad Aamir, 14, 55, 59, 61
Khan, Sameera, 230, 239–40, 241
Khasnabish, Alex, 17–18
Killer Mike, 5–6
Kohan, Jenji, 14, 70–86
Kohler-Hausmann, Issa, 22–23n15
Kovic, Christine, 23n16
Krishnan, Kavita, 232, 239, 244
Kurian, Alka, 13, 16, 17, 230–47, 238

Latinx people: immigration to Texas and, 23n16, 132–33, 191–92 (*see also* Mayan Indigenous day laborers); Los Tigres Del Norte and, 137, 139n14; in *Orange Is the New Black* (television series), 73, 78–79, 80. *See also* Peruvian Armed Conflict (1980–2000)
Lebron, Christopher, 22n6
LeFlouria, Talitha, 9
Lempert, Lora, 86n4
Lerman, Amy E., 106n26
Leyva, Selenis, 78–79
Liberation Prison Yoga, 166, 172–73
Liebb, Stefan, 180–81, 183
Lieder, Frances K., 239, 240
life sentences, 80, 182, 223–24, 225–26n7
Little, Cassandra D., 13, 19, 35–51
Lockup (television series, 2005–), 43–44
Lorde, Audre, 1, 2–3, 38
Los Tigres Del Norte, 137, 139n14
"Lost Letter #27: John Peters to Phillis Wheatley Peters, 1784" (Jeffers), 10, 12, 34
Lucas, Anneke, 166, 168–69, 172–84
Lull, James, 73

Maidment, MaDonna, 19, 25n52
Mandela, Nelson, 9
Manrique, Marie, 222
Mariátegui, Carlos, 224–25nn2–3
Martin, Trayvon, 7
Maryland, Schools Under Registration Review (SURR schools, Baltimore), 2–3, 22n7

262   Index

masculinity/manliness, 115, 118, 121, 159, 212, 218, 234, 242, 243

Mayan Indigenous day laborers, 131–39; disaster recovery work of, 132, 135, 138n3; First Amendment free speech rights of, 131–32, 136; Fourteenth Amendment equal protection rights of, 136–37; immigration challenges faced by, 132–33; *Jornaleros de las Palmas v. City of League City, Texas,* 15, 131–32, 135–39; labor organizing and, 135; stolen wages and lack of health care benefits, 132, 136–37

Mbembe, Achille, 8

MCI Framingham, ix

McKinney, Coy, 145

mediation, 158–59

Medicaid fraud, 40–43

Mehta, Punam, 172

Meiners, Erica, 9

Menon, Nivedita, 236

Merfish, Beth Matusoff, 13, 14, 20, 93–107

Mexican American Legal Defense Fund (MALDEF), 135

Michigan, "Broken Windows" policing in Detroit, 24n38

Middle of Nowhere (2012 film), 25n46

military-industrial complex, 87n11, 170, 202

Miller, Amara, 180

mindfulness practices, 166, 174, 177, 182

"A Minefield Called My Heart" (Argüelles), 133–35, 137, 138

Minh-ha, Trinh T., 10

Mirkin, Harris, 78

Misdemeanorland (Kohler-Hausmann), 22–23n15

Mitra-Kahn, Trishima, 240, 241

money laundering, 42–43

Moraes, Esther, 235

Morris, Ruth, 147

Morrison, Toni, 3–4, 137

Morrissey, Megan, 77, 87n20

Mulgrew, Kate, 78

Munshi, Swapan, 182

Murakawa, Naomi, 8

Musial, Jennifer, 5, 16, 18, 166–89

music: Johnny Cash and, 139n14; for *The Jeffersons* (television sitcom), 76, 87n17; rap music, 5–6; Los Tigres Del Norte and, 137, 139n14; "You've Got Time" (Spektor), 11, 25n41, 74–76

Muslims: anti-Muslim stance in India, 54, 55, 58–63, 231, 236, 238, 245; patriarchy inside/out of prison and, 77–78; post-9/11 discrimination against, 190, 193, 194–95, 202; U.S. Muslim Ban and, 190–92, 195, 196

Nair, Lakshmi, 171–72

Narwal, Natasha, 245

National Day Laborer Organizing Network, 135

National Women's Studies Association (NWSA), "Forty Years after Combahee" panel (2017), ix-x, 4–5

Native peoples. *See* Indigenous peoples

Navar-Gill, Annemarie, 86–87n8

Negri, Antonio, 7

neoliberalism: carceral liberalism as secret formula of, 2, 6–11, 75; in colonialism and racialized capitalism, 137–38; prison work details as slavery, 21, 44, 100–101, 116–17, 121, 182, 214, 215; settler colonialism in prison yoga programs and, 167–72, 175–84; state apparatus of the prison vs., 75

Nevada: Give (nonprofit), Clark County, 8; queer communities of color and, 38–49; Ujima Youth Services legal case, 39–42, 44

New Deal, 20

New Jim Crow, The (Alexander), 7, 9, 10, 99, 106n27

New York City: "Broken Windows" policing, 22–23n15, 24n38; Central Park jogger case (1989), 2; Howard Beach incident (1986), 1–2; impact of immigration in, 22n5; minors incarcerated as adults and, 181–82; Rikers Island, 181–82

Nixon administration, 35

Nocella, Anthony J., 146, 147

No Mercy Here (Haley), 19

Nussbaum, Emily, 76

Obama administration, 132, 190, 191–92

Okazawa-Ray, Margo, 4

Orange Is the New Black (television series, 2013–19), 70–89; backstories of characters, 70, 71, 74, 76–80; dissident feminist solidarities and, 81–86; heteronormative romance and marriage in, 71–72, 79–81; intersectional narratives and, 76–77; Latinx femininity and, 78–79; memoir as basis of, 71–74; patriarchy/prison-

Index 263

Orange Is the New Black (continued)
archy and, 70, 72, 73, 75, 77–81, 84–85, 88n28, 88n31; trans-figure in, 20, 76–77; as viewed by incarcerated women, 43, 46–47; white homonarrative ideal and, 71–72, 82; white privilege/gaze and, 14, 71–77, 79–83, 85–86, 87n20; "You've Got Time" (Spektor), 11, 25n41, 74–76
other/othering: in carceral liberalism, 5–6; dehumanization and, 18, 44, 48–49, 74–75, 87n15, 95–96, 98–99; fetishizing gaze in photographing prison yoga programs, 166, 173–75, 178–84; Indigenous people and, 167; Jim Crow/New Jim Crow and, 7, 10, 19, 20, 70, 81, 88n32, 99, 106n27; in *Orange Is the New Black* (television series), 70, 74, 85; in poetry, 10, 12–13; racialized "us. vs. them" in Texas Prison Museum, 103–4, 105n5

Page, Enoch, 183
Panopticon (Bentham), 9, 63, 192–93
"Pantoum for a Black Man on a Greyhound Bus" (Jeffers), 12, 33
Parenti, Christian, 89n37
Patagonia Clothing, 47–48
Paton, Alan, 8
patriarchy: capitalism and, 243–44; Indian female university student resistance to (*see* Pinjra Tod/Break the Cage movement [India]); intersections with carcerality and imperialism, 6–8, 10; *Orange Is the New Black* (television series) and, 70, 72, 73, 75, 77–81, 84–85, 88n28, 88n31; Peruvian gender discrimination in prisons and, 211–24; terrorism as strategy to control women, 243–44
pedagogy of the oppressed (Freire), 3
People's Union for Civil Liberties (India), 66n2
Perkinson, Robert, 94, 105n8, 182
Peruvian Armed Conflict (1980–2000), 211–26; Communist Party-Shining Path (PCP-SL), 17, 211–23, 224–25nn1–3, 225–26nn5–7; Fujimori government and, 213, 215–16, 220, 224n1, 226n9; gender discrimination in prisons, 213–24; nature of the Peruvian prison system, 213–17; Repentance Law (1993), 221–22; summary of conflict, 224n1; Truth and Reconciliation Commission (CVR) analysis of, 211–13, 216, 224n1, 226n10; Tupac Amaru

Revolutionary Movement (MRTA), 17, 211–23, 224n1, 225n3, 225–26n7
Peters, John, 12
Phadke, Shilpa, 230, 239–40, 241
photography: of male bodies in prison yoga programs, 166, 173–75, 178–84; of migrants to Texas, 23n16; *Prison Obscura* (photography exhibit on prisoners), 85; self-representations of prisoners vs., 184
PIC. *See* prison industrial complex (PIC)
Pillai, Shreerekha, 1–29, 61, 70–92, 103, 137, 143, 168, 190, 193, 214, 231
Pinjra Tod/Break the Cage movement (India), 230–46; awareness-raising campaigns, 231, 233, 237–38, 239–40, 246n1; curfew rules for female Indian university students, 230–34, 239, 240, 242–43, 244; female infantilization and, 230–31, 233, 235; as fourth-wave feminist resurgence, 17, 233, 236–42; hostel housing for university women and, 13, 230–31, 233–34, 235, 238, 242–45; mainstream Indian Women's Movement (IWM) and, 233, 236–42; nature of the movement, 230–33; personal aspects of the movement, 242–45; Jyoti Singh rape and murder protests (2012) and, 232, 233, 234, 236, 238; state response to agitating women, 233–35
poets and poetry, 12–13; "Against Innocence" (Ravi Shankar), 12, 13, 109; "Citizenship" (Javier Zamora), 12, 13, 249; Audre Lorde, 1, 2–3, 38; "Lost Letter #27: John Peters to Phillis Wheatley Peters, 1784" (Honorée Fanonne Jeffers), 10, 12, 34; "A Minefield Called My Heart" (Pancho Argüelles), 133–35, 137, 138; "Pantoum for a Black Man on a Greyhound Bus" (Honoré Fanonne Jeffers), 12, 33; "Reaching Guantánamo" (Solmaz Sharif), 12–13, 125; "Reagan" (Killer Mike), 5–6; "Space" (Jeremy Eugene), 10, 12, 13, 15, 18, 129–30; "Sunday School" (Ravi Shankar), 12, 110; "To a Girl Sleeping in the Street" (Nazik Al-Mala'ika), 198–99
police/professionalized policing: abuse of Peruvian prisoners, 218, 219; arrest of Pinjra Tod leaders (India) and, 232, 233; Black Lives Matter (BLM) movement, 7, 10, 21n1, 81, 195; "Broken Windows" policing, 22–23n15, 24n38; curfew rules

264   Index

for female Indian university students, 230–31, 233–34, 239, 240, 242–43, 244; origins of professionalization, 20; "thin blue line" and, 20

Policing the Planet (Camp and Heatherton), 10

political prisoners: in Turkey, 53–54, 62. *See also* Peruvian Armed Conflict (1980–2000)

poverty: criminalizing the poor and, x, 82–83, 87–88n23, 214; *Orange Is the New Black* (television series) and, 73, 76, 82, 86n5; television portrayals of upward mobility and, 76, 87n17. *See also* employment restrictions; immigrants and immigration

power dynamics: in anarchist communities, 149; in colonial contact zones, 86n3; control of time in prisons, 10–11, 64, 75, 216–17; "count" in prison education programs, 118–19; employment and (*see* employment restrictions); food in prisons, 63–64, 65, 120–21, 221; Foucault and, 8, 53, 54, 60, 63, 114, 142, 170, 173; inmate deference to educators in prisons, 117–18; masculinity/manliness and, 115, 118, 121, 159, 212, 218, 234, 242, 243; in the Peruvian Armed Conflict, 212, 216, 223; settler colonialism and prison yoga programs, 167–72, 175–84; white savior trope and prison yoga programs, 89n40, 174, 177–81. *See also* patriarchy

Pratt, Mary Louise, 86n3

pregnancy, in prison, 24–25n40, 45–46, 72, 79–80, 219

prison (generally): abolition democracy and, 13, 14, 16, 75–76; birth of modern prison empire, 9; contraband/contraband searches, 43, 101, 115, 218; daily routines of inmates, 44, 64, 216–17; education programs (*see* education/educators; prison yoga programs); Foucault's philosophy of power and, 8, 53, 54, 60, 63, 114, 142, 170, 173; growth of U.S. prison population, x, 18, 101, 142, 143, 170, 214; life sentences, 80, 182, 223–24, 225–26n7; as political confrontation site, 14, 53–54, 62 (*see also* Peruvian Armed Conflict [1980–2000]); privatization movement, x, 75, 82–83, 89n37, 141–43; Scared Straight initiatives in public schools, 3, 22n9; school dropout

rates compared with incarceration rates, 200–201; solitary confinement as human rights violation, 9, 74–75; women in (*see* women's incarceration)

Prisoner No. 100 (Habib), 14, 55, 59–61, 63–65, 67n8, 68n12

Prisoner's Wife, The (Bandele), 80

prison industrial complex (PIC): carceral epistemology and, 11; characteristics of incarcerated people, x; children/grandchildren of the incarcerated and (*see* children and youth); dominant discourse in reinforcing, 214; growth of U.S., x, 18, 101, 142, 143, 170, 214; military-industrial complex and, 170; parallels with the colonial state, 21; policy shifts and, 18; prison work details as enslavement, 21, 44, 100–101, 116–17, 121, 182, 215; privatization in, x, 75, 82–83, 89n37, 141–43; in producing "bad" women, 81; stereotyping prisoners and, 171, 174–77, 183; surveillance technology in, 139n8, 193; women in (*see* women's incarceration); yoga industrial complex and, 16, 18, 167–72, 173, 180, 182–83

Prison Obscura (photography exhibit on prisoners), 85

Prison Rape Elimination Act (2003), 114

prison yoga programs, 166–87; *Elephant Journal* series on, 166, 168–69, 172–84; "going native/going carceral" and, 16, 167–69, 171, 172, 178–79, 183–84; mindfulness and, 166, 174, 177, 182; need for systemic analysis of, 181–83; New Age movement and, 16, 168–69; in *Orange Is the New Black* (television series), 72–73; photography and, 166, 173–75, 178–84; settler colonialism and, 167–72, 175–84; South Asian models of yoga teaching vs., 16, 171–72, 178; stereotyping prisoners and, 171, 174–77, 183; white supremacy and, 167, 171–73, 177–81, 183; yoga industrial complex and, 16, 18, 167–72, 173, 180, 182–83

Prison Yoga Project, 177, 179–81, 186n65

public education. *See* education/educators

queer communities of color, 38–49

radical Black feminism: intersectionality and, 2; mainstream feminism vs., 5; memoir as form of resistance, 5, 35–50;

Index   265

radical Black feminism: (*continued*)
resistance to violence of neoliberalism, patriarchy, and carcerality, 8. *See also* Combahee River Collective (CRC); Davis, Angela
Radical Imagination, The (Haiven and Khasnabish), 17–18
Ranada, Shilpa, 230, 239–40, 241
Rao, Varavara, 52
rape. *See* sexual/gender violence
rap music, 5–6
Rathbone, Christine, 47
"Reaching Guantánamo" (Sharif), 12–13, 125
"Reagan" (Killer Mike), 5–6
Reagan administration, 1, 5–6
rehabilitative programming, 16, 18, 75, 113, 142, 177, 183. *See also* education/educators; prison yoga programs
resistance/activism, 18–21; alternative justices in (*see* alternative justices [Alt-J]); Black Lives Matter (BLM) movement, 7, 21n1, 81, 195; Civil Rights Movement, 1, 7, 19–20; coalition building by the Combahee River Collective in, 1–2, 8, 15, 18–19, 21, 84, 243, 245; cohabitation/coalition building by women in Peruvian prisons, 217, 218–23 (*see also* Peruvian Armed Conflict [1980–2000]); dissident feminist solidarities in *Orange Is the New Black* (television series), 81–86; from exteriority vs. interiority, 81; feminism in (*see* feminism); films and television series in, 10–11, 25n46, 43–44, 87n15 (*see also Orange Is the New Black* [television series, 2013–19]); in India (*see* Indian prison writings; Pinjra Tod/Break the Cage movement [India]); legal action by day laborers, 15, 131–32, 135–39 (*see also* Mayan Indigenous day laborers); music in (*see* music); U.S. Constitution rights and (*see* U.S. Constitution); writing in (*see* Indian prison writings; poets and poetry; writing/creative writing)
restorative justice (RJ), 145; as alternative to prison and punishment, 146–47; comparison with transformative justice, 147, 148, 149; critiques and new directions for, 149; critiques of the criminal justice system, 151–52; origins of, 146; principles of, 146

retributive justice, 10–11
Reuleaux Triangle, in Venn diagrams, 6
Rikers Island (New York City), 181–82
Rios, Victor, 176
Robinson, Cedric, 8
Rodriguez, Dylan, 168, 173–74
Romero-Delgado, Marta, 16, 17, 18, 211–29
Root and Rebound, 48–49
Ross, Luana, 171
Ruiz, David, 95–96, 105n8
Russia, size and growth of prison population, 214

Sahasranaman, Vinita, 235
Said, Edward W., 183
Salime, Zakia, 235–36
San Quentin State Prison (California), 36, 166, 175, 177, 179–80, 183
Santeria, 78–79
Sarsour, Linda, 195
Schwann, Anne, 83
Scott, John, 66n1
sentence reduction, 18
Sentencing Project, 23n17
September 11, 2001 terrorist attacks: Indian Prevention of Terrorism Act (POTA, 2002), 55, 56, 58–59, 60; post-9/11 discrimination against Muslims and, 190, 193, 194–95, 202
Sered, Danielle, 24n33
sexual behavior: female imprisonment and pregnancy in prison, 24–25n40, 45–46, 72, 79–80, 219; female staff members and incarcerated men, 121
sexual/gender violence: alternative justices and (*see* alternative justices [Alt-J]); Central Park jogger case (1989, New York City), 2; criminal justice system failure to address, 141, 144–45, 152; Federal Prison Rape Elimination Act (2003), 114; forms of, 152; in immigration detention centers, 132; intentional communities and, 141, 152–53; involving United Nations Human Rights Commission personnel, 196; in Peruvian prisons, 218–19, 226n10; protests against rape in India, 232, 233, 234, 236, 238; protests against sexual harassment of women in India, 231–32, 234, 236–37, 239, 241–42, 244; rape culture, 144, 152, 159, 218, 234; sex trafficking, 8–9, 201; sexual violation of Black women, 19, 144; strip and cav-

266   Index

ity searches as, 43, 218; Syrian and Iraqi refugees and, 201–2; U.S. Prison Rape Elimination Act (2003), 114; victim-blaming, 78, 152, 237

Shakur, Assata, 2–3

Shakur, Sanyika, 80, 88n28

Shange, Savannah, 8

Shankar, Ravi, 12, 13, 109, 110

Sharif, Solmaz, 12–13, 125

Sharma, Shailza, 13–14, 21, 52–69

shoes, in prison, 43, 116

Simpkins, Antwann M., 24n36

Singh, Ujjwal Kumar, 56, 58, 60, 61, 67n7

Sjoberg, Laura, 79

slavery/enslaved people: immigrant la-borers as slaves, 135–37; master-slave relationship in prisons, 60, 63; prison work details as slavery, 21, 44, 100–101, 116–17, 121, 182, 214, 215; sexual viola-tion of Black women and, 19; Thirteenth Amendment rights, 116, 182

Sloan, Barbara, 99–100

Smith, Barbara, 4

Smith, Nat, 20–21

Smith, Stephen Wm., 131–32

social class/caste systems: African Ameri-can prisoners as undercaste in Texas prisons, 99; anti-Dalit (rural/working-class) stance in India, 231, 234, 236, 241, 244, 245; criminal justice system and, 11; Pinjra Tod/Break the Cage movement (India) and, 231–32, 234–36, 241–42. *See also* poverty

social confinement (Blu Wakpa), 176, 183

social death, 25n46, 89n38, 168–70, 184n5

solitary confinement/segregation units: as human rights violation, 9, 74–75; as ongoing violence, 170, 181

Soules, Dale, 84

South Africa, 8, 9

"Space" (Eugene), 10, 12, 13, 15, 18, 129–30

Spektor, Regina, 11, 25n41, 74–76

Spivak, Gayatri, 174

Stanley, Eric A., 20–21

state of exception (Agamben), 53, 60–61

Stephens, Bill, 95

stereotyping: Peruvian female activists and, 212, 213–14; U.S. prison industrial complex (PIC) and, 171, 174–77, 183

Story, Brett, 22–23n15

Sturman, Robert, 166, 173, 174–75, 178–81, 182, 184

Sudbury, Julia, 9, 17, 18, 19

Sufrin, Carolyn, 24–25n40

suicide, 40, 42, 181

"Sunday School" (Shankar), 12, 110

surveillance/surveillance technology: cell/smart phones and, 198, 201, 202–3, 234, 241; Panopticon (Bentham) and, 9, 63, 192–93; in the prison industrial complex (PIC), 139n8, 193; privacy and, 192–94; women in India and, 234, 239

Syrian and Iraqi refugee women in Hous-ton, Texas, 16–17; carcerality of the mind and, 16, 192, 194–97, 201, 202; cell phone technology and, 198, 201, 202–3; children of, 12, 195–98, 200–202; English language instruction and, 195–96, 201; Houston as sanctuary city, 190, 191–92, 194; medical services and, 196–97; mi-croaggressions experienced by, 194–95; Muslim Ban and, 190–92, 195, 196; poli-tics of vulnerability and, 195–98, 200–202; post-9/11 discrimination and, 190, 193, 194–95, 202; rationalizing carceral violence toward, 194–95; resettlement and sense of home, 190, 197–99; surveil-lance/surrender of privacy and, 192–94

Talve-Goodman, Sarika, 8

Taylor, Keeanga-Yamahtta, 21n1, 84, 193

television programs: *The Jeffersons* (televi-sion sitcom), 76, 87n17; *Lockup* (televi-sion series, 2005–), 43–44. *See also Or-ange Is the New Black* (television series, 2013–19)

terrorism: accusations in the Peruvian Armed Conflict, 213, 216; Indian anti-terrorism laws in supporting imprison-ment, 53, 54–61, 66n4; as a patriarchal strategy to control women, 243–44; post-9/11 discrimination against Mus-lims and, 190, 193, 194–95, 202. *See also* September 11, 2001 terrorist attacks

Texas: criminalization of immigrants in, 23n16, 131–39, 191–92; day laborers in (*see* Mayan Indigenous day laborers); Jeremy Eugene poem, 10, 12, 13, 15, 18, 129–30; historic Spanish Inquisitions, 191; Hurricane Harvey and, 112, 113, 132; legal consequences of school absence/truancy in, 200–201; state refusal of federal resettlement funding, 191–92, 200, 202; Syrian and Iraqi refugees (*see*

Index   267

Texas: (*continued*)
Syrian and Iraqi refugee women in Houston, Texas)
Texas Department of Corrections (TDC): claims of Eighth Amendment violations, 95–96, 105n8; educators in prisons and, 102–3, 104, 111–23; history of, 95–96; Holliday Transfer Unit and, 93, 102–3; Hurricane Harvey and, 112, 113; importance of property vs. inmates, 112, 113, 121; inmate uniforms, 98–99; lack of air conditioning in prison quarters, 96, 114, 115; massive expansion of, 101; prison museum (*see* Texas Prison Museum [Huntsville]); prison work details as slavery, 100–101, 116–17, 121
Texas Prison Museum (Huntsville), 14, 20, 93–106; architectures of separation and, 102–3; blank-faced mannequins, 98–99, 103; dark tourism and, 94, 96–98; disembodied objects in, 93, 94, 98–100; electric chair ("Old Sparky") exhibit, 93, 94, 99–100, 103; intentional neutrality and, 94, 95–96, 101; introductory welcome video, 95–96, 97–98; prison cell recreation, 98, 103; reforms and, 95–96; unpaid prisoner-made objects, 100–101
Thiong'o, Ngugi Wa, 55–56, 138
Thirteenth Amendment prohibition of slavery, 116, 182
Thomas, Clarence, 144
Thuma, Emily, 9
Tillet, Salamishah, 22n4
Tillman, Korey, 8
"To a Girl Sleeping in the Street" (Al-Mala'ika), 198–99
torture: in Indian prisons, 61; methods of, 170; in Peruvian prisons, 211, 216–24; power dynamics in prisons and, 170
transformative justice (TJ), 145, 147–48; as alternative to prison and punishment, 147–48; comparison with restorative justice, 147, 148, 149; critiques and new directions for, 149; critiques of the criminal justice system, 151–52; principles of, 147
trauma: carcerality of the mind and Syrian/Iraqi refugees, 16, 192, 194–97, 201, 202; of children/grandchildren of the incarcerated, 35–40, 44–49, 78–79; posttraumatic stress and, 16, 145, 194, 202; resistance to (*see* resistance/activism)

treatment industrial complex, 75
Trump administration, 132, 190, 191–92, 196, 200
Tubman, Harriet, 4
Tupac Amaru Revolutionary Movement (MRTA), Peru, 17, 211–23, 224n1, 225n3, 225–26n7
Turkey, political prisoners in, 53–54, 62

Ujima Youth Services (foster care support service in Nevada), 39–42, 44
Unaccompanied (Zamora), 12
United Kingdom (UK): American Revolutionary War and, 34n; India as British crown colony, 57–58, 62–65; prison tourism in, 97
United Nations (UN): High Commissioner for Refugees (UNHCR), 195–96; Minimum Rules for the Treatment of Prisoners, 216–17; sexual/gender violence involving personnel of, 196; solitary confinement as human rights violation, 9
United States: American Revolutionary War and, 34n; Muslim Ban, 190–92, 195, 196; Prison Rape Elimination Act (2003), 114; size and growth of prison population, x, 18, 101, 142, 143, 170, 214. *See also* Federal Bureau of Prisons; *names of specific states;* New York City
U.S. Constitution: First Amendment rights, 131–32, 136; Eighth Amendment rights, 95–96, 105n8; Thirteenth Amendment rights, 116, 182; Fourteenth Amendment rights, 136–37
U.S. Marshals Service (USMS), 49–50n11, 50n17
United States v. Cassandra Little, 40–46
University of Houston-Clear Lake, "Transforming Lives by Degrees" program in prison, 3–4
Urquhart, Diane, 97

Van Melik, Bart, 176, 179
Vick, Jason, 8–9
victim-blaming, 78, 152, 176, 232, 237
Victim-Offender Conferencing (VOC), 146, 159
Victorville prison camp (California), 42–45
Vishwavijai, 54, 60, 61, 63–64, 65, 66n3

268   Index

Wacquant, Loïc, 214
Wang, Jackie, 9, 24n30
War Bonnett, Darcy K., 80–81
War on Drugs, 6, 132–33
Wheatley, Phillis, 10, 34
white supremacy: prison yoga programs and, 167, 171–73, 177–81, 183; settler colonialism and prison yoga programs, 167–72, 175–84; white privilege/gaze in *Orange Is the New Black* (television series), 14, 71–77, 79–83, 85–86, 87n20; white savior trope and, 89n40, 174, 177–81. *See also* police/professionalized policing
"wilding," 2
Wilson, Jacqueline Z., 97
women and gender studies, 18–19
women's incarceration: children/grandchildren of the incarcerated and, 35–40, 44–49, 78–79; comparison with men's incarceration rate, 6, 23n17; daily routines and, 44, 64, 216–17; domesticity as form of, 1, 77–78, 243, 244; Jeremy Eugene poem and, 10, 12, 13, 15, 18, 129–30; federal policy for location of incarceration of parents, 44–46; *Lockup* (television series, 2005-), 43–44; medical/reproductive care and protection, 19, 24–25n40, 45–46, 62, 72, 78–79, 80, 196–97, 217, 218; memoirs of formerly-incarcerated women, 35–50 (*see also* Indian prison writings; *Orange Is the New Black* [television series, 2013–19]); Peruvian activists and (*see* Peruvian Armed

Conflict [1980–2000]); pregnancy in prison and, 24–25n40, 45–46, 72, 79–80, 219; refugee women and (*see* Syrian and Iraqi refugee women in Houston, Texas); *United States v. Cassandra Little* case, 40–46
work. *See* employment restrictions
writing/creative writing, 111–23; educator responses to writing by inmates, 112–22; as exposure therapy, 122–23; genre in, 119–20; Master of Arts programs in prison and, 111–23; memoir as form of resistance, 35–50, 71–74, 80–81 (*see also* Indian prison writings; *Orange Is the New Black* [television series, 2013–19]); reading by inmate students and, 115, 117. *See also* poets and poetry
Wynter, Sylvia, 8
Wyoming, legal consequences of school absence/truancy, 200–201

yoga. *See* prison yoga programs
youth. *See* children and youth
"You've Got Time" (Spektor), 11, 25n41, 74–76
Yparraguirre, Elena, 225–26n7

Zamora, Javier, 12, 13, 249
Zehr, Howard, 146
Zindanama (Azad), 14, 54, 59–63, 65, 66n3, 67n8, 67–68nn10–11
Zindanama (Vishwavijai), 54, 60, 61, 63–64, 65, 66n3

Index   269

Dissident Feminisms

Hear Our Truths: The Creative Potential of Black Girlhood *Ruth Nicole Brown*

Muddying the Waters: Coauthoring Feminisms across Scholarship and Activism
 Richa Nagar

Beyond Partition: Gender, Violence, and Representation in Postcolonial India
 Deepti Misri

Feminist and Human Rights Struggles in Peru: Decolonizing Transitional Justice
 Pascha Bueno-Hansen

Against Citizenship: The Violence of the Normative *Amy L. Brandzel*

Dissident Friendships: Feminism, Imperialism, and Transnational Solidarity
 Edited by Elora Halim Chowdhury and Liz Philipose

Politicizing Creative Economy: Activism and a Hunger Called Theater
 Dia Da Costa

In a Classroom of Their Own: The Intersection of Race and Feminist Politics in
 All-Black Male Schools *Keisha Lindsay*

Fashioning Postfeminism: Spectacular Femininity and Transnational Culture
 Simidele Dosekun

Queer and Trans Migrations: Dynamics of Illegalization, Detention,
 and Deportation *Edited by Eithne Luibhéid and Karma R. Chávez*

Disruptive Archives: Feminist Memories of Resistance in Latin America's
 Dirty Wars *Viviana Beatriz MacManus*

Being La Dominicana: Race and Identity in the Visual Culture of Santo Domingo
 Rachel Afi Quinn

COMPUGIRLS: How Girls of Color Find and Define Themselves in the
 Digital Age *Kimberly A. Scott*

Carceral Liberalism: Feminist Voices against State Violence
 Edited by Shreerekha Pillai

The University of Illinois Press
is a founding member of the
Association of University Presses.

University of Illinois Press
1325 South Oak Street
Champaign, IL 61820-6903
www.press.uillinois.edu